DATE DUE

A WOI

FE 28 '98			
FE 16 '98			
MR 19 '98			
MR 24 '98			
AP 08 '98			
MR 31 '98			
MR 28 '01			
AP 11 '01			

emco, Inc. 38-293

D0840870

A WOLF IN THE GARDEN

*The Land Rights Movement and
the New Environmental Debate*

Edited by
PHILIP D. BRICK
and
R. McGREGGOR CAWLEY

ROWMAN & LITTLEFIELD PUBLISHERS, INC.

ROWMAN & LITTLEFIELD PUBLISHERS, INC.

Published in the United States of America
by Rowman & Littlefield Publishers, Inc.
4720 Boston Way, Lanham, Maryland 20706
3 Henrietta Street
London WC2E 8LU, England

British Cataloging in Publication Information Available

Library of Congress Cataloging-in-Publication Data

A wolf in the garden : the land rights movement and the new environ-
mental debate / edited by Philip D. Brick and R. McGreggor Cawley.
p. cm.
Includes bibliographical references and index.
1. Environmentalism—United States. 2. National parks and
reserves—Government policy—United States. 3. Landscape changes—
United States. 4. Nature conservation—United States. 5. Man—
Influence on nature—United States. 6. Environmental policy—
United States. I. Brick, Philip D. II. Cawley, R. McGreggor.
GE197.W65 1996 333.7315'0973—dc20 96-433 CIP

ISBN 0–8476–8184–x (cloth: alk. paper)
ISBN 0–8476–8185–8 (pbk.: alk. paper)

Printed in the United States of America

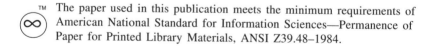

For Susan, and the river we share.
—Philip D. Brick

For Sondra, Aaron and Leif.
—R. McGreggor Cawley

Contents

Acknowledgments   ix

1   Knowing the Wolf, Tending the Garden   1
Philip D. Brick and R. McGreggor Cawley

Part 1: The Land-Rights–Environmental Debate

2   Overcoming Ideology   15
Ron Arnold

3   The Pristine Silence of Leaving It All Alone   27
Donald Snow

4   Property Rights Movement: How It Began and Where
It Is Headed   39
Nancie G. Marzulla

5   Environmentalism: The Real Movement to Protect
Property Rights   59
Glenn P. Sugameli

6   Protecting Community Stability and Local Economies:
Opportunities for Local Government Influence in Federal
Decision- and Policy-Making Processes   73
Karen Budd-Falen

7   The County Supremacy Movement: Mendacious Myth
Marketing   87
Scott W. Reed

Part 2: Analyzing the Debate

8   Environmentalists and the New Political Climate:
Strategies for the Future   107
Gus diZerega

9   Taking the Land Rights Movement Seriously   115
Kirk Emerson

10 The Logic of Competing Information Campaigns:
    Conflict over Old Growth and the Spotted Owl   135
    Jonathan I. Lange

11 War of Words   151
    Jon Christensen

Part 3: New Directions

12 Wising Up to the Wise Use Movement   161
    Karl Hess, Jr.

13 The Economic Role of Environmental Quality in Western
    Public Lands   185
    Ray Rasker and Jon Roush

14 Wise Use Movement and the National Parks   207
    John Freemuth

15 End of the Progressive Era: Toward Decentralization
    of the Federal Lands   215
    Robert H. Nelson

Part 4: Coming Back into the Country

16 Community and the Politics of Place   235
    Daniel Kemmis

17 Settling America: The Concept of Place in Environmental
    Politics   249
    Mark Sagoff

18 Peril on Common Ground: The Applegate Experiment   261
    Brett KenCairn

19 Tough Towns: The Challenge of Community-Based
    Conservation   279
    Graham Chisholm

20 The Wilderness Killers   293
    Tom Wolf

    Epilogue: Taming the Wolf   303
    Philip D. Brick and R. McGreggor Cawley

    Index   309
    About the Contributors   319

Acknowledgments

The editors would like to thank all the contributors to this volume for their help in organizing and finally producing this volume. Special thanks to Shirley Muse of Whitman College for her skilled and dedicated administrative assistance, as well as the folks at Rowman & Littlefield for their patience and professional work. Thanks also to Paul Hoornbeek for preparing the index on short notice.

We would also like to gratefully acknowledge permission to reprint the following chapters:

Chapter 3 first appeared in *Northern Lights Magazine,* Winter 1994. A slightly different version entitled "Wise Use and Public Lands in the West" appeared in the May/June 1994 issue of *Utne Reader.* Reprinted by permission of the author.

Chapter 4 previously appeared in *Land Rights: The 1990s' Property Rights Rebellion,* edited by Bruce Yandle, © 1995 Rowman & Littlefield. Reprinted by permission of the author and publisher.

Portions of chapter 5 previously appeared in *Virginia Environmental Law Journal* 12, no. 439 (1993) as "Taking Issues in Light of the Sound and Fury (Signifying Nothing?) of *Lucas v. South Carolina Coastal Council.*" Reprinted by permission of author and publisher.

Chapter 7 is adapted from a longer version that previously appeared in *Idaho Law Review* 30, no. 3 (1993-94). Reprinted by permission of author and publisher.

A longer version of chapter 10 previously appeared in *Communication Monographs* 60, no. 3 (1993). Reprinted here by permission of author and publisher.

A longer version of chapter 13 previously appeared as "A New Look at Old Vistas: The Economic Role of Environmental Quality in Western Public Lands" by Raymond Rasker in *University of Colorado Law Review* 65 (1994). Reprinted by permission of the author and publisher.

Chapter 15 is a revised version of "Government as Theater: Toward a New Paradigm for the Public Lands" in *University of Colorado Law Review* 65 (1994). Reprinted by permission of the author and publisher.

Chapter 16 was condensed from *Community and the Politics of Place* by Daniel Kemmis, © 1990 University of Oklahoma Press, by permission of the author and publisher.

Portions of chapter 17 previously appeared in *Journal of Energy, Natural Resources, and Environmental Law* 12, no. 2 (1992). Reprinted by permission of the author and publisher.

Chapter 20 previously appeared in *Colorado's Sangre de Cristo Mountains* by Thomas J. Wolf. © 1995 University of Colorado Press. Reprinted by permission of the author and publisher.

1

Knowing the Wolf, Tending the Garden

Philip D. Brick and R. McGreggor Cawley

> In a historical sense, we are all to blame for the loss of wolves. In the
> nineteenth century, when the Indians on the plains were telling us that
> the wolf was a brother, we were preaching another gospel. Manifest
> Destiny. What rankles us now, I think, is that an alternative gospel still
> remains largely unarticulated. You want to say there never should have
> been a killing, but you don't know what to put in its place.
>
> —Barry Lopez, *Of Wolves and Men*

Throughout literature, including familiar fables and fairy tales from
Aesop and the Brothers Grimm, the wolf appears from the dark forest
to embody cunning evil and powerful cowardice. There seems to be
no limit to the wolf's avarice: Aesop's wolf threatens to devour even
the crane who generously offers to dislodge a bone from the wolf's
throat. In the European-American mind of the eighteenth and nineteenth centuries, the wolf had to be eradicated before civilization could
be carved out of a dense and impenetrable wilderness. By the mid-
twentieth century, there were no wolves remaining to greet Little Red
Riding Hood as she strayed from her straight and narrow path.

Today, the wolf appears not just in our imaginations, but also in
our national forests. Once confined to the Superior-Quetico region of
Northern Minnesota, wolves are being brought back to the lower
forty-eight states by elaborate federal reintroduction schemes pushed
by wolf advocates and the environmental movement. But the wolves
that now populate Yellowstone are not the wolves of Aesop or the
Brothers Grimm. They are part of a "new environmental paradigm,"
which sees the wolf as a symbol of a wildness that is to be loved, not
feared.

The "new" wolf emerges from the wild not to devour innocent Little
Red Riding Hood or to trick her into believing a hairy creature could

1

be her grandmother, but to satisfy our yearnings for a paradise lost. That is not all, for the new wolf also has therapeutic powers: reintroducing the wolf can also "bring balance back to damaged ecosystems." In the words of Interior Secretary Bruce Babbitt, "At last, the wolves are coming home, and Yellowstone will be a complete ecosystem. . . . It's an extraordinary achievement and it's an important statement about who we are as Americans."[1]

Of course, the old wolf did not become the new wolf over night. In a 1930s version of the fairy tale, James Thurber has Red Riding Hood shoot the wolf with a pistol hidden in her basket. The moral, says Thurber: "It's not so easy to fool little girls nowadays as it used to be."[2] But shooting a wolf these days in the lower forty-eight states is a federal offense. There is clearly something more involved here than the surface issue of killing or saving wolves.

When hated, wolves were hunted and tortured with bitter cruelty. When courted, the wolf appears in glossy wildlife calendars as clean and sympathetic as a household pet. It is hardly a matter of simply hating or loving the wolf then. Instead, the various images of the wolf (the various clothes put on it) represent differing worldviews, and the status of the wolf signifies the effort to assert one worldview over another. So even though wolves are back in the Rocky Mountain West, natural-resource policy continues to be paralyzed and polarized by the competing worldviews symbolized by the old wolf and the new wolf.

The wolf is not the only metaphor capturing the underlying turmoil in contemporary federal land policy. The garden is also a locus of significant struggle. Consider the curious twists and turns in Roderick Nash's classic work, *Wilderness and the American Mind.* Nash begins his treatise by suggesting "'Wilderness' has a deceptive concreteness at first glance. The difficulty is that while the word is a noun it acts like an adjective. The term designates a quality (as the "-ness" suggests) that produces a certain mood or feeling in a given individual and, as a consequence, may be assigned by that person to a specific place."[3] Yet, in speculating about a future for wilderness, he warns: "the greatest long-term threat to the interests of people who covet the wild may reside in the *garden scenario*. It too ends wilderness but beneficially rather than destructively" [emphasis his].[4] Nash's garden scenario is a direct allusion to the manicured and thoroughly managed landscapes—"artificial wildernesses"—proposed by Martin Kreiger, Rene Dubos, and others.[5]

To see the possible confusion in separating wilderness from garden we need only look to Yellowstone National Park. It was created in 1872 as a "public park or pleasuring-ground for the benefit and enjoyment of the people," and the secretary of interior was charged with developing regulations that provided for "the preservation, from injury or spoilation, of all timber, mineral deposits, natural curiosities, or wonders within said park, and their retention in their natural condition." The secretary was also directed to prevent the "wanton destruction of the fish and game found within said park."[6]

To our modern ear, this language sounds very much like a call for preservation of wilderness. However, the act also granted the secretary of interior discretion to permit the construction of "buildings for the accommodation of visitors" as well as "roads and bridle-paths." A park with hotels, restaurants, roads, and bridle-paths suddenly seems more gardenlike than wildernesslike. And where does the wolf—which is neither fish nor game—fit into the wilderness/garden of Yellowstone?

Further confusion (clarification?) emerged forty-four years later with the creation of the National Park Service (NPS). The 1916 Organic Act directed the NPS to "promote and regulate the use" of national parks, monuments, and reservations "by such means and measures as conform to the fundamental purpose . . . to conserve the scenery and the natural and historic objects and the wildlife therein and to provide for the enjoyment of the same in such a manner and by such means as will leave them unimpaired for the enjoyment of future generations."[7] But the Organic Act also authorized the cutting of timber "in order to control the attacks of insects or disease or otherwise conserve the scenery" and the "destruction of such animals and of such plant life as may be detrimental to the use" of the parks, monuments, and reservations. The rest of the Yellowstone story is, as the saying goes, history.

The zeal of the NPS in protecting the park's natural scenery throughout the twentieth century created the conditions necessary for the spectacular fires of 1988. With equal zeal, the early NPS carried out a war against predators in the park, ostensibly following the belief that elk, deer, and antelope were the primary wildlife to be preserved.[8] Primary among the eradicated predators, of course, was the wolf.

Now, we envision plans to *restore* Yellowstone. Hoping to dodge the problematical wilderness/garden, we call Yellowstone an *ecosystem*, defined as: "living organisms together with their nonliving environment forming an interacting system inhabiting a defined area of interest."[9] Yet, as the recent controversies over ecosystem management at Yellowstone demonstrated, even the apparent objectivity of this language does not provide enough room to avoid the underlying tension.[10] A garden is as much an interacting system as a wilderness.

Indeed, organic gardeners have long appreciated the advantages of understanding the interactions among the various components of their gardens. Skillful application of this knowledge allows the gardener to harness the powers of nature, and thereby minimize the need for artificially produced pesticides and fertilizers. Thus, Interior Secretary Babbitt's assertion that wolves have made Yellowstone a complete ecosystem could be read either as a statement about wilderness, or as the boast of a proud gardener.

Government and the Illusion of Control

Whatever our visions of the wolf and the garden, government has been the conduit for advancing and enforcing our illusions. National parks and wilderness areas, despite their natural character, are artifacts of government, owing their current conditions to the intervention of bureaucratic managers. Tom Wolf rightly points out that the wolf never could have been eradicated in gardens of the lower forty-eight states without the persistence of hunters enticed by government bounties.[11] And it is not without great irony, as Karl Hess notes, that environmental activists have relied on the power of the federal government to reintroduce wolves into the American West.[12]

Yet, we view this irony as containing the potential for clarifying the current state of federal land policy. The battle between environmentalists and their opponents is not for control of resources; it is a struggle for control of government. The protagonists believe that control of government will allow them to claim the federal estate in their own image of the wolf and the garden. But this belief is an illusion of control that is always transitory. As one observer put it, "we can't buy solutions from the government, we can only rent them for a while until the landlord changes his mind."

In this regard, both environmentalists and their opponents confront a much larger problem. Public faith in progressive, benevolent government appears to be fading as more and more citizens see government as a wolf mucking about in what should be their private gardens. Recent polls indicate that Americans increasingly view government as a cause of current problems, rather than a solution. In some vague (yet clearly articulated) sense, some people fear government in much the same way they used to fear the wolf. Although wolves rarely if ever attack humans, the belief that they might turn their gaze upon us fuels our fears of the mythological wolf. Mistrust of government bears much the same imprint.

Roughly a decade ago, one of the leading Sagebrush Rebels explained that their protests were animated both by policies adopted in the 1960s and 1970s, and by "apprehensions and fears of what's coming next." Then secretary of interior James Watt was able to defuse these fears with his promise of a "good neighbor policy," which shifted the illusion of control from environmentalists to western commodity resource users. This strategy worked because, despite the states' rights rhetoric of the Sagebrush Rebellion, the central argument focused on the *way* federal lands were managed, not the legitimacy of federal management—a point affirmed by the Sagebrush Rebels' opposition to the Reagan administration's ill-fated proposal to privatize the federal estate.[13]

In the current political climate, it seems unlikely that such a strategy would succeed. Seeking to defend themselves from a seemingly endless barrage of criticisms, federal land managers have hitched their wagon to "ecosystem management," apparently oblivious to the fact that Americans increasingly associate bureaucratic management of any social problem with inefficiency and ineptitude. The central issues raised by the land-rights movement—wise use, property rights, county supremacy—challenge not just the direction of federal land management, but also the underlying philosophical and legal concepts upon which it is based. Perhaps even more important, the environmental movement, which seemed invulnerable during the 1970s, now finds itself struggling with a fundamental identity crisis.

Frustrated by events over the past decade, elements within the environmental community have diagnosed the root problem as emerging more from faults in the movement's strategies than from the efforts of its opponents. For example, some critics charge that the environmental movement has become too moderate and too institutionalized, allowing corporations to capture the "green" agenda, leaving the movement without a separate and defining mission.[14] At the same time, other critics accuse the movement of embracing ideas that are too radical, moving the environmental community's posture beyond what it can sustain politically. For these critics, biodiversity, animal rights, and ecofeminism may be appropriate vanguard concepts for a movement out to remake modern society, but in the contemporary political climate where Americans feel insecure about their economic future, such concepts only highlight a perception that environmentalists are out of touch with mainstream America.[15] Still others indict environmental groups for their elitism, detachment from the public, indifference to working class interests, and staunch support of big government.[16]

It is not at all clear, then, what direction the environmental movement might take should it regain the illusion of control that it enjoyed throughout the 1970s. Moreover, recent events cast serious doubts about whether or not the movement will ever recover its lost stature. The optimism so prevalent during the early Clinton administration has now yielded to holding a Maginot line against a flood of anti-environmental, regulatory reform measures in the 104th Congress. At this writing, it is too early to assess whether this power shift will have lasting consequences. However, it is clear that we have entered a period of uncertainty and possible change.

As troublesome as recent setbacks to the environmental movement may seem to many environmentalists, there is little reason to believe that Americans are abandoning their interest in the environment. Indeed, the current turmoil should ultimately strengthen the movement. Uncertainty and chaos, as many ecologists have come to appreciate, best describe the dynamism of natural ecosystems, producing the diversity of life that we today celebrate.[17] The challenge today, then, may be to shape an environmentalism that can survive and thrive in uncertain times, and with less reliance on government. We believe that there is much in the current land-rights–environmental debate that can help move this process forward.

The Land-Rights–Environmental Debate: Background

In contentious natural-resource and land-use debates, the environmental movement has always squared off against powerful industrial and agricultural interests. But with the rise of land-rights groups in the late 1980s and early 1990s, that opposition is now better organized and more ideologically coherent. The result is a striking transformation of natural-resource debates. The shift in the debate is startling, especially since the "land-rights movement" was considered to be politically marginal just a few years ago.

Many environmentalists had come to treat environmental laws passed twenty years ago as etched in stone, a view supported by the fact that most environmental laws were passed with bipartisan support or were signed by Republican presidents. Yet, the laws protecting our air, water, public lands, and endangered species rely heavily on the regulatory power of the federal government. In consequence, they are now juicy targets for ideological and budgetary attacks from zealous conservative legislators.

Supporting these legislators at home is a well-organized cadre of land-rights groups, who provide them with regulatory horror stories (farmer goes to jail for killing a kangaroo rat, logger loses family wage job because of a spotted owl, etc.) and barrage them with complaints about experiences with federal environmental regulators in sophisticated fax and letter-writing campaigns. Land-rights groups have been defining the contours of natural-resource debates, putting the environmental movement constantly on the defensive. Too often, environmental groups seem to see no other option than to defend federal regulations that even they admit don't work as well as they should.

The land-rights movement is diverse and broadly based, including property-rights groups nationwide, with wise-use and county-supremacy groups strongest in the West. Wise-use is a coalition of loggers, ranchers, miners, farmers, fishermen, oil and gas interests, real estate developers, and off-road vehicle enthusiasts, while county-supremacy groups, made up of both property-rights advocates and wise-use interests, focus on using county government as a weapon against federal agencies, which in their view are conspiring with environmentalists to take land away from traditional commodity uses. Although estimates vary, it is clear that land-rights groups have proliferated quickly in recent years. The movement grew from two hundred groups in 1988 to over fifteen hundred groups nationwide in 1995, with most growth occurring in the past two or three years.[18]

The land-rights movement draws much of its strength from combining interests that formally had little in common with one another. For example, ranchers have been traditionally suspicious of mining interests or real estate developers. But the movement has been able to create a united front, linked primarily by fear and loathing of environmental regulations.

Environmentalists have had a difficult time coming to terms with angry land-rights activists. From a position of presumed innocence (Little Red Riding Hood), the environmental movement's first instinct was to pull out a concealed pistol and fire away at the "wolf in sheep's clothing." As wise-use, property-rights, and county-supremacy groups surged in the early 1990s, environmental groups initially tried to marginalize them by portraying them as puppets of big industry (which funds land-rights groups to a greater or lesser extent, depending on the group), and more recently trying to connect land-rights activists with still more extreme militia groups. For example, some environmentalists, especially after the bombing of the Federal Building in Oklahoma City, point out that the National Federal Lands Conference, which promotes county supremacy, endorsed the militia movement as a useful tool to intimidate "out of control" federal bureaucrats in its October 1994 newsletter.

Other environmentalists point to the cunning wolf who manipulates workers in natural-resource industries to identify with their bosses. For example, an influential wise-use group, People for the West!, is funded almost exclusively by the mining industry, even though its rhetoric (and much of its local support) is populist. Environmentalists also charge that the cynicism of land-rights groups is thinly veiled. They cite Ron Arnold's blueprint for developing popular citizen activists who advance industry's agenda as an example of the cunning wolf misleading an unsuspecting public. Environmentalists are particularly enraged that timber corporations fund organizations to fight environmental laws that "cost jobs," while far more jobs, they claim, are lost to log exports, mill modernization, and unsustainable forest practices.

The growth of land-rights groups suggests that these arguments are falling on deaf ears. It was not enough to simply label land-rights groups "astroturf" (phony grassroots groups). Environmentalists thought they could eradicate the land-rights wolf by demonstrating that a real wolf (industry) lay beneath the popular veneer of appeals for property rights, individual liberty, and jobs. But what they did not see, at least initially, were the sources of the land-rights movement's strength, which go far deeper than they first suspected, reaching deeply into evolving ideological preferences and latent class tensions in rapidly changing regional economies.

Environmentalists could not help but notice the land-rights movement's success in mobilizing a committed grassroots constituency that is convinced that it must fight all environmental laws with an ideological fervor formally reserved only for foreign enemies. Environmentalists often cannot understand why a local farmer might be more worried about an endangered bald eagle nesting on his property (which could trigger federal endangered species proceedings) than the takeover of his farm by corporate agribusiness. Certainly, more family farms have been lost to the latter than to the bald eagle, which seems reminiscent of the ever-elusive communist in Bob Dylan's song, "Talkin' John Birch Paranoid Blues."

To dismiss these concerns as idle paranoia misses the point. To many in the land-rights movement, the greens have replaced the reds as the greatest threat to free enterprise and democracy in America. As a popular joke among land-rights activists goes, "Environmentalists are watermelons . . . green on the outside and red on the inside." Strong ideological commitments have a way of energizing activists and propelling them beyond parochial goals. It is the stuff of coherent social movements, bringing together interests that had hitherto been discrete and largely unconnected. In the process, environmental issues become inextricably linked with contentious issues of federalism, taxation, and individual rights, where kindred ideological spirits can be mobilized and constituencies widened.

Environmentalists also have difficulty coming to terms with issues of class latent in what they see as the land-rights–industry wolf. With few exceptions, environmental groups have had no coherent strategy to engage rural Americans in environmental programs. At the same time, environmental goals have expanded ever further into the rural West's traditionally exclusive domain, as environmentalists moved beyond "saving special places" to a wider concern for "biodiversity," a term virtually unknown just a decade ago. But the most biologically productive land is most often connected with private interests, a fact not lost on many landholders and public-land ranchers who fear they may lose their way of life if environmental restrictions grow. These long latent fears were just waiting to be mobilized by land-rights activists who understood their concerns, and gave them an organizationally powerful and ideologically charged expression.

More recently, some environmental leaders have recognized that there is much to be learned from the rise of land-rights groups. In short, the big bad wolf has become a more benevolent one (though we doubt it will soon adorn any glossy calendars). For example, Jon Roush, president of the Wilderness Society, suggests that the recent congressional assault on the environment reflects shortcomings in environmental strategies, including inattention to social and economic problems, especially in rural areas: "If we can't sustain communities around wilderness areas, then we can't have sustainable wilderness areas."[19] Or, as Audubon Society president John Flicker remarks, "we are moving into a new era of conservation. We are out of the era of major command and control frameworks and into an era much more focused on solving problems at the state and local level. We need to organize accordingly."[20] In most cases, this means organizing in rural communities and paying more attention to social-justice issues.

When the wolf is viewed as less a threat than an opportunity, there is much that can be done to move the debate to new and more productive levels. The land-rights wolf, much like the Yellowstone wolf, can help restore political vision to the environmental movement—it can help bring the environmental movement back home to defend real homelands and communities, both human and natural, instead of defending abstract philosophical principles and unpopular regulations. We will return to the subject of "taming the wolf" in the final essay in this volume.

Navigating the Land-Rights–Environmental Debate

Our aim in this volume is to explore what implications the rise of the land-rights movement might have on the environmental movement. Although some in the land-rights movement suggest that their aim is to defeat *environmentalism* not the *environment*, to many people this is simply splitting hairs.[21] Environmentalism is deeply rooted in American culture, and environmental groups continue to enjoy a high measure of public support. In poll after poll, no matter how the questions are asked, Americans consistently voice concern about environmental issues.

However, disarray in the environmental movement, coupled with the rise of land-rights groups, suggests that there is much to be done. The land-rights movement can offer a lesson or two, but it is important to note that land-rights criticisms of the environmental movement parallel criticisms that appear from within the movement.[22] We use the word "parallel" with some care here. Obviously, the land-rights critique of environmentalism and criticisms within it are moving in different directions. The former seeks to discredit environmentalism, and the latter seeks to strengthen it. Our goal in this volume is to facilitate a dialogue between these two opposing factions in an effort to help restore political vision to the environmental movement.

Restoring political vision is far different from finding some "middle ground" or "balance" between land-rights and environmental groups, as some observers of the debate have suggested is the answer.[23] We are not interested in finding a middle ground in the current debate, since we are not convinced anyone would want to occupy it. Indeed, if the bitter land-use struggles of recent decades tell us anything at all, it is what any Texan knows—there are only two things you will find in the middle of the road: a double yellow line and a dead armadillo. We need not add public-land and natural-resource policy to the list. Instead, we hope to help redefine the debate by exploring the promise and perils of "place-centric" environmental activism, stimulated by the appearance of a wolf that is both old and new.

This book is organized in four sections. Our goal in part 1 is to offer the reader an opportunity to explore the current land-rights–environmental debate, drawing on writings from leading figures from each side. Each of the three main branches of the land-rights movement are addressed—wise-use, private-property rights, and county-supremacy. Part 2 offers a "debate about the debate," analyzing how the struggle to define the high ground in natural-resource debates plays itself out in national and local policy contexts, and in the media. Part 3 explores ideas that will be crucial to moving the debate beyond its current limits, encouraging us to reconceptualize our attitudes toward public lands and the human communities and economies that sustain them. Finally, part 4 explores the concept of place and the challenges of environmental activism at the local level, which, despite difficulties, will be central in the effort to "tame the wolf."

Notes

1. Michael Milstein, "The Wolves Are Back, Big Time," *High Country News*, 6 February 1995, 12.
2. Barry Lopez, *Of Wolves and Men* (New York: Scribner, 1978), 264.
3. Roderick Nash, *Wilderness and the American Mind*, 3rd ed. (New Haven: Yale University Press, 1982), 1.
4. Ibid., 380.
5. Ibid., 238–71.
6. 25 Stat. 32–33 (1872).
7. 408 Stat. 535–36 (1916).
8. Alston Chase, *Playing God in Yellowstone: The Destruction of America's First National Park* (Boston: Atlantic Monthly Press, 1986).
9. United States Forest Service and United States National Park Service, *A Vision for the Future: A Framework for Coordination in the Greater Yellowstone Area* (Washington, D.C.: Government Printing Office, 1990), G-2.
10. R. McGreggor Cawley and John Freemuth, "Tree Farms, Mother Earth, and Other Dilemmas: The Politics of Ecosystem Management in Greater Yellowstone," *Society and Natural Resources* 6:41–53.
11. See Tom Wolf, "Wilderness Killers," chapter 20 in this volume.
12. See Karl Hess, Jr., "Wising Up to the Wise Use Movement," chapter 12 in this volume.
13. R. McGreggor Cawley, *Federal Land, Western Anger: The Sagebrush Rebellion and Environmental Politics* (Lawrence: University Press of Kansas, 1993).
14. See Paul Watson and Warren Rogers, *Sea Shepard: My Fight for Whales and Seals* (New York: W. W. Norton, 1982); Bill Devall and George Sessions, *Deep Ecology, Living as if Nature Mattered* (Salt Lake City: Peregrine Books, 1985); Murray Bookchin, *Remaking Society: Pathways to a Green Future* (Boston: South End Press, 1990); Christopher Manes, *Green Rage: Radical Environmentalism and the Unmaking of Civilization* (Boston: Little Brown, 1990); Dave Foreman, *Confessions of an Eco-Warrior* (New York: Harmony Books, 1991); Howie Wolke, *Wilderness on the Rocks* (Tucson: Ned Ludd Books, 1991); Barry

Commoner, *Making Peace with the Planet* (New York: New York Press, 1992); and Peter List, *Radical Environmentalism: Philosophy and Tactics* (Belmont, Calif.: Wadsworth, 1993).

15. See Robert Cahn, ed., *An Environmental Agenda for the Future* (Washington, D.C.: Island Press, 1985); Peter Borrelli, ed., *Crossroads: Environmental Priorities for the Future* (Washington, D.C.: Island Press, 1988); Donald Snow, ed., *Inside the Environmental Movement: Meeting the Leadership Challenge* (Washington, D.C.: Conservation Fund, 1992); Bob Pepperman Taylor, *Our Limits Transgressed: Environmental Political Thought in America* (Lawrence: University Press of Kansas, 1992); Martin W. Lewis, *Green Delusions: An Environmentalist Critique of Radical Environmentalism* (Durham: Duke University Press, 1994); and Charles T. Rubin, *The Green Crusade: Rethinking the Roots of Radical Environmentalism* (New York: Free Press, 1994).

16. See discussion in Robert Braile, "What the Hell Are We Fighting For?" *Garbage* 6: 28–35.

17. Daniel B. Botkin, *Discordant Harmonies: A New Ecology for the Twenty-First Century* (New York: Oxford University Press, 1990). See also Lisa Jones, "The End of Certainty," *High Country News*, 13 November 1995, 8.

18. Ron Arnold, Center for the Defense of Free Enterprise, personal communication with the authors, 12 June 1995.

19. Cited in Phil Shabecoff, "DC's Power Brokers Look for a New Home," *High Country News*, 13 November 1995, 22. In chapter 13 of this volume, Jon Roush and Ray Rasker offer some thoughts on how wilderness preservation and economic development can go hand in hand for small communities in the rural West.

20. Ibid., 22.

21. The distinction between environmentalism and environment is a key premise in Ron Arnold, *Ecology Wars: Environmentalism As If People Mattered* (Bellevue, Wash.: Free Enterprise Press, 1987).

22. See Mark Dowie, *Losing Ground: American Environmentalism at the Close of the Twentieth Century* (Cambridge, Mass.: MIT Press, 1995).

23. Alston Chase, *In a Dark Wood* (New York: Houghton Mifflin, 1995).

Part 1

The Land-Rights–Environmental Debate

2

Overcoming Ideology

Ron Arnold

It was 1964, the year of the Wilderness Act. Historian Leo Marx began his classic, *The Machine in the Garden,* with the assertion that "the pastoral ideal has been used to define the meaning of America ever since the age of discovery, and it has not yet lost its hold upon the native imagination."[1] A little more than thirty years after, we have the present volume, *A Wolf in the Garden,* echoing Marx less than tolling a sea change in American notions of exactly what is meant by the pastoral ideal. Marx saw it as a cultivated rural "middle landscape," not urban, not wild, but embodying what Arthur O. Lovejoy calls "semi-primitivism"; it is located in a middle ground somewhere between the opposing forces of civilization and nature.[2]

The pastoral ideal is not simply a location but also a psychic energy condenser: it stores the charge generated between the polarities of civilization and nature. Ortega y Gasset recognized this as long ago as 1930 in *The Revolt of the Masses:* "The world is a civilized one, its inhabitant is not: he does not see the civilization of the world around him, but he uses it as if it were a natural force. The new man wants his motor-car, and enjoys it, but he believes that it is the spontaneous fruit of an Edenic tree."[3]

There was a certain truth to this blind sight: producers in the middle landscape invisibly yielded the raw materials for the motor-car (and everything else). The labor power of dwellers in America's middle landscape has always been reified as an Edenic tree to be plucked by distant capital and unappreciative consumers, and the dwellers felt it keenly.

Since 1964, the rise of environmentalist ideology has pushed the pastoral ideal increasingly toward nature, striving to redefine the meaning of America in fully primitivist terms of the wild. Eco-ideologists

15

have thrust their metaphoric raging Wolf into every rank and row of our civilized Garden to rogue out both the domesticated and the domesticators. The Wolf howls "wild land, wild water, wild air." Whether Wild People might have a proper place in Wolf World remains a subject of dispute among eco-ideologists.[4]

Public-policy debate over the environment and the meaning of America has been clamorous these thirty years. Its terms were succinctly put by Edith Stein:

> The environmental movement challenges the dominant Western worldview and its three assumptions:
>
> * Unlimited economic growth is possible and beneficial.
> * Most serious problems can be solved by technology.
> * Environmental and social problems can be mitigated by a market economy with some state intervention.
>
> Since the 1970s we've heard increasingly about the competing paradigm, wherein:
>
> * Growth must be limited.
> * Science and technology must be restrained.
> * Nature has finite resources and a delicate balance that humans must observe.[5]

That fairly delineates the public debate. However, in order to critique an ideology, one needs an accurate statement of that ideology. The environmentalist ideology striving to redefine the meaning of America was expounded most realistically by author Victor B. Scheffer in a *Northwest Environmental Journal* article, "Environmentalism's Articles of Faith." The five tenets Scheffer proposed appear to be the core of shared beliefs actually held most widely by environmentalists:

1. *All things are connected.* "[N]ever will we understand completely the spin-off effects of the environmental changes that we create, nor will we measure our own, independent influence in their creation." Scheffer adds, "I use the word *nature* for the world without humans, a concept which—like the square root of minus one—is unreal, but useful."

2. *Earthly goods are limited.* "As applied to people, carrying capacity is the number of individuals that the earth can support before a limit is reached beyond which the quality of life must worsen and *Homo*, the human animal, becomes less human. One reason we hu-

mans—unlike animals in the wild—are prone to exceed carrying capacity is that our wants exceed our needs."

3. *Nature's way is best.* "Woven into the fabric of environmentalism is the belief that natural methods and materials should be favored over artificial and synthetic ones, when there's a clear choice. Witness the vast areas of the globe poisoned or degraded by the technological economy of our century."

4. *The survival of humankind depends on natural diversity.* "Although species by the billions have vanished through natural extinction or transformation, the present rate of extinction is thought to be at least 400 times faster than at the beginning of the Industrial Age. Humankind's destruction of habitats is overwhelmingly to blame."

Scheffer adds, "No one has the moral right, and should not have the legal right, to overtax carrying capacity either by reducing the productivity of the land or by bringing into the world more than his or her 'share' of new lives. Who is to decide that share will perhaps be the most difficult social question for future generations."

5. *Environmentalism is radical* "in the sense of demanding fundamental change. It calls for changes in present political systems, in the reach of the law, in the methods of agriculture and industry, in the structure of capitalism (the profit system), in international dealings, and in education."[6]

One can see the Wolf skulking in each of Scheffer's five tenets of eco-ideology. Actual organizations and individuals comprising the environmental movement stress different clusters of these tenets. Although the environmental movement's structure is complex and amply textured, three distinctive axes of influence dominate environmental politics in America:

1. Establishment interventionists—acting to hamper property rights and markets sufficiently to centralize control of many transactions for the benefit of environmentalists and their funders in the foundation community, while leaving the market economy itself operational, they tend to emphasize the need for natural diversity and in some cases to own and manage wildlife preserves. Notable organizations in this sector are the Nature Conservancy, National Wildlife Federation, and National Audubon Society.

2. Eco-socialists—acting to dislodge the market system with public ownership of all resources and production, commanded by environmentalists in an ecological welfare state, they tend to emphasize the limits of earthly goods. Greenpeace, Native Forest Council, and Maine Audubon Society are representative groups.

3. Deep ecologists—acting to reduce or eliminate industrial civilization and human population in varying degrees, they tend to emphasize that nature's way is best and environmentalism is radical. Earth First!, Sea Shepherd Conservation Society, and Native Forest Network are in this category.[7]

The Wolf in these varieties of sheep's clothing is rapacious, not simply protecting nature but also annihilating the livelihoods of dwellers in the middle landscape. Today the Wolf is firmly entrenched in Washington, D.C., where important environmental groups have established headquarters or major operating bases. Eco-ideologists have written many laws, tested them in the courts, and pressured many administrative agencies into compliance with their ideology. They have, in brief, become the Establishment. The apparatus of environmentalism is no longer represented merely by nonprofit organizations, but has grown to encompass American government at all levels.

Since the inception of the Environmental Grantmakers Association (EGA) in 1985, the foundation community has usurped substantial control of the environmental movement. The standard philanthropic model, "non-profit organization submits its proposal to foundation for funding," has given way to "a combine of foundations selects and dictates grant-driven programs to non-profit organization." In the instance of the Ancient Forest campaign in the Pacific Northwest, a cluster of six EGA foundations even went so far as to create their own projects because of dissatisfaction with the capabilities of the Washington, D.C., environmental community. The foundations derive their income from managed investment portfolios representing the power elite of corporate America.[8]

As the environmental debate developed during the late 1980s, the "dominant Western worldview" gained an organized constituency and advocacy leadership: the wise use movement. Incipient and gestating more than a decade in the bosom of those who had been most wounded by environmental ideology, the new movement congealed at a conference in Reno, Nevada, in 1988. It was centered around a hodgepodge of property-rights groups, antiregulation legal foundations, trade groups of large industries, motorized-recreation-vehicle clubs, federal-land users, farmers, ranchers, fishermen, trappers, small forest holders, mineral prospectors, and others who live and work in the middle landscape.[9]

It came as a shock to environmentalists. The "competing paradigm" unhappily found itself confronted with a competing paradigm. The free ride was over. A substantial cluster of nonprofit grassroots organizations now advocated unlimited economic growth, technological progress, and a market economy. They opposed the eco-ideologists' proposals using the tactics of social-change movements, such as mobilizing grassroots constituencies, staging media events including protest demonstrations, and orchestrating letter-writing campaigns to pressure Congress.

It was a pivotal shift in the debate. No longer were eco-ideologists able to face off against business and industry, pitting greedy for-profit corporations against environmentalism's nonprofit moral high ground. Now it was urban environmentalists defending their vision of the pastoral ideal against those who actually lived the pastoral ideal in the middle landscape.

This simple structural rearrangement of the debate went virtually unnoticed, but was crucial: it was nonprofit against nonprofit, one side promoting economic growth, technological progress, and a market economy, the other opposing.

The emergent wise use movement held up a mirror to the embarrassing questions posed by the "competing paradigm": Just *who* will limit our economic growth? Who will restrain America's science and technology? Who will decide what "delicate balance humans must observe"? The answer was clear: only environmental ideologists, and not those who create economic growth, science, technology, or the market economy.

Asserting such onerous control over others was not attractive and clarified the environmental movement as just another special interest protecting its selfish economic status. Economics is not about money, it is about the allocation of scarce resources. The wise use movement bared the environmental movement's ambition to be resource allocator for the world.[10]

Environmentalism's efforts to turn America's pastoral ideal wild stood out in sharp contrast to the wise use movement's actual stewardship of the land, the water, and the air. Wise users were not perfect, to be sure, but they were down to earth, real, and necessary. They created economic growth, employed science and technology, and drove the market economy.

Environmentalism, by contrast, appeared in the same light as pastoral literature in critic William Empson's *Some Versions of Pastoral*: "about the people but not by or for them."[11] Environmentalism, like pastoral literature, was about those pastoral rural dwellers who produced dinner, dress, and domicile for everyone, but was generated by the educated elite, not by those who lived the pastoral ideal. Environmentalism's ideology was promulgated for the ruling elite, not for the farmer or rancher or family forest owner or mineral prospector.

When the wise use movement arose to demystify ecofetishism, the environmental movement lost its grip on the debate.

The first environmentalist reaction to the emergence of the wise use movement was passive denial—ignore it and it will go away. That lasted from 1988 to early 1992. The present phase of active denial began with a study of the wise use movement by the W. Alton Jones Foundation, dated February 1992, portraying the rising social force as a mere front for industry, created by industry, paid for by industry, and controlled by industry. The fact that foundation analysts sincerely believed this assessment points up how unprepared the environmental movement was to lose its favored "non-profit versus for-profit" moral high ground in the debate. Industry *had* to be the opponent. The wise use movement *had* to be a mere front. So that's what they saw.[12]

This humbuggery lasted only half a year. Further research, sponsored by the Wilderness Society and conducted by the Boston-area media strategy firm MacWilliams Cosgrove Snider, disclosed a disturbing truth: "What we're finding is that wise use is really a local movement driven by primarily local concerns and not national issues. . . . And, in fact, the more we dig into it, having put together over a number of months a fifty state fairly comprehensive survey of what's going on, we have come to the conclusion that this is pretty much generally a grass roots movement, which is a problem, because it means there's no silver bullet."

The words are those of Debra Callahan, then director of W. Alton Jones Foundation's Environmental Grass Roots Program, at the 1992 Environmental Grantmakers Association annual fall retreat. Her session, titled "The Wise Use Movement: Threats and Opportunities," capped off the three-day convocation of foundation executives.[13]

Callahan's source, the MacWilliams Cosgrove Snider report, titled "The Wise Use Movement: Strategic Analysis and Fifty State Review," affirmed that the wise use movement was the greatest threat the environmental movement had ever faced.[14]

"What people fundamentally want, what people fundamentally believe about environmental protection," Callahan said polls revealed, "is that no, it's not just jobs. And no, it's not just environment. Why can't we have both?"

> The high ground is capturing that message, okay? The wise use movement is trying to capture that message. What they're saying out there is that "We are the real environmentalists. We are the stewards of the land. We're the farmers who have tilled that land and we know how to manage this land because we've done it here for generations. We're the

miners and we're the ones who depend for our livelihood on this land. These environmentalists, they're elitists. They live in glass towers in New York City. They're not environmentalists. They're part of the problem. And they're aligned with big government. And they're out of touch. So we're the real environmentalists."

And if that's the message that the wise use movement is able to capture, we are suddenly really unpopular. The minute the wise use people capture that high ground, we almost have not got a winning message left in our quiver.

Judy Donald of the Washington, D.C.-based Beldon Fund, and Callahan's copresenter, took the conclusion a step further. "There are, as Deb has made clear, ordinary people, grass roots organizations, who obviously feel their needs are being addressed by this movement," said Donald. "We have to have a strategy that also is addressing those concerns. And that cannot come simply from environmentalists. It can't come just from us. That's the dilemma here. It's not simply that people don't get it, it's that they do get it. They're losing their jobs."

Barbara Dudley, then executive of the Veatch Fund, now head of Greenpeace, stated: "This is a class issue. There is no question about it. It is true that the environmental movement is, has been, traditionally . . . an upper class conservation, white movement. We have to face that fact. It's true. They're not wrong that we are rich and they are up against us. We are the enemy as long as we behave in that fashion."

These commanders of environmentalism had acknowledged they were destroying jobs and hurting those who produce our material goods. They admitted themselves the enemy. This moment of self-comprehension was a tremendous opportunity to repent and reach out to wise users, dwellers in the middle landscape who felt betrayed by big government and big business.

Instead, the foundations and their environmental cohort deliberately fell back on their stereotype, portraying wise use as a front for corporations, and risking a frontal assault against wise use with new tactics: "Attack Wise Use. . . . Find divisions between Wise Use and Wise Use and exploit them. . . . We need to . . . talk about the Wise Use agenda. We need to expose the links between Wise Use and other extremists."

In other words, a smear campaign would be mounted to tie wise users to unpopular extremists such as the John Birch Society, the Unification Church, Lyndon LaRouche, and to violent factions such as the militias. They knew they couldn't shoot down the message, so they settled for shooting the messenger.

To implement the smear campaign, W. Alton Jones Foundation helped found the Clearinghouse on Environmental Advocacy and Research (CLEAR) in 1993 with two grants totaling $145,000. In the same year, Jones gave numerous grants in the $20,000 to $30,000 range to small local organizations that agreed to conduct smears against wise use.[15]

The Sierra Club engaged private investigator David Helvarg to write an anti–wise use tirade titled *The War Against the Greens* claiming a conspiracy of violence by wise users against environmentalists. Helvarg's sponsors also funded a road show for him to tie wise use to an alleged far-right terrorist network.[16]

The EGA foundations and their grant-driven environmentalist dependents spent millions on related media saturation projects designed to identify the words "wise use" with "violence" in the public mind. Reliance on the Big Lie revealed grant-driven environmentalists as intellectually and morally bankrupt, and the technique backfired, just as EGA members Donald and Dudley foresaw.

Grassroots environmentalists saw that big-money foundations controlled the mainstream environmental movement, which they felt had sold out true reform for pallid incrementalism. They deserted by the hundred thousands, preferring to form scattered local and regional groups of their own. The Wilderness Society and Sierra Club were hit particularly hard, losing 125,000 members and 130,000 members, respectively, in 1994.[17]

Most devastating for the foundations, author and syndicated columnist Alexander Cockburn, an icon of the Left, aired their dirty laundry in the progressive flagship, *The Nation*. "For years now," wrote Cockburn in August 1995, "David Helvarg has been backed by environmental groups such as the Sierra Club to investigate and smear the Wise Use movement by any means necessary. This goes back to the early 1990s when the Environmental Grantmakers Association offered a de facto bounty for material discrediting Wise Users as (a) a front for corporations or (b) part of a far-right terrorist network."

Cockburn—an equal-opportunity critic who routinely berates the wise use movement for its failings—deplored the smear tactic. He wrote, "And so we have the unlovely sight of Helvarg behaving like an F.B.I. agent. He prowls across literature tables at Wise Use meetings and ties all the names on the pamphlets, letterheads and books into his 'terror network.' The trouble is, he never makes his case. Helvarg never comes up with the terrorist conspiracy he proclaims, because there hasn't been one."[18]

Indeed. What there has been, and what environmentalists cannot confront, is a potent movement subversive of environmentalism's articles of faith. That is why they resort to a hoax rather than lively debate on the issues.

Although it would be rash to propose wise use's articles of faith—it is a diverse movement—some of the following principles would probably find wide agreement among those who provide the material goods to all of humanity:

1. *Humans, like all organisms, must use natural resources to survive.* This fundamental verity is never addressed by environmental ideology. The simple fact that humans must get their food, clothing, and shelter from the environment is either ignored or obliquely deplored in quasi-suicidal plaints such as, "I would rather see a blank space where I am—at least I wouldn't be harming anything."

If environmentalism were to acknowledge our necessary use of the earth, the ideology would lose its meaning. To grant legitimacy to the human use of the environment would be to accept the unavoidable environmental damage that is the price of our survival. Once that price is acceptable, the moral framework of environmental ideology becomes irrelevant and the issues become technical and economic.

2. *The earth and its life are tough and resilient, not fragile and delicate.* Environmentalists tend to be catastrophists, seeing any human use of the earth as damage and massive human use of the earth as a catastrophe. An environmentalist motto is "We all live downstream," the viewpoint of hapless victims.

Wise users, on the other hand, tend to be cornucopians, seeing themselves as stewarding and nurturing the bountiful earth as it stewards and nurtures them. A wise use motto is "We all live upstream," the viewpoint of responsible individuals.

The difference in sense of life is striking. Environmentalism by its very nature promotes feelings of guilt for existing, which naturally degenerate into pessimism, self-loathing, and depression. Wise use by its very nature promotes feelings of competence to live in the world, generating curiosity, learning, and optimism toward improving the earth for the massive use of future generations.

The glory of the "dominant Western worldview" so scorned by environmental ideologists is its metaphor of progress: the starburst, an insatiable and interminable outreach after a perpetually flying goal. Environmentalists call humanity a cancer on the earth; wise users call us a joy.

If there is a single, tight expression of the wise use sense of life, it has to be the final stanza of Shelley's *Prometheus Unbound.* Wise users, I think, will recognize themselves in these lines:

To suffer woes which Hope thinks infinite;
To forgive wrongs darker than death or night;
To defy Power, which seem omnipotent;
To love, and bear; to hope till Hope itself creates
From its own wreck the thing it contemplates;
Neither to change, nor falter, nor repent;
This, like thy glory, Titan! is to be
Good, great and joyous, beautiful and free;
This is alone Life, Joy, Empire, and Victory![19]

3. *We only learn about the world through trial and error.* The universe did not come with a set of instructions, nor did our minds. We cannot see the future. Thus, the only way we humans can learn about our surroundings is through trial and error. Even the most sophisticated science is systematized trial and error. Environmental ideology fetishizes nature to the point that we cannot permit ourselves errors with the environment, ending in no trials and no learning.

There will always be abusers who do not learn. People of goodwill tend to deal with abuse by education, incentive, clear rules, and administering appropriate penalties for incorrigibles.

4. *Our limitless imaginations can break through natural limits to make earthly goods and carrying capacity virtually infinite.* Just as settled agriculture increased earthly goods and carrying capacity vastly beyond hunting and gathering, so our imaginations can find ways to increase total productivity by superseding one level of technology after another. Taught by the lessons learned from systematic trial and error, we can close the loops in our productive systems and find innumerable ways to do more with less.

5. *People's reworking of the earth is revolutionary, problematic, and ultimately benevolent.* Of the tenets of wise use, this is the most oracular. Humanity is itself revolutionary and problematic. Danger is our symbiote. Yet even the timid are part of the human adventure, which has barely begun.

Humanity may ultimately prove to be a force of nature forwarding some cosmic teleology of which we are yet unaware. Or not. Humanity may be the universe awakening and becoming conscious of itself. Or not. Our reworking of the earth may be of the utmost evolutionary benevolence and importance. Or not. We don't know. The only way to see the future is to be there.

As the environmental debate advances to maturity, the environmental movement must accept and incorporate many of these wise-use precepts if it is to survive as a social and political force. Establishment interventionism, as represented by the large foundations and their grant-driven client organizations, must find practical ways to accommodate private property rights and entrepreneurial economic growth. Eco-socialism's collectivist program must find practical ways to accommodate individual economic liberties in its bureaucratic command-and-control approach. Deep ecology's biocentrism must find practical ways to accommodate anthropocentrism and technological progress.

To accomplish this necessary reform, environmentalists of all persuasions will have to face their ideological blind spots and see their own belief systems as wise users see them, that is, in a critical and practical light. This is a most difficult change for ideological environmentalists. Failure to reform environmentalism from within will invite regulation from without or doom the movement to irrelevancy as the wise use movement lives the pastoral ideal in the middle landscape, defining the meaning of America.

Notes

1. Leo Marx, *The Machine in the Garden: Technology and the Pastoral Ideal in America* (New York: Oxford University Press, 1964), 3.

2. Arthur O. Lovejoy, et al., *A Documentary History of Primitivism and Related Ideas* (Baltimore: Johns Hopkins Press, 1935), 369.

3. José Ortega y Gasset, *The Revolt of the Masses*, trans. anon. (1930, reissued New York: W. W. Norton & Company, Inc., 1993), 82.

4. Bill Devall and George Sessions, eds., *Deep Ecology: Living as if Nature Mattered* (Salt Lake City: Peregrine Smith Books, 1985).

5. Edith C. Stein, *The Environmental Sourcebook* (New York: Lyons & Burford, 1992), 6.

6. Victor B. Scheffer, "Environmentalism's Articles of Faith," *Northwest Environmental Journal* 5, no. 1, (1989): 99–108.

7. Ron Arnold and Alan Gottlieb, *Trashing the Economy: How Runaway Environmentalism Is Wrecking America* 2nd ed. (Bellevue, Wash.: Free Enterprise Press, 1994), 57–67 et passim. This analysis of the environmental movement's structure is part of the larger analytical treatment throughout the text.

8. Taped sessions of the Environmental Grantmakers Association 1992 Annual Fall Retreat, Conference Recording Service, Berkeley, California, 1992. Session 2: "North American Forests: Coping with Multiple Use and Abuse"; Session 19: "Environmental Legislation: Opportunity for Impact and Change"; Session 23: "Media Strategies for Environmental Protection."

9. Alan M. Gottlieb, ed., *The Wise Use Agenda* (Bellevue, Wash.: Free Enterprise Press, 1989). This document was the result of the 1988 Wise Use Strategy Conference and consists of recommendations for natural resource use from 125 of the 250 conference participants.

10. Michael Kelley, "The Road to Paranoia," *The New Yorker* 72, no. 17 (1995): 60.

11. William Empson, *Some Versions of Pastoral* (New York: New Directions, 1974), 6.

12. W. Alton Jones Foundation, *The Wise Use Movement* (Charlottesville, Va.: W. Alton Jones Foundation).

13. Taped session of the Environmental Grantmakers Association 1992 Annual Fall Retreat, Conference Recording Service, Berkeley, 1992. Session 26: "The Wise Use Movement: Threats and Opportunities."

14. The Wilderness Society, *The Wise Use Movement: Strategic Analysis and Fifty State Review*, prepared by MacWilliams Cosgrove Snider, Boston, 1992. Distributed by Clearinghouse on Environmental Advocacy and Research, Washington, D.C.

15. W. Alton Jones Foundation, Form 990 Annual Report to the Internal Revenue Service, 1993, Page 10, Part 15, Line 3a, Grants and Contributions Paid This Year. Anti-wise-use grant recipients included Environmental Defense Fund ($75,000): Idaho Conservation League ($30,000); Kentucky Coalition ($30,000); Maine Audubon Society ($26,250); Missouri Coalition for the Environment Foundation ($20,000); Pennsylvania Environmental Council ($30,000); Piedmont Environmental Council ($25,000); Society for the Protection of New Hampshire Forests ($26,250); Southern Utah Wilderness Alliance ($30,000); Vermont Natural Resources Council ($26,250); Western States Center ($20,000).

16. David Helvarg, *The War against the Greens: The "Wise Use" Movement, the New Right, and Anti-Environmental Violence* (San Francisco: Sierra Club Books, 1994).

17. Keith Schneider, "Big Environment Hits the Recession," *New York Times*, 1 January 1995, F4. See also, Stephen Greene, "Environmental Groups Advised to Slim Down," *Chronicle of Philanthropy*, 12 January 1995, 29.

18. Alexander Cockburn, "Exchange," *The Nation* 261, no. 5 (1995): 150.

19. Percy Bysshe Shelley, "Prometheus Unbound," in *The Works of Percy Bysshe Shelley* (Roslyn, N.Y.: Black's Reader Service, 1951), 180.

3

The Pristine Silence of Leaving It All Alone

Donald Snow

When I was in junior high, I loved to read the super-hero comics. Green Lantern was my favorite. Innately rational and often scientific in his use of logic, the Green Lantern could evoke mysterious powers through his ring. He would hold the ring in the robin-hood-green glow of a lantern given to him by the dying spaceman, Abin Sur, and recite these lines: "In brightest day, in blackest night, no evil will escape my sight! Let those who worship evil's might beware my power, GREEN LANTERN'S LIGHT!" The ring would recharge with mystical energy, and Green Lantern would fly off strong and true. He took himself quite seriously, this Guardian of the Universe, and at age twelve, so did I.

I wasn't nearly as keen on Superman, who by comparison seemed so crass and obvious. Big muscles. Krypton. Mild-mannered reporter (I've never been fond of journalism). That dysfunctional galactic family. But there was one storyline I loved in Superman: his visits to the world known as Bizzarro. You remember: there was a planet that was earth's reverse. Everything revered on earth was hated on Bizzarro, and vice versa. Ugliness and evil were prized. Hate and rudeness on Bizzarro were as cherished as love and kindness on earth. Children were rewarded for bad deeds; crime was normal and the greatest criminals became heroes. People had blue flesh, and their faces were cracked and pocked. You could almost smell their breath emanating from the colored newsprint pages.

This chapter first appeared in *Northern Lights Magazine*, Winter 1994. A slightly different version entitled "Wise Use and Public Lands in the West" appeared in the May/June 1994 issue of *Utne Reader*. Reprinted by permission of the author.

❅   ❅   ❅   ❅   ❅

Environmentalists in the West are now facing what must seem like Bizzarro to them. It's the wise use movement, a strange reverse-mirror of environmentalism. Go line by line down the list of environ-mentalist policy accomplishments since around 1970, and in almost every case you'll find a wise use counterattack. Wise users are out to weaken the Endangered Species Act, preserve the old rattle-bones Mining Law of 1872, change a host of provisions in the National Forest Management Act (especially those granting citizens the right to chal-lenge timber sales), block serious efforts at ecosystem management on the public lands, and weaken pollution-control regulations. With the bulk of its reactionary agenda resting on public lands issues, wise use started in the West but quickly took root in other regions. Any place you find a living tradition of natural resource-industries tapping publicly owned resources, you're apt to find wise use.[1]

Some have argued that the movement rose from the ashes of the Sagebrush Rebellion, the Reagan-era effort, beginning in Nevada, to "return" federal lands to the states, who had never owned them in the first place. The Sagebrush Rebels had a friend in the White House when President Reagan, proclaiming himself a Rebel, too, appointed some of the Rebellion's own leaders to key positions in the adminis-tration. The infamous Jim Watt, a born-again Christian who blended apocalyptic theology with latter-day Manifest Destiny, ran the Depart-ment of the Interior and tried to sell off twenty-seven million acres of federal land through something he coyly labeled the Assets Man-agement Program. This was asset management by divestiture, but Watt had at least the preponderance of western history right: the primary motive driving federal lands policy until, officially, 1976 was *disposal*, or privatization, of the federal domain.

The Sagebrush Rebellion per se was too nitwitted to succeed, but it did manage to produce a fine learning curve. In the end, some of the Rebels themselves came to question the wisdom of their own move-ment. Why would the commodity interests—ranchers, loggers, et al.—want to *own* federal lands that already offered such a bounty of subsidies? With absurdly cheap grazing fees, free minerals, and a fed-eral road-building program that gave loggers subsidized access to tim-ber that the market would never pay for, the federal lands turned out to be a bargain too good to be true. But that's not what killed the Sagebrush Rebellion. Torn between the demands of western rancher-legislators, who wanted state control of federal lands, and the promptings of Reagan administration libertarians, who demanded private ownership, not state control, the Rebellion split ideologically in two. The national press helped, as well. Unpalatable to all but a handful of doctrinaire free marketeers, the Sagebrush Rebellion died a simple, political death. Federal land disposal belonged to the last century. Americans are in love with their public lands, even if most of them still think the national forests are managed the same as Yellowstone. All but the most obstreperous western senators finally had to give up their dream of privatizing the public lands.

Wise use came along with a less blatant but more effective agenda. Its clear aim is to secure the hegemony of private commodity interests on the federal lands by stripping away all environmental "impediments" to development. If wise use is successful, federal-lands management would give the commodity interests the best of all worlds: immunity from the risks of real markets (under the aegis of "preserving community stability"), the continued bounty of federal subsidies, and a monopoly of land uses favoring both the extraction of natural resources and forms of recreation (mostly motorized) beloved by the wise use constituency.

It's an oversimplification to see wise use merely as the next step following the failed Sagebrush Rebellion, for wise use is a much broader movement. If you look carefully at the emerging wise use agenda—said to have first congealed in Reno at a 1988 "Multiple Use Strategy Conference"—you'll see plenty of elements that have non-Sagebrush roots. There's a very strong stripe of Christian fundamentalism, a heavy dose of property rights protectionism, solid ties to the gun lobby, and a potent element of motorized recreation advocacy. These bear evidence that wise use organizers have done their homework and footwork. They have broadened their movement by making alliances with important constituencies that alone are only marginal players in the great public-lands debate, but linked together make a powerful force in western politics.

The broad strategies of the wise use movement, as well as I can make them out, seem obvious. First, solidify into firm and lasting policy the federal prejudice favoring the commodity interests who reap profits and livelihoods from the public domain. These interests represent the traditional industries of the West—mining, logging, and agriculture. But it's a mistake to view wise use as a mere front for profit-taking corporations. All over the West, there is a large wise use constituency that represents livelihood, not profit, and is anything but corporate in outlook. These are working people who see their own economic survival tied to the continued health of natural-resource industries. Wise use unites management and labor in a common cause.

Second, identify the enemy and keep it as busy as possible so that its efforts are deflected into holding-the-line rather than moving ahead into new initiatives. The enemy is clearly environmentalism. National, state, and local environmental organizations, while often disagreeing over their own strategies, have for more than twenty years shared the broad goal of reforming public lands management to make it more ecologically responsible. In the face of this effective activism, wise use is a truly reactionary movement. It sees itself fighting environmentalism *mano-a-mano*—putting before every conceivable policy arena a series of new initiatives directly attacking national and state environmental laws. Most of these initiatives probably seem as zany to the general public today as environmentalism must have seemed twenty years ago, but zaniness and American politics are a well-loved comedy team. Take a look at some of the titles of wise use policy proposals, and you can begin to see their reactionary origins: the Private Rights in Federal Lands Act; the Truth in Regulation Act; the Public Rangeland Improvement Act; Obstructionism Liability; Standing to Sue in Defense of Industry; Economic and Community Impact Statements.

Third, win the hearts and minds of the public by portraying wise use as the last hurrah for the little guy. One nagging problem for the Sagebrush Rebels was the public's view of them as a cabal of rich, white ranchers making a grab for the public's land. Wise use struggles to portray itself as a loose alliance of hardworking yeomen—loggers in jackboots, leather-faced family ranchers, sunburned farmers bouncing behind the wheel of the antique combine, hardscrabble miners with clear eyes and dirty faces. The public relations message is simple: these folks are the salt of the earth, and a bunch of pasty-faced overeducated eco-bunnies hooked together by modem are out to take their jobs away.

Anyone who's not allergic to politics can see the wisdom behind these strategies. They work in concert to build coalitions and improve public relations. But wise use continues to be hamstrung by some of its proponents' outrageous theories and proclamations. Environmentalists have taken joy in repeating the wise use mantra of oddball ideas, forgetting how oddball many of their own ideas still seem to an urban public confused about nature. Here's a quick grab bag of wise use ideas:

- Forests found in our national parks are being improperly managed because they are "left to nature." As any professional forester can tell you, managing them properly requires logging. We should be routinely logging the national parks.
- In addition to national wilderness and park reserves, we should be setting aside "logging and grazing reserves" where these two primary commodity uses of the land would be paramount and not allowed to be interrupted by any other competing uses, such as recreation.
- County governments in counties that contain large amounts of federal land can and should pass ordinances prohibiting federal land managers from any actions that invade the prevalent "custom and culture" of the county. If the custom and culture is ranching, then the feds can do nothing that is deemed inimical to the settled expectations of local ranchers. Federal bureaucrats who fail to obey these local ordinances should be subject to severe penalties, including imprisonment.
- In addition to Environmental Impact Statements, the federal government should require Economic Impact Statements and Property Rights Impact Statements for any environmental or land-use planning policies that are likely to force adjustments in human activities.
- Some scientists who possess a hidden agenda to overthrow capitalist democracies are deliberately exaggerating the effects of global warming, acid rain, and ozone depletion. In reality, the preponderance of scientific opinion says that these are very minor problems that can easily be solved by small decreases in our consumption of fossil fuels and large increases in our reliance on nuclear power to take care of future energy needs.
- Farmers, ranchers, loggers, and miners are the original and best environmentalists. Because of their productivity on the land, larger populations of wildlife exist now than have ever existed before. Farmers and ranchers spend enormous sums of money building dams to keep water from washing away the soil. Loggers inevitably improve forest habitat; they do for the West's forests what wildfires once did, rejuvenating landscapes by removing mature trees. Even miners improve habitat. By revegetating mined sites and applying irrigation to make new grasses grow, their efforts feed the abundant wildlife that returns almost immediately to mined sites. This is usually an improvement over premining conditions.

- Many treaties between the federal government and American Indian tribes are null and void because they offer preferential rights to Indians based solely on race. Indian fishing rights, for example, are invalid unless they are identical to non-Indian fishing rights. Moreover, Indian tribal sovereignty is a myth. There is no constitutional basis for tribal governance over non-Indian people either on or off the reservations.
- Ranchers, miners, and loggers are now "the New Indians," or "endangered species." The federal government, thoroughly infiltrated by "watermelon environmentalists" (green outside, red inside), is deliberately trying to force them from the land. Laws and ordinances should be passed giving people equal protection with endangered species (or, similarly, giving these New Indians special protection as a distinct "culture").

❊   ❊   ❊   ❊   ❊

When urban environmentalists encounter such ideas, they surely must start thinking about selenium in the well water. Few of these ideas emerge from serious centers of scholarship, though some of them have proponents in academia who try to give them intellectual justification. Most are homecooked, emerging from a distinctly rural context and lacking the sober respectability of scholarship. That's not surprising. Many rural Americans are strangely prone to conspiracy theories, strict constitutionalism, and oddball legal constructions. But if their general mindset is often paranoia, who can blame them? The rural quarter has been shrinking dramatically since the Second World War; many of the verities of rural life are by now mythic. Wise use, daffy as if often sounds, is at the core a pleading to maintain, somehow, somewhere, a dignified rural existence. But ideas like those recited above make easy fodder for the enemies of wise use.

There's another, even stronger tool to fight wise use, and environmentalists and some journalists have used it freely: the issue of funding. Determined to discredit the movement, every knowledgeable wise use opponent can recite the proof that wise use organizations are "industry fronts," raising most of their money from corporations invested in natural resources and doing the political bidding of big business under the guise of grassroots activism. They have a point. As of 1994, an untidy bundle known as the Western States Public Lands Coalition/People for the West!, then based in Pueblo, Colorado, reportedly received most of its $1.7 million annual budget from two hundred corporate members, mostly mining companies. The coalition is a national leader in the fight against federal mining-law reform. The Idaho-based Blue Ribbon Coalition, which claims to represent the interests of over a half-million off-road vehicle enthusiasts, gathered up half of its annual $185,000 budget from Japanese ORV-makers. Looking at these kinds of groups alone, it's easy to make the case that wise use merely represents corporate efforts to increase profits by removing environmental impediments. I've yet to see an article or news report on the movement that failed to make that point.

But is wise use an irrelevant fringe movement, as many environmentalists claim? Is it the last gasp of the West's natural resource industries as they fall into eclipse, soon to be replaced by a new economy of scenic, wilderness and recreational resources? A lot of environmentalists seem to think so. Few critics of wise use seem to think the movement can last, or have much effect.

I think they're wrong.

❆ ❆ ❆ ❆ ❆

Wise use is no fringe movement. It is an inevitable and logical extension of the early conservation movement from which it took its name. The early conservationists emphasized the *wise use* of natural resources over their outright protection and were more often than not the leading opponents of land preservation schemes. Throughout this century, use-oriented conservationists—who were never environmentalists in the modern sense—learned to use coalitions of commodity interests to do the political bidding for the West's continued development, much of it subsidized by the federal government.

Gifford Pinchot and Franklin Roosevelt probably did more than any others to cement the relationship between the federal land and water agencies and the West's commodity interests. In the name of "scientific conservation," Pinchot, first chief of the Forest Service and the greatest of the federal lands empire-builders, figured out that the only way to gain the West's acceptance of the massive national forest reserves was to buy off the commodity interests. Irrigators got federal dams if they agreed to drop their opposition to logging the forested watersheds; ranchers got preferential grazing rights in national forests; miners continued to receive the unique dispensation of the 1872 mining law, which allowed them to assume free ownership of federal lands where they discovered valuable mineral deposits. FDR added his own ingredients to the West's bizarre pork stew. He created enormous, environmentally destructive public works projects—mostly dams on the greatest rivers in North America—and labeled them "conservation." Throughout the twentieth century, management of the West's public lands has become increasingly politicized. As legal scholar James Huffman says, we call these lands "public" lands, but we should really be more honest. They are *political lands*, and their fate has always been tied to congressional horse-trading.

The coalition politics that have grown from those roots have been a long time coming and make sense. Until wise use came along, there was little or no central coordination of the advocacy that has always been necessary to buy votes to maintain the West's antique natural-resource economy. Each piece of the old economy historically did its own bidding, and many segments fiercely battled one another, much in the way that homesteading once waged a direct war against the depredations of the open range. Though prototypes of it have been around since the middle-1970s, the wise use movement never got off the ground until environmentalists seized the economic initiative and began attacking federal subsidies, both hidden and overt, that prop up the natural resource economies of the West's dry states. When environmentalists finally got around to the federal budget, wise use organizing went ballistic. The commodity interests—those dyed-in-the-wool advocates of "free-market capitalism"—have rallied around the maintenance of the subsidies they all require to survive. They've all gotten the idea now: holding most of the subsidies in place brings political power to the elected officials and federal agencies who grant the subsidies, and economic power to the commodity interests. Wise use is the most effective alliance, to date, among the pillars of the old economy.

Here's another reason why wise use, or something like it, is here to stay. In the West at least, wise use is innately much more mainstream than environmentalism. The wisest of the wise users understand the West's politics and essential character much better than environmentalists ever have or perhaps ever will. Against strong contrary evidence, most Westerners still believe that their economy is based on natural resource industries—that these industries are the "engines" of all other economic activity, and without them the region's economy soon would collapse. The facts say something else.

In Montana, a 1992 Department of Commerce study revealed that 64 percent of the state's workforce was employed in services (defined as education, law, health, and consumer services), retail trade, and government. Only 7 percent worked in agriculture and 6 percent in all of manufacturing, which included the wood-products industry. *Forty percent* of all personal income in Montana came from "unearned" sources such as retirement benefits, pensions, and investments. The report concluded with this: "Montana's economy has become different from what we are accustomed to thinking it is. It is not an economy that is going to change—it is an economy that has already changed."

But wise use wisely ignores these kinds of facts—true now in varying degrees throughout the Rockies—and continues to propagate the myth of the Natural Resource West. It plays to the public's misunderstanding of economic matters, even as it allows the West's senators to look like heroes when they go to bat for those subsidies that help keep the mines, mills, and marginal ranches alive.

Cutting trees, plowing soil in long, clean rows, crushing hard, igneous rock to get at the mineral grains—those were the things Westerners always did to support their kids and put a big bird on the table come holidays. People feel productive when they measure the tangible results of their work. They can look at a haystack and know it's sixty-five tons of nicely baled alfalfa. They can measure a deck of logs with their eyes and guess its sale value within a few dollars. Wise use is making the most of an effective interplay of these western icons, which are very powerful political tools, even if they no longer have much to do with ordinary life in the urbanized West. If you don't believe it, look at the 1994 Senate filibuster over grazing fees. Not exactly one of the nation's most pressing issues, a grazing fee increase that would have brought uncountable change to the treasury slammed the Senate to a halt in the name of hometown heroics. When did anyone ever do that for a serious western environmental issue?

Those who dismiss wise use because it's "not a grassroots movement" are simply wrong. Plenty of wise use groups really are industry fronts, but plenty are not, and even the ones that are represent mainstream interests of at least a few thousand hardworking Westerners. The interests of those thousands does a movement make, and environmentalists, of all people, should understand that.

Environmentalists must come to grips with the fact that they do not hold exclusive rights to the concept and practice of grassroots organizing in the West. The wise use movement is now beating them at their own game, yet many environmentalists seem incredulous that other ordinary people can have expectations of the land that differ so vastly from their own. Lots and lots of folks back home, in little hamlets like Deer Lodge and Burley and Salida, don't really want the new economy of environmental amenities. They want the old one, because that's where they find dignity, livelihood, and the completion of what they and their ancestors saw as destiny. Mythic or not, it's the story of the West: the "settling" of the land; the "improvement" of nature through agriculture and industry; the "reclamation" of the hideous barren wilderness. Lots of folks who live next door still *believe* in those things, and they're willing to support anyone—including big business masquerading as "grassroots associations"—who promises to deliver. There is a large, and potentially larger, grassroots constituency for wise use, and if its organizers get clever enough, they'll find it.

Wise users stand on some pretty secure institutional bedrock, and they know it. In the West, the deck has always been stacked in favor of commodity interests who were given all manner of special protections under federal and state policy. Water law, mining law, grazing and timbering policies are all deftly skewed to ensure the continuing development of the West's resources. The policies that protect these once-vital industries have endured most of this century, and lately have all stood firm against the attacks of environmentalists. Until these revered western institutions are fundamentally altered (and they won't be merely by tinkering with payment schedules like grazing fees and below-cost logging subsidies), they will continue to guide the West's environmental destiny.

Wise use exists to ensure that these time-encrusted policies remain intact. That's precisely why wise users have their gunsights on the few true environmentalist inroads into national policy—laws like the National Forest Management Act, the Endangered Species Act, and the Wilderness Act. These recent shifts in federal policy, while easily subverted by western senators and prodevelopment bureaucrats, signal an era of threatening change to the settled interests of the West. Wise use will be increasingly important in making sure that the West's commodity favoritism continues, precisely because the movement understands so well the West's fundamental beliefs about itself. These beliefs may be mythic, but they are stronger than any mountain of facts.

✳   ✳   ✳   ✳   ✳

Instead of attacking wise use, environmentalists should sit down and study it, simply to learn why it appeals. It offers something environmentalism has never offered (but interestingly, the early conservation movement did): a cogent focus on both livelihood and equity. The early conservationists were quite keen on both. They wanted to grow "forests for the home-builder first of all," and that popular slogan linked them to every American family struggling to make a living.

Livelihood speaks to people, to their sense of both survival and pride. The heart of Jefferson's vision of the West was a vision of individual livelihood, agrarian land ownership, and the civic virtue that he believed grew from it. The central problem with environmentalism is that it lacks a cogent, convincing focus on livelihood, and that has made it vulnerable to wise use attacks. The grand cause of protecting the environment *from humans* means that lots of humans now feel unwelcome in what they see as the environmentalists' visionary world. It doesn't take too many thousands of the unwelcome to form a counter movement, if somebody's willing to organize them, and that's precisely what has happened.

Wise use as a cogent social-political movement is well constructed to last a long time and perhaps succeed, if not nearly as well as environmentalism at least well enough to have a substantial and lasting impact on key policies in the West. Its historic and philosophic roots are deep in the West's soil, and if some of its proponents are too fast to be making grandiose claims to "culture," they are nonetheless correct in their reach to reclaim the moral high ground seized by environmentalists.

But before wise use can succeed, it's going to have to rid itself of the kind of fringe thinking that will brand it as a movement of crackpots. What wise users must learn to articulate more clearly and convincingly than they have is why Americans should be willing to protect the West's resource-dependent communities without converting them into silly little Old Economy theme parks. Rather than trying to freeze the West in mythic time, wise users ought to be joining environmentalists in an earnest search for both livelihood and community. Livelihood in the emerging economies of the West implies diversification, a rich mixture of the old and the new; it implies paying all the bills—which is to say, making sure that we don't continue propping up local economies with national subsidies, or making recreational uses of public lands hostage to commodity uses that pad agency budgets. Community implies a loosening of one's grip on ideology and a willingness to participate in shared experience.

What we have discovered at Northern Lights through our efforts in dispute resolution and community-building is this: If you can keep people from addressing policy per se, and direct their efforts toward solving problems that are tangible, workable, and local, you get an entirely different result. The West, as some have argued, may be the most fractious political community in the country, where Earth First! and People for the West! quibble over priority rights to the exclamation point. But it's also a place where the simple traditions of neighborliness and social goodwill can be parlayed into cooperative problem solving.

The great challenge for the West is to innovate. But the old battle lines—now merely carved deeper in the sand by the arrival of wise use—hold us to a false and frozen view of the West as the Region of Either-Or: either we maintain the Old Economy of mining, logging, and ranching propped up here and there by hidden supports, or we witness the collapse of the "basic industries," the continued depopulation and impoverishment of the rural quarter, and the loss of the West's essential character, to be replaced by an 865,000 square-mile Soul of the Rockies subdivision containing very, very large playgrounds. Either it's boom-bust-rape-scrape (described in a shrill voice as "conservation" or "multiple use"), or it's the pristine silence of leaving it all alone. Clearly, it's time to try something new.

Note

1. I am indebted to numerous sources for their information and valuable insights. Ralph Maughan and Douglas Nilson of Idaho State University have written the best summary of wise use ideology I've seen yet: "What's Old and New about the Wise Use Movement." Thanks to Barbara Rusmore for sending it. Margaret Kriz's "Land Mine" in the *National Journal*, 23 October 1993, provides valuable information on the land rights movement and its funding sources. *Western Horizons*, the newsletter of the Wise Use Exposure Project of the Western States Center in Portland, provides month-by-month tracking of the emerging wise use agenda. Mary Chapman's "Observations from the Back of the Pumpkin Truck" (Center for the New West, in Denver, October 1993) offers a spirited critique of New West tendencies toward becoming a "politically correct, smoke-free, white wine tofu culture of appropriate conspicuous consumption." Conversations with Karl Hess, Jr., John Baden, Tom Wolf, Gerald Mueller, and Charles Wilkinson have enriched my thinking about both environmentalism and wise use and have helped frame public-lands issues more clearly in my mind.

4

Property Rights Movement: How It Began and Where It Is Headed

Nancie G. Marzulla

In the waning days of the Carter administration, outgoing secretary of the interior Cecil Andrus bragged, "We have seen more wilderness and national parks, and more wildlife refuges than all other administrations combined."[1] Few realized that voters' reactions to the massive conversion of Bureau of Land Management (BLM) holdings to national parks and wildlife refuges during the Carter years was a major reason why his administration was not being returned to the White House.

The Carter administration more than doubled the size of the National Wildlife Refuge System. An additional five million miles of rivers entered the National Wild and Scenic River System—a fourfold increase in just four years. This reduced the likelihood of conversion to private ownership, setting off the tinderbox that became known as the property rights movement.

Roots of the Property Rights Movement

In 1964, the Department of the Interior marked a turning point in U.S. land policy when it announced a moratorium on claiming desert land for farming purposes. Previously, the federal government considered public lands as temporary holdings to be claimed, privatized, and homesteaded as the nation matured.

This chapter previously appeared in *Land Rights: The 1990s' Property Rights Rebellion*, edited by Bruce Yandle, ©1995 Rowman & Littlefield. Reprinted by permission of author and publisher.

The moratorium provoked distinct outrage in the West, especially Nevada. The federal government administers approximately forty-six million acres of the state—roughly 87 percent of its total land (much of it desert). If other states had been closed to land claims at the same point in their development, Nevadans argued, it would certainly have provoked a civil war. Robert List, Nevada's attorney general at the time, brought suit against the Interior Department in an attempt to end the moratorium. Secretary Andrus finally capitulated, lifting the moratorium in 1978.

Dubbed the "Sagebrush Rebellion" by the national media, the suit created a movement founded on the principle that the federal government had a trust obligation to dispose of public lands. The momentum of the rebellion swept List into the governor's mansion.

During the List administration, Deputy Attorney General Harry Swainston decided to go one step further. Amending the original suit in an attempt to force the BLM to completely relinquish public lands in Nevada, he claimed that a state so federally dominated could not be considered on an "equal footing" with other states (the federal government controls only about 3 percent of the land in other states).[2] He contended that such an overwhelming presence lessened the state's sovereignty.

In April of 1981, however, U.S. District Judge Ed Reed rejected Swainston's argument, writing, "No state legislation may interfere with Congress' power over the public domain." Reed also said Congress possessed the ability to withdraw public lands from use for indefinite periods of time. When pressed he denied a rehearing by the state.[3]

Judge Reed's decision, however, was too late to stem the tide of change. People's frustration over federal opposition to resource development in their region was peaking. Western states are a treasure trove of natural resources, containing an estimated fifteen billion barrels of oil and one hundred trillion cubic feet of natural gas, producing 40 percent of the nation's coal, holding enormous reserves of metals, and yielding vast productivity in the timber and cattle industries.[4] What the region lacks is political power. With less than 5 percent of the nation's population, Westerners found themselves at the mercy of a Congress dominated by populous urban states that viewed the West as a wilderness playground that must be preserved and not developed, even at the cost of local poverty and unemployment. One national newspaper noted "a diffuse and ill-focused feeling of uneasiness, powerlessness, and anger that cuts through political and socioeconomic boundaries."[5]

The first to actively organize were those dependent on federal lands for their livelihoods—farmers, ranchers, miners, loggers, and "inholders" (property owners bordering or surrounded by federal land). While trade associations represented select constituencies, there was still no real "network." The establishment of organizations like the Center for the Defense of Free Enterprise, National Inholders Association (now the American Land Rights Alliance), and People for the West! in the mid-1970s created this network, and gave the movement a name—wise use.

Bill Burke of the left-wing Political Research Associates authored a highly critical report of the wise use movement, but, according to Scott Allen of the *Boston Globe*, even Burke had to admit the movement raises "valid issues about protecting property rights and about environmentalists' exaggerations."[6]

Property Rights Comes Into Its Own

Property rights emerged from within the wise use movement to become a force in its own right. Infringement on the Fifth Amendment's guarantee—"nor shall private property be taken for public use, without just compensation"—is not just a problem out West, but is also a national concern. Starting in the 1960s, federal, state, and local governments increasingly began to regulate property through environmental protection policies.[7] In the 1970s, they came almost exclusively from Washington. According to a study by Thomas D. Hopkins of the Rochester Institute of Technology, environmental-regulation costs rose from $41 billion a year in 1973 to $126 billion in 1993 (stated in constant 1988 dollars).[8] These estimates, however, do not account for regulation's drag on productivity or the value of lost consumption that accompanies higher prices generated by regulation. Whether it was in repairing a car air conditioner, replacing linoleum, or disposing of tires and insecticides, millions of people suddenly became aware of this new regulatory maze. The loss of jobs because forest and agricultural property were placed off limits communicated the problem in even starker terms.

Roots of Today's Property Rights Movement

Ordinary people began confronting the regulators, feeling they were being unfairly singled out to bear the burden of implementing environmental policies. Most simply wanted to be paid when their property was taken. The government, on the other hand, was not prepared to pay for valuable land, species and habitat protection, historic corridors, and other things it considered to be important priorities. Through its ability to regulate, the federal government increasingly began to "take" without compensation everything but the actual title to the property. The government then argued that it should not have to pay—regardless of the severity of the regulation—since it had not actually taken the property away from its owner.

It is this infringement of constitutional rights, not opposition to environmental protection, that fuels the property rights movement. Its central idea is that no objective, no matter how laudable, can justify violating the Constitution.[9] The strong antagonism between property rights activists and environmentalists stems from the fact that environmentalism has promoted the regulations creating this threat. As Justice Oliver Wendell Holmes noted over seventy years ago, "a strong public desire to improve the public condition is not enough to warrant achieving the desire by a shorter cut than the constitutional way of paying for the change."[10]

Fueling the Property Rights Backlash

Federal regulations relating to the environment can be traced back to early conservationists like John Muir, Gifford Pinchot, and Theodore Roosevelt. The birth of the modern environmental regime, however, was on 22 April 1970—the commemoration of the first Earth Day. On the heels of creating the Environmental Protection Agency (EPA), Congress rapidly passed a string of environmental statutes that created a regulatory net covering virtually every aspect of property use and ownership. The 1970 National Environmental Policy Act (NEPA), one of the first comprehensive statutes, requires the preparation of an Environmental Impact Statement (EIS).[11] This encompasses permits and authorizations for things like road construction and mineral and timber sales as well as generic programs like oil leasing and gas exploration on federal lands. Opponents of such development use NEPA as a means of stopping projects on the grounds that an EIS was not prepared or is inadequate.

Originally passed in 1970, significantly amended in 1977, and massively overhauled in 1990, the Clean Air Act regulates the emissions into the atmosphere.[12] It requires permits for "major sources" of air pollution, implemented through state legislation that must be submitted for federal review in the form of a State Implementation Plan

(SIP). Failure to enact legislation satisfactory to the federal government can result in the imposition of a federal plan as well as sanctions such as the cutoff of highway construction funds or punitive cutbacks in allowable emissions.

Discharges into the waters of the United States are the target of the Clean Water Act.[13] Passed in 1972, it has never been significantly amended. Unlike Clean Air, the Clean Water Act has no SIP; instead, the federal government prescribes water quality standards for states to achieve. Section 404 of the act serves as the authority for federal regulation of approximately one hundred million acres of wetlands. While Congress has yet to establish a legal definition of wetland based on scientific or other criteria, the EPA's wetlands delineation notes that 75 percent of what is considered wetlands are privately owned. Unlucky landowners must leave their property untouched, and will rarely receive any payment for doing so. They must still pay property taxes, and their heirs may still pay inheritance taxes based on its fair market value before being declared wetland.

The Resource Conservation and Recovery Act (RCRA) prescribes a "cradle-to-grave" program for the management of hazardous waste.[14] Toxic waste must be labeled, manifested, and tracked to its ultimate place of disposal. Treatment, storage, and disposal facilities must obtain RCRA permits and comply with stringent regulations concerning construction, allowable wastes, groundwater monitoring, closure plans, and financial responsibility. Permitting programs are often delegated to states, where additional requirements are frequently imposed.

The Comprehensive Environment Response, Compensation, and Liability Act (CERCLA or "Superfund") imposes joint and several strict liabilities upon the owner, operator, transporter, or person arranging for the disposal of hazardous substances, whenever those substances are released into the environment.[15] Literally hundreds of companies and organizations—even the EPA itself—can be counted among the potentially responsible parties in a Superfund site.[16] Each party has an incentive to sue the others to avoid paying the full cleanup costs for the site, which currently averages $25 million. More than a thousand Superfund sites have been identified nationwide, but fewer than one hundred have been cleaned up since 1980.

The Endangered Species Act of 1973 (ESA) forbids the "taking" of any species of animal or plant listed by the U.S. Fish and Wildlife Service (FWS).[17] "Taking" is interpreted so broadly that even the act of making undue noise that might disturb a listed species can constitute a violation of the law. Initially funded to acquire sensitive habitat from private owners, FWS purchased 735,396 acres of private land for habitat and other protective purposes between 1966 through 1989.[18] Currently without funding, FWS still routinely engages in regulatory takings, locking up hundreds of thousands of acres of privately owned land in the process.

Protected species are sometimes found to be in competition with important public services, causing concern for the livelihoods and welfare of large populations. For example, the protection of salamanders feeding off the Edwards Aquifer in San Antonio, Texas, threatens the operation of a thriving city's water supply. In Cherokee County, Georgia, a planned water reservoir "needed to alleviate water shortages" was blocked "when it was determined that two types of tiny fish living downstream from the dam would be endangered by the project."[19]

To an ordinary citizen, the open-ended nature of ESA recovery can also be ominous. The plan for the painted snake coiled forest snail, for example, merely says, "If landowners are not in agreement, investigate other options for protecting habitat." For the swamp pink, the plan advises that "nontraditional avenues for endangered species protection . . . will be investigated."[20] In practice, these "nontraditional" options have included using everything from wetlands legislation to soil erosion control requirements to shut down private land use.

State and Local Regulation

Every state has adopted some sort of environmental protection schemes that mirror, or even exceed, federal requirements. Logically, they adapt to the state's own ecological, economic, and social needs, but they also add another layer of rules and regulations. It is often the state regulatory scheme, in fact, that most directly touches people on a regular basis.

Many federal environmental statutes set minimums (or floors) for state plans so states cannot become "pollution havens" where industry may flee to avoid regulation. They provide substantial flexibility in determining how to achieve compliance, and allow for the adoption of additional and more stringent regulations. California, New York, and Colorado, for example, have adopted highly specialized air-pollution regulations to address their unique and very different climatic conditions, geographies, and population distributions. State "mini-superfunds," SEPA (the state equivalent of NEPA) requirements, recycling laws, labeling rules, and community right-to-know requirements are all examples of state analogies to federal statutes that either embroider federal regulatory programs or extend to activities not otherwise regulated. On the flipside, however, they often deny flexibility for innovative homegrown solutions that might better suit a given group of people.

The area of public health and safety has traditionally been the domain of the states, although recent years have seen significant federal encroachment on this formerly exclusive preserve. The same can be said for zoning and land-use restrictions on federal provinces. States have similarly expanded their land-use regulations to include historic preservation, battlefield protection, scenic designations, setbacks along waterways and streams, farmland protection, establishment of "greenways," buffer zones, designation of parks and preserves, and restrictions on natural-resource development.

These economic incentive/disincentive policies can effectively prohibit or eliminate many otherwise feasible and productive human activities. Richard Delene has a 2,400-acre nature preserve in the Upper Peninsula of Michigan.[21] He and his wife wanted to relive the life of Henry Thoreau, whose words marked a sign on their property: "In the wilderness, there is preservation of the world." Protected with lock and key were 26 acres of duck ponds and more than 100 acres of enhanced habitat the Delenes had built. Additional work was under way until armed agents of the Michigan Department of Natural Resources disturbed their preserve. Because they did not obtain state permits for moving dirt, the Delenes now face potential fines in excess of $1.2 million, and are under a permanent restraining order to cease all their construction activities.

The Property Rights Movement Responds

These regulations also challenge the ability of communities to maintain a tax base. This has left a bitter taste in the mouths of millions of people across the United States who, in the 1990s, are fighting back yet again by founding organizations, learning more about their rights, and seeking relief from invasions of property that have become so rampant in this country.

With the sentiments of the Sagebrush Rebellion raging through the West in 1980, many Westerners were drawn to the presidential campaign of former California governor Ronald Reagan, who ran on the theme of "get government off our backs and out of our pockets." Using the support of these activists and others to propel himself to the White House, Reagan returned the favor by appointing Westerners to key positions in his administration. These appointments included BLM director Bob Burford and EPA administrator Ann Gorsuch of Colorado, and James Watt of Wyoming as secretary of the interior. When he started at interior, Watt found it "to be in bad need of good management," noting that national parks—land so zealously acquired by his predecessor—had deteriorated in "a shameful way" while wildlife refuges "had been ignored."[22] Watt's property-rights and wise use approach to environmental policy made him an archenemy of environmentalists and the focus of environmental rallies and direct-mail campaigns, and indirectly made him a major fund-raising tool.

One windfall of his notoriety was that "exaggerated accusations forced Congress to see what Jim Watt is really doing." This resulted in what he considered to be a "phenomenally successful" tenure.[23] Although constant pressure did eventually lead to his resignation— and that of Ann Gorsuch at EPA—his legacy lives on. Many of Watt's appointees served through the Bush administration and even into the Clinton years.

In the courts, property rights also made substantial gains during the Reagan years. This was especially true in the Supreme Court. Until the 1980s, the Court showed little interest in property-rights law. Back in 1922, Justice Oliver Wendell Holmes announced the bedrock principle of takings law: "The general rule, at least, is that while property may be regulated to a certain extent, if regulation goes too far it will be recognized as a taking." Despite that, the Court showed no interest in cases that would actually enforce this doctrine. In 1978, the issue of regulatory takings had received so little attention that Justice William Brennan declared he was "unable to develop any 'set formula' for determining when 'justice and fairness' require that economic injuries caused by public action be compensated by the government rather than remain concentrated on a few persons."[24] The only guidance Brennan could offer was to order courts to review the circumstances of alleged takings by creating an ad hoc three-factor factual inquiry.

It was not until 1987, following the elevation of William Rehnquist to chief justice and the appointments of Sandra Day O'Connor and Antonin Scalia, that the Court seemed willing to take another look at the takings issue. During that year's term, the justices agreed to hear the trilogy of *Hodel v. Irving, First English Evangelical Church v. County of Los Angeles*, and *Nollan v. California Coastal Council*.

In *First English*, the Court for the first time held that a regulation could violate the Fifth Amendment. In that case, the issue was whether a county was required to compensate a church barred from reconstructing a summer camp destroyed by a flood due to a flood control ordinance. In *Nollan*, the Court ruled that the California Coastal Commission could not require the owner of a home next to a beach to donate a third of his land to the state in order to obtain a permit to rebuild his home, without paying the owner just compensation. *Hodel* secured property rights pertaining to future interest in a property.

In 1992, the Court gave property-rights proponents another victory with *Lucas v. South Carolina Coastal Council*. After David Lucas purchased two lots of beachfront property for the sole intent of development, he was told he could not develop the land because of recently enacted state environmental regulations. The central holding of *Lucas* is that "regulations that deny the property owner of all 'economically viable use of his land' constitute one of the discrete categories of regulatory deprivations that require compensation without the usual case-specific inquiry into the public interest advanced in support of the restraint." Because of this ruling, the court need not engage in ad hoc inquiry, thus keeping the government from introducing countervailing evidence to defeat the claim. *Lucas* also dealt with ripeness. The Court noted that ripeness was a state concern that should not hold up the Supreme Court review. It remarked: "In these circumstances, we think it would not accord with sound process to insist that Lucas pursue the late-created 'special permit' procedure before his takings claim can be considered ripe."

In addition, the appointment of jurists like Jay Plager to the Court of Appeals for the Federal Circuit, Alex Kosinski (1981–85) and Loren Smith (1985–present) as chief judge of the Court of Federal Claims, and Moody Tidwell as a judge in the same court secured property rights victories in cases like *Loveladies Harbor v. U.S.* and *Florida Rock v. U.S.* The Supreme Court has also remained active, hearing *Dolan v. City of Tigard* in its 1993 term.

In *Dolan*, the Court reversed and remanded a decision by the Oregon Supreme Court compelling a property owner to give almost 10 percent of her land to the city for the creation of a greenway and bike path. A permit to enlarge a plumbing supply business hinged on her agreement to donate the land. In his majority opinion, Chief Justice Rehnquist wrote: "We see no reason why the Takings Clause of the Fifth Amendment, as much a part of the Bill of Rights as the First Amendment and Fourth Amendment, should be relegated to the status of a poor relation in these comparable circumstances."[25]

Property rights, however, did seem to be that poor relation when the Court ruled in favor of government regulation in the case of *Bab-bitt v. Sweet Home*. On 29 June 1995, the Court upheld a U.S. Fish and Wildlife Service definition of Section 9 of the Endangered Species Act, allowing the definition of "harm" to include "habitat protection." The decision provides the government with a blank check with which it can destroy an individual's entire investment in land or private enterprise—not because an endangered species lives on a plot of land, but because it might want to someday.

The *Sweet Home* decision points up only too clearly that courts are simply not curtailing the wholesale destruction of private property rights. Given that neither they nor the executive branch are living up to their commitment, the property rights movement is looking to Congress for a solution. In the 104th Congress, Senator Slade Gorton (R-WA) introduced reform legislation addressing the problem presented by *Sweet Home*, and codifying the property rights ruling of the lower court. A major shortcoming of the bill, however, is that it fails to require the government to compensate a property owner if his or her land is unavoidably taken.

The biggest boost for private property rights to come out of the Reagan administration, however, was Executive Order 12630—"Governmental Actions and Interference With Constitutionally-Protected Property Rights."[26] EO 12630 recognizes that the government, short of the formal exercise of its eminent domain authority, can take private property through regulation or "inverse condemnation." Modeled after requirements for NEPA's EIS, the order calls for a "takings impact analysis" of new government regulations to prevent unnecessary takings and allow the government to budget funds for compensating those actions involving necessary takings without hindering the enforcement of any environmental program.[27]

The purpose of the order is "to assist Federal departments and agencies in . . . proposing, planning, and implementing actions with due regard for the constitutional protection provided by the Fifth Amendment" and "to reduce the risk of undue or inadvertent burdens on the public fisc resulting from lawful government actions." The attorney general, in consultation with executive departments and agencies, is responsible for promulgating "Guidelines for the Evaluation of Risk and Avoidance of Unanticipated Takings." Agencies are required to report identified takings implications and actual takings claims to the Office of Management and Budget for planning and budgetary purposes, with U.S. Supreme Court decisions serving as the touchstone for formulating these guidelines. EO 12630 does not enlarge or fix the scope or definition of regulatory takings. The Fifth Amendment itself still sets the floor upon which the government may exercise its power. The order simply requires decision makers to ascertain whether a proposed act will activate the Constitution's guarantee that private property not be taken for public use without just compensation.

The Bush U-Turn

While the Reagan years were a boon to property rights, they inadvertently created a complacency within the movement that dealt it a savage blow after Reagan left office. By changing from an adversarial to a cooperative attitude with property owners, the Reagan administration essentially took the wind out of the sails of the burgeoning movement—effectively disarming landowners and resource users. As reported by the *New York Times*: "Mr. [Bob] Burford . . . said he helped end the Sagebrush Rebellion . . . by seeing to it that the Federal Government . . . is sensitive to the needs of all users of the public range."[28] This left Westerners vulnerable to the unexpectedly adversarial Bush administration. On the campaign trail, then-vice president George Bush claimed he wanted to be known as the "environmental president." Under Bush, the EPA issued a new wetlands delineation manual in 1989 that broadened the definition of "navigable waters" by redefining land that held water for short periods of time each year as "wetlands"—almost doubling the amount of land over which the federal government exercises control (from one hundred to two hundred million acres). Seventy-five percent of this land was privately owned. Indiana Farm Bureau president Harry Reardon noted at the time, "Few people realized that the laws governing wetlands and private property have not changed in twenty years. What has changed is the interpretation of those laws by several bureaucrats. . . . The intent is to control all land, not just wetlands."[29]

The Bush administration was simply unable to cope with the property rights movement. Having distanced itself from the Reagan agenda by appeasing the environmental lobby, it could not accommodate the revolt from the heartland. "The Bush administration," reported the *Washington Post*, "finds itself straddling an awkward ideological fence. Many members of the core Republican constituency are active in the property rights movement. . . . However, President Bush has indicated his support for the environment."[30]

What Has Regulation Wrought?

Federal wetlands regulations, more than anything else, may have been the spark that ignited the renewed property-rights revolt. Wetlands statutes were the basis for many of the cases underscoring the arbitrariness and injustices committed by the enforcement regime under which people are sent to jail for acts done on their privately owned land. For example:

- The EPA and Federal Bureau of Investigation (FBI) began staking out the property of Marinus Van Leuzen after he challenged the government to "buy his land or put him in jail." Van Leuzen, who owns a house on stilts on the Bolivar peninsula of Texas, put sand under the house to park his truck and set up lawn furniture. The U.S. Army Corps of Engineers and the EPA ordered him to stop this development because it was deemed an illegal destruction of wetlands. A decision was made to prosecute Van Leuzen at the close of a six-hour meeting held in Washington with the assistant attorney general for environment and natural resources and representatives of the Army Corps, EPA, and FBI.
- Ocie Mills and his son Carey served twenty-one months in a federal penitentiary and were fined $10,000 for the crime of dumping sand on Ocie's Florida property while building a home for Carey. Federal District Judge Roger Vinson later ruled that "at the time in question, Mills' land was probably not a wetland for the purposes of the Clean Water Act."[31]
- Marine engineer Bill Ellen was sentenced to six months in jail and six months of home supervision in 1990 for building a wildlife sanctuary on Maryland's eastern shore. The man who hired Ellen for the job, millionaire commodities trader Paul Tudor Jones, II, escaped incarceration by paying a $1 million fine and making a $1 million donation to an environmental group. The "wetland" Ellen disturbed was so dry and dusty that construction workers were forced to wear surgical masks and keep the ground wetted down while they worked. Attempts by property-rights activists to win a pardon for Ellen from President Bush were met with silence from the White House.

Rise of the Grassroots Property Rights Group

By 1992, property rights had become such an active issue at the grassroots level that even the *New York Times* took note of what was happening, writing: "The strength of the property rights movement, as it is often called, comes from joining the old wings of the 1970s Sagebrush Rebellion in the West—miners, loggers, ranchers, energy companies—with private landowners in the East and South."[32]

One way landowners are fighting back is by taking their cases to court. They gained legal muscle after the founding of the Pacific Legal Foundation (PLF) in 1973. The PLF was the first of many nonprofit, public-interest law firms litigating in defense of individual and economic freedoms, including property rights. "We see the '90s as our decade," noted PLF founder and president Ron Zumbrum. "We have the weapons—court precedent, experienced personnel, and credibility."[33]

There has also been a wealth of property-rights activism at the grassroots level. When property is affected, especially when a community or select group is threatened, an organization is inevitably formed to provide a unified front against the attempted intrusion on their rights. David Lucas, the plaintiff in the U.S. Supreme Court case of *Lucas v. South Carolina Coastal Council*, received so many calls and letters from property owners with problems similar to his own that he formed his own group called the Council on Property Rights.

The Alliance for America serves as a loose confederation of over six hundred property-rights organizations. The alliance communicates with its members through an extensive fax network, and hosts the "Fly-In for Freedom," which brings in property owners and users from all over the country to meet with their elected officials in Washington.

In Hollow Rock, Tennessee, Henry Lamb runs the Environmental Conservation Organization (ECO). Lamb was appalled by the number of people who considered private property a public resource. As a building contractor, he realized that he could not conduct business in this atmosphere. He set about linking together groups concerned about the threat to private property rights. From an initial coalition of seventeen organizations, ECO now boasts over five hundred member organizations.

Fred Nims, a career military officer turned farmer, founded Oregonians in Action in 1981. What was originally conceived as a coalition became an educational center focusing on property rights and land-use regulation reform. The organization has become very influential in state politics, promoting ten bills to protect the rights of farmers and land users in the 1993 legislative session. It later expanded to include the legal center that provided Florence Dolan with the legal assistance she needed to take her case before the U.S. Supreme Court.

Grassroots activism has been highly effective as well, unifying many people and serving as a catalyst for coalition-building. Large rallies and parades organized around the issue have been held in places like Boise, Idaho, and Tallahassee, Florida. The *Washington Post* noted "the growing number of small-scale property owners who, over the last two years, have coalesced into a political force aggrieved with government regulation of their land," and concluded that "the private property rights movement consists of 'moms and pops' who have joined together to fight to use their land as they see fit."[34]

In the midst of all this new property-rights activism, it became clear that there was a need for a national organization to formulate and execute a comprehensive, litigative, legislative, and grassroots strategy. This need was met in 1991 with the founding of Defenders of Property Rights. Set up by lawyers who saw the distinct need for a central hub to unite the diverse aspects of the property-rights movement, Defenders was constructed to bring about a sea change in property-rights law through strategically filed lawsuits, groundbreaking property-rights legislation, and public education about the issue. This new initiative, designed to forge a unified national and state strategy in cooperation with existing grassroots forces, proved that times had changed for the property rights movement.

The 1990s: The Tide Turns

Senator Ben Nighthorse Campbell of Colorado (then a Democrat) wrote in a letter to Secretary of the Interior Bruce Babbitt: "People working under your command at the Interior Department seem bent on offending and double-dealing everyone west of Oklahoma." These bureaucrats, wrote Campbell, are on a "crusade to push through public lands reforms that fit their own elitist vision of the world."[35] (Campbell switched to the Republican Party in 1995.)

By then, even Cecil Andrus—whose 1981 boast as interior secretary extolling the growth of federal lands opened this chapter—had had enough. In a 1994 letter to Babbitt, Andrus (now the governor of Idaho) claimed that BLM director Jim Baca "didn't know what he was talking about" with regard to land policy. "Frankly, my friend," warned Andrus, "you don't have enough political allies in the western United States to treat us this shabbily."[36] This was a direct slam against Babbitt, who was governor of Arizona prior to his run for president in 1988. After that, he became the president of the environmentalist League of Conservation Voters. Baca resigned shortly after the arrival of Andrus's letter in Washington. When the Greenwire press service asked Babbitt what happened, he replied, "The Western governors were unhappy with Jim Baca."[37]

What's Going On Right Now

A marked change in property-rights policy is currently afoot at the legislative level. In the 104th Congress, the new Republican majority placed property rights high on its "Contract with America" agenda. On 2 March 1995, the House voted overwhelmingly to pass the Property Rights Protection Act of 1995, requiring the government to pay just compensation to property owners whose land is devalued by 20 percent or more.[38] Property owners have the option of requiring the government to buy all of their affected property if the extent of the taking goes over 50 percent, but are barred from compensation where actions are considered a "nuisance." The legislation is limited to wetlands, endangered species, and lesser statutes. Broader legislation that includes the implementation of a "takings impact analysis" (TIA) and judicial reform is progressing through the Senate.[39]

The House of Representatives also passed a reauthorization of the Clean Water Act in early 1995 that contained several reforms, including the same protections found in the Property Rights Protection Act of 1995.[40] Senator John Chafee (R-RI), the chairman of the Environment and Public Works Committee, however, is cool to the House bill, saying he is in no hurry to act on Clean Water legislation. This, plus the threat of a veto by the Clinton White House, have dampened hopes of reauthorizing the statute in the 104th Congress. Earlier in the session, a bill sponsored by Senators Phil Gramm (R) and Kay Bailey Hutchison (R) of Texas placing a moratorium on the listing of endangered species or habitat—prompted by the listing of the golden-cheeked warbler, affecting thirty-three Texas counties—was signed into law.

Even more activity is present at the state level. In the past few years, especially in 1995, there has been an explosion of legislation being signed into law. The states are serving as both a laboratory and a role model for federal legislation, as states like Washington and Florida now have laws that mandate compensation for any percentage of land that is taken. Many more have TIAs and special statutes affecting wetland and ESA policy enforcement. In all, twenty-two states now have property rights protections of some sort signed into law, with many of these states boasting more than one law on the books.

In presidential politics, property rights is also a major factor, with Republican front-runners Senators Bob Dole of Kansas and Gramm giving the issue high priority.

Property Rights: The Civil Rights Issue of the 1990s

Although rooted in the land-oriented Sagebrush Rebellion of the 1970s, the property-rights battle has evolved into a fight for freedom and individual rights, with property recognized as more than just land. Just as segregation led to the civil rights movement of the 1960s, government intrusion on property rights—largely in the name of protecting the environment—has sparked a new crusade to protect an individual's right to own and use all forms of and interests in private property. Noah Webster, the great eighteenth-century American educator and linguist, noted that the link between liberty and private property rights is intrinsic: "Let the people have property and they will have power— a power that will forever be exerted to prevent the restriction of the press, the abolition of trial by jury, or the abridgment of any other privilege."

Steadily increasing regulation at the federal, state, and local levels now touches every conceivable aspect of property use. Through its ability to regulate, the government now more than ever takes the uses and benefits of property rather than condemning it and paying its owner the fair market value. This violates the Fifth Amendment's guarantee, "nor shall private property be taken for public use, without just compensation." Like civil rights movements of the past, people have organized to pressure the government through their elected representatives and the courts to change current policies and promote property-rights protections.

Today, property rights has become the line drawn in the sand between tyranny and liberty. As a result, the American public is coming to realize that the environmental ethic is based less on environmental protection and more on the false pretense that people should have only limited rights to own and use their property, and only when it is deemed acceptable to government regulators. Indeed, the environmental movement is predicated on the notion that the world would be better off without people and their activities: "Legal experts like Joe Sax and John Echeverria envision a future in which land is treated not as individual castles behind a moat, but as cooperating units of larger natural and economic systems. In fact, says Echeverria, it is inevitable that a crowded earth will demand more of each of its citizens. 'I think this [environmental backlash] is sort of a burp,' he says, 'an anachronistic movement appealing to the myth of the Boone frontier, which is not what we have anymore.'"[41] An examination of statutes passed to protect the environment reveal their antihuman animus. For example, the Clean Water Act is designated to restore the chemical and biological integrity of our nation's waterways. Needless to say, everyday human endeavors like taking a shower involve the discharge of water into the nation's waterways, thereby creating a violation of the act. Superfund addresses cleaning up soils and groundwater, but has no limit on the extent of this cleanup, basically requiring that land be restored to the way it was when there were no people.

Government policy makes criminals out of ordinary people. A bureaucratically created wetlands enforcement program never authorized by Congress, which sentences people to jail for violation of vague and arbitrary rules (even though there may be no actual harm to the environment) and requires property owners to spend hundreds of dollars to create new wetlands as so-called mitigation, calls to mind a passage from Ayn Rand's classic novel *Atlas Shrugged*, when government bureaucrat Dr. Ferris tells industrialist Hank Rearden:

> There's no way to rule innocent men. The only power government has is the power to crack down on criminals. When there aren't enough criminals, one makes them. One declares so many things to be a crime that it becomes impossible for men to live without breaking laws. Who wants a nation of law-abiding citizens? What's there in that for anyone—but just pass the kind of laws that can neither be observed nor enforced nor objectively interpreted—and you created a nation of lawbreakers—and then you cash in on the guilt.[42]

The environmental ethic also hinders the natural human impulse to own things and protect that right to ownership. The property rights movement of the 1990s is rooted in the recognition that a "better" solution is to recognize property rights and acknowledge the importance of working with the property owners (rather than against them) to achieve environmental protection. While the "commons" will always be at the mercy of politically powerful special interests who may hold no stake in the land, it should be recognized that exclusive ownership of property creates the only effective, long-term incentive to conserve resources and minimize pollution. A property owner who blights his or her land destroys his or her own estate and that of his or her heirs. A bureaucrat who blights "public" land bears no cost whatsoever. When land belongs to everyone, it actually belongs to no one, which is the source of the "tragedy of the commons." Experience also teaches that uncompensated takings in the name of environmentalism often creates perverse disincentives that prove themselves to be antienvironmental. If the price of creating habitat is losing property without compensation, where is the motivation to create or maintain habitat in the first place? The property rights movement is not seeking less environmental protection; it asks only that the few unlucky landowners who do lose their property to regulation no longer be forced to bear an unfair share of the burden.

Ultimately, uncompensated takings are not just a problem of economic efficiency, but of justice. The danger was outlined by Chief Justice Holmes in 1922: "The protection of private property in the Fifth Amendment presupposes that it is wanted for public use, but provides that it shall not be taken for such use without compensation. . . . When this seemingly absolute protection is found to be qualified by the police power, the natural tendency of human nature is to extend that qualification more and more until at last private property disappears."[43]

The Supreme Court noted further in 1972: "The dichotomy between personal liberties and property rights is a false one. Property does not have rights. People have rights. The right to enjoy property without unlawful deprivation, no less than the right to speak or the right to travel, is in truth a 'personal' right. . . . In fact, a fundamental interdependence exists between the personal right to liberty and the personal right to property. Neither would have meaning without the other."[44]

To defend human rights and ensure that we live in a world where the environment is protected by the rule of law as embodied in the Constitution, we must ensure that forced transfers of property—not just through the power of eminent domain, but also through regulatory takings—be allowed only when just compensation is paid. We are already at a major constitutional and governmental crossroads. Property-rights advocates are committed to see to it that property rights are vigorously protected.

Notes

1. Cy Ryan, United Press International, 6 January 1981.
2. The federal government owns 82.265 percent of Nevada's total state acreage (U.S. Department of the Interior, Bureau of Land Management, *Public Land Statistics* [Washington, D.C.: GPO], Tables 4 and 5). Other states include Ala-

bama, Connecticut, Illinois, Indiana, Kansas, Maine, New Jersey, New York, Ohio, Oklahoma, Pennsylvania, Rhode Island, South Carolina, Texas, Michigan, Minnesota, Missouri, North Carolina, North Dakota, Tennessee, and Wisconsin, Ibid. (at Table 4).

3. Cy Ryan, United Press International, 18 July 1981.

4. David F. Salisbury, "Energy: The Varmint That May Spoil America's West, *Christian Science Monitor*, 3 September 1981, B26.

5. Ibid.

6. "'Wise Use': Groups on Move against Enviros in New England," *Greenwire*, 22 October 1992.

7. Although all government regulation can potentially violate the Fifth Amendment, this chapter is limited to a discussion of environmental regulation. See *Hodel v. Riving*, 481 U.S. 704 (1987) (federal law that provided for escheat of tribal property interests); *Richardson v. City and County of Honolulu*, 759 F. Supp. (D. Ha. 1991) (city ordinance that sets a dollar ceiling on renegotiated historic rental property); *Seawell Assoc. v. City of New York*, 542 N.E.2d 1050 (N.Y. 1989) (city ordinance prohibiting the demolition, alteration, or conversion of single-room occupancy rental properties); and *United Artists Theater Circuit v. City of Philadelphia*, 595 A.2d 6 (Pa. 1991) (city ordinance designating property as historic).

8. Thomas D. Hopkins, *Cost of Regulation* (Rochester, N.Y.: Rochester Institute of Technology, 1991), table 5a.

9. U.S. Constitution, Amendments 5 and 14; *Pennsylvania Coal Co. v. Mahon*, 260 U.S. 393, 416 (1922).

10. *Pennsylvania Coal* 260 U.S. at 416.

11. A useful compendium of the various federal statutes discussed in this text is Federal Environmental Laws (St. Paul, Minn.: West, 1993).

12. 42 U.S.C. §§ 7401-7671q (1988 & Supp. 1991).

13. 33 U.S.C. §§ 401-26p, 441-54 (1988).

14. 42 U.S.C. §§ 6901-911, (1988).

15. 42 U.S.C. §§ 99601-75, (1988).

16. See Brett Dalton, "Superfund: The South Carolina Experience," in *Taking the Environment Seriously* edited by Roger E. Meiners and Bruce Yandle (Lanham, Md.: Rowman & Littlefield, 1993), chapter 5.

17. 16 U.S.C. §§ 1533-44 (1988).

18. See Thomas R. Dunlap, *Saving America's Wildlife* (Princeton: Princeton University Press, 1988). Also, National Research Council, *Setting Priorities for Land Conservation* (Washington, D.C.: National Academy Press, 1993).

19. Paul Kaplan, "Those Little Fish Still Delaying Cherokee County Reservoir," *Atlanta Journal/Atlanta Constitution*, 3 July 1994.

20. National Wilderness Institute, "Going Broke? Costs of the Endangered Species Act as Revealed in Endangered Species Recovery Plans," 27.

21. See Margaret Ann Reigle, "FLOC Members under Armed Siege over Duck Ponds," *News from the FLOC* (Cambridge, Md.: Fairness to Landowners Committee, February 1994).

22. Robyn C. Walker, United Press International, 23 January 1982.

23. Ibid.

24. *Penn Central Transp. Co. v. City of New York*, 438 U.S. 104, 124 (1978).

25. *Dolan v. City of Tigard*, No. 93-518, Slip. Op., at 17 (U.S. June 24, 1994).

26. Upon assuming office, President Clinton and Vice President Gore immediately expressed their intent to rescind Executive Order 12, 630. 53 Fed. Reg. 8859 (1988).

27. See Roger J. Marzulla, "The New 'Takings' Executive Order and Environmental Regulation—Collision or Cooperation" 18 Envnt. L.Rep. (Envtl L. Inst.) 10254 (July 1988). Marzulla, also a Westerner and former president of the Mountains States Legal Foundation, was the chief architect of the executive order and was appointed by President Reagan to serve as assistant attorney general for the then Land and Natural Resources Division of the U.S. Department of Justice.

28. Philip Shabecoff, "Farewells, Fond and Otherwise, for Land Director," *New York Times*, 5 July 1989, A18.

29. Harry Pearson, *Hoosier Farmer*, September-October 1991, 3.

30. Kristin Downey, "A Conservative Supreme Court Addresses Property Rights," *Washington Post*, 16 February 1992, H1.

31. *United States v. Mills*, 817 F. Supp. 1546, 1548 (1993).

32. Keith Schneider, "When the Bad Guy Is Seen as the One in the Green Hat," *New York Times*, 16 February 1992.

33. H. Jane Lehman, "Owners Aren't Giving Ground in Property Battles," Chicago Tribune, 9 February 1992, E1.

34. H. Jane Lehman, "A Changing Tide in Wetlands Decisions: Violators Caught in a Tug of War over Property Rights, Environmental Protection," *Washington Post*, 18 January 1992, E1.

35. Letter from Senator Ben Nighthorse Campbell to Interior Secretary Bruce Babbitt, 5 March 1994. For contrast, see "'Wise Use': Groups on the Move against Enviros in New England," *Greenwire*, 22 October 1992, in which the idea of "land-grabbing elitists" is depicted as a "right-wing" fantasy.

36. Letter from Idaho governor Cecil D. Andrus to Secretary of the Interior Bruce Babbitt, 25 August 1993.

37. "Babbitt Outlines Priorities for Coming Year," *Greenwire*, 28 March 1994.

38. H.R. 925, 104th Cong., 1st Sess., The Property Rights Protection Act of 1995.

39. S. 605, 104th Cong., 1st Sess., The Omnibus Property Rights Act of 1995.

40. H.R. 961, 104th Cong., 1st Sess., The Clean Water Amendments of 1995.

41. "Landowners turn the Fifth into Sharp-Pointed Sword," *High Country News* 24, no. 2 (1993), 12.

42. Ayn Rand, *Atlas Shrugged* (New York: Random House, 1957).

43. *Pennsylvania Coal Co. v. Mahon*, 260 U.S. 393, 415 (1922).

44. *Lynch v. Household Finance Corporation*, 405 U.S. 538, 552 (1972).

5

Environmentalism: The Real Movement to Protect Property Rights

Glenn P. Sugameli

The self-styled "property rights" movement is based on two unfounded claims: that "takings" bills will protect private property and that such bills codify the Constitution's Fifth Amendment clause "nor shall private property be taken for public use, without just compensation." Neither claim is true.

In fact, the two claims are closely related—takings bills would harm the property and other rights of average American citizens because they would impose standards that are contrary to the Fifth Amendment's balanced approach. The result would be massive costs to taxpayers, a litigation explosion, and an inability to enforce protections for people and property. We all live, work, and recreate downstream, downwind, downhill, and near property on which takings bills would allow developers, factories, and others to be bad neighbors: extracting profits at the expense of nearby people and property, and the public.

Conservation and environmental laws were enacted to deal with threats to people and property—from the Dust Bowl to Love Canal. Examples abound—wetland laws prevent pollution, flooding, and loss of recreational and commercial fishing jobs. Passage of the Surface Mining Control and Reclamation Act of 1977 was prompted by the 1972 collapse of a massive coal company waste refuse pile that had dammed a stream. The resulting twenty- to thirty-foot tidal wave killed

Portions of this chapter previously appeared in *Virginia Environmental Law Journal* 12 (1993): 439-91 as "Takings Issues in Light of *Lucas v. South Carolina Coastal Council*: A Decision Full of Sound and Fury Signifying Nothing." Reprinted by permission of author and publisher.

over 125 people, devastated sixteen communities, and destroyed a thousand homes.[1]

The property rights and values of American citizens are protected by environmental laws that prevent pollution, flooding, and other threats to their health, homes, and businesses. Proposed federal and state "takings" bills would radically redefine property rights in a way that threatens fundamental safeguards for people, neighboring homes, and communities.

Those who support environmental protection and oppose takings bills are the genuine private property movement, not the self-styled "property rights" advocates. The National Wildlife Federation and others strongly support the Fifth Amendment's balanced protection of private property. If a court determines that a government limit on use of private property goes so far as to be a taking, just compensation must be paid. We oppose takings bills because they will delay, block, or be so expensive as to force repeal of a wide range of protections of property and people that do *not* take private property rights.

Takings Bills Versus the Constitution

Takings bills use standards that are contrary to the Fifth Amendment's test for determining when compensation is required because private property has been taken for public use. For example, both H.R. 925, which passed the House of Representatives on 3 March 1995, and S. 605, which was introduced by Senator Robert Dole (R-KS), would mandate unlimited payments from taxpayers to corporations and others whose property has not been taken according to every justice of the Supreme Court.

In the 1993 *Concrete Pipe* decision, the Supreme Court unanimously reaffirmed its long-standing rejection of two premises that lie at the heart of these and other takings bills that require payments when there is (1) a specific diminution in the value of (2) any affected portion of property. First, because takings decisions must consider many factors, including impacts on neighboring property owners and the public, the Supreme Court said that its cases "have long established that mere diminution in the value of property, however serious, is insufficient to demonstrate a taking." Second, determining whether property has been taken requires looking at the overall property, which cannot "be divided into what was taken and what was left for the purpose of demonstrating the taking of the former to be complete and hence compensable."[2]

In contrast, takings bills that focus on only "the affected portion" of the property guarantee that almost any company can meet the bills' percentage diminution of value test. It would not be enough that a company can fully use 99.9 percent of its property. Payments would be required even in a situation where a small buffer strip requirement actually increases the value of tens of thousands of acres that a company can develop.

Bills such as S. 605 would extend this new entitlement to impacts of a broad sweep of federal actions on any property, including contract rights and other intangibles. The result would be a flood of costly litigation. Claims would be filed whenever worker safety or other concerns affect one machine out of a thousand in a factory, or one truck in a fleet.

As the Justice Department told Congress, this would threaten enforcement of civil rights and disabilities laws and laws that ensure the safety of food, drugs, airplanes, trucks, and the sound operation of pension funds and banks. Said associate attorney general John R. Schmidt, "[T]his bill and similar proposals are based on a radical premise that has never been a part of our law or tradition: that a private property owner has the absolute right to the greatest possible profit from that property, regardless of the consequences of the proposed use on other individuals or the public generally."[3]

Thirty-three state attorneys general wrote Congress in September 1994 that: "[Takings bills] purport to implement constitutional property rights protections, but in fact they promote a radical new takings theory that would severely constrain the government's ability to protect the environment and public health and safety." Legal scholars had previously written that takings bills are "flawed caricatures of constitutional rules that would impose wholly new and burdensome requirements on Congress and the federal agencies when they seek to protect private property and public health and safety."[4]

Payoff (Compensation) Takings Bills

Many takings bills would pay developers, factories, and others to comply with laws that protect the rights of all Americans. These bills do not offer "compensation" for property that has been taken. Rather, they would use funds from federal, state, or local taxpayers to pay off property owners whenever a regulation reduces the speculative value of any portion of property by more than a certain percentage. As discussed above, this takings test has been repeatedly rejected by the

Supreme Court in two major respects. Indeed, the test has never been endorsed by a single Supreme Court justice.

Budget-Busting Takings Bills

Proposed takings legislation would force repeal of basic protections by making them too expensive to enforce. The Office of Management and Budget has estimated the costs of S. 605 to "be several times the $28 billion [over seven years] of the House-passed legislation." (The Congressional Budget Office "has no basis for estimating the additional amounts of compensation" for larger claims.) A 1995 study by the University of Washington Institute for Public Policy Management revealed that Washington state's defeated Referendum 48 could have cost local governments up to $1 billion annually for takings studies alone and exposed them to payments to takings claimants of up to $11 billion.[5]

People Reject Takings Bills

Voters have consistently and overwhelmingly rejected statewide takings referenda. In November 1995, Washington state's Referendum 48 was rejected 60 to 40 percent, as was an Arizona takings impact assessment bill in a November 1994 statewide initiative vote. Even supporters of takings recognize that the American people oppose these bills: the *Seattle Times* reported that "R. J. Smith of the conservative Competitive Enterprise Institute, a Washington, D.C. think tank, said the defeats in Washington and Arizona may have taught another lesson—that property rights leaders shouldn't take the issue directly to voters through initiative or referendum."[6]

For state and local governments, takings laws would have a host of disastrous consequences.[7] For example, these bills could reverse the results of cases where courts have rejected takings claims brought by businesses affected by local efforts to protect people, property, and communities by controlling drunk driving, drinking in public, and all-night bars.[8]

The National Governors Association, the National Conference of State Legislatures, the National League of Cities, the U.S. Conference of Mayors, the National Institute of Municipal Law Officers, and the Western State Land Commissioners Association all have approved resolutions opposing takings payment bills for budgetary and other reasons.[9] Dozens of newspaper editorial boards opposed takings bills in 1995 alone.[10] In December 1995, President Clinton notified Senate Judiciary Committee Chair Orrin G. Hatch of his "intention to veto [S. 605] or any similar compensation entitlement legislation."[11]

Takings is being used in a backdoor administrative, legislative, and judicial attack on laws and regulations that are too popular to modify or repeal on the merits. The scope of the takings agenda has ignited broad opposition. This includes citizens representing civil rights, labor, environmental, and other concerns who are working to conserve protections for people and property. For example, takings-bill opponents range from the League of Women Voters to the United Cerebral Palsy Associations, from the United States Catholic Conference to the American Public Health Association.

Extreme Breadth of the Takings Agenda

Justice Holmes, in *Pennsylvania Coal Co. v. Mahon*—the very opinion that created the concept of a regulatory taking—warned that "government could hardly go on if to some extent values incident to property could not be diminished without paying for every such change in the general law. As long recognized some values are enjoyed under an implied limitation and must yield to the police power [to protect health, safety and welfare]." [12]

State and federal takings bills target a wide variety of protections. Senator Dole's S. 605 applies to virtually every federal law, from civil rights to banking regulations. This extraordinarily wide scope reflects the ideas of intellectual proponents of the takings movement. In his 1987, book which provided a major spark for takings bills, Professor Richard A. Epstein wrote: "It will be said that my position invalidates much of the twentieth century legislation, and so it does. . . . The New Deal *is* inconsistent with the principle of limited government and with the constitutional provisions designed to secure that end."[13] Similarly, the Cato Institute's Roger Pilon has written that "except when issues of endangerment arise, regulations of lot sizes, setback requirements, or restrictions on types of construction are all illegitimate. . . . Likewise with rent controls or antidiscrimination measures: private individuals have a perfect right to offer their properties for sale or rent to whomever they choose at whatever prices they wish."[14] As one commentator has written: "The resurrection—or construction—of an absolutist view of property is an attempt to re-open many of the issues previously resolved in the 19th century (nuisance law, the police power, the taxing power) and the 20th century (social regulation, regulation of private enterprise, fees and charges)."[15]

Civil Rights and Takings

Historically, takings and "property rights" claims have been invoked by those who oppose a wide variety of laws that limit activities that profit at the expense of the basic human rights and property of average citizens. An Atlanta motel operator challenged the Civil Rights Act's requirement that the motel rent rooms to people of color. The Supreme Court found that while this fundamental public accommodation provision may have reduced the fair market value of the motel, it was *not* a "taking" of the motel's property.[16] After a customer had to crawl into the restroom, an International House of Pancakes (IHOP) franchisee resisted complying with the Americans with Disabilities Act's provisions requiring access to public accommodations. The court rejected the franchisee's claim that requiring him to remove tables and spend money to make the restrooms accessible to people who use wheelchairs was a taking.[17]

Safeguards of Homeowners from Mining

Courts have rejected a series of takings claims against laws that protect the safety and property of coalfield residents from the devastating effects of strip mining and underground mining. In *Hodel v. Indiana*, the Supreme Court found that the Surface Mining Control and Reclamation Act "prohibition against mining near churches, schools, parks, public buildings, and occupied dwellings [was] plainly directed toward ensuring that surface coal mining does not endanger life and property in coal mining communities."[18]

Takings advocates tend to ignore the Supreme Court's major 1987 *Keystone* decision, which ruled that a law requiring that 50 percent of coal beneath homes be left in place to prevent subsidence damage did not take the coal that had to be left. The Court found the State acted "to protect the public interest in health, the environment, and the fiscal integrity of the area."[19]

In a subsequent case, the M & J Coal Company removed so much coal from an underground mine that huge cracks opened on the surface rupturing gas lines, collapsing a stretch of highway, and destroying homes. When the federal Interior Department required M & J Coal to reduce the amount of coal it was mining to protect property and public safety, the company sued. The court rejected M & J Coal's claim that, despite the company's 34.5 percent annual profit, mining regulations had "taken" its property.[20]

Takings Bills versus Civil Rights and Homeowner Protections

These results would be altered by takings bills that ignore the benefits of safeguards and focus only on impact on value of any affected portion of property, rather than on the entire property. The affected portion could be viewed as the lost tables in the IHOP case or the coal needed to support the homes in the *Keystone* and *M & J Coal* cases.

Nuisance Law

Takings proponents often attempt to rely on a very narrow exception in takings bills for actions to prevent a nuisance. Historically, however, nuisance (unwritten law developed by judges) did not prevent massive pollution and other harms to people and property. Pollution control and other laws were passed because nuisance law proved extremely inadequate.

For example, nuisance does not cover cumulative damage to health and property from many sources. The Civil Rights Act and Americans with Disabilities Act were needed precisely because discrimination in public access on the basis of race or disability was not a nuisance. A state nuisance exception might not apply to the *M & J Coal* case because the state authorities refused to protect the homes.

Nuisance is also extraordinarily murky. The greatest authority on nuisance law, Dean William Prosser, wrote that there is "no more impenetrable jungle in the entire law than that which surrounds the word 'nuisance.'" Therefore, the test in takings bills is not only inaccurate, it is anything but clear. Complex litigation would be required to determine whether the nuisance exception applied to every conceivable case.

Radical Federal Administrative Takings Agenda

Former solicitor general Charles Fried (1985–89) has described the Reagan administration Justice Department as determined to misuse the Takings Clause to thwart regulation:

> Attorney General [Edwin] Meese and his young advisers—many drawn from the ranks of the then fledgling Federalist Societies and often devotees of the extreme libertarian views of Chicago law professor Richard Epstein—had a specific, aggressive, and, it seemed to me, quite radical project in mind: to use the Takings Clause of the Fifth Amendment as a severe brake upon federal and state regulation of business and property. The grand plan was to make government pay compensation as for a taking of property every time its regulations impinged too severely on a property right—limiting the possible uses for a parcel of land or restricting or tying up a business in regulatory red tape. If the government labored under so severe an obligation, there would be, to say the least, much less regulation.[21]

Government compensation for actual takings of property is required by the Fifth Amendment.[22] The "radical" agenda of the Meese Justice Department, however, was to require compensation or force repeal of regulations, not only for actual takings, but in thousands of other instances *"as for* a taking."

The embodiment and legacy of this radical agenda is President Reagan's Executive Order 12630 on takings.[23] The order requires that all federal regulations be approved by agencies and the attorney general under a takings test that the Congressional Research Service and others have demonstrated severely misrepresents Supreme Court rulings on takings law.[24] For example, it omits any reference to Supreme Court principles that weigh against finding a taking and includes insupportable limits on preventive actions and margins of safety—requiring that health and safety protections "should be undertaken only in response to real and substantial threats to public health and safety," and "be no greater than is necessary to achieve the health and safety purpose."

Relying on this flawed Executive Order, the Interior Department proposed a rule that would have nullified the Surface Mining Control and Reclamation Act of 1977's protection for sensitive national lands and private property.[25] The rule would have opened not only the national parks but also the nation's backyards, schoolyards, churchyards, and graveyards to strip mining. *The New York Times* reported, in a widely syndicated front-page article, on the Bush administration's plan to finalize the rule after the 1992 presidential election.[26] As a result of the firestorm of public and editorial criticism that followed, the rule was blocked by Congress[27] and withdrawn.

This example illustrates the flaw in takings bills that ignore competing property interests by asserting that government should minimize the impact of its actions on "the" property interest involved. Allowing mining may harm surface owners of the property that is mined and those who live nearby.

Red Tape (Assessment) Takings Bills

State and federal takings bills that are patterned after Executive Order 12630 generate costly and obstructive red tape under the guise of assessing potential takings liability. In 1990, former senator Steve Symms (R-ID) offered an unsuccessful amendment to require certain regulations to comply with "Executive Order 12630 or similar procedures."[28] In 1991, the Senate approved an expanded Symms amendment applicable to all federal agencies, but it was removed in conference committee with the House.[29]

At the state level, too, numerous takings bills have been introduced and some have been enacted.[30] Most of these bills would require the state attorney general or state agencies to develop guidelines to assess potential takings and to plan for the resulting liability that might occur from proposed regulations or other agency actions.

Many of these takings-impact-assessment bills are based on an impossible premise—they purportedly would require a takings determination and a dollar assessment at the time any regulation is proposed. Such a requirement would conflict with the Supreme Court's consistent takings rulings, which emphasize that there cannot be an inflexible test for takings. Takings can only be decided after a particular regulation has been applied to a specific piece of property. This allows consideration of individual and cumulative impacts of proposed uses on neighboring and downstream property and the public.[31]

The Delaware attorney general's experience under a 1992 state takings assessment law confirms this.[32] The office conducts a "canned" regulatory review noting that virtually all regulations involving real property might result in a taking and that a more meaningful analysis can only be done on a property-specific basis. Ralph S. Tyler, deputy attorney general of Maryland, concluded that the Delaware example underscores "the central conceptual flaw" of a similar proposed Maryland bill, "it is impossible to conduct a meaningful 'takings' analysis in the abstract."[33]

These problems with takings assessment or "liability planning" bills have even been recognized by Nancie G. Marzulla, president and chief legal officer of Defenders of Property Rights (and wife of Roger Marzulla, Chairman of Defenders of Property Rights, who authored the Reagan takings Executive Order when he was an Assistant Attorney General). She has written that "Planning Bills . . . do have serious weaknesses. As Maryland [deputy] attorney general Ralph S. Tyler points out, 'no meaningful analysis can be done' of the liability at stake in a taking when so much depends not only 'upon the particular circumstances' of the case, but on the philosophy of the particular judge hearing the case. . . . When judges take this ad hoc approach to takings law, liability planning becomes a shot in the dark."[34]

Thus, the real purpose and effect of these bills is not to assess or plan for takings liability, but to delay or block needed protections of people and property. Liability planning can never work because the only categorical rules in takings law are negative—that is, they only say when there is not a taking, not when there is. For example, property restrictions never cause a taking if they track limitations in the title to property, as defined by "background principles of property and nuisance law." This requires property- and use-specific analysis, including "the degree of harm to public lands and resources, or adjacent private property, posed by the claimant's proposed activities."[35]

It is possible to write guidelines that state these negative rules and some of the factors that the Constitution requires to be taken into account. Any effort to assess the likelihood of a taking or the amount of compensation, however, would necessarily be so speculative as to be meaningless.

While such efforts cannot yield any useful estimates of potential government liability or the number or cost of takings of private property, they are not harmless. They can require taxpayers to bear high costs. They can function, intentionally or not, to delay or block implementation of laws that protect people, property, and communities.

Myths and Facts—Endangered Species, Wetlands, and Floodplains

Unfortunately, much of the protakings bill rhetoric consists of argument by mythical anecdote. This is especially true of unfounded assertions that property rights are being taken every day by species protection laws and laws that protect private property, health, and safety by limiting destruction of wetlands and floodplains.

In fact, for a variety of reasons, takings claims under wetlands and species-protection laws have been rejected by federal and state courts in the overwhelming majority of cases. For example, in the over twenty-year history of the Endangered Species Act (ESA) (16 U.S.C. §§ 1531-1544 [1988]), courts have only decided two Fifth Amendment taking cases on their merits, both of which have found that the ESA did not take private property.[36]

Federal and state courts have recognized several reasons why government protections of people, property, and the environment rarely take private property.[37] These include the threshold test that takings are limited to actions that eliminate property rights, as defined by "background principles of property and nuisance law." Also, it is not a taking to regulate only part of the "property as a whole," prohibiting only particular uses of land does not cause a taking; and variances, permits, and other administrative remedies can preclude takings.

Takings advocates, however, often misinterpret takings cases.[38] In the *Lucas* decision, one of the Supreme Court's examples of "background principles" clearly states that there can never be a taking from prevention of harm to private property by denying Clean Water Act Section 404 permits to dredge and fill lake beds and other wetlands "that would have the effect of flooding others' land."[39]

Takings proponents also erroneously charge that Section 404 requires leaving land untouched. As the Supreme Court has unanimously held: "a permit system implies that permission may be granted, leaving the landowner free to use the property as desired. Moreover, even if the permit is denied, there may be other viable uses available to the owner. Only when a permit is denied and the effect of the denial is to prevent 'economically viable' use of the land in question can it be said that a taking has occurred."[40]

Very few wetland permits are denied. In Fiscal Year 1994, out of over 48,000 applications to the Army Corps of Engineers for Section 404 wetland dredge and fill permits, 82 percent were covered by general permits in an average of 16 days and only 0.7 percent (358) were denied. Denial of a permit does not impact uplands or developable wetlands within the same parcel. And, as the Supreme Court recognized, there are uses of wetlands that do not require permits to dredge and fill wetlands, which include normal farming, grazing, and forestry activities.

Conclusion

Thus, takings bills endanger the property and other rights of Americans by incorporating standards that are contrary to the Constitution's balanced approach. We all depend upon environmental and other laws to safeguard our children, our homes, and our communities. Takings bills would impose massive and unjustifiable costs, litigation, and enforced rollbacks of these fundamental protections. Opponents of takings bills are the real guardians of property rights.

Notes

1. Gerald M. Stern, *The Buffalo Creek Disaster* (New York: Vintage Books, 1976), prologue.
2. *Concrete Pipe & Products v. Construction Laborers Pension Trust*, 113 S. Ct. 2264. 2264, 2290-91 (1993).
3. Testimony on file with the author.
4. Letters on file with the author.
5. 7 June 1995 letter from OMB Director Alice Rivlin to Senate Judiciary Committee chairman Orrin Hatch and 17 October 1995; letter from E. O'Neill to Senate Judiciary Committee chairman Orrin Hatch. Both letters on file with author.
6. "Ref. 48 defeat has louder echoes: A property rights stall now in Congress, too?" 9 November 1995, A1, 16.
7. See "Legislature Should Quickly Kill Measure to Scrap Land-Use Controls," *Tampa Tribune*, 9 March 1993, at 6 (editorial): "Under this measure, a factory could be built beside a retirement village, a massage parlor next to a church, or a night club on a quiet residential street. One irresponsible developer could spoil a neighborhood and ruin property values of its residents without fear of governmental interference. This apparently, is some legislator's idea of property rights."
8. See. e.g., *Get Away Club, Inc. v. Coleman*, 969 F.2d 664 (8th Cir. 1992) (tavern claim that highway sobriety checkpoints took its property by reducing drinking on premises); *Glasheen v. City of Austin*, 840 F. Supp. 62 (W.D. Tex. 1993) ("to-go beer windows" takings challenge to restriction on consumption of alcohol "in or on" public streets and sidewalks in designated areas of city); *Midnight Sessions, Ltd. v. City of Philadelphia*, 945 F.2d 667 (3d Cir. 1991), *cert denied*, 112 S. Ct. 1668 (1992) (takings challenge to denial of license for all-night dance hall).
9. NGA 1995 Annual Meeting Resolution 18; NCSL policy resolution passed 28 July 1994; NLC Resolution #1 adopted 4 December 1994; USCM Resolution Adopted June 1995; NIMLO Resolution adopted 8 April 1995; WSLCA Resolution adopted 12 January 1995.
10. For example, "Environmental Reform via Sledgehammer," *Los Angeles*

Times, 8 March 1995; "Polluters Loophole," *Mesa Tribune* (Arizona), 27 February 1995; "The 100 Day Hurricane," *New York Times*, 9 April 1995; "The Twisted 'Takings' Bill," *News And Observer* (Raleigh, N.C.), 1 March 1995; "Wrong Way on Takings," *Washington Post*, 9 March 1995; "A Law That Would Take the Public," *Chicago Tribune*, 20 February 1995.

11.   Letter on file with the author.

12.   "[W]hile property may be regulated to a certain extent, if a regulation goes too far it will be recognized as a taking" (260 U.S. 393, 413, 415 [1922]) also 260 U.S. at 413.

13.   *Takings, Private Property and the Power of Eminent Domain* (Cambridge: Harvard University Press, 1985), 281.

14.   "Property Rights, Takings, and a Free Society," *Harvard Journal of Law and Public Policy* 6 (1983): 188.

15.   James M. McElfish, Jr., *Property Rights, Property Roots: Rediscovering the Basis for Legal Protection for the Environment*, Envtl.L Rep. (Envtl.L. Inst.) 24 (1994): 10,231, 10,246.

16.   *Heart of Atlanta Motel, Inc. v. United States*, 379 U.S. 241 (1964)

17.   *Pinnock v. International House of Pancakes Franchisee*, 844 F. Supp. 574 (S.D. Cal. 1993), *cert. denied before judgment*, 114 S. Ct. 2726 (1994).

18.   452 U.S. 314, 329 (1981). This statutory protection was later threatened by a proposed rule relying on a flawed Takings Executive Order to open these areas to mining, as discussed below.

19.   *Keystone Bituminous Coal Ass'n v. DeBenedictis*, 480 U.S. 470, 488 (1987).

20.   *M & J Coal Co. v. United States*, 47 F.3d 1148 (Fed. Cir. 1994), *cert. denied*, 116 S. Ct. 53 (1995).

21.   Charles Fried, *Order and Law: Arguing the Reagan Revolution—A Firsthand Account* (New York: Simon & Schuster, 1991), 183.

22.   "So long as compensation is available for those whose property is in fact taken, the governmental action is not unconstitutional." (*United States v. Riverside Bayview Homes, Inc.*, 474 U.S. 121, 128 [1985] [unanimous Supreme Court decision]).

23.   3 C.F.R. § 554 (1988), *reprinted in* 5 U.S.C. § 601 (1988).

24.   See the author's article, *Virginia Environmental Law Journal*, 12 (1993): 444.

25.   56 Fed. Reg. 33, 152-65 (1991). The author submitted National Wildlife Federation's extensive comments opposing the proposal. Sensitive national lands and private property are protected by 30 U.S.C. § 1272(e) (1988).

26.   Keith Schneider, "U.S. Set to Open National Forests for Strip Mining," *New York Times*, 28 September 1992, A1.

27.   See Energy Policy Act § 2504(b) as reported at 138 Cong. Rec. H12,146 (daily ed. 5 October 1992).

28.   136 Cong. Rec. S10,909-17 (daily ed. 27 July 1990).

29.   See 137 Cong. Rec. S7542-49, S7552-62 (daily ed. 12 June 1991) regarding the Symms amendment. See H.R. Conf. Rep. No. 404, 102d Cong., 1st Sess. 354 (1991), reprinted in 1991 U.S.C.C.A.N. 1734 regarding removal.

30.   See Larry Morandi, "Takings for Granted," *State Legislatures*, June 1995, 22.

31. It is "a question of degree—and therefore cannot be disposed of by general propositions" (*Pennsylvania Coal Co. v. Mahon,* 260 U.S. 393, 416 [1922]). The process relies on "factual inquiries into the circumstances of each particular case" (*Connolly v. Pension Benefit Guar. Corp.,* 475 U.S. 211, 224 [1986]). The Court uniformly insists "on knowing the nature and extent of permitted development" of a particular piece of property (*MacDonald, Sommer & Frates v. Yolo County,* 477 U.S. 340, 351 [1986]).

32. Del Code Ann. tit. 29, § 605 (1992).

33. Letter from Ralph S. Tyler, deputy attorney general of Maryland, to Delegate Donald B. Elliot, Maryland House of Delegates 1 (26 March 1993).

34. Nancie G. Marzulla, "State Private Property Rights Initiatives as a Response to 'Environmental Takings,'" in *Regulatory Takings: Restoring Private Property Rights,* edited by Roger Clegg (Washington, D.C.: National Legal Center for the Public Interest, 1994), 87, 107.

35. *Lucas v. South Carolina Coastal Council,* 112 S. Ct. 2886, 2899-902 (1992). See also *Dolan v. City of Tigard,* 114 S. Ct. 2309, 2317-20 (1994) (in "physical takings" claims, a "roughly proportional" relationship between a mandated transfer of ownership—for example, of land for sidewalks—and the nature and extent of the potential impacts from development can defeat a takings claim).

36. *Christy v. Hodel,* 857 F.2d 1324, 1335 (9th Cir. 1988) (rancher fined for killing grizzly bears that were eating sheep), cert. denied, 490 U.S. 1114 (1989); *United States v. Kepler,* 531 F.2d 796, 797 (6th Cir. 1976) (ban on interstate transport of endangered species that were lawfully possessed before passage of the ESA).

37. See the author's article, *Virginia Environmental Law Journal* 12 (1993): 454-91.

38. For example, they have stated or implied that the *First English* and *Florida Rock* cases found takings (Marzulla, 98). In *First English,* the Supreme Court declined to decide whether barring reconstruction of a summer camp destroyed by a flood was a taking. The Court let stand a later state court decision finding no taking (*First English Evangelical Lutheran Church v. County of Los Angeles,* 482 U.S. 304 [1987] [focusing on remedy once a taking is found], *decision on remand,* 210 Cal. App. 3d 1353, 1372-73 [1989], *cert. denied,* 493 U.S. 1056 [1990]). In *Florida Rock,* the Supreme Court denied the company's petition to review the Federal Circuit's decision that overturned a trial level finding of a taking (*Florida Rock Indus. v. United States,* 18 F.3d 1560, 1566 [Fed. Cir. 1994], cert. denied, 115 S. Ct. 898 [1995]).

39. *Lucas v. South Carolina Coastal Council,* 112 S. Ct. 2886, 2900-01 (1992). See 33 U.S.C. § 1344 (1988).

40. *United States v. Riverside Bayside Homes, Inc.,* 474 U.S. 121, 126-27 (1985) (emphasis added).

6

Protecting Community Stability and Local Economies: Opportunities for Local Government Influence in Federal Decision- and Policy-Making Processes

Karen Budd-Falen

It seems to this author that one of the biggest problems facing local governments in rural America is the loss of the local tax base. The loss of this tax base means that less money is available for locally funded projects such as schools, needy families, health care, police and fire protection, roads, and other basic services. Although there can be numerous causes for this economic hardship, certainly in the West two common reasons are (1) the transfer of private property owner-ship from tax-paying citizens to tax-exempt organizations and (2) the loss of jobs dependent on the use of private and federal lands. With-out payment of taxes from local businesses, wage earners, and prop-erty owners, local governments and their rural constituents will continue to suffer. The purpose of this chapter is to advocate a method that can be used by local governments to advance the protection of local tax bases and private property rights through involvement in federal land-management decisions.

Community Stability Defined

Congress has a long history of concern for the protection of the eco-nomic stability (i.e., the local tax base) of those communities and counties containing and surrounding federal lands. Congress, the courts, and federal agency regulation all require that federal land-management agencies, specifically the U.S. Bureau of Land Management (BLM) and the U.S. Forest Service, protect the economic or community stability of those communities and localities surrounding the national forest and BLM-managed lands.

However, although community stability is an important consideration in the management of federal lands, neither the Congress, the courts, nor the federal agencies have defined economic or community stability. These national agencies and institutions cannot define economic or community stability because there can be no national definition of community stability. Rather, community stability must be defined on a local level. As described by the Forest Service in its detailed history of federal land law:

> Forest reserves are for the purpose of preserving a perpetual supply of timber for home industries, preventing destruction of the forest cover which regulates the flow of streams, and protecting local residents from unfair competition in the use of forest and range. . . . We know that the welfare of every community is dependent upon a cheap and plentiful supply of timber; that a forest cover is the most effective means of maintaining a regular stream flow for irrigation and other useful purposes, and that the permanence of the livestock industry depends upon the conservative use of the range.[1]

The first congressional mandate that the Forest Service should manage its lands with a concern for the stability of local economies arose during the debates regarding the Organic Administration Act of 1897.[2] Specifically, these debates illustrated the concern for protecting the forests from fire and insect damage, therefore ensuring that they would be managed for economic purposes.[3] For example, after describing the conditions of the forests, one Senate document concluded:

> A study of the forest reserves in relation to the general development and welfare of the country, shows that the segregations of these great bodies of reserved lands can not be withdrawn from all occupation and use; that they must be made to perform their part in the economy of the nation. According to a strict interpretation of the rulings of the Department of the Interior [the federal agency managing the national forests at that time], no one has a right to enter a forest reserve, to cut a single tree from its forests, or to examine its rocks in search of valuable minerals. Forty million acres of land are thus theoretically shut out from all human occupation or enjoyment. Such a condition of things should not

continue. For unless the reserved lands of the public domain are made to contribute to the welfare and prosperity of the country, they should be thrown open to settlement and the whole system of reserved forests abandoned.[4]

Congressman Shafroth echoed this concern:

The forestry question is not a matter of great concern from a national standpoint, because the purposes for which these reservations are set aside are merely local. It is a matter of interest to people in the West only as to whether these reservations are properly established. It is on account of the waters which are to irrigate our agricultural lands that we are interested in forest reservations. The timber question can never be a matter of national concern in connection with these reservations. . . . The timber reserves of that [Rocky Mountain] region can never be a subject of National concern, although it may be of great interest to the people of that particular locality—the people of Colorado, Utah and other Western communities.[5]

Congress has never changed its concern for local communities. Eleven years following the passage of the Organic Administration Act, Congress passed the Twenty-Five Percent Fund Act, under which 5 percent of the revenues generated from the commodity use of the national forests are to be returned to state and county governments for schools and roads.[6] In 1913, Congress directed that an additional 10 percent of the revenues generated from timber, mining, and live-stock use on the national forests be returned to local counties as funding for road construction and maintenance.[7] In 1976, Congress amended the Twenty-Five Percent Fund Act, thus increasing payments to state and local governments by adding certain timber sale receipts and timber purchaser credits to the revenue fund.[8]

The Forest Service's admission of its obligation to provide for the economic stability of communities adjacent to forest lands is also well settled. The first chief of the Forest Service wrote: "In the management of each reserve, local questions will be decided upon local grounds. . . . Sudden changes in industrial condition will be avoided by gradual adjustment after due notice."[9]

Current Forest Service regulations also recognize the obligation of the agency to provide for community stability.[10] For example, agency regulations state that Forest Service land and resource-management plans must "be designed to aid in providing a continuous supply of national forest timber for the use and necessities of the citizens of the United States."[11]

Congress and the courts have also considered the importance of livestock grazing on BLM lands to the economic stability of surrounding communities. For example, the courts in interpreting the Taylor Grazing Act have recognized, "the purpose of 43 U.S.C. §§ 315 *et. seq.* [the Taylor Grazing Act] is to stabilize the livestock industry and to permit the use of public range according to needs and qualifications of the livestock operators with base holdings."[12] In other cases, the courts also have stated: "[The purpose of the Taylor Grazing Act] is at least twofold. First, it is designed to provide the most beneficial use possible of public range. . . . The livestock industry of the West is an important source of food supply for the people of the nation. . . . Second, the Act is intended, in the interest of the stock growers themselves, to define their grazing rights and to protect those rights by regulation against interference."[13]

Once it is recognized that the federal agencies have the duty to consider community stability in making land-management decisions, the question becomes how to enforce this mandate. The answer is through local government participation in federal land-management decisions.

Opportunities for Local Governments to Protect Community Stability

Once "community stability" has been defined, there are numerous opportunities available to local governments to assert and protect local tax bases and economies dependent upon the use of natural resources on the federal lands. One of these ways is through involvement in federal land-use planning.

Forest Service Land-Use Planning Processes

Forest Service regulations specifically invite local governments to participate in and to influence regional and forestwide land-use plans. For example, agency regulations stipulate that prior to the development of any agency land-use plan, the Forest Service must meet with local governments to establish a "coordination process" to be used during the development of the federal land-use plan. At a minimum, this coordination process shall include participation by the local government prior to the agency's selection of a preferred alternative.[14]

Forest Service regulations state:

(d) In developing land and resource management plans, responsible land officers shall meet with a designated state official and other representatives of federal agencies, local governments, and Indian tribes at the beginning of the planning process to develop procedures for coordination. At a minimum, such conferences shall also be held after public issues and management concerns have been identified and prior to recommending the preferred alternative. Such conferences may be held in conjunction with other public participation activities, if the opportunity for government officials to participate in a planning process is not thereby reduced.[15]

Note that these regulations apply specifically to local governments; the general public does not have these additional opportunities for participation and influence. Rather, these procedures suggest that local governments are to be held apart from the general public during the development and implementation of land-use plans.

In addition, the Forest Service is required to review and coordinate regional and local planning efforts with "the equivalent and related planning efforts of other federal agencies, state and local governments, and Indian tribes."[16] The results of this review shall be displayed in the environmental impact statement (EIS) for the land-use plan.

Again, Forest Service regulations state:

The review [of local land-use plans and policies by the Forest Service] shall include

(1) Consideration of the objectives of other federal, state and local governments and Indian tribes as expressed in their plans and policies;

(2) An assessment of the inter-related impacts of these plans and policies;

(3) A determination of how each Forest Service plan should deal with the impacts identified; and

(4) Where conflicts with the Forest Service planning are identified, consideration of alternatives for their resolution.[17]

Forest Service planning regulations also discuss methods to assist the agency in resolving management conflicts. Agency regulations require the federal government to seek input from other federal, state, and local governments to help resolve management concerns in the planning process and to identify areas where additional research is needed. "This input should be included in the discussion of research needs of the designated forest planning area."[18]

Finally, Forest Service regulations require that the agency implement monitoring programs to determine how its land-use plans are affecting the local economies and "communities adjacent to or near the national forest being planned."[19] The monitoring plan will determine if the agency is, in fact, protecting local economies or community stability. This monitoring plan should also evaluate effects of local land-use plans on national forest lands.[20]

Bureau of Land Management
Land-Use Planning Processes

Federal law also provides opportunities for local governments to participate in, and to influence BLM land-use policies, plans, and programs. BLM regulations state:

> (a) In addition to the public involvement . . . the following coordination is to be accomplished with other federal agencies, state and local governments, and Indian tribes. The objectives of coordination are for the state directors and district and area managers to keep apprised of non-Bureau of Land Management plans; assure that consideration is given to those plans that are germane in the development of resource management plans for public lands; assist in resolving, to the extent practicable, inconsistencies between federal and non-federal government plans; and provide for meaningful public involvement of other federal agencies, state and local government officials, both elected and appointed, and Indian tribes in the development of resource management plans, including early public notice of proposed decisions which may have significant impact on non-federal lands.
>
> (b) State directors and district and area managers shall provide other federal agencies, state and local governments, and Indian tribes opportunity for review, advice and suggestions on issues and topics which may affect or influence other agency or [local] government programs.[21]

The regulation, entitled "Coordination of Planning Efforts," gives local government the opportunity to influence BLM land-use planning to protect local economies. The regulation directs the BLM to give local governments early notification of proposed decisions "which may have a significant impact on non-federal lands" and requires that the federal agency take all practical measures to resolve conflicts between federal and local land-use plans.[22]

In order that local governments have advance notice of land planning, BLM's coordination regulations also require: "(d) A notice of intent to prepare, amend, or revise a resource management plan shall be submitted, consistent with State procedures for coordination of

Federal activities, for circulation among State agencies. This notice shall also be submitted to Federal agencies, the heads of county boards, (and) other local government units."[23]

In addition to BLM's coordination regulations, BLM regulations require consistency between federal land-use plans and local plans. BLM regulations mandate:

> (a) Guidance and resource management plans and amendments to management framework plans shall be consistent with officially approved or adopted resource related plans, and policies and programs contained therein, of other federal agencies, state and local governments and Indian tribes so long as the guidance and resource management plans are also consistent with the purposes, policies and programs of federal laws and regulations applicable to public lands, including federal and state pollution control laws implemented by applicable federal and state air, water, noise and other pollution standards or implementation plans.

> (c) State directors and district and area managers shall, to the extent practicable, keep appraised of state and local governmental and Indian tribal policies, plans and programs, but they shall not be accountable for ensuring consistency if they have not been notified, in writing, by state and local governments or Indian tribes of an apparent inconsistency.

> (e) Prior to the approval of a proposed resource management plan, or amendment to a management framework plan or resource management plan, the state director shall submit to the governor of the state(s) involved, the proposed plan or amendment and shall identify any known inconsistency with state or local plans, policies or programs.[24]

Again, BLM regulations require BLM plans to be consistent with local community stabilization plans. To ensure that such consistency reviews occur, the local government is responsible for notifying the BLM of conflicts between local and federal plans. Once the BLM is notified of the inconsistencies, the agency must consider alternatives to alleviate these problems. This consideration should appear as part of the environmental impact statement (EIS).

Local Government Participation under the Endangered Species Act

The 1988 amendments to the Endangered Species Act (ESA) require the U.S. Fish and Wildlife Service (FWS) to notify state and local governments regarding all proposed listings of threatened or endangered species, all proposed additions or changes in critical habitat designations, and all proposed protective regulations or recovery plans.[25] Once the local government is notified of the proposed species listing or delisting or the proposed critical habitat designation, the local government can offer comments to appraise the FWS of the effect of the proposed action or regulation on local economies.

Purpose and Listing Requirements under the Endangered Species Act

The purposes of the ESA are to (1) provide a means to conserve the ecosystems upon which endangered and threatened species depend, and (2) provide a program for the conservation of such threatened and endangered species.[26] A "threatened" species is a species likely to become endangered throughout all or a significant portion of its range within the foreseeable future.[27] An "endangered" species is a species that is endangered throughout all or a significant portion of its range.[28]

The ESA has certain strict procedural requirements for species listing and critical habitat designation. The listing of a threatened or endangered species is to be based on the best scientific and commercial data available, after taking into account a state's efforts to protect the species.[29] The listing determination is a numerical calculation *only*; there is no consideration of the economic impacts of the listing of that species.

Critical habitat is the specific area within the geographical area occupied by the species at the time it is listed, containing those physical or biological features essential to the conservation of the species, which may require special consideration or protection.[30] Critical habitat may also include areas outside the geographical area occupied by the species at the time it is listed, if the secretary determines that those areas are essential for the conservation of the species.[31]

Critical habitat designations are based on scientific data, *economic impacts,* and other relevant information. The secretary may exclude an area from critical habitat if he or she determines that the benefits of such exclusion outweigh the benefits of specifying the area as critical habitat. Areas may be excluded unless, based on the best scientific and commercial data available, the failure to designate such an area as critical habitat will result in the extinction of the species.[32]

The ESA also grants authority to the FWS to issue protective regulations and recovery plans that detail the steps that all state agencies and private individuals must follow in order to "conserve" the species.[33] Protective regulations and recovery plans are based on the best scientific and commercial data available.

Finally, federal agencies have been notified that they are to give "additional consideration" to those plant and animal species that the FWS may be considering, but does not have the adequate data to list, as threatened or endangered. Often this is called the "sensitive species" program.[34]

Local Government Participation
under the Endangered Species Act

The Endangered Species Act was amended in October 1988 to allow state and local governments the opportunity to participate in and to influence all proposed species listings as well as the proposed designations of critical habitat. Specifically, the 1988 amendments require that local governments are to be notified of the listing, delisting, or reclassification of a threatened or endangered species or its critical habitat. This notification must be "actual notice."[35] Actual notice means that the local government must receive a letter regarding any of the above endangered-species actions. General newspaper or *Federal Register* notice is not enough. Once notified, the local government has the opportunity to comment on the proposed species listing or critical habitat designation. If the local government disagrees with the FWS decision, the FWS must specifically respond to that local government's comments.[36] In addition, the ESA requires other land-management agencies also to consider local government and public comments regarding the listing of a species or its habitat.[37]

Local Government Protection of Community Stability
and Private Property Rights

Based on the above, this author asserts that local governments have the regulatory and legislative authority allowing them to influence federal agency decisions and protect the stability of local economies. The Bureau of Land Management and the U.S. Forest Service are directed to consider community stability and local land-use plans during their decision-making processes and to propose and consider alternatives if local and federal plans and policies conflict. The U.S. Fish and Wildlife Service must consider and respond to the comments of local governments. However, the ability of the local government to protect local economies is dependent upon (1) the willingness of the local government to initiate participation in land and resource planning processes and (2) the support the citizens give to their local governments in this effort. Both the citizens and their local governments must be committed to complete local land-use and economic planning, to notify the federal agencies of the county's interest in land-use planning, and to insist that the regulations outlined above are followed to their full extent.

Local Government Participation in Federal Decision-making Activities

To take advantage of the above authority, this author advocates that local governments (1) notify all federal agencies that they want to be informed of, and participate in, all federal decision-making activities occurring within the county, and (2) complete and adopt a local definition of community stability through a land-use plan.

Again, both BLM and Forest Service regulations charge local governments with the task of notifying the federal agencies of the county's desire to participate in land-use planning.[38] Without written notification from the local government regarding its desire to participate, the federal agency is under no obligation to consider the county's economic needs.

Once the federal agency has been notified, BLM and Forest Service regulations require that federal land-use planning efforts be both coordinated and consistent with local land-use plans and policies.[39] Thus based on these regulations, it logically follows that local governments must legally adopt local land-use plans and policies. The development of a local land-use plan is completely different than completion of a local zoning regulation. Zoning entails the description of a certain use that will be allowed on a specific parcel of land. On the other hand, land-use plans describe the general industrial, environmental, and social bases necessary for support of the county. Although zoning may be based upon land-use planning, zoning does not have to be completed, or even contemplated, for local elected officials to participate in federal planning processes through the completion of local land-use plans.

Citizens' Participation with the Local Government in Federal Decision-making Processes

Although the federal laws and regulations are written to give local governments authority to influence decisions made at the federal level, local governments also depend upon the support of the people. The U.S. Constitution gives to the citizens the power to support or influence their elected officials through a Petition for Redress of Grievances.[40] The First Amendment of the Constitution states, "The Congress shall make no law abridging the right of the people to petition the government for a redress of grievances."[41] This provision guarantees to citizens the right to petition the government without intervention or prohibition by the federal or state authorities.[42] Petitioning a local government through this process not only encourages those elected officials toward a certain viewpoint, but will protect the elected officials from harassment by state and federal officials as those officials protect the citizens. The Petition for Redress of Grievances should be used to encourage local elected officers to adopt county ordinances or resolutions protecting and defining property rights, to intervene on behalf of the citizens in federal land-use planning efforts, to enact local land-use planning, and to establish endangered or threatened species recovery plans that protect the species while protecting the economic base of the community.

Citizen Participation

It is this author's belief that citizens and their local governments have the authority to protect private property, local tax bases, and economic stability through local land-use planning and participation with federal agencies in their decision-making processes. It is simply a matter of whether the citizens and their governments are willing to expend the time and effort to participate in these decisions.

Notes

1. Forest Service, United States Department of Agriculture, *The Use Book*, 13 (1906 ed.).
2. The Organic Administration Act of 1897 (Organic Act) created the National Forest System. 30 Stat. 34 (1897) (16 U.S.C. §§ 473-75, 477-78, 479-82, 551). Specifically, the Organic Act gave the federal agencies the authority to fight fire on the forest lands. See 16 U.S.C. § 551 (1988). Additionally, the record indicates that the government was receiving criticism from what the National Academy of Sciences claimed to be a policy of allowing individuals to cut timber from the forest lands without regulation. However, note that more forests have been destroyed from fire than from illegal timber cutting.
3. See S. Doc. No. 105, 55th Cong., 1st Sess. 10, 21-23 (1898).

4. Id.

5. 30 Cong. Rec. 984 (1897).

6. 16 U.S.C. § 500 (1988) (as amended).

7. 16 U.S.C. § 501 (1988) (as amended).

8. Id. National Forest Management Act of 1976, Report of Senate Committee of Agriculture and Forestry, S. Rep. 94-893 (May 1976) 1, 22-23.

9. Forest Service, *The Use Book*, 17.

10. 36 C.F.R. § 221.3(a)(1)(1944).

11. See also C. Schallau, and R. Alston, "The Commitment to Community Stability: A Policy or Shibboleth?" *Environmental Law* 17(1987): 429.

12. The Taylor Grazing Act 43 U.S.C. § 315-315r (1988) recognized the practice, established by the livestock industry, of utilizing the public lands for livestock grazing. The act also established regulations governing such use of those lands and created the agency which was later known as the Bureau of Land Management (BLM). The regulations are found at 43 C.F.R. Part 4100. For interpretation of the grazing act see *Chournos v. United States*, 193 F.2d 321, 322 (10th Cir. 1951), denied 343 U.S. 977 (1952).

13. *Red Canyon Sheep Co. v. Ickes*, 98 F.2d 308, 314 (1938); *United States v. Fuller*, 442 F.2d 504, 507 (9th Cir. 1971), *rev'd on other grounds*, 409 U.S. 488 (1973). ("The purpose of the Taylor Grazing Act was to develop and stabilize the western cattle business.")

14. 36 C.F.R. § 219.7 (1994).

15. 36 C.F.R. § 219.7(d) (1994).

16. 36 C.F.R. § 219.7(a) (1994).

17. 36 C.F.R. § 219.7(c) (1994).

18. 36 C.F.R. § 219.7(e) (1994).

19. 36 C.F.R. § 219.7(f) (1994).

20. Id.

21. 43 C.F.R. § 1601.3-1 (1994).

22. Id.

23. 43 C.F.R. § 1610.3-(d) (1994).

24. 43 C.F.R. § 1610.3-2 (1994).

25. Pursuant to the Endangered Species Act, the U.S. Fish and Wildlife Service (FWS) is the agency responsible for species listing and for critical habitat, protective regulation and recovery plan determinations. Once a species is listed, state and private landowners must comply with the FWS determinations regarding that species' protection. Federal land-managing agencies, that is, the BLM and Forest Service, are required to consult with the FWS regarding species protection, but the FWS does not have a veto power over the actions of another federal agency, even in the name of the ESA (*National Wildlife Federation v. Coleman*, 529 F.2s 359 [1976], *cert. den.* 429 U.S. 979 [1977]); see also 16 U.S.C. § 1533(b)(5)(A).

26. For purpose and listing requirements under the Endangered Species Act see 16 U.S.C. §§ 1531 *et seq.* ESA purposes are at 16 U.S.C. § 1531(b).

27. 16 U.S.C. § 1532(20)

28. 16 U.S.C. § 1532(6).

29. 16 U.S.C. § 1531(b).
30. 16 U.S.C. § 1532(5)(A)(i).
31. 16 U.S.C. § 1532(5)(A)(ii).
32. 16 U.S.C. § 1533(b)(2).
33. 16 U.S.C. § 1533(d).
34. The sensitive species program requires federal agencies to give special protection to species that are not legally or formally listed as threatened or endangered pursuant to the Endangered Species Act. These species and their habitat may be "protected" even though (1) they may not meet the strict scientific review requirements under the ESA, and (2) the public has had no opportunity to review or comment on the special protection program as required by the ESA.
35. 16 U.S.C. § 1533(b)(5)(a)(ii).
36. 16 U.S.C. § 1533(i).
37. 16 U.S.C. § 1533(f)(5).
38. 36 C.F.R. § 219.7 (1994) and 43 C.F.R. § 1610.3-1 (1994).
39. Id.
40. U.S. Constitution Amendment 1.
41. This right is guaranteed to the individuals of the states through the Fourteenth Amendment to the U.S. Constitution.
42. W. C. Skousen, *The Making of America, The Substance and Meaning of the Constitution*, 2d ed. (Washington, D.C.: National Center for Constitutional Studies, 1986), 689.

7

The County Supremacy Movement: Mendacious Myth Marketing

Scott W. Reed

For the past century, major grievances of many people living in the western United States have swirled about public lands owned by the United States. The "county supremacy movement" promoting adoption of county ordinances asserting supremacy over public lands is the latest skirmish. Continuing controversy is inevitable and endemic when more than half of the land in the twelve western states is owned by the federal government as compared with only 4 percent in the other thirty-seven continental states.

With environmental interests regaining some influence in the Clinton administration, the private users of public lands through their Western senators are fulminating about a new "War on the West" as they did with the Carter administration. "War within the West" is more apt. The county supremacy movement is a new version of the Sagebrush Rebellion, which in turn was simply another spin on how to place the public lands under control of the private commercial users. The Sagebrush Rebellion called for transfer of public lands to private ownership by ranchers with grazing permits. Such transfers would have given the basis for enforceable local control. The county-supremacy movement originates in the same cattle country, but its remedy lacks any basis for legal enforceability. The county supremacy ordinances have the durability of cow chips. County supremacy is a gaseous myth. The methane falls mainly on the plain.

This chapter is an abridged version of an article previously published in *Idaho Law Review* 30, no. 3 (1993-94): 525-53 under the same title. Reprinted by permission of author and publisher.

However, it is folly to underestimate the political power of myths. A remarkable collection of powerful thinkers in what became the United States in the late eighteenth century shaped the myth that became the United States. "All men are created equal" begins the Declaration of Independence, a statement of principles that resonated around the world and still does. Two centuries later our government works best when its people and its elected officials are in agreement upon those high principles set forth by our deepest political thinkers, Thomas Jefferson, Abraham Lincoln, and Martin Luther King, Jr.

In a democracy and, perhaps to an even greater degree, in all other types of governments, the direction is shaped by myths. The ongoing constant battle for the minds, hearts, and guts of men and women is to form, initiate, and then implement the most popular and shared myths; but not all myths are benign, noble, productive, peaceful, cohesive, or sensible. Some are just plain bad. The county supremacy movement is the newest Western myth, very different in fact from its outside appearances. It has been hauled into a host of mostly rural county courthouses. In June of 1993, the National Federal Lands Conference claimed to have 175 to 200 counties enlisted in the county movement.[1]

From Co-opting to Confrontation in Cattle Country

The county supremacy movement originated in Catron County, 2,563 people in 6,897 square miles of high and dry cattle country in southwestern New Mexico. The cattlemen, angered by threatened reductions in grazing allotments on federal lands, saw their traditional control over the local U.S. Forest Service and the Bureau of Land Management slipping away.[2] From the time the West was won, the ranchers had run the range, both on their own land and on the land ostensibly in public ownership, by a combination of friendship and good-old-boy relationships with the forest ranger or BLM supervisor combined with intimidation of the occasional independent public employee who showed some concern over the condition of the land and the water instead of the cow.

The environmental tide that created a flood of new legislation at the national level in the 1970s has been battering Western land management for two decades and finally is beginning to seep through. There are new directions to reduce animal unit months (AUMs) and to recognize that "multiple use of public lands" could include recreation and wildlife.[3] The cattlemen were losing control of the federal bureaucracy, but they still controlled and were part of the county government. So surfaced the disingenuous scheme to give the county government control of the federal lands and take back what was slipping away—hence the Catron County Interim Land Use Policy Plan.[4] The plan was a land grab by which the county asserted jurisdiction (i.e., control) over all federal and state land, waters, and wildlife within the county. The Catron County plan directs that no federal agency may undertake a change in management or operation without approval by the county commissioners. No acquisition of land or disposal can be made without county commissioner approval. A stated objective is to promote an actual reduction in federal and state ownership by disposal of "isolated tracts," compelling sale to private interests. No wilderness is allowed and no wild and scenic rivers may be created without county concurrence. The county is the designated planning agency for all future actions on state and federal lands.

The Continuing American Revolution

As with state rights, county rights has a simplistic appeal. Rebelling against government has been in the hearts of the ordinary American citizens ever since colonial days. To a considerable degree, the American Revolution never came to an end. No sooner had the British left than we began bashing the Continental Congress. Shay's Rebellion led to the Philadelphia Convention and the creation of the Constitution for the United States.[5] The creation of the Constitution was a rebellion against the Continental Congress and the existing government.

Even in times of popular presidents—George Washington, James Monroe, Teddy Roosevelt, Franklin Roosevelt—there have always been strident dissenters complaining about the federal government. There is a stream that sometimes widens into a river flowing through our history from the Whiskey Rebellion through the Know-Nothing movement to the Populists to Ross Perot. The best government is the least government. The next best government is local government. Those people back there don't understand our territory or our ways.

The authors of the Catron County plan came up with the mantra of "custom and culture," words of indefinite and uncertain meaning.[6] To an anthropologist whose profession is a study of customs and of culture, the combination of the terms in the Catron County plan is meaningless.[7] In the nine thousand years of prehistory in which traces of Native Americans can be identified in the Southwest, there was no single culture or custom but rather an ever-changing and shifting of ways in which people lived.[8] White men, who conquered the American West and sought to eradicate the natives and their ways of life, had an ephemeral culture: light, multiply, and move on.[9]

It is entirely appropriate that the major commercial, mythic figure for the Southwest is Billy the Kid, a reckless, marauding, gun-slinging juvenile delinquent who died early without any significant accomplishments to his name other than a number of unmotivated murders. This reckless punk lacked even the social affability to lead or participate in a gang yet he idealized rebellion, albeit, without a cause.[10] The promoters of the county supremacy movement sought, as all myth-makers must, to find and claim deep historical roots. It is easier to believe in an idea given rebirth, to believe in the good old days that never were.

States Supreme under Articles of Confederation

The National Federal Lands Conference claims the origin of its effort to protect the private, commercial utilization of public property in the U.S. Constitution.[11] The historical roots exist for the county supremacy movement, but they are in the Articles of Confederation, not the Constitution. The Articles of Confederation were agreed upon in the Continental Congress by the thirteen colonies, which became states on 15 November 1777 after commencement of the American Revolution. The combative purpose was stated in Article III: "The said states hereby severally enter into a firm league of friendship with each other, for their common defence, the security of their Liberties, and their mutual and general welfare, binding themselves to assist each other, against all force offered to, or attacks made upon them, or any of them, on account of religion, sovereignty, trade, or any other pretense whatever."[12]

This system of government did not work well in wartime. The inability of the Continental Congress to provide leadership and, more important, adequate funding to support the army made the achievements of George Washington and the ultimate victory all the more remarkable. When peace came, the national government fell apart, or more accurately, never came together. In his speeches to the New York Ratifying Convention in June of 1788, Alexander Hamilton said he found in the existing government "weaknesses to be real, and pregnant with destruction."[13]

The foremost weakness was the total independence of each state. The financing arrangement of the national government was similar to what exists in the United Nations today and was subject to the same erratic compliance. Congress would make requisitions for funds prorated among the several states. It was up to the states to comply or not according to their desires and financial abilities. When Hamilton was speaking, New York and Pennsylvania were the only states that had fully complied with the requisitions issued by the Continental Congress. All the other states were delinquent and New Hampshire and North Carolina had paid nothing at all.

The problems with the Articles of Confederation went far beyond the ability to raise sufficient money to accomplish national purposes. These states were acting as independent sovereign nations:

> The New Jersey merchant shipping his products across his own borders paid a tariff duty either at New York or at Philadelphia, a situation which James Madison compared to a cask tapped at both ends. The Connecticut farmer similarly found himself charged excises either at New York or Boston; while on the Chesapeake, fishermen discovered that they were caught in a net of taxes and others in retaliation from both Maryland and Virginia, since both states claimed jurisdiction over the main waters of the bay.[14]

Foreign countries refused to bargain with Congress, which had little authority to enforce a new treaty that it might sign. The certificates issued by the Continental Congress were not redeemed; states were manufacturing their own money, which was not accepted across the border.

In an exchange of correspondence with John Jay in 1786, George Washington described the Confederation as "error to correct" and was pessimistic as to the likelihood of changes occurring:

> I do not conceive we can exist long as a Nation, without having lodged somewhere a power which will pervade the whole Union in as energetic a Manner, as the authority of the different State governments extends over the several States. To be fearful of vesting Congress, constituted as that body is, with ample authorities for national purposes, appears to me the very climax of popular absurdity and madness. Could Congress exert them for the detriment of the public without injuring themselves in an equal or greater proportion? Are not their interests inseparably connected with those of their constituents?[15]

Constitutional Convention Creates a Nation

Madison, Hamilton, and the majority of the delegates in Philadelphia sought to forge the authority that would create a nation. Hamilton told the delegates that the Constitution was intended to remedy the existing situation where either a federal standing army could be called upon to enforce the requisitions or the federal treasury would be bereft: "What, Sir, is the cure for this great evil? Nothing, but to enable the national laws to operate on individuals, in the same manner as those of the states do."[16]

Especially for a lawyer who drinks in the Constitution as his mother's milk, it is difficult to believe that there could ever have been opposition to its adoption. With Founding Fathers of the stature of Madison, Hamilton, Jefferson, Adams, John Jay, James Wilson, and John Marshall, supported by respected and popular leaders such as Benjamin Franklin, George Washington, and Edmund Randolph, who would dare oppose? In fact, the opposition was formidable.

By most any measure, the Articles of Confederation were an abysmal failure, but many believed that the Constitutional Convention far exceeded the intent expressed by the Continental Congress in creating it. That intent was understood to be only to find the necessary changes to make the existing system work better.

The New York delegates, New York supreme court justice Robert Yates, and speaker of the New York Assembly John Lansing, wrote to New York governor George Clinton explaining that they had left before the conclusion of the Constitutional Convention because they felt their charge had been limited to revising the Articles of Confederation: [17]

> From these expressions we were led to believe, that a system of consolidated government could not, in the remotest degree, have been in the contemplation of the legislature of this state; for that so important a trust as the adopting measures which tended to deprive the state government of its most essential rights of sovereignty, and to place it in a dependent situation, could not have been confided by implication; and the circumstance, that the acts of the convention were to receive a state approbation in the last resort, forcibly corroborated the opinion, that our powers could not involve the subversion of a constitution, which being immediately derived from the people, could only be abolished by their express consent, and not by a legislature, possessing authority vested in them for its preservation.[18]

The arguments of the anti-Federalists are the same heard today in

Catron County and now in Boundary County and wherever the county government folk gather. The national government will subvert "the legislative, executive and judicial powers of the individual states."[19] The new federal government will be "destitute of accountability to its constituents."[20]

Anti-Federalists: Preserve States' Rights

Luther Martin, attorney general of Maryland, who had been a delegate to the Constitutional Convention, was a major player and speaker in those deliberations. In the debate that followed, Martin carried forth all of the doubt and criticisms he had voiced loudly during the Constitutional Convention to become the most outspoken opponent of the delegates who had been in Philadelphia. Martin's anti-Federalist writings are redundant with italics. In reading them, you can almost hear his voice rising in excitement as he railed against the Constitution: "It was urged, that the government we were forming was not in reality a *federal* but a *national* government, not founded on the principles of the *preservation*, but the *abolition* or consolidation of all State governments."[21] Martin voiced the view that was reiterated by the anti-Federalists that a central government would be too far distant from the people being governed:

> If the inhabitants of the different States consider it as a grievance to attend a *county court* or the *seat* of their *own government*, when a little inconvenient, can it be supposed that they would ever *submit* to have a *national government* established, the *seat* of which would be *more than a thousand miles removed from some of them?* It was insisted that the governments of a *republican nature*, are those *best* calculated to *preserve* the *freedom* and *happiness* of the citizen—That governments of *this kind*, are *only calculated* for a territory but *small* in its extent; that the *only* method by which an extensive continent like America could be *connected* and *united* together consistent with the principles of freedom, must be by having a *number* of *strong* and *energetic State governments* for securing and protecting the rights of *individuals* forming those governments, and for regulating all their concerns.[22]

The fundamental change made at the Constitutional Convention was the abolition of the wording and the intent expressed in Article II of the Articles of Confederation: "Each state retains its sovereignty, freedom, and independence, and every Power, Jurisdiction and right, which is not by this confederation expressly delegated to the United States, in Congress assembled."[23] Martin saw in the change the creation of "not in reality a *federal* but a *national* government, not founded on the principles of the *preservation*, but the *abolition* or *consolidation* of all *State governments*."[24]

Melancton Smith, a prominent New York and Poughkeepsie businessman who had served in the first Provincial Congress in New York, in the Continental Congress, and as sheriff of Duchess County, was the principal anti-Federalist spokesman opposing Alexander Hamilton in the debate at the New York Ratifying Convention.[25] Smith saw the adoption of the Constitution as being nothing less than the abolition of state constitutions, which would be an event fatal to the liberties of Americans: "These liberties will not be violently wrested from the people; they will be undermined and gradually consumed."[26]

The preamble to the Catron County Interim Land Use Policy Plan states a demand to reclaim those liberties phrased in terms Smith could have used in 1788:

> Further, we reaffirm the fundamental rights of mankind as enumerated in the Declaration of Independence and acknowledged the limited nature of government as intended by the nation's Founding Fathers. Based on these cherished traditions, We declare that all natural resource decisions affecting Catron County shall be guided by the principles of protecting private property rights, protecting local custom and culture, maintaining traditional economic structures through self-determination, and opening new economic opportunities through reliance on free markets.[27]

Melancton Smith reiterated the point that the country was too big for adequate representation from such a distance: "It is not possible," he said, "to collect a set of representatives, who are acquainted with all parts of the continent."[28]

With the approval of the Constitution, it became clear that there would indeed be a United States rather than a confederation of independent states. The anti-Federalists were soon enough dead and buried, but their ideas have continued to resurface even though constitutionally unsustainable. The Civil War, for example, was a dramatic manifestation of the power of the federal government over the states. The states' rights movement in the South in the Truman and Eisenhower years with all its racist overtures was an effort to refight the Civil War politically. The Southern descendants of the slave owners lost again both constitutionally and at the ballot boxes. But the maverick myth retains its appeal. Return the power to the people, more accurately to "our kind" of people. Never mind the Constitution. Never mind the Civil War. Forget about the crushing of Calhoun, the defeat of George Wallace. Let the county claim control.

Catron Plan to Nullify Federal Control

The Catron County Interim Land Use Ordinance seeks county supremacy over the federal government in many areas, eliminating wilderness, requiring county approval of land, wildlife, and timber management plans, and directing the sale of isolated federal tracts. In other areas the ordinance stresses coordination. However worded, it is difficult to distinguish the objective sought in Catron County from the nullification, not of all federal laws, but of those federal policies, plans, and practices related to land, water, and wildlife that were not to the liking of the county government.

The Catron County "Interim Land Use Policy Plan Concerning the Use of Public Lands and Public Resources and Protection of the Rights of Private Property" is all encompassing.[29] It purports to assert county control over all public lands, waters, and wildlife in the county owned by the State of New Mexico and the United States. The intent to subordinate state and federal management to county control is explicit: "all federal and state agencies shall comply with the Catron County Land Use Policy Plan and coordinate with the County Commission for the purpose of planning and managing federal and state lands within the geographic boundaries of Catron County, New Mexico."

State and federal agencies must submit written reports on all proposed actions to the county before the state and federal agency may undertake any action. Neither the state nor the federal government may add additional land to its public holdings without offsetting an equivalent acreage by transfer to private ownership from existing public land ownership. Prior county approval is required before a state or federal agency can make any changes in wildlife habitat, wildlife recovery plans, timber sales, volume projections, restricted access, road closures, and primitive or wilderness state designation. The preparation of economic impact statements must be made before any federal or state agency can change any land uses. Catron County is the designated lead planning agency for all federal and state lands, waters, and natural resources. Any federal proposal for wild and scenic river designation in Catron County must comply with the county water-use plan. The ordinance prohibits the designation of any wilderness area within the county. "Isolated" federal tracts of land are to be disposed of.

The rebirth of the Sagebrush Rebellion, intent to have virtually all federal lands transferred to private ownership, is set forth in the introduction with a "demand" that all lands not designated as "specific lands" be "relinquished to the citizens." There are twenty-seven "shall" and "shall nots" directed to the federal agencies, occasionally including the state agencies.

Supreme Court: Congress Is Supreme

Article IV of the U.S. Constitution, known as the Property Clause, provides: "Congress shall have power to dispose of and make all needful rules and regulations respecting the territory or other property belonging to the United States; and nothing in the constitution shall be so construed as to prejudice any claims of the United States, or of any particular state." The power of Congress over federal lands under the Property Clause is virtually without limitation. The clearest statement came in *Kleppe v. New Mexico.*[30] New Mexico had enacted a law giving the state power to control wild horses on federal lands. Congress had enacted the Wild Free-Roaming Horses and Burros Act to prohibit the taking of wild horses.[31] New Mexico argued that under the Property Clause the powers granted to Congress were narrowly limited and did not include protection of wild animals living on federal property but not belonging to the United States. Justice Marshall for a unanimous court gave the Property Clause an expansive reading granting Congress complete power over public lands: "And while the furthest reaches of the power granted by the Property Clause have not yet been definitively resolved, we have repeatedly observed that '[t]he power over the public lands thus entrusted to Congress is without limitations.'"[32]

While states did have jurisdiction over federal lands within their boundaries, Congress retained the power under the property clause to enact laws respecting those lands and when it did, such laws overrode state laws under the Supremacy Clause. When the state law conflicted with federal law, federal law must prevail: "A different rule would place the public domain of the United States completely at the mercy of state legislation."[33]

Ten days earlier the Supreme Court held that the State of Kentucky could not require federal installations to obtain state air contaminant permits even though the Clean Air Act arguably directed coordination between the states and the Environmental Protection Agency.[34] Congress had exclusive legislative authority over federal property through the Supremacy Clause as carried out in the plenary powers clause so that the "activities of the Federal Government are free from regulation by any state."[35]

The Catron Plan attempts to tell the federal and state agencies how they must run their shop and what they can and cannot do on state and federal public lands. These county provisions deliberately attempt to interfere with federal management as directed by a number of federal statutes including the Endangered Species Act: "Congressional enactments that do not exclude all state legislation in the same field nevertheless override state laws with which they conflict. U.S. Constitution, Article VI."[36] When Congress acts, the effect of the Supremacy Clause may be to preempt state law:

> State law can be pre-empted in either of two ways. If Congress evidences an intent to occupy a given field, any state law falling within that field is pre-empted. If Congress has not entirely displaced state regulation over the matter in question, state law is still pre-empted to the extent it actually conflicts with federal law, that is, when it is impossible to comply with both state and federal law, or where the state law stands as an obstacle to the accomplishment of the full purposes and objectives of Congress.[37]

Any attempt under the Catron County-type ordinance to interfere with the management of public lands by the Forest Service or the Bureau of Land Management would be an unconstitutional "obstacle to the accomplishment and execution of the full purposes and objectives of Congress."[38]

Just how narrow is the area in which states are allowed to impose some control in federal lands matters was illustrated in *California Coastal Commission v. Granite Rock Co.*[39] In a very sharply controverted five-to-four decision, the U.S. Supreme Court reversed the Ninth Circuit decision that held that the effect of the federal public lands statutes upon the Coastal Zone Management Act was to preempt the California Coastal Commission's requirement that a mining company obtain a state permit to work its unpatented mining claims located in a national forest.[40] Justice O'Connor, writing for the majority, drew a distinction between the land-use planning and the state environmental regulation:

> Land use planning in essence chooses particular uses for the land; environmental regulation, at its core, does not mandate particular uses of the land but requires only that, however the land is used, damage to the environment is kept within prescribed limits. Congress has indicated its understanding of land use planning and environmental regulation as distinct activities. As noted above, 43 U.S. §1712(c)(9) requires that the Secretary of Interior's land use plans be consistent with state plans only "to the extent he finds practical." The immediately preceding subsection, however, requires that the Secretary's land use plans "provide for compliance with applicable pollution control laws, including State and Federal air, water, noise or other pollution standards or implementation plans." § 1712(c)(8)[41]

Justice O'Connor found similar distinctions in the National Forest Service regulations. The permit requirement sought by the California Coastal Commission was an environmental regulation; otherwise it would have been invalid: "Federal land use statutes and regulations, while arguably expressing an intent to pre-empt state land use planning, distinguish environmental regulation from land use planning."[42]

The dissenting justices, Justices Powell and Scalia, joined with Justices Stevens and White, argued strongly that permit requirement from the coastal commission was a land use regulation and therefore most certainly preempted.[43]

The Catron Plan concerning the use of public lands and public resources and protection of the rights of private property would under any interpretation be "state land use planning," which all nine justices in *California Coastal Commission v. Granite Rock Co.* would agree was preempted by federal law.

In response to requests by two county attorneys facing commissioners wanting to adopt local supremacy ordinances, Montana attorney general Joseph P. Mazurek issued an informal opinion concluding that "any proposed county ordinance that prohibits or limits such action by the federal government is in direct conflict with the United States Constitution and federal legislation."[44]

Attorney General Mazurek reviewed in historical detail the comprehensive federal-land legislation and regulations, which literally covered the earth. The constitutional inhibitions against state control specifically extended to denial of any authority by the county to prevent the federal government from acquiring lands within the county.

Custom and Culture Claptrap

The Catron County Interim Land Use Policy Plan is founded upon the premise articulated by Karen Budd-Falen that federal laws allow special deference to local "custom and culture," defined almost entirely by the local extractive or resource-dependent industries such as logging, mining, ranching, and farming.[45] The Budd-Falen theory is that once these customs and cultures are identified, the federal agencies must by law and federal regulation defer to them to allow counties to determine policy. Neither the Supremacy Clause nor the Property Clause then become involved because Congress has allowed for state and local control. It is a plausible theory. Congress can certainly yield federal power to allow state and local control. The prime example on federal lands is game management where states are explicitly given authority to set seasons and limits and to enforce those regulations on all federal lands.[46]

The Clean Water Act and the Clean Air Act each provide detailed and specific arrangements for the states to assume the federal programs. However, "custom and culture" is no "Open Sesame" to local control. National Federal Lands Conference spokesmen are similar to the seventeenth-century European geographers proclaiming the certainty of the Northwest Passage. Laws recognizing deference to custom and culture do not exist. The custom and culture theory teeters upon the slenderest of reeds. The National Environmental Policy Act, relied upon by Budd-Falen as authority, contains in some 350 words of the introductory declaration of policy, the following as one of six broad general policy directions: "(4) preserve important historic, cultural, and natural aspects of our national heritage, and maintain, wherever possible, an environment which supports diversity and variety of individual choice."[47]

From this paragraph Budd-Falen has first condensed to "historic, cultural, and natural aspects," then gone to Webster's dictionary to find that "culture" is defined as including "customary beliefs" and then gone to Bouvier's law dictionary (1867 edition!) to find a definition of "custom."[48] The Budd-Falen syllogism is to take "cultural" out of context, alter the word to "culture," find an outdated dictionary that includes "customary" within a definition of "culture" and then transmute "customary" to "custom." Voila! "Custom and Culture." The result is not statutory construction but creative distortion.

Nowhere in the statutes or regulations related to the U.S. Forest Service, the Bureau of Land Management, the Fish and Wildlife Service, the Endangered Species Act, the Wild and Scenic Rivers Act, or the National Environmental Policy Act are the words "custom and culture" to be found. Although the word "custom" may appear by itself in other federal statutes not identified in or related to the Catron County Plan, it does not appear alone in any of the above contexts. Neither does the word "culture" appear alone.

> The First Amendment allows anyone to hawk any political nostrum without regard to truth or accuracy. It is the politician, not the Supreme Court justice, who can make the laws mean what he or she wants them to. The National Federal Lands Conference is avidly peddling falsehoods to promote its political agenda: "Did you know that the National Environmental Protection Act (NEPA) *requires that the federal agencies protect your custom, culture and community stability . . .* ? Catron County, New Mexico's Model Interim Land Use Plan . . . will help you protect your civil rights and property rights while you define your custom, culture and community stability."[49]

Unlike political rhetoric or commercial advertising, statutory construction is a very precise and rigid discipline commencing always with the written word. But if in the beginning there is no word, there can be no tenable interpretation. Words are literally the building blocks for statutory construction. "Custom and culture" do not exist. There is nothing there.

Continuing Problems

In the two hundred years since the formal creation of these United States of America by the adoption of the Constitution, enormous changes have occurred at a rate and scale without precedent. Thirteen states have become fifty. The population has exploded with an incredible diversity of race, creed, and color. Yet despite marvels of modern communication and transportation, the problems perceived by the opponents of the Constitution continue. It took George Washington and Thomas Jefferson many days to travel from home in Virginia to Philadelphia and then to Washington, D.C., a task that can be accomplished in person in hours and by voice and fax in seconds. Yet the nation's capital is perceived by many, perhaps by most, Americans as being as far removed from local citizens as predicted in Luther Martin's polemics.

Although the federal public lands are managed on a day-to-day basis by men and women who live here rather than there, those who would derive a living or a profit from the use of those public lands decry distant domination particularly when past practices are curtailed or eliminated by national directive. The county supremacy ordinances are a reaction to assert local control. The motives of those behind the adoption of those local ordinances can be questioned, but their popularity is undeniable.

The validity of the county supremacy ordinances is not questionable. The Property Clause and the Supremacy Clause of the U.S. Constitution totally and completely eliminate any possibility of local control of any nature. Until and unless Congress explicitly grants to the states authority over federal public lands, and the state legislatures in turn grant that authority to the counties, there will be no local control.

Notes

1. *National Federal Lands Conference Update* (June 1993).

2. The cowboy myth is powerful politics. In October of 1993 a filibuster by Western Senators to stop a rise in federal grazing fees held up the $12 billion Interior budget. Grazing permit holders numbered only 28,000 in twenty-two western states with a population of fifty million, but Senator Alan K. Simpson (R-WY) characterized the filibuster as "defending a Western life style" (Timothy Egan, "Wing Tip 'Cowboys' in the Last Stand to Hold on to Low Grazing Fees," *New York Times*, 29 October 1993, A1, A8).

3. Randal O'Toole, *Reforming the Forest Service* (Washington, D.C.: Island Press, 1988), 166–69; Denzel Ferguson and Nancy Ferguson, *Sacred Cows at the Public Trough* (Bend, Ore.: Maverick Publications, 1983), 228–31.

4. *Catron County Interim Land Use Policy Plan* adopted by Catron County, May 21, 1991, reprinted in *National Federal Lands Conference Update* (August 1992).

5. Gordon S. Wood, *The Creation of the American Republic 1776–1787* (New York: Norton, 1969).

6. The words "custom and culture" appear in the introduction, the preamble and under "Land Disposition," "Agriculture," "Timber and Wood Products" (twice), and "Cultural Resources, Recreation, Wildlife and Wilderness" (*Catron Plan*, 1–3).

7. In *Boundary Backpackers v. Boundary County*, District Court, Boundary County, Idaho (No. 93-9955), one of the plaintiffs is Lew Langness, Ph.D., a retired U.C.L.A. anthropology professor. In an affidavit dated 4 October 1993, Professor Langness described any attempt to define "custom and culture" in the county or to direct planning in accordance with custom and culture as completely lacking scientific, political, or legal validity.

8. In his chapter on the Indians of the Southwest, Alvin M. Josephy identifies seven cultures. The identifiable prehistory of each evolved from a previous cul-

ture and then in turn evolved into another up to the first exposure to the Spaniards: Desert Culture, Mogollon Culture, Anasazi Culture, Hobokan Culture, Hakataya Culture, Pueblo Culture, and Cochise Culture. These cultures were adapted and modified by the different tribes and subtribes (Alvin Josephy, *The Indian Heritage of America* [Boston: Houghton Mifflin, 1991], 146).

9. "Rather than 'settling' the region, mining rushes picked up the American West and gave it a good shaking" (Patricia Nelson Limerick, *The Legacy of Conquest* [New York: Norton, 1987], 100.

10. In an article entitled "Billy the Kid Country," biographer Robert M. Utley observed that "respectable New Mexico historians lament the public's obsession with Billy the Kid" (Robert M. Utley, "Billy the Kid Country," *American Heritage* 42 [April 1991], 65).

11. Madison provided in Federal Papers No. 45 a lengthy discussion about the sovereignty of the state versus the federal. He stated that, in conflict, the state must be superior as it is the entity that creates the federal government, and the people must be superior to the state, as it is the people who created the states. Thus, in the design of the Founding Fathers, "it was the people who were the sovereigns of our nation" (Wray Schildkrecht, "Hope for the Future—Why the County Government Movement was Born," *National Federal Lands Conference Update* [June 1993]).

12. "The Articles of Confederation," in *The Complete Anti-Federalist*, Vol. 1, edited by Herbert J. Storing (Chicago: University of Chicago Press, 1981), 101.

13. "Alexander Hamilton, Remarks in the New York Ratifying Convention," (20 June 1788), in *Selected Writings and Speeches of Alexander Hamilton*, edited by Morton J. Frisch (Washington, D.C.: American Enterprise Institute, 1985), 196.

14. William F. Swindler, "The Letters of Publius," *American Heritage* 12 (June 1961): 4, 6.

15. Richard B. Morris, "The Jay Papers II: The Forging of the Nation," *American Heritage* 20 (December 1968): 4, 24, 96–97.

16. Frisch, *Selected Writings and Speeches of Alexander Hamilton*, 199.

17. The departure of Yates and Lansing left Hamilton as the only New York delegate. The Constitution was not all that he wanted, but it was sufficiently superior to the Articles that he willingly signed for New York and then carried a laboring oar in the Federalist papers and at the New York convention to win ratification (Catherine Drinker Bowen, *John Adams and the American Revolution* [Boston: Little, Brown, 1950], 290-91).

18. "Letter from Robert Yates and John Lansing to George Clinton (21 December 1787), in *The Complete Anti-Federalist*, Vol. 2, 16–17.

19. "Essays of Brutus (October 1787–April 1788)," in *The Complete Anti-Federalist*, Vol. 2, 420.

20. "Letters of Centinel (October 1787–April 1788)," in *The Complete Anti-Federalist*, Vol. 2, 157.

21. "Luther Martin, Esq., The Genuine Information Delivered to the Legislature of the State of Maryland Relative to the Proceedings of the General Convention Lately Held at Philadelphia (1788)," in *The Complete Anti-Federalist*, Vol. 2, 45 (emphasis in original).

22. "Luther Martin, Esq., The Genuine Information Delivered to the Legislature of the State of Maryland Relative to the Proceedings of the General Convention Lately Held at Philadelphia (1788)," in *The Complete Anti-Federalist*, Vol. 2, 48. In addition to the basic emphasis, Martin used dashes, commas, and semicolons but never periods so that he wrote not in sentences, but in paragraphs or pages.

23. "The Articles of Confederation," in *The Complete Anti-Federalist*, Vol. 1, 101.

24. Luther Martin, Esq., "The Genuine Information Delivered to the Legislature of the State of Maryland Relative to the Proceedings of the General Convention Lately Held at Philadelphia (1788)," in *The Complete Anti-Federalist*, Vol. 2, 45 (emphasis in original.).

25. "Speeches by Melancton Smith (June 1788)," in *The Complete Anti-Federalist*, Vol. 6, 148.

26. Ibid., 171.

27. *Catron Plan*, preamble, sec. 1. The Boundary County Interim Land Use Policy Plan preamble is identical.

28. "Speeches by Melancton Smith (June 1788)," in *The Complete Anti-Federalist*, Vol. 6, 171.

29. All references will be to *Catron Plan*. The ordinance subject to challenge in *Boundary Backpackers v. Boundary County*, Boundary No. 93-9955 has virtually identical wording. The National Federal Lands Conference urges the counties not to change the language from the *Catron County* model without changes.

30. 426 U.S. 529 (1976).

31. Ibid. 16 U.S.C.§ 1332 et seq. (1985). The act is arguably the most ecologically unsound "conservation" legislation passed in recent times. Wild horses and burros are exotic species that compete with native wildlife for forage, destroy vegetation, and cause soil compaction and erosion just as do their twins, the domestic livestock. The emotional appeal of horses led to the initial passage of the act and continues to erupt at any effort for control. When the National Park Service proposed removing twenty wild horses from the Ozark National Scenic Riverways, one-thousand people protested including the local congressman. The removal decision was narrowly upheld on appeal (*Wilkins v. Lujan*, 995 F2d 850 [8th Cir. 1993]).

32. Kleppe, 426 U.S. at 539.

33. Ibid., 543 (citing *Camfield v. United States*, 167 U.S. 518-526 [1897]).

34. *Hancock v. Train*, 426 U.S. 167 (1975).

35. Ibid., 178 (quoting *Mayo v. United States*, 319 U.S. 441, 445 [1943]).

36. *Jones v. Rath Packing Co.*, 430 U.S. 519-525-30 (1977).

37. *Silkwood v. Kerr-McGee Corp.*, 464 U.S. 238, 248 (1984) (citation omitted).

38. *Ventura County v. Gulf Oil Corp.*, 601 F.2d 1080, 1086 (9th Cir. 1979) (quoting *Hines v. Davidowitz*, 312 U.S. 52, 67 [1941], affirmed without opinion, 445 U.S. 947 [1980]).

39. 480 U.S. 572 (1987).

40. *California Coastal Commission*, 480 U.S., 594.

41. Ibid., 587.

42. Ibid., 593.

43. Ibid., 594–614.

44. Letter from Joseph P. Mazurek, Montana attorney general, to Mike McGrath and Keith Haker, County Attorneys, Lewis and Clark, and Custer County (11 June 1993).

45. Karen Budd-Falen was the luncheon speaker at a Soil Conservation Service meeting at Idaho Falls, Idaho on 13 December 1991:

> National Environmental Policy Act has as its goals to, and I quote, "Use all practicable means to preserve important historic, cultural, and natural aspects of our national heritage." What we started doing was looking up those terms, you know, if you go with the standard definition of "cultural and natural aspects", what you think of is Indian ruins, dinosaur bones and that's what you think the National Environmental Policy Act is out there to protect. When you start legally defining custom and culture, though, custom and culture is defined as "a right of usage or practice by the people which, by unvarying habit, has become compulsory and has acquired the force of law." (Transcript Narrative from videotape from Boundary County files produced in *Boundary Backpackers v. Boundary County*, Boundary No. 93-9955).

46. Federal Land Policy and Management Act of 1976, § 302, 43 U.S.C. § 1732(a) (1988). State control of hunting and fishing was given precedent over federal regulation in *Geer v. Connecticut*, 161 U.S. 519,535 (1896), on the now rejected theory of state ownership. The Forest Service enters into cooperative arrangements with the states on hunting and fishing (36 C.F.R. § 241.1 *et seq.* [1993]; see also Michael J. Bean, *The Evolution of National Wildlife Law* [New York: Praeger, 1983], 136–45).

47. 42 U.S.C., § 4331(b)(4)(1988). The word "cultural" also appears in the Wild and Scenic Rivers Act.

48. Karen Budd-Falen, *Protecting Community Stability—List of Citations*, six-page handout at National Federal Lands Conference meetings.

49. In this promotional letter to "Dear Friend," printed in the 1 July 1992 *National Federal Lands Conference Update*, National Federal Lands Conference Vice President Bert N. Smith was selling the *Update* for $65 per year (regular price $75). *Update* is six pages published monthly on cheap stock. The last page typically is an order form for audio tapes ($29.98), videotape ($59.95) and the *County Government and Federal Lands Handbook* ($99.95). *Update* gives notice of upcoming conferences that despite industry sponsorship still carry a $50.00 registration fee. The now completed Catron County Comprehensive Land Plan (250–300 pages) is sold by the National Federal Lands Conference for "a mere $250."

Part 2

Analyzing the Debate

8

Environmentalists and the New Political Climate: Strategies for the Future

Gus diZerega

Conservative senator James Buckley helped write the Endangered Species Act. Arguing in defense of snail darters, Buckley said the act "represents a quantum jump in man's acknowledgment of his moral responsibility for the integrity of the natural world." It could not have been said better by Dave Foreman, cofounder of Earth First!. Environmental values do not fit easily into a liberal/conservative political spectrum, and it is a mistake to try to make them do so.

To a disturbing extent the environmental movement hitched its wagon to the political fortunes of liberal Democrats. In doing so it entwined its fate with theirs. The result has been mixed. We will be paying the cost of that strategy for a while. One reason propelling this strategy is that most national environmental organizations do not have an active grassroots membership. They are mostly a mailing list, a staff, and a magazine. Given this structure, they naturally tend to focus their attention on Washington, D.C., and national solutions to environmental problems. It is here that the few speaking on behalf of the many can be most influential.

Beginning with the New Deal, the Democratic Party has long been more receptive to energetic national legislation than have the Republicans. It was therefore only natural that national environmental organizations would focus primarily upon the Democrats. But their efforts shifted much of our movement's energy and focus to the national level. This was a serious mistake for two reasons. First, by becoming overly identified with the party that dominated political power for so long, environmental organizations gave their opponents largely unchallenged access to the other party. Pre-1994 election public polls indicated that while 63 percent of Democrats regard themselves as "environmentalists" so did 55 percent of Republicans. But because of their preoccupation with Democratic politics, environmental activists largely gave the game to the "takings" and "wise use" crowd in the Republican Party. Most environmental eggs were placed in the Democratic basket.

Second, knowing we had no where else to go, Democrats did not have to worry about keeping our support. A few crumbs would keep us loyal because they were the least of two evils. They would never have to *fight* on our behalf; and usually they did not. I do not know any other explanation for the miserable environmental performance of the Clinton-Gore administration while Congress was in Democratic hands. It had the votes to pass many measures, but lacked the commitment to fight for them.

Many environmental advocates who are exquisitely and sensitively aware of the complexities of old growth forests, desert streams, and alpine tundra are often simple minded in their view of human society. Too often their model of society is as linear and simplistic as that of those western ranchers who never met a good predator or a bad steer. Our dominant strategy of relying primarily upon centralized national solutions to problems of extraordinary complexity has backfired. This approach has been the political equivalent of industrial agricultural monoculture, with its reliance on huge fields of uniform crops maintained by artificial fertilizers and pesticides. It has similar weaknesses and dangers. We, too, became dependent upon unreliable, insensitive, and often destructive "technologies": in this case, the liberal Democratic Party and central bureaucracies.

Policy Options

The realm of choice is wider than this. Three broad environmental policy strategies exist. The first seeks national legislation, regulation, and protection of environmental values. The second involves local communities in protecting and enhancing their immediate environment. The third utilizes market mechanisms to encourage and reward environmentally sensitive behavior. Each appeals to different political positions. Each has strengths and weaknesses. In most cases hybrid mixes may be best; but until we understand these three, our hybrids may be infertile. Once we understand them, our range of possibilities is greatly expanded.

National strategies promise immediate impact upon our public lands, where many of our most valuable natural areas remain. Further, they are countrywide in their impact. Sometimes this is the best scale for approaching a problem, such as air pollution. Here a national strategy reduces the likelihood that polluters will threaten to go elsewhere if they are held accountable for their actions. In addition, it can protect distant victims of pollution where the specific culprits cannot reasonably be held responsible, such as the case of automobile exhaust. Handled properly, national strategies are also highly visible, thereby helping create a wider consensus for change. National environmental organizations have been skillful at these tactics.

This approach also has significant weaknesses. First, national policy making proceeds slowly. Our system of government gives disproportionate power to those who would obstruct it. This assists us when we are on the defense but obstructs us when seeking new laws. Second, regulatory and administrative agencies and their clienteles have agendas of their own, ones often not in harmony with ours. The near imperviousness of the Forest Service and Bureau of Land Management (BLM) to internal reform are cases in point. Third, even if legislation is passed, affected interests will continue to jockey for influence over its enforcement. Implementation is as important as legislation, and more vulnerable to sabotage. Fourth, national approaches are often not sensitive to local environmental conditions. Thoughtless fire-suppression policies are good examples. Fifth, national strategies can appear to local communities as hostile impositions. The "wise use" movement is one result.

A different mix of strengths and weaknesses holds for community-based approaches. (1) When local communities are responsible for preserving and enhancing environmental values, the results can be breathtaking. Swiss and Japanese villages have successfully managed their community forest and meadow commons for as long as eight hundred years, dwarfing the record of the Forest Service.[1] (2) Local focus can bring unparalleled sensitivity to local circumstances and opportunities, allowing a fine-tuning unavailable to centralized management. (3) A community-oriented strategy maximizes points for innovation, while minimizing the impact of failures because of their small scale. Successes can be copied, failures avoided. (4) Community strategies can involve large numbers in environmental protection.

There are weaknesses as well. (1) The scale of some problems is not conducive to local solutions. (2) Local communities, particularly in ecologically critical areas, are often not wealthy, and therefore are subject to strong economic pressure for hasty development. This situation afflicts the rural West, where in some cases population growth approaches Third World rates. (3) They are often dominated by local elites tied emotionally as well as economically to extractive industries. Catron County, New Mexico, home base for the "county supremacy" movement is the most notorious example. (4) They can be extraordinarily myopic to the wider impact of local decisions.

Market-oriented strategies have their own strengths. (1) They encourage people to act in environmentally sensitive ways even when they themselves are not committed to such values. For example, if emission permits are bought and sold, polluters will have a powerful economic incentive to minimize their pollution and expose those polluting in excess of their permits. If I have a permit and you are polluting without one, or in excess of what you are allowed, the economic value of *my* permit falls. Markets therefore waste fewer resources than do centrally planned economies. (2) A market strategy probably provides the best framework for encouraging innovative solutions to problems. (3) These strategies are widely perceived to be voluntary. (4) They foster efficiency in the use of resources, enabling a given amount to go further than would otherwise be the case. This is partly why Julian Simon won his bet with Paul Ehrlich that natural resource prices would fall over time.[2]

The weakness of market strategies is that values not easily or appropriately put into monetary terms will be systematically short-changed. Among these values are wilderness and endangered species—two of my strongest reasons for being an environmentalist. The market's primary value is economic efficiency, and although a powerful asset in some contexts, it can be a weakness in others. Perhaps most fundamentally, investment in the market is based upon the rate of interest, creating a time horizon often not in harmony with nature. Practices that should adhere to ecological cycles if they are to be sustainable are linked instead to the rate of interest.

While no single strategy is always best, advocates of one usually compare the strengths of their preferred approach to the weaknesses of the alternatives. We need to become pragmatic when considering strategies and policies. No single strategy is suitable for every problem. Society is as complex as an ecosystem, and ideological or political rigidity on public policy is hardly a wise approach.

The State as Environmental Despoiler

Because of our prevailing bias in favor of centralized solutions, I want to expand briefly upon the costs we continue to pay for an overly one-sided approach. Government has often not proven a very reliable tool, even when Democrats controlled the House and Senate, and sometimes the presidency. Rick Sutherland was president of the Sierra Club Legal Defense Fund until his untimely death in 1991. In the final year of his life, he wrote, "My experience in the last two decades has led me to conclude that the government is all too often the environment's worst enemy."[3] To a large extent this was because the government refused to enforce environmental laws that were on the books. In addition, the regulations issued by responsible agencies frequently went against the intent of the laws that gave them their power. Further, not only does the government not always enforce desirable laws, it is frequently the architect of very bad ones. All too often the business interests that most vociferously oppose needed environmental reforms do so because they have grown dependent upon government subsidies. One of the greatest frauds put over on the American people is that Western ranchers, agribusiness, people who build in flood plains and barrier islands, the lumber industry, and the mining industry are proponents of "free enterprise" rather than of a welfare state for themselves and an ill-fare state for the rest of us. They are on the dole despite, and often because of, their wealth.[4]

If government did not subsidize these people at our expense, the following environmentally destructive activities would now be absent or taking place on a much smaller scale: most dams on the Columbia, Colorado, and Snake Rivers, logging in the Rocky Mountains, extractive agriculture in the arid and semi-arid West, most Sierra Nevada dams and the agribusinesses they serve, much ranching on BLM lands, and many roads and highways. Patterns of population and land use would be much different from what they are today, largely to the advantage of the environment. For example, while California would still have abundant agriculture, it would no longer grow low-value water-intensive crops such as alfalfa, rice, cotton, and hay.[5]

Laws are a necessary *part* of a successful environmental strategy. Without laws we would not have wilderness areas or national parks. Without laws we would likely have lost all our Pacific coast old growth forest by now, not just most of it. But we should not kid ourselves that laws alone are the key to a green future. Setting aside the fact that these lands have often been poorly managed, neither wilderness areas nor national parks alone can protect the ecosystems within their boundaries. They have become islands, isolated from the larger systems that sustained them for thousands of years; and it is unlikely that Washington will substantially increase the size of the national parks we have, even should the Democrats regain power.

We must tailor proposals in terms appealing to Republicans who care about the environment, and want to preserve it, but who distrust centralized government and regulatory bureaucracies. In addition, we should target local communities in environmentally sensitive areas, developing strategies seeking to harmonize community life with sustainable environmental practices. Hybrid strategies are necessary, but they need to emphasize communities and markets rather than regulation from On High.

The Endangered Species Act (ESA) demonstrates how this new strategy might work. The central political weakness of the ESA is that it is opposed by many private landowners. At this time, the last thing the average landowner wants to find on his or her land is an endangered species. All too often their response to such a discovery is "shoot, shovel, and shut up." Its second weakness is the very slow and litigious path by which a species becomes listed as endangered. Many species might become extinct before they are even listed. This weakness is connected with the first, for it is their dismay at having resident species listed that encourages landowners to litigate. A third weakness should concern us even more. So far the ESA has failed to make much difference in reversing the decline of endangered species. Since 1966, 1,354 species have been listed as endangered or threatened. Of them, 822 are native to the United States. Only 20 have been removed from the list. Eight were dropped because they were listed in error, seven because they are now extinct. Of the five delistings, one is the bald eagle, one is a plant in Utah, and three are birds native to a single Pacific island. In short, seven extinctions and five successes. As of 1990, the General Accounting Office found that 80 percent of species listed were still declining.

If landowners had incentives to encourage reproduction in the wild of endangered species, the picture would be completely different. People would want species to be listed and would create conditions on their land encouraging them to settle there and to reproduce. Rather than simply preserving relic populations, at least in some cases species could be put well on the road to recovery. Important work has already been done on this question. In 1993, Defenders of Wildlife published *Building Economic Incentives into the Endangered Species Act*.[6] This is a collection of fourteen studies by experts in government, education, and research organizations analyzing how perverse incentives existing between private landowners and endangered species can be reversed.

Among the best proposals, in my view, are those presented by John Baden and Tim O'Brien of the Foundation for Research on Economics and the Environment, and by Randal O'Toole of Cascade Holistic

Economic Consultants. Baden and O'Brien point out that the ESA needs to elicit innovative ideas and enthusiastic cooperation from many private landowners if it is to achieve its goals. To this end they propose establishing a "national Biodiversity Trust Fund with regional, state, and local member organizations (e.g. the Crazy Mountains Biodiversity Trust Fund). Each fund would be managed by a board of trustees and would have as its key mandate, the conservation of species and habitat."[7]

Baden and O'Brien suggest that funding for these projects could come from foundations, private donations, corporations, and a percentage of the revenues from activities on public lands that infringe upon wildlife habitat, such as logging, mining, and recreation. They and O'Toole suggest 10 percent of the revenue raised from making these activities pay fair market value should go to the trust funds. This percentage would yield between $500 million and $1 billion annually. For comparison's sake, the Fish and Wildlife Service currently spends about $50 million a year to protect endangered species. O'Toole argues that no more than 2 percent of biodiversity trust funds should be spent on overhead and 10 percent on research; and "the remainder must be spent on activities that actually improve biodiversity or help protect a rare or endangered species."[8]

The trust funds could purchase conservation easements (thereby committing owners to preserving their natural environment) buy land outright, or pay "bounties" to landowners who provide breeding or otherwise crucial habitat for endangered species. Environmental groups and landowners would compete in developing proposals for trust fund funding. The fund managers would award grants and purchase land or easements from the most promising proposals. O'Toole describes one possibility where in order to preserve spotted owls in California's Sierra, the biodiversity board would purchase timber from the Forest Service to remove it from logging, pay private landowners to practice select cutting, and pay $5,000 per pair to any landowner or public agency with spotted owls nesting on its property.

These examples are only a few of the many included within the Defenders of Wildlife study. Most proposals are in keeping with the kind of values espoused by Republicans. Were they well known, the new Republican Congress *might* end up making quite positive contributions to the protection of endangered species.

A reform such as this would encourage other reforms. For biodiversity trust funds to do their job adequately, users of public lands should pay "fair market value" for their use. Further, a government strapped for money will favor uses that generate income. If recreational fees were pegged to their market value, and the Forest Service could keep some of the money it raised from these fees, the service itself would value preserving old growth, clean water, and free-running rivers. Fair market value could be discovered only by allowing *anyone* to bid on grazing and timber allotments, even if they chose not to graze or log them. The Sierra Club, Nature Conservancy, Ducks Unlimited, Trout Unlimited, Biodiversity Trust Fund, and others, could purchase protection of national lands of great ecological value—a better use of funds than paying lobbyists and lawyers.

Interestingly, these reforms are more in keeping with Republican than Democratic biases, because they emphasize local communities, independent organizations, and market processes. Public policy and environmental protection are too important to be shackled by ideological blinders. Such shackling helped hatch the wise use movement. It is time to drop them and act more wisely ourselves.

Notes

1. A. McKean, "Management of Traditional Common Lands (*Iriaichi*) in Japan," *Making the Commons Work: Theory, Practice and Policy* (San Francisco: Institute of Contemporary Studies, 1992), 63–98; Elinor Ostrom, *Governing the Commons: The Evolution of Institutions for Collective Action* (New York: Cambridge University Press, 1990), 58–69, 88–102.

2. See John Tierney, "Betting the Planet," *New York Times Magazine*, 2 December 1990, 52.

3. Frederic Sutherland, "The Government Is the Environment's Worst Enemy," *Earth Island Journal*, Fall 1991, 39.

4. Marc Reisner, *Cadillac Desert: The American West and Its Disappearing Water* (New York: Penguin, 1987); High Country News, *Western Water Made Simple* (Washington, D.C.: Island Press, 1987).

5. Mark Reisner and Sarah Bates, *Overtapped Oasis: Reform or Revolution for Western Water* (Washington, D.C.: Island Press, 1990).

6. *Building Economic Incentives into the Endangered Species Act* can be obtained for $10.00 from Caroline Kennedy, Defenders of Wildlife, 1101 14th St. N.W., Suite 1400, Washington, D.C. 20005.

7. Ibid., 95.

8. Ibid., 105–6.

9

Taking the Land Rights Movement Seriously

Kirk Emerson

This chapter offers a preliminary analysis of the burgeoning land rights movement, its origin, and the nature of its concerns. A variety of theories might explain the origins of this movement, suggesting that in combination, several events, agents, institutions, and forces have played a role in this development. Arguing that the movement is neither uniform nor monolithic, I identify five dominant rationales that together represent and distinguish the different political and ideological interests that have coalesced into the land rights movement. These include equity claims, new populist principles, privatization arguments, market transaction reasoning, and libertarian assertions. Each of these rationales incorporate several underlying conceptions of property in land. Opportunities for public deliberation, I conclude, reside with these conceptions and the policy arguments they generate.

Origins of the Movement

Analyzing the land rights movement requires some understanding of its origins. Given its multifaceted nature, however, no single source can be authoritatively assigned. As would be expected, popular opinions and theories abound, falling generally into one of four categories: critical events, agency theories, institutional causes, and deterministic models. Discussing each of these diagnoses is informative, for each of them informs a broader understanding of the combination of different events, agents, institutions, and forces that have contributed to the rise of this movement.

Critical events (big bang or last straw theories) are often pointed to as the genesis of the land rights movement. Nancie G. Marzulla, president of the Defenders of Property Rights, a Washington, D.C., legal defense firm for property owners, places the moment in 1964 when the U.S. Department of Interior announced its intentions to halt further conversion of publicly owned lands to agricultural use. She suggests that the Sagebrush Rebellion was set into motion by this event, which in turn lead to the contemporary property rights movement.[1] Alternatively, Richard Miniter has pointed to 1989 as the critical date, when President Bush announced his "no net loss" wetlands policy that "sparked a national grassroots movement against a broad array of environmental and other government imposed land-use restrictions."[2]

The second set of theories, what one might call agency theories, assigns responsibility for the land rights movement to specific agents of change, not unlike elite theories of political agenda setting. These explanations credit specific policy entrepreneurs or political activists with an instrumental role. Some point to the agent provocateurs, like Chuck Cushman and Ron Arnold, whose individual efforts are seen as catalysts for the formation of hundreds of local property rights groups, representing thousands of members, hooked up to millions of fax machines. Or to Richard Epstein, the academic godfather of the reconstituted (or reconstitutionalized) takings doctrine, who has provided legal ammunition for aggressive litigators to represent property owner plaintiffs around the country.[3] Or to the policy entrepreneurship (and the litigation skills) of Mark Pollot and Roger Marzulla (Nancie's husband), the authors of President Reagan's 1987 Executive Order 12630 requiring takings impact analyses as well as subsequent property rights legislation.[4] These agency theories can be easily elaborated (and wrongly so, in my opinion) into conspiracy theories of a movement orchestrated by a few key elites.

A third explanatory model places the blame or the honor with institutional variables. For example, Jack Walker has found that certain legal and institutional factors can provide the impetus and opportunity for interest group formation.[5] Contrary to the prevailing wisdom, voluntary groups often develop after, rather than before, key legislative acts. Walker observed that many environmental groups formed after the spate of environmental laws in the early 1970s, suggesting that "influences for change come as much from inside the government as from beyond its institutional boundaries."

It can be argued that the institutional responsiveness of an increasingly conservative federal court system to property rights claimants has served to precipitate further legal challenges and embolden the movement. In its recent rulings on regulatory takings cases, the Supreme Court has been scrutinizing the nature and necessity of regulations more carefully and has placed a greater burden on the government to defend the legitimacy and efficacy of its regulatory actions.[6] New categorical rules that limit the effect of regulations have been added to the changing takings doctrine. These judicial developments have prompted more legal action, more willingness to appeal, and more financial support for appeals. Successful compensation claims before the U.S. Claims Court may have prompted the growing number of suits in that federal court. The very hearing of takings cases, which previously the Supreme Court routinely declined to accept, has provided a signal to policy entrepreneurs and public interest litigators seeking to broaden the takings doctrine.

Another example of an institutional argument, is the impact of President Reagan's executive order, which represented a new policy opportunity for controlling rogue regulators within the administration.[7] Although it has rarely been used by federal agencies, if at all, the takings impact analysis concept has developed into a policy proposal now being exported to the states, precipitating organization of state property rights lobbies. Likewise, the model legislation promoted by the American Legislative Exchange Council and the Defenders of Property Rights for capping lost property values due to regulations has provided a vehicle for political action in both state and federal legislatures.[8]

One additional institutional theory can be found in certain failures of institutions, which encourage property rights claims. Here the culprit is the recognized pattern of abuse by public officials who pushed the regulation of wetlands and endangered species "too far"; or the repeated excesses of land-use planners and local officials who turned development reviews into extortion for off-site improvements; or the fault line between the radical ecologists and the inside-the-beltway envirocrats that left grassroots environmentalists unprepared for the allegations of property rights advocates.[9]

Finally, deterministic models offer plausible explanations as well, where larger forces beyond the manipulation of individual agents, institutions, or events are at play. These theories work at various scales and contexts. For example, early pluralist theories of interest-group formation predict the rise of countervailing pressure groups in reaction to the hegemony of a dominant group.[10] The increasing strength and influence of environmental interest groups in the 1970s, according to this model, gave rise inevitably to the organization of offsetting conservative forces during the Reagan era. This is how O'Connor and Epstein, for example, characterize the origins of conservative public interest law groups, such as the Pacific Legal Foundation, in the early 1980s.[11] This general group theory lends some credence to the "environmental backlash" hypothesis, but within the broader dynamic context of interest group pluralism.

A second deterministic model is based on more cyclical views of history. Building on the work of Samuel Huntington, William Futrell, president of the Environmental Law Institute, presents the history of environmental law and the environmental movement generally as a series of swings from conservative convictions to creedal passions for reform: "Environmental politics follows this pattern and oscillates between a period of public purpose and a time of private rights, a period of positive government emphasizing planning for the public interest and a time of negative government, demanding freedom from regulation, a period when environmental values and resource protection are emphasized and a time when development takes priority over social concerns."[12] While this may raise some doubts about the survival of Inglehart's postmaterial "culture shift" and Milbraith's "New Ecological Paradigm," perhaps such swings are limited to our domestic scene, since such patterns are sometimes explained as peculiar to our American political culture.[13] Richard Ellis, for example, sees political conflict in the United States as rooted in rival cultures.[14] He might explain the rise of the land rights movement as a resurgence of the dominant individualistic strain suppressing our egalitarian lineage, at least for the moment.

Another deterministic theory might drawn on the work of public-opinion scholars, such as James Stimson, who trace large public mood swings, and suggest that now the country is cycling back toward a more conservative era, hence the rise of the New Right and the silence of the liberal Left.[15] This theory would encompass the rise of the larger deregulation movement as well, which has been building since the late 1970s. The initial targets for deregulators were economic measures and the rules that accompanied federal assistance. But now attention has turned to environmental and land use regulations, which have expanded significantly through federal wetlands regulation, the Endangered Species Act, and more aggressive growth management policies at state and local levels.

In reviewing these different perspectives on the rise of the land rights movement, one can begin to appreciate the multiplicity of forces and conditions that have contributed to this emergence. Rather than one single factor, many different events, agents, institutions, and forces acting over time and in different locales have helped create a rather complicated, diverse coalescence of interests. But what binds this complex assemblage of membership groups, group entrepreneurs and patrons together into a recognizable movement? There is no national federation of card-carrying property rights protectors. Indeed, several different national networks exist, such as the Alliance for America, the Land Rights Letter, and the American Land Rights Association.

The unifying interest of the land rights movement is land, the real property at stake. Rights in land, whether publicly or privately owned, set the boundary of the substantive concerns that bind these groups into a movement. But this doesn't move our understanding forward very far; the interests in land represented in this movement vary considerably: from east to west, from inclusion on public lands to exclusion from private lands. All of us have interests in land. Of the 92 million households in this country, two-thirds own homes. According to the 1990 U.S. Census figures, over 59 million households live in owner-occupied units, while close to 33 million live in rental units—and even renters exercise certain property rights. The American Planning Association has an interest in land; so do most environmental organizations. We all have some degree of commitment to property in land.

What distinguishes the land rights movement, in all its complexity and across its many constituents, I suggest, is a latticework of interconnected, complementary understandings of property in land. Behind the rhetoric of property-rights talk are substantive conceptions of property that include its value, how rights in property are to be governed, property ownership, the stability of the rules that define property, and the autonomy afforded by private property. I am intentionally *not* framing the debate exclusively around rights. As Dennis Coyle notes, "The language of rights permeates controversies over the uses of land."[16] Behind those rights claims, however, are more substantive and foundational conceptions about property that need to be unraveled and looked at. In the next section of this chapter, I discuss the rationales that incorporate these conceptions of property and help us further articulate the dimensions of the land rights movement.

Defining Rationales

In order to take the land rights movement seriously and engage in more substantive and productive deliberation, we need a more discriminating understanding of the rationales that guide this complex coalition. By rationales, I mean the basic arguments or fundamental reasoning about property expressed by and motivating its adherents.

These rationales provide the outside boundaries of the land rights movement as well as differentiate among the various personal, political, and ideological interests that compose the movement. Together these arguments also lend some insight to the origins of the movement, its likely staying power, and its connections to other ongoing political and policy debates.

I have identified five rationales from my readings of the movement's own membership materials and background papers, legal argumentation in regulatory takings cases, legislative proposals for state and federal property rights protection, as well as both critical and supportive commentary on the movement. These rationales include equity claims, new populist principles, privatization arguments, market transaction reasoning, and libertarian assertions. Each of these rationales represent a facet of the land rights movement and is articulated by key actors and associations who draw predominantly on that line of argumentation.

These are not meant to be mutually exclusive rationales. Rather they tend to be mutually consistent and reinforcing (like intersecting spheres in a Venn diagram). However, these rationales are sufficiently distinct to enable a useful classification of the central claims and priority principles. It is important to note that several groups endorse many, if not most, of these rationales of the land rights movement. Nonetheless, one need not embrace all of these principles, and certainly not in their extreme forms, to identify oneself as a supporter of the land rights movement. (That is what makes membership counts an irrelevant measure of the movement's strength.) I see the land rights movement as a coalescence of political activists, policy entrepreneurs, patrons, organizers and organized groups, as well as unorganized supporters, all sharing complementary, mutually reinforcing rationales. That is one of the sources of the movement's strength—an associational commitment that incorporates expected material benefits with the sharing of compatible conceptions of property.

The equity rationale represents concerns for fairness and justice that are raised when private landowners bear unanticipated or burdensome costs due to public regulation or direct condemnation. The demands for compensation spring from this rationale. Equity concerns are also expressed when private users of public lands are restricted in ways that are perceived as unfair and unjustified. These equity concerns are perhaps the most compelling and most intractable of the movement's rationales. They require weighing the relative values of property with respect to different competing interests—private owners, public agencies, and the public at large. Three major equity arguments stand out, most of them well developed within the legal reasoning presented in regulatory takings claims.

The most familiar of these is the argument that some individual property owners are bearing a disproportionate regulatory burden imposed for the positive benefit of the rest of society. The constitutional restriction on eminent domain in the Just Compensation Clause is the foundational principle here. The private value of the property is being diminished, it is argued, well beyond the positive public value being preserved for hard-to-quantify, broadly enjoyed, often delayed or future benefits. It is one thing to be restricted from creating a nuisance or jeopardizing public health or safety; private value should not include an unrecognized right to harm others. It is quite another thing, it is argued, to pay excessive costs for what are perceived as public uses or benefits for which just compensation should be paid. Unfortunately, the line distinguishing public harm from public benefit, as Justice Scalia admitted in his 1992 *Lucas v. South Carolina Coastal Council* opinion, is not well drawn, particularly with respect to wetlands and biodiversity values. Nor is the composition and source of "private" value straightforward. Fair market value, for example, is not necessarily the exclusive product of private investment.

Much, if not most, of the unresolved doctrinal issues over regulatory takings have to do with sorting out these values in land (many, potentially indeterminate) in order to balance fairly majoritarian interests with individual rights. Whether or not to compensate, how much to compensate, or on what basis to compensate property owners for their lost property value in exchange for protection of public value remain open questions.

A second equity argument challenges the justification for direct condemnation or regulation of private land that does not serve a valid public purpose or is not legally authorized by statute or by the Constitution. For example, Peggy Reigle's group, Fairness to Landowners Committee (claiming 8,800 property-owning members in thirty states) fights the legitimacy of wetlands regulations and promotes more restrictive field definitions and less protective standards. Here the declared public value in private land is questioned. If there is no legitimate public value, then it is unfair and unreasonable to diminish the private property value. This argument most often takes the form of substantive due process claims against "arbitrary and capricious" public decision making. A companion claim is expressed by private users of public lands who defend their "vested rights" or use privileges by denying the legitimacy of the federal government's exercise of the Property or Supremacy Clauses of the Constitution.

A third, closely connected set of equity claims is about the efficacy of governmental actions; are the regulations really going to
achieve the intended public purpose? If not, it is argued, then they
place an unfair and unjustifiable burden on property owners who must
forgo private value in exchange for unrealized, if not unrealizable,
public gains. This was the line of reasoning pursued in the 1987 *Nollan v. California Coastal Commission* ruling, in which the "essential
nexus" doctrine for exactions originated and again in the 1994 *Dolan
v. City of Tigard* decision's "rough proportionality" test. Despite one's
reading of these Supreme Court rulings, the demand for efficacious
regulation is certainly a justifiable concern for property owners and
taxpayers alike.

This equity rationale then motivates a distinct set of issues around
the multiple values of property and the "calculus of fairness" for resolving competing claims over those values.[17] This presents one critical area for deliberation with property rights advocates. Much of the
current discourse on these issues has been conducted through the courts
and in legal briefs. Several conservative legal foundations and defense
funds field litigators, join law suits, and provide amicus briefs on cases
that are driven by these equity claims.[18] Legal scholars debate these
issues in law review articles and law school symposia.[19] As the efforts
increase to provide legislative remedies for losses in private property
value, the debate is shifting to the political and public arena as well,
however, the issues are being cast more as "rights talk" than equity
claims.[20]

A second major line of reasoning within the land rights movement
is the new populism rationale, which raises questions about the governance of property. Who should be making decisions ultimately affecting the property of the common man and woman and their local
communities? The neopopulist response is that competent, accountable,
and decent government should stay close to home. Bureaucrats and
legislators back in Washington, D.C., do not have the knowledge or
commitment to plan or regulate or adjudicate local or state land and
natural resource issues. Only decentralized and limited government can
foster responsible self-determining individuals and communities. These
are the perennial arguments of supporters for rejuvenated federalism
and stronger states rights. But they have been emboldened by reactions to the cumulative reach of a growing number of federal regulations for environmental cleanup and natural resource protection, worker
safety, and consumer protection that now extend into the affairs of
individual proprietors, small farms and businesses, school boards, and
property owners. Enforcement of these regulations has also been con-

siderably strengthened; now violators can be criminally liable for unauthorized polluting activities or property damage. The new populists are responding to these multiple intrusions into "their" lives and onto "their" lands.

What is perceived as the arrogance of federal bureaucrats abusing their powers of office, be they from the Bureau of Land Management, the Fish and Wildlife Service, the Army Corps of Engineers, or the Environmental Protection Agency, is a major source of neopopulist anger. This has been a continuing theme for inholders (private property owners living in or adjacent to publicly owned and managed lands) who are often subject to direct condemnation, or prolonged threats of condemnation, and to stringent development standards or restrictions.[21] Nasty behavior, lack of notice, exclusion from public discussion or timely involvement, and below-market compensation offers are recurrent complaints. Most critically, these property owners contend they have no political recourse, since unelected bureaucrats from federal or state agencies are often the final decision makers over the disposition of their property.

These neopopulist arguments can be found in the self-presentation of essentially all the local and national property rights groups. The Alliance for America describes its membership as follows:

> We are farmers, cattlemen, private landowners, fishermen, miners, loggers, teachers, carpenters, truck drivers, and a thousand more . . . the people, families and communities that make America the greatest nation on earth. This nation, however, seems to no longer be one whose government is of, by, and for the people, but one which is of, by, and for the unelected bureaucrats and regulators. Today government and environmental regulations, some of which seem to be based on tea leaf readings and Tarot card predictions, have made criminals of ordinary citizens doing ordinary things. It is time for the common sense people of this land to wake up and take back the control of their lives and futures.[22]

For additional examples, see Pendley's catalogue in *It Takes a Hero*, or the *Land Rights Letter* (where one column, entitled "Reluctant Warriors," features profiles on regular people who have made the movement a success).[23]

Admittedly the populist rhetoric is self-conscious and has been exploited by the political and policy entrepreneurs of the land rights movement. Nonetheless, the new populism rationale represents deeply felt values and the extension of a long-standing political tradition in this country. Classic questions about representation, accountability, the regulatory role of government generally, and the limit of federal authority specifically, are central to deliberation along this line of reasoning.

The privatization rationale focuses on the ownership of property through two lines of argumentation. The first is the standard efficient management argument; that private ownership of land is a necessary, if not sufficient, condition for the most efficient and environmentally sound stewardship practices. This is coupled with an entitlement argument that supports private rights to public lands. The core of the wise use movement's case rests on these twin claims, rallying support from ranchers, miners, loggers, oil drillers, and those dependent on the resource extraction industries. The second entitlement claim is particularly important when squaring the seeming contradiction between support for private ownership with protection of public subsidies for low mining fees and grazing permits. However, since the twentieth-century federal land retention policies are not recognized as valid by many wise users or by those in the newly dubbed "county ordinance movement," such nominal fees are seen as interferences with vested or promised rights, not as undeserved subsidies. The escalating protests and civil disobedience in eastern Nevada over new grazing restrictions by the U.S. Bureau of Land Management and the U.S. Forest Service demonstrate this entitlement perspective.[24]

The documentation and economic reasoning behind this privatization rationale have been elaborated on by free-market environmentalists and new-resource economists out of the Political Economy Research Center (PERC).[25] Their intellectual heritage of economic liberalism reaches way back to John Locke and Adam Smith and is intertwined with the conservation lineage from Pinchot. Wise, multiple-use principles for management of natural resources, it is argued, can be carried out by those who know the land, know the resources, and have the greatest incentives to manage for long-term productivity. Indeed, the incentive structure of this rational-actor model is the central logic. Public regulations, for example, such as those in the Endangered Species Act, can provide perverse incentives to private property owners to defy their stewardship principles and destroy listed species on their property rather than come under the jurisdiction of the ESA.[26] Admittedly the wise use groups' interests go beyond this privatization rationale and incorporate many of the other lines of reasoning being presented, but their originating rationale resides with the privatization argument. At the very least, the wise users give the most direct expression of and priority to privatization interests. This makes sense, of course, given the western provenance of these groups, where more than a third of the land is federally owned.[27]

Dueling anecdotes of egregious mismanagement of both public and private lands abound. These are familiar and persistent indictments. The dichotomous assumption behind the rationale that there are only two forms of ownership in land, public and private, and both are absolute, is the real culprit here.[28] It becomes particularly dysfunctional when applied by either side to the challenges of ecosystem management, where legal boundaries between private and public lands are rarely coincident with natural system delineations. Rather than confront this directly, unfortunately, the battles are fought over legalistic interpretations of congressional intent and administrative discretion, and such arcane doctrines as *noscitur a sociis* (where words are known by the company they keep), as in the 1994 *Sweet Home v. Babbitt* ruling by the D.C. Circuit Court of Appeals.

As one further example on the entitlement side of this argument, take the case against the U.S. Forest Service's regulation of Crooked Lake in Michigan's Upper Peninsula. This is now on appeal in the Sixth Circuit; the Mountain States Legal Foundation is representing the property owners. The foundation's central argument is that the federal government when it purchases private lands assumes only those rights previously owned and cannot then call on the Property Clause of the Constitution to exercise its sovereign rights to restrict use of the lake.[29]

The market transaction rationale, although closely akin to the privatization argument, emphasizes property's role in the productive workings of the economy as a whole. The rules that govern property in land, it is argued, must be clearly and consistently applied so that expectations about the future use of land can be realized. Stable, predictable property rights and values reduce transaction costs, minimize risk, and encourage investment. Unanticipated changes or burdensome regulations concerning the institutions of property, its administration, protection, and adjudication, will discourage private risk taking and the productive use of resources.

This market transaction rationale originates in Ronald Coase's seminal work on social cost theory and has been extended by political economists and transaction costs analysts as well as by legal scholars of the law and economics tradition. One extreme extension of this reasoning has been developed by Richard Epstein at the University of Chicago. Epstein has played a pivotal intellectual role in raising the takings issue to its current prominence. Many of his colleagues and students form the cadre of policy entrepreneurs and public interest litigators who have pushed for revisions in the judicial takings doctrine and new statutory limits on regulatory impacts on property values.[30]

The private business interests supporting this rationale are those with speculative interests to protect; owners of undeveloped land, the real estate industry, and the home builders' associations. Rule changes, such as the redefinition of regulated wetlands or local rezoning (particularly down zoning), or lengthy, uncertain permit approval processes, in the long run, it is argued, hinder risk-taking investments necessary for economic development. This rationale comes across in the strategy to correct the takings dilemma through statutory rather than judicial means. What we now see in Congress and in statehouses around the country are proposals for brightline rules that would reduce the risk of investment in land and provide insurance against future rule changes that cannot be ensured from the muddled judicial doctrine on takings. One thing did become clear in the *Lucas* decision was that even Justice Scalia, writing for the majority, could not adequately define a total taking, let alone a partial taking (cases where less than 100 percent of all productive use of the land is taken by regulation). Indeed, Scalia's efforts at a categorical ruling for total taking were compromised by upholding the nuisance exceptions based on background principles in state property and common law. Categorical rules can be accomplished more bluntly, at least in theory, by statute.

The libertarian rationale is evoked quite simply by Professor Epstein's philosophy that all regulation is theft.[31] I distinguish this last rationale in its emphasis on private property as an essential element of personal autonomy. The right to exclude is consonant with freedom, as Bruce Yandle explains, "The ability to exclude, to select who may enter and use a resource, is powerful evidence of freedom and liberty."[32] Expressed in the NIMBY syndrome, adherents to the libertarian rationale want exclusive control not only over their backyards but their back pockets as well. Compulsory shelling out for the public interest is an infringement on individual liberty and any lost property value from governmental regulation ought to be compensated. The libertarian rationale offers the natural rights argument for private property and recognizes few, if any, justifiable constraints on individual freedom.

It is from this rationale that property rights are defended as co-equal with civil and political rights and in need of the same diligent constitutional protections.[33] Erasing the "double standard" will restore "fundamental rights, rights that are crucial to individual freedom and democracy."[34] This "double standard" for judicial review originated with a famous footnote by Justice Harlan Stone in a 1938 ruling by the Supreme Court, *United States v. Carolene Products.* Deference was given to regulatory impositions on property that passed a simple "rational basis" test, while closer scrutiny was given to governmental actions that might jeopardize free speech and criminal procedure rights, political rights such as voting, and the rights of "discrete, insular minorities." In a recent, well-documented study of judicial treatment of land-use regulation, Coyle states, "In its zeal to justify an expanding regulatory state, the land use establishment . . . has undermined the freedom critical to the American polity and has supported the dilution of the Constitution beyond the bounds of credible interpretation."[35]

The more radical libertarian extension of this rationale is expressed by the "freedom fighters" of the movement, given to the most radical rhetoric and emotional "rights talk." While Robert Nozick articulates best the modern libertarian philosophy, those drawn to this rationale in the movement tend to cite our revolutionary Founding Fathers as their main inspiration and refer to the land rights movement as a revolt.[36] The most radical activists and organizers of the movement tend to argue the extreme libertarian rationale, including the radical recreationists, hunters and bikers who defend their right to ride the desert free and clear.

This libertarian argument is particularly challenging to objectify into a domain for critical deliberation. It is one thing to acknowledge the opposition to, say, a rails-to-trails program that could diminish privacy and present security concerns for private homeowners; it is another to understand the withdrawal from civic engagement or any responsibility for a collective public interest. Through the lens of this rationale, however, regulations are seen as unjustifiable constraints on individual freedom: the "negative" freedom from governmental intrusion. The forgotten half of the equation, as opponents have countered, are those governmental measures that enable the "positive" freedom to pursue one's own course, to have educational opportunities that enable informed choices, to live in a safe civil society, to have some stable expectations about the behavior of one's neighbors or the quality of the air one breathes. Deliberation about libertarian premises is essential to reengage individual rights with collective responsibility.

Opportunities for Deliberation

If there is any consolation to be found in the rise of the land rights movement, it is in the opportunities that have been created for public deliberation about property and its role in connecting, not just delimiting, public and private rights and responsibilities. This is unfinished business not only for the environmental movement, but also for our American political culture. Some might say unresolvable business, and hence the pendulum swing from reform to conservation, or from collective welfare to robust economic liberalism. If we are to moderate that arc of action-reaction, which it is in the interests of environmental integrity to do, then we need to take hold of this new opportunity for deliberation.

In some regards, I am arguing for an approach not unlike Cass Sunstein's articulate defense of regulation and reconstruction of the activist state in *After the Rights Revolution*.[37] Let me illustrate with just a few of the opportunities for deliberation presenting themselves right now in the growing public debate. The new populism rationale, described above, provides the underpinning for policy proposals to limit the reach of regulation at its source, that is, by reducing the authorized scope of what constitutes a legitimate governmental action. One of the ways this is being approached is by redefining and narrowing the justification for regulations to only those situations that would prevent "imminent and identifiable 1) hazard to public health and safety or 2) damage to specific property other than the property whose use is limited" (the current language in H.R. 925). A more subtle companion approach is to excise the word "welfare" from the heretofore standard rubric of "health, safety and welfare," as the general domain for the exercise of traditional police powers of the state. This omission occurs, for example, in the model assessment bills that specify guidelines that state attorneys general would convey to state agencies for required reviews of the "constitutional takings implications" of proposed regulations.[38]

Dropping the term "welfare" from the scope of affirmative duties of government has more than symbolic significance and, of course, represents the essence of the current deregulatory fervor. Land-use planning and zoning, for example, are based on public welfare reasoning. Ironically, the protection of property values was an original justification for separating land uses through zoning and has been understood and interpreted as a legitimate public welfare goal of government.[39] If the nuisance definitions of state courts or the "imminent and identifiable hazard" language of statutes become the sole basis for governmental regulation, innumerable public protections that people have come to expect from state and local government may well be withdrawn.

Engaging with the new populist argumentation on this requires discussion of the role of government in the definition and protection of property. Rather than quietly substituting environmental protection into the equation (we now hear on occasion "health, safety, and environmental protection"), we need to address the legacy and meaning of welfare more directly. Before banishing "public welfare" to the politically incorrect ashpile along with the "L" word, let's discuss more fully the sources of value in property and the role of government in providing that value. Are the majority of people really willing to write off all provision of public amenities such as natural corridor protection or historic preservation or future public resources, such as those provided by a diverse species gene pool? Do we simply abandon all prospective welfare duties because contemporary budget exigencies now prohibit them?

Ideas are now beginning to emerge that address some of these questions, particularly with respect to determining value. For example, the concept of "givings" or "makings" of value by government-financed infrastructure or insurance that enhances private property values is revealing the complexity of what constitutes property value. Local zoning restrictions add potential value in future use provisions for not only your property but neighboring property as well. Discussions on the fluidity of property value are now starting; how are fair market values obtained, what is their margin of error, how stable are they, how dependent are they on other factors, like changing interest rates and market dynamics? Federal, state, and local governments actually play several roles that affect property value, not just that of regulator. At the same time, the government is not the only determinant of influence on property values.

As a final example of an opportunity for deliberation, a major equity-based policy proposal is the categorical definition of a compensable taking as a specific percentage reduction in property value. Traditionally, judicial determinations of whether or not a taking has occurred are based on a case-specific, contextual balancing of the nature of the governmental action with the economic burden on the property owner and his or her investment-backed expectations.[40] The categorical proposal provides a predetermined cap on lost property value, which, if exceeded and proved to be due to the effect of the regulation, would be automatically compensable. The earliest proposals of this sort appeared in 1991 model language sponsored by the American Legislative Exchange Council for state takings bills and recommended 50 percent reduction as the limit of regulatory impacts. On its face, that sounds reasonable. Looked at another way, property owners would willingly or at least legally sustain losses of up to 50 percent in fair market value due to governmental intrusions before a statutory taking would be triggered. That sounds rather generous. Why not lower the limit to, say, 35 percent or 25 percent? The official bargaining position of the Congressional Republican's Contract with America began at 10 percent, then moved to 33⅓, then returned to 10.

The problem is that there is no rational basis for choosing one categorical cap over another—10 percent or 80 percent. Did 10 percent sound fair, or was it the most politically palatable, or merely beyond the average margin of error for most real estate appraisals? At issue is the problematic of imposing a uniform decision rule for complicated phenomena, such as property in land, that derive value and ownership from multiple sources and conditions. It looks simple on its face, but a raft of administrative rules will be needed to determine which cases meet the cut off. How do we determine what 10 percent is and of what base? And what happens to those who lose only 9.5 percent? This legislation turns a muddled judicial doctrine into a bureaucratic nightmare. Nonetheless, there are legitimate equity issues here and by attending more closely to the property values at issue, perhaps the complexity of such calculations can return us to a more reasonable balancing approach, not unlike, perhaps, but more definitive than, the court's contextual balancing of public purpose and private burdens.

In sum, to take the land rights movement seriously requires an acknowledgment of the various rationales behind the rhetoric and an understanding of their relation to different conceptions of property in land and to specific policy initiatives. Opportunities now exist for public deliberation around all of these rationales. If not taken, we risk a descent into a pathogenic environmental politics (to extend David Truman's phrase), where lines are drawn and never crossed. This should prompt public regulators and environmentalists to reevaluate and reaffirm their own underlying rationales and refresh the public's understanding of the "essential nexus" between private interests and public responsibility.

Cases Cited

Agins v. City of Tiburon, 447 U.S. 255 (1980).

Dolan v. City of Tigard, No. 93-518. U.S. Supreme Court (1994).

Florida Rock Industries v. U.S. Claims Court, Case No. 266-82L (1990).

Keystone Bituminous Coal Association v. DeBenedictus, 480 U.S. 470 (1987).

Loveladies Harbor, Inc. v. United States, 2 Cl. Ct. 153 (1990).

Lucas v. South Carolina Coastal Council, 112 S.Ct. 2886 (1992).

Nollan v. California Coastal Commission, 483 U.S. 825 (1987).

Penn Central Transportation v. New York City, 438 U.S. 104 (1978).

Pennsylvania Coal v. Mahon, 260 U.S. 393 (1922).

Sweet Home Chapter of Communities for a Great Oregon v. Babbitt, 17 F.3d 1463 (D.C. Cir. 1994).

United States v. Carolene Products Co., 304 U.S. 144 (1938).

Village of Euclid v. Ambler Realty, 272 U.S. 365 (1926).

Whitney Benefits v. United States, 926 F2d 1169 (1991).

Yee v. City of Escondido, 112 S. Ct. 1522 (1992).

Notes

1. See Nancie Marzulla's discussion in chapter 4 of this volume.
2. Richard Miniter, "You Just Can't Take It Any More," *Policy Review* 70 (1994): 40–46.
3. Richard A. Epstein, *Takings, Private Property and the Power of Eminent Domain* (Cambridge: Harvard University Press, 1985).
4. Charles R. Wise, "The Changing Doctrine of Regulatory Taking and the Executive Branch," *Administrative Law Review* 44 (1994): 403–23.
5. Jack L. Walker, "The Origins and Maintenance of Interest Groups in America," *American Political Science Review* 77: 390–406.
6. Charles R. Wise and Kirk Emerson, "Regulatory Takings: The Emerging Doctrine and Its Implications for Public Administration," *Administration & Society* 26 (1994): 305–36.
7. Robin E. Folsom, "Executive Order 12,360: A President's Manipulation of the Fifth Amendment's Just Compensation Clause to Achieve Control over

Executive Agency Regulatory Decisionmaking," *Boston College Environmental Affairs Law Review* 20 (1993): 637.

8. Kirk Emerson and Charles R. Wise, "Statutory Approaches to Regulatory Takings: State Property Rights Legislation Issues and Implications for Public Administration," paper presented at the American Political Science Association Conference in Chicago (31 August 1995).

9. Christopher Boerner and Jennifer C. Kallery, "Restructuring Environmental Big Business," Occasional Paper 145 (St. Louis: Center for the Study of American Business, Washington University, 1994).

10. David B. Truman, *The Governmental Process*, 2d ed. (New York: Knopf, 1971).

11. Karen O'Connor and Lee Epstein, *Public Interest Group Law Groups: Institutional Profiles* (New York: Greenwood Press, 1989).

12. Celia Campbell-Mohn, Barry Breen, and J. William Futrell, *Environmental Law: From Resources to Recovery* (St. Paul: West Publishing Co., 1993), 5.

13. Ronald Inglehart, *Cultural Shift in Advanced Industrial Society* (Princeton: Princeton University Press, 1990); Lester W. Milbraith, *Environmentalists: Vanguard for a New Society* (Albany: SUNY Press, 1984).

14. Richard J. Ellis, *American Political Cultures* (New York: Oxford University Press, 1993).

15. James A. Stimson, *Public Opinion in America: Moods, Cycles, and Swings* (Boulder: Westview Press, 1991).

16. Dennis J. Coyle, *Property Rights and the Constitution Shaping Society through Land Use Regulation* (Albany: SUNY Press, 1993), 6.

17. Mark L. Pollot, *Grand Theft and Petit Larceny* (San Francisco: Pacific Research Institute for Public Policy, 1993).

18. The Pacific Legal Foundation (PLF), for example, has filed amicus briefs for virtually every takings case that has reached the Supreme Court since 1981, and successfully brought the Nollan appeal before the Court. It should be noted that on the other side, environmental organizations as well as other national professional and public interest associations also file supportive briefs, for example, American Planning Association and the National Trust for Historic Preservation.

19. For particularly insightful critiques of the Lucas decision, see the special issue published by the *Stanford Law Review* (vol. 45, May 1993) with articles by Richard Epstein, Joseph Sax, Richard Lazarus and William Fisher. As another example, a three-day symposium, "Regulatory Takings and Resources: What Are the Constitutional Limits," was sponsored in summer 1994 by the Natural Resources Law Center and the Byron R. White Center for American Constitutional Study, University of Colorado School of Law.

20. The House debate on March 2–3 over H.R. 925 may be the first nationally televised public exchange on these and other property rights concerns. The fall 1994 referendum in Arizona on Proposition 300 provided a forum for state deliberation, but the equity issue was not highlighted as such.

21. The *Land Rights Letter* in the east and the National Inholders Association (now named the American Land Rights Association) have been the most prom-

inent national networks for inholders and other property owners faced with un-
wanted federal government action.

22. Alliance for American, *Information Sheet*. P.O. Box 449, Caroga Lake,
N.Y. 12032 (1994).

23. William Perry Pendley, *It Takes a Hero* (Bellevue: The Free Enterprise
Press, 1994).

24. Tom Kenworthy, "Dueling with the Forest Service," *Washington National
Weekly Edition* (27 February–5 March 1995), 31.

25. See Terry L. Anderson and Donald R. Leal, *Free Market Environmentalism* (San Francisco: Pacific Institute for Public Policy Research, 1991), and John
Baden and Richard Stroup, *Natural Resources: Bureaucratic Myths and Environmental Management* (San Francisco: Pacific Institute for Public Policy Research,
1983).

26. A frequently cited example is of the Riverside, California, fires in 1993
where the property owners who defied the prohibition against disking their fields
to protect an endangered gnatcatcher saved their homes and any remaining habitat
by building firebreaks. In the Hill Country in Texas, potential restrictions on
treecutting to save the golden-cheeked warbler and the black-capped vireo nesting
habitat have led some property owners (including Ross Perot it is claimed) to
clearcut trees prematurely. As Richard Stroup has explained, the ESA has created
a "Shoot, shovel, and shutup" response on the part of potentially affected property
owners.

27. Over 25 percent of the land in twelve western states is owned by the federal
government. In five of the states (Alaska, California, Idaho, Nevada, and Utah)
federally owned land comprises over 60 percent of the states' acreage.

28. See Lyton K. Caldwell and Kristin Shrader-Frechette, *Policy for Land,
Law, and Ethics* (Lanham, Md.: Rowman & Littlefield, 1993).

29. Mountain States Legal Foundation, "Michigan Property Rights on Appeal,"
The Litigator, winter 1995, 2.

30. See Mark Pollot, *Grand Theft and Petit Larceny* (San Francisco: Pacific
Research Institute for Public Polity, 1993); Roger Clegg, Michael DeBow, Jerry
Ellig and Nancie G. Marzulla, *Regulatory Takings: Restoring Private Property
Rights* (Washington, D.C.: National Legal Center for the Public Interest); Hertha
L. Lund, *Property Rights Legislation in the States: A Review* (Bozeman: Political
Economy Research Center [PERC] 1994); Bruce Yandle, "Regulatory Takings,
Farmers, Ranchers and the Fifth Amendment" (Clemson: Center for Policy Stud-
ies Property Rights Project, 1994); and Paul Heyne, "Economics, Ethics and Ecol-
ogy," in *Taking the Environment Seriously*, edited by Roger E. Meiners and Bruce
Yandle (Lanham, Md.: Rowman & Littlefield, 1993), 25–50.

31. Richard A. Epstein, *Takings, Private Property, and the Power of Eminent
Domain* (Cambridge: Harvard University Press, 1985).

32. Bruce Yandle, "Property Rights, Bootleggers, Baptists, and the Spotted
Owls" (Presentation to the South Carolina Agricultural Council, Cayce: 23 April
1993), 11.

33. Chief Justice Rehnquist opined in the Tigard ruling, "We see no reason
why the Takings Clause of the Fifth Amendment, as much a part of the Bill of

Rights as the First Amendment or the Fourth Amendment, should be relegated to the status of a poor relation."

34.   Coyle, *Property Rights and the Constitution Shaping Society through Land Use Regulation*, 13.

35.   Ibid; see also Stanley Brubaker, "Up (Sort of) from Footnote Four: In the Matter of Property Rights," *Public Interest Law Review* (1993): 97–126.

36.   Robert Nozick, *Anarchy, State, and Utopia* (New York: Basic Books, 1974).

37.   Cass R. Sunstein, *After the Rights Revolution: Reconceiving the Regulatory State* (Cambridge: Harvard University Press, 1990).

38.   "Welfare" has been deleted from the recently defeated Arizona statute. For example, "State agencies whose governmental actions are specifically to protect public health and safety are ordinarily given broader latitude by courts before their actions are considered takings. However the mere assertion of a public health and safety purpose is insufficient to avoid a taking." They must, it goes on, constitute real and substantial threats to public health and safety; significantly advance but be no greater than necessary to achieve the public health and safety purpose, etc. Not only is welfare not included here, but public health and safety actions are expressly limited. From Title 37. Arizona Revised Statutes, Article 2.1, Section 37-221(b)(4).

39.   See: *Village of Euclid v. Ambler Realty*, 272 U.S. 365 (1926).

40.   See: *Penn Central Transportation v. New York City*, 438 U.S. 104 (1978), and *Agnis v. City of Tiburon*, 447 U.S. 255 (1980).

10

The Logic of Competing Information Campaigns: Conflict over Old Growth and the Spotted Owl

Jonathan I. Lange

As "the environment" has emerged as a predominant issue of the American scene, environmental advocacy and counteradvocacy have become a central political drama. Nuclear accidents and waste disposal, air and water degradation, chemical and oil spills, ozone depletion and the greenhouse effect, species displacement and vanishing wilderness are only a small sample of the environmental concerns currently played out by assorted publics, interest groups, government agencies, and representatives in the theaters of American media, courts, and policy-making bodies.

Natural-resource utilization is at center stage within the environmental drama; indeed, some scholars have argued that the perception of scarce resources is an essential—and therefore necessary—condition of any conflict.[1] Since the economic health of so many communities depends on what are now dwindling natural resources, environmentalists, "counterenvironmentalists," and government agencies continually clash over resource utilization, allocation, replacement, and depletion.[2] Resource conflict has become a quintessential feature of the American political drama.

Discursive practices inherently determine the "social construction" of any environmental conflict. What humans say about the issues—

This chapter is an abridged version of an article previously published in *Communications Monographs* 60, no. 3 (1993): 239–57 under the same title. Reprinted here by permission of author and publisher.

even how the issues are defined—will determine interpretation, treatment, and outcome of the public debate. This study explores the communicative character of what is arguably the nation's most wrenching natural-resource conflict of the late twentieth century: the dispute over old growth forests and the spotted owl.

As with other disputes, both environmentalists and industry representatives choose strategies that are dependent on and responsive to their antagonist. This analysis reveals how disputants' *interactive logic*—a mirroring and matching of each other's strategies—is achieved with little to no direct communication between parties. They learn of each other's tactics primarily through the mass media as they pursue duplicate or antithetical rhetorical strategies with various audiences. In studying this conflict, I followed standard qualitative data gathering techniques and field work recommendations.[3] My analysis is based on four years of field research, including extensive interviews on both sides of the debate, participation in planning meetings and conferences, and written material from both environmental and timber industry groups. This chapter offers five categories, which are not meant to be exhaustive or discrete. Evidence is conveyed primarily by illustration and example. Those quotes not referenced are taken from interviews and *in situ* fieldwork or are conclusions drawn from daily newspaper accounts.

Background

Old growth timber, located in what environmentalists call "ancient forests," has been the subject of increasing controversy for at least two decades, ever since environmental groups began efforts to reduce or prevent industry clearcutting. Clearcutting—as opposed to select cutting—is the most economically efficient method of logging timber because every tree is cut. However, a desolate and unsightly landscape of tree stumps and cleared brush is left behind; what was once a magnificent section of forest—a complex habitat for dozens of plant and animal species—is transformed into a barren spectacle. This transformation notwithstanding, the timber industry would have to lay off thousands of workers were it unable to continue clearcutting trees; communities and regions whose economy and social fabric rely on timber would suffer dramatically. Those who oppose clearcutting mourn the loss of biological diversity, animal habitat, scenic beauty, spiritual retreat, and recreation areas previously available in the ancient forests. Reforestation efforts—only sometimes successful—produce rows of small, single-species trees in monocultured "tree farms," and can not replace the majestic, environmentally precious, and biologically diverse virgin forest. Though federal foresters offer some hope with "the new forestry," in which logging and reforestation processes are modified and improved, all agree that current forestry methods can not truly reproduce old growth. Old growth certainly cannot be replaced within a single lifetime; the trees are generally between two hundred and one thousand years old.

The vast majority of this country's remaining old growth (approximately 10 percent of the original) is on public lands, "owned" by the citizenry and "managed" by the United States Forest Service (USFS) and the Bureau of Land Management (BLM), divisions of the U.S. Departments of Agriculture and Interior, respectively. Both are charged by law to regulate the multiple use of the forests. The controversial policy of multiple use is designed to protect and preserve watersheds, wildlife, and wilderness, while still allowing for recreation, grazing, mining, and timber sales. Under the multiple-use policy, timber is auctioned by the government to private timber companies that "harvest" logs for milling into lumber.

Over the past two decades, environmental groups have gone to the courts as part of their attempt to protect old-growth ecosystems from alleged abuse by government agency or industry. Lawsuits and appeals were initiated to require correction of ill-prepared environmental assessments and environmental impact statements, to prevent "overcutting" a specified acreage, to stop logging in areas unsuitable for reforestation, and to deter cutting where resultant erosion would destroy fish habitat and endanger watersheds. Until recently, however, environmental groups usually lost in court or had suits prohibited by federal legislative riders.

The spotted owl controversy has complicated matters considerably. In 1973, Congress passed the Endangered Species Act, one of this nation's most stringent environmental protection laws. The act required that any threatened or endangered species be listed and that recovery plans be developed and implemented by all federal land-managing agencies. The legislative history of the Ninety-third Congress states that the purpose of the act was "to provide a means whereby the *ecosystems* [author's emphasis] upon which endangered and threatened species depend may be conserved, protected, or restored."[4] A second critical law is the National Forest Management Act (NFMA) of 1976, the same law that mandated multiple use. This legislation further required the USFS to protect and maintain the diversity of species on its lands and to identify "indicator species" *representing* the health of the biotic community (since the agency could not monitor all species within a single ecosystem). For biological reasons, including its role in the food chain, the USFS chose the Northern spotted owl as one of the indicator species of old growth forests. Environmental groups therefore liken the owl to the canary in the coal mine; if the owl is threatened or endangered, so too are the old growth ecosystems.

Although timber advocates dispute the findings, studies by government agencies confirm that the owl's survival is dependent upon the health of old growth forests; that is, the owl would perish without old growth. Since the drastically dwindling number of owls was well documented, environmentalists in 1986 sought its listing as a threatened or endangered species to protect both the owl and the ecosystems upon which it depends, old growth forests. In 1987, the U.S. Fish and Wildlife Service (USF&WS) denied the request. Twenty-six environmental groups sued, and the courts ordered the USF&WS to reconsider the owl's listing. In April of 1989, the agency proposed to list the owl as threatened. However, official listing could occur only after a period of further study, public comment, and biological assessment.

This seemed a great victory for environmental groups. It meant that at least some proposed auctions of timber from USFS and BLM old growth lands would now be enjoined by law since the lands constituted the habitat of a potentially threatened indicator species. However, the entire timber industry now brought its full might to bear on the controversy. Central to the entire economy of the affected geographical regions, and requiring a "steady and predictable" supply of old growth logs to survive without massive personnel layoffs and loss, the industry and its members worked steadily to stave off economic damage to the industry and social turmoil in the timber-dependent regions.

The period between the proposal to list the owl and actual listing was thus characterized by intense debate, fervent lobbying, and congressional deal-making. Both the industry and environmental groups waged extensive and intense information campaigns to gain the support of various groups and federal agencies, including the general public. The campaigns were marked by media depiction of demonstrations, counterdemonstrations, threats, and passionate rhetoric from both sides. Though occasional formal and informal events allowed for face-to-face interaction, negotiation, and attempted mediation, members of the industry and environmental groups rarely met in collaborative circumstances. The owl was officially listed in June of 1990.

A bevy of remaining issues sustains the competing information campaigns. Chief among them is how much and which old growth acreage should be set aside as owl habitat. Bitter controversy surrounds the agencies' long-term forest management plans. Congress's continuous debates on reauthorization of the Endangered Species Act maintains attention on old growth (as well as dozens of other natural-resource conflicts). When making timber policy, the federal agencies and Congress will diligently attempt to assess and include the general public's position. As the sympathetic chair of an influential congressional committee told one environmentalist, "I agree with you, but you have to get me more letters." All of these occurrences indicate continuation of intense political communication designed to mobilize public support.

Mirroring and Matching

Analysis of the information campaigns as waged through 1992 shows how both timber and environmental groups used the same five major and overlapping strategies as they mirrored or matched each other's communicative behavior: (1) frame and reframe; (2) select high or select low; (3) vilify and ennoble; (4) simplify and dramatize; and (5) lobby and litigate. The term "matching" indicates communicative behavior that copies or repeats the other party's strategy; "mirroring" describes communicative behavior that duplicates the other party's tactic by presenting antithetical, polar, or "mirror image" information. On occasion, parties engage in both processes. The five categories provide an understanding of the primary features of the information campaigns. The first strategy discussed, framing and reframing, shows how disputants attempt to contextualize the entire dispute.

Frame and Reframe

Across a wide variety of communicative forums—including newsletters, financial appeals, propaganda materials, press releases, interviews granted reporters, newspaper advertisements, television commercials, legal briefs filed, letters to congresspersons, and presentations to Rotary, Kiwanis, and like groups—each side frames issues in accordance with its particular ends.[5] Facts, explanations, and interpretations are contextualized to discursively construct a reality favorable to one's rhetorical goals. Frames are then predictably followed by a mirroring or matching strategy in which reality is *reframed*, by the other group, with an antithetical or oppositional context. Where it begins is, of course, a matter of arbitrary punctuation.

Representative examples will illuminate this category. The first involves mirroring and matching moves that focus on economic and employment issues such as lumber mill shutdowns, the resulting loss of jobs, and retraining displaced forest products workers for alternate vocations. In media cited above, environmental groups acknowledge the pain of transition, yet suggest it is inescapable: old growth is finite; we will eventually run out; it is now time to acknowledge the inevitable reduction of timber-related work. They further argue that the problem of timber supply stems primarily from poor planning, decades of overcutting, and increasingly sophisticated logging and milling technology. They note that increasing timber harvests have been accompanied by a decreasing workforce throughout the 1970s and early 1980s—all prior to any effects of the spotted owl controversy; the bird is "only a scapegoat." They attempt to create a context in which the timber industry is framed as destroyer of the forest, out to get the last bit of old growth. They argue that the trend in workforce reduction will continue inevitably as an effect of technology even apart from timber supplies. One environmentalist commented, "I think the jobs issue is tragically irrelevant. . . . The jobs aren't going to be around that much longer anyway. . . . We won't have these jobs for our children, so let's slow (logging) down now."[6] Environmentalists point out that if the industry really cared about its workers, owners would be helping with retraining efforts instead of fighting the inevitable.

An antithetical frame—or reframe—is offered by timber industry supporters at every opportunity. They attempt to make jobs the primary issue. Overcutting is sometimes acknowledged, yet they portray trees as "a renewable resource." The owl is to blame for supply problems and mill closures. They suggest that advanced technology is "only a scapegoat" in explaining jobs lost. As one timber spokesperson argued: "Automation never closed a mill. Lack of logs will close mills."[7] Timber workers accuse environmentalists of trying to ruin their communities. They scoff at suggestions that they give up a way of life that their fathers and grandfathers enjoyed. Typical of this point, one spokesperson noted: "Working in the woods or a mill, trucking logs, well, that can hardly be replaced with a minimum wage tourism job. And those computer jobs everyone talks about—do I look like I'm cut out for a desk job? It's easy for them to say, 'Stop logging,' but I've got a family to feed." The industry works diligently to press the jobs issue in nearly every discussion while environmentalists attempt to reframe it with equal fervor.

Three additional and representative examples further illustrate the framing and reframing process. In these cases, industry and environmentalist representatives match each other's moves with mirrored content as they react to news reports. (For brevity's sake, frames and reframes are indicated but not fully detailed.) In 1990, a press-announced "new environmental agenda" by the U.S. Forest Service was followed with: "Environmentalists are reacting with skepticism, calling the new agenda a 'public relations ploy,' and a timber industry association says the logging restrictions are too tough."[8] When a Bush administration task force announced a likely reduction in 1991 timber sales, the executive director of the American Forest Resource Alliance called the plan "unbalanced" in favor of "environmental special interests"; the vice president of the Wilderness Society was moved to say the proposal was "a dismal display of politics over science and an attempt to undermine the Endangered Species Act and other federal laws that protect the environment."[9] Immediately following the 1992 Forest Service announcement of its plan to protect the owl (later rejected as inadequate by a federal judge), a timber representative offered this to the press: "We are extremely disappointed that the Forest Service has placed the spotted owl before tens of thousands of Pacific Northwest families" while an environmentalist spokesperson said, "This is completely inadequate. . . . This clearly can't stand on the grounds of being a credible plan for the owl."[10] These frames or reframes represent hundreds of similar reactions, as offered to the press or other media. They are further advanced and bolstered as both groups employ a second strategy, selecting high or low.

Select High/Select Low

In the contest to win public opinion, each side selects studies, "expert opinions," and interpretations of each that offer numbers that promote its point of view. Hardly a new process on the American political scene, sides select high or low numbers in accordance with their rhetorical ends while simultaneously rejecting opposing figures. For example, timber industry spokespersons cite sources that herald catastrophic job losses. Environmentalists, on the other hand, present information that minimizes job losses. A deputy undersecretary in the Department of the Interior, acting as coordinator of a government task force developing plans for the owl's recovery, complained: "We've had studies [reported to us] over the past year with job losses ranging from 14,000 to 102,000 jobs."[11] The range is actually wider: "The Wilderness Society has portrayed the risk at only 12,000 jobs. At the other extreme, the industry-sponsored American Forest Resource Alliance placed the risk at more than 147,000 jobs."[12]

A second illustration involves the very definition of old growth forest itself—and therefore, the amount actually remaining. There are a number of definitions of old growth, ranging from the broadest (mature timber not yet cut) to the most narrow (an area with trees two hundred years or older, thirty-two inches or larger in diameter, with specific types and numbers of trees, tree canopies, and downed trees per acre). Environmentalists and industry groups offer different definitions depending on the purpose at hand. For example, if environmentalists want to demonstrate how little old growth is left, they use the narrow, more restrictive definition. If, however, they want to argue that large sections of old growth forest and spotted owl habitat must be off limits to logging, they employ a broad, inclusive one. Of course, the reverse scenario is true for the industry.

Similar processes of selecting high or low occur with nearly every other aspect of the controversy. Citing different sources, groups offer different counts on the number of owls remaining, the acreage of national lands already protected from logging, the amount of Pacific Northwest lumber needed by the nation, the success rate of tree-replanting efforts, and other numerical "facts" that can be differentially found or interpreted. Each group points to the other's "misuse" of these facts as evidence of its villainous nature.

Vilify/Ennoble

In her case study of pro-life and pro-choice rhetoric, Vanderford outlines four forms and functions of vilification as a rhetorical strategy.[13] They include formulating specific adversarial opponents, casting them in an exclusively negative light, attributing diabolical motives to them, and magnifying their power. All four forms and functions are present in this environmental conflict. The counterpoint to vilification is also present, as environmentalists and timber advocates ennoble their own cause and motives. Taken together, this creates a mirror effect in which each side castigates the other while proclaiming its own virtue.[14]

In an industry with a volatile union-management history, the current internal solidarity results in part from management's success in framing environmentalists as devil figures, particularly radical environmental groups like Earth First! The majority of workers and owner-operators now view environmentalists as "radical preservationists" who want to "lock up the forests" preventing their "wise use." These "so-called environmentalists" are actually "eco-terrorists" using "raw generalizations, bum science, and half truths" in creating conditions that will "be the death of many [Pacific Northwest] communities." Workers and owners both depict national environmental groups as wealthy, highly organized, outside "obstructionists" who should leave decisions about Pacific Northwest resources to those who live there; "enviros" are "East Coast carpetbaggers trying to tell us our economy is going to have to transition." One informant, an owner of a struggling lumber company, told me that, "we can solve this conflict, but only if we keep it local."

Many in the environmental community believe that the intent of the owners in particular is, as one informant said, to "take every last possible stick while the taking is still good." Pacific Northwesterners are being duped by an industry of "timber beasts" who, like the coal barons of Appalachia, will ruin the landscape and long-term economy after depleting the natural resources. The view of environmentalists is perhaps best represented in a local newspaper opinion piece that said, "The timber side is headed by a few giant corporations with almost unlimited resources, highly unified and closely associated with other large companies, including perhaps newspapers and television stations. The environmental side consists of a loose coalition of volunteer labor, not very unified or very well organized."[15] An environmental informant told me that their best hope was to nationalize the issue: "People in the East think national forests are like national parks and will remain untouched. They need to know that these forests are being destroyed. Then they need to write letters and complain. This is the only way we can fight an insensitive multi-million dollar industry."

As each group vilifies the other, so too does each side ennoble itself. Both sides claim they have "compromised"; both hold that "science" favors their position; both imply "morality" and "the common good" as their guiding forces.[16] Environmental groups point out that since only 10 percent of the nation's original old growth forests are left, to compromise on that paltry amount is to employ an unfair starting point. That is, a true compromise is impossible, since 90 percent has already gone to timber interests.[17] Timber groups argue that millions of acres of potentially harvestable timber are now "locked up"; it is they who have compromised, now to the point of economic ruin. Similarly, when a federally appointed panel of scientists advised a significant reduction in timber harvests in order to save the owl from extinction, environmental supporters referred to the group as "our very best scientists" and "the bluest of blue ribbon committees." Timber groups labeled the report "bum science" maintaining that the public is not learning the true "science of forestry." Finally, inferences about moral ends and the common good are made by both groups. The industry claims to be saving jobs as well as a way of life that spans generations. One industry leader marched in a pro-timber demonstration to call attention to the nation's growing number of homeless, connecting the harvesting of timber and milling of lumber to the need for additional housing. Environmentalists maintain they are preserving nature for our children's children. One environmentalist told me that, "history will eventually show that we were the heroes of our generation." Another says, "Environmentalists make great ancestors." Such images and slogans are characteristic of the third category: simplify and dramatize.

Simplify and Dramatize

A third mirroring and matching dynamic entails the simplification and dramatization of an issue of staggering complexity. Sproule's comparison of "old" and "new" rhetorics is useful here. He describes self-contained slogans as the "persuasive staples" of the new rhetoric—as compared to the enthymematic operation of the old. He further postulates images in new rhetorics as replacing the world of ideas common to the older suasion.[18] Zarefsky argues that American audiences find complexity "unbearable" and that we "simplify what can not be avoided."[19] Sproule's and Zarefsky's arguments are borne out in the two information campaigns as simple, easily absorbed and dramatic images and slogans are substituted for analysis or explanation of phenomenally complicated issues.

Other than the images and slogans, there is little simple about the spotted owl conflict. Interrelated and inordinately complicated biological, economic, social, and political issues defy assimilation. John Turner, the head of the USFWS, said the spotted owl is "one of the most complex resource issues in this nation's history." This complexity makes it difficult to navigate between the conflicting claims of both sides, to differentiate between "thousands" or "millions" or "billions" of revenue dollars lost or generated, directly or indirectly affected jobs, board feet milled or not milled, board feet sold in the United States or exported, profitable or below-cost timber sales, current or lost wilderness acres, private versus public acres, reforested or spotted owl habitat acres or habitat conservation acres, and so on. The jargon and endless acronyms further confuse.

Yet disputants work to simplify the issues so that they may be dramatized for mass consumption. The timber industry has at least partially succeeded in creating an "owls versus people" scenario in the media. *Time* magazine ran an eight-page cover story entitled, "Owl vs. Man," with photographs inside of an owl opposite a logger.[20] The *Wall Street Journal* wrote that the issue "sets about 1500 pairs of spotted owls against the people who make their living cutting down trees in the Pacific Northwest."[21] Timber supporters and Senators Hatfield, Packwood, and Gorton are repeatedly quoted on the forced choice between people and owls.

The owls-versus-people sloganeering is only one example of simplification and dramatization. As the two groups struggle for the most novel, media-attention-getting device, attempting "photogenic discord," they intentionally create additional images and slogans for mass audience consumption.[22] Environmentalists drew television and photojournalist attention by camping on platforms placed high in old growth trees; others demonstrated at USFS offices, wearing owl costumes while carrying signs bemoaning loss of habitat. The industry held "counter-demonstrations," during which thousands of loggers and log truckers rallied in Northwest cities, driving through lumber towns with industry-symbol yellow ribbons attached to limbs, hard hats, and belts. They wore tee shirts and displayed bumper stickers offering phrases like "I Like Spotted Owls . . . Fried," and "Save a Logger, Eat an Owl." Environmental groups countered with slogans like "Owls Don't Destroy Forests, People Do," and "Save an Owl, Educate a Logger." "This Family Supported by Timber Dollars" was later mirrored with "This Family Supported by Intact Ecosystems." As environmentalists promoted the phrase "ancient forests," timber groups warned of turning "mill towns into ghost towns." Environmentalists renamed an industry-approved owl "preservation plan" to the owl "extinction plan." When a congressperson from Indiana sponsored a bill (which eventually failed) to end all logging of old growth, an Oregon congressperson proposed turning one-and-one-third million acres of rural Indiana into a national park.[23] Perhaps the ultimate matching behavior in the simplification and dramatization category was the petition actually submitted by the Washington Contract Loggers Association to the Department of the Interior seeking declaration of loggers as a threatened species.

Members of both groups acknowledge the "low-level" nature of these public appeals. When I discussed this simplification and dramatization analysis with one informant—he could have been from either side—he said, "The process of raising public awareness is not centered on trying to educate the public about the details of the problem as much as it is on making the public aware that there is an injustice which needs their attention." Both groups hold workshops on "dealing with the media" in which participants practice delivering "sound bites."

Departure from the simplification/dramatization strategy occurs when audiences are perceived as better informed; in these cases there is often detailed, rich, and more straightforward discussion. One such context includes antagonists' internal communication forums, such as meetings, conferences, newsletters, and interpersonal encounters, where simple and dramatic communication is accompanied by more complex, straightforward discussion. As Pearce notes, "Discourse *within* various groups in society is usually richer than that *between* groups."[24] But those media are less a part of the two information campaigns and less a part of an interactive logic than two additional sites. It is in the litigation and lobbying arenas where more sophisticated audiences evoke more sophisticated rhetoric.

Lobby and Litigate

Both groups believe that the most serious theaters for the conflict are in the courts and in Washington, D.C. Both sides lobby extensively and file lawsuits and appeals that ask the courts to change unfavorable agency decisions (i.e., USFS, BLM, USF&WS) or lower court decisions. While lobbying and litigation processes reflect many of the rhetorical strategies discussed above, they additionally constitute what both groups view as the ultimate culmination of the information campaigns. Each process has a distinct set of attributes and rules.

Both groups have office space in the nation's capital, replete with full-time staff, media consultants, and the latest office technology. The "Western Ancient Forest Campaign" is "networked" with the major national environmental groups ("The Big Ten") and many "local" or "grassroots" environmental groups in the Northwest. The American Forest Council, part of the "wise-use movement," coordinates with oil, coal, and other natural resource extraction industries as well as local grassroots timber groups. In both camps, staffers do their own lobbying and support lobbying efforts from visiting Northwesterners. At both offices, pamphlets provide information on "face to face lobbying" such as who to visit, how to dress, and what to talk about. Materials to take home instruct supporters on how to hold demonstrations, conduct "outreach" and phone campaigns, what to say when making phone calls, and how to write the most effective letters to congresspersons and local newspaper editors.

While litigation used to be the sole province of environmental groups, recently, lumber companies and timber associations have matched the strategy, filing appeals that challenge timber inventory accuracy, clarity of guidelines and even use of indicator species to test the health of a forest. "We've gone to school on the way environmentalists use the courts," said an executive director of a timber association. Environmental groups continue filing appeals of agency plans; their appeals are based on violation of the Endangered Species Act, the National Environmental Policy Act or the National Forest Management Act. And as environmentalists file lawsuits against private companies for alleged illegal logging, timber companies sue environmentalists for economic loss sustained during "downtime" caused by demonstrations at logging sites. Both sides carefully choose from dozens of potential issues for suit or appeal, as they are costly and time-consuming processes. Gain and loss are measured not only by the outcome of the issues in question, but by favorable or unfavorable publicity as well, showing the connection between these processes and the overall information campaign for public opinion.

Interpreting the Environmental Discourse

This study reveals at least two important principles about contemporary environmental—and in a larger context, political—discourse. First, though the antagonists seldom address each other, their communicative behavior has its own peculiar logic, a logic of duplication and antithesis, of matching and mirroring. And while this synchronous spiral of noninteraction is composed of messages directed not to each other, but to the public and members of government and government agencies, communicative behavior is still based on the previous or predicted moves of the other group. Parties learn of each other's communication tactics through indirect means, usually the mass media, supporting the contention that media are "relied upon increasingly to let members of concerned groups know what . . . the opposition is doing and thinking."[25] At least a large part of what the opposition is doing and thinking in this case is plotting how to respond to the other group. The interactive, interdependent, and almost symbiotic nature of the disputants was revealed as I listened to their internal discussions that so often focused on responding to, anticipating, or copying the other's moves. A recent meeting of one environmental group was held to determine whether or not they should "counteract the effects of" an industry-produced television commercial with one of their own in order to "set the record straight." Of course, the industry engaged in similar kinds of deliberations, as when they so often discussed, for example, how to respond to environmentalist lawsuits and appeals.

The second precept suggests a new framework for analyzing contemporary political communication. While dozens of writers bemoan the character of this discourse, and while many insightful explanations (and remedies) are offered, there is little mention of how competing political information campaigns interact. The current analysis implies that one reason it is so difficult for campaigns to rise above the current debased state of affairs is that their cocreated systems preclude it.

In describing interpersonal interactions, Pearce notes how logics of interaction have assorted "senses of obligation." Parties are compelled to respond to each other in ways determined by the system they constitute. The system is the best explanation for itself. A specific communicative act by one interlocutor practically "forces" a predetermined response by the other as parties become locked into a systemic, self-reinforcing, patterned, and repetitive practice.[26] Such a dynamic is clearly present here. For example, if one group vilifies the other, it is incumbent on the other to respond, refuting the charge and/or providing one's own. When timber representatives frame the major issue as job loss, environmentalists must attempt to reframe it; otherwise, a fully unfavorable context, from their point of view, would prevail. If one party neglected to lobby or litigate, the other party's practices in these areas would transform the entire conflict in their favor. The consequences of not mirroring or matching one's antagonist are untenable. Thus, the sorry state of political communication as reflected in information campaigns may partially derive from a cocreated sense of constraint, necessity, and logical force. Political communication campaigns may result more from a logic cocreated with the competing candidate or group than the audience or other exigencies. Until parties who create American political information campaigns break out of this inherently flawed system—from which they retreat, paradoxically, only at their peril—it seems our political discourse is doomed to remain impoverished and dysfunctional.

Notes

1. See, for example, L. A. Coser, *Continuities in the Study of Social Conflict* (New York: The Free Press, 1967); Joyce Hocker and William Wilmot, *Interpersonal Conflict* (Dubuque, Ia.: Wm. C. Brown, 1991).

2. I take the term "counterenvironmental" from the work of Richard P. Gale, "Social Movements and the State: The Environmental Movement, Countermovement and Government Agencies," *Sociological Perspectives* 29 (1986): 202–40. It should be noted here that neither "environmentalist" nor "timber industry" is a monolithic entity.

3. These draw from a number of authors, especially John Lofland and Lyn Lofland, *Analyzing Social Settings: A Guide to Qualitative Observation and Analysis* 3d ed. (Belmont, Calif.: Wadsworth, 1995) and W. Barnett Pearce, *Communication and the Human Condition* (Carbondale: Southern Illinois University Press, 1989).

4. Cited in Julie Norman, "USFS/BLM Ignore Substitutes for Old Growth and Trigger Political Bail-Out That Threatens U.S. Constitution," *Headwaters* (1989): 12–13.

5. For foundational discussions on the "framing" of issues, see Erving Goffman, *Frame Analysis: An Essay on the Organization of Experience* (Cambridge, Mass.: Harvard University Press, 1974) and Charles T. Salmon, ed., *Information Campaigns: Balancing Social Values and Social Change* (Newbury Park, Calif.: Sage, 1989), 24–28.

6. Cited in Mark Freeman, "F & W Owl Ruling Upsets Both Sides," *The Mail Tribune*, 10 January 1992, 1A.

7. Cited in Alex C. Zacoreli, "Timber Workers Frustrated," *The Ashland Daily Tidings*, 12 September 1991, 1.

8. Ken Grubb, "Feds Restrict Logging in California Forests," *The Ashland Daily Tidings*, 9 February 1990, 3.

9. See "Owl Backers See Plan as Basis for Talks," *The Mail Tribune*, 22 November 1990, 1A; see also Andrew Lamar, "White House Timber Plan Takes Flak," *The Ashland Daily Tidings*, 22 September 1990, 1.

10. "Forest Service Adopts Thomas Plan," *The Ashland Daily Tidings*, 5 March 1992, 1.

11. Cited in Kathy Durbin, "Owl Team Allotted 9 Months for Report," *The Oregonian*, 6 March 1991, D2.

12. Cited in Jim Kadera, "Latest Guess: Owl Will Cost 34,000 Jobs." *The Oregonian* 14 March 1992, E-5.

13. Marsha L. Vanderford, "Vilification and Social Movements: A Case Study of Pro-Life and Pro-Choice Rhetoric," *Quarterly Journal of Speech* 75 (1989): 166–82.

14. See W. Barnett Pearce, Stephen W. Littlejohn, and A. Alexander, "The New Christian Right and the Humanist Response: Reciprocated Diatribe," *Communication Quarterly* 35 (1987): 171–92.

15. Harry Cook, "Timber Managers Put Industry First If Uses Conflict," *The Ashland Daily Tidings*, 20 October 1989, 15.

16. See Sally A. Freeman, Stephen W. Littlejohn, and W. Barnett Pearce, "Communication and Moral Conflict," *Western Journal of Communication* 56 (1992): 311–29.

17. For a full account of this argument, see Jonathan I. Lange, "Refusal to Compromise: The Case of Earth First!," *Western Journal of Speech Communication* 54 (1990): 473–94.

18. J. Michael Sproule, "The New Managerial Rhetoric and the Old Criticism," *Quarterly Journal of Speech* 74 (1988): 468–86.

19. David Zarefsky, "Spectator Politics and the Revival of Public Argument," *Communication Monographs* 59 (1992): 410–14.

20. Thomas Gup, "Owl Vs. Man," *Time*, 25 June 1990, 55–56.

21. Cited in "Other Editors Say: People Suffer to Help Protect Spotted Owls," *The Mail Tribune*, 11 April 1990, 15A.

22. Glasgow University Media Group, *Bad News* (London: Routledge and Kegan Paul, 1976).

23. Bill Manny, "Rep. Smith Vows to Turn Tables on Indiana Old-Growth Advocate," *The Mail Tribune*, 4 April 1990, 1.

24. Pearce, *Communication*, 43.

25. Clarice N. Olien, Phillip J. Tichenor, and George A. Donohue, "Media Coverage and Social Movements," in *Information Campaigns: Balancing Social Values and Social Change*, edited by Charles T. Salmon (Newbury Park, Calif.: Sage, 1989).

26. Pearce, *Communication*, 40.

11

War of Words

Jon Christensen

> We had fed the heart on fantasies.
> The heart's grown brutal from the fare.
>
> —W. B. Yeats
> "Meditations in Times of Civil War"

"This is a war we're in. We're choosing up sides," thundered Gene Gustin, chairman of the public lands use advisory committee for Elko County, Nevada. Shouts of approval rose from a crowd of 350 people, in cowboy hats and gimme caps, jammed into an old theater in Alturas, California, near the border with Nevada, for a Win Back the West rally.

This was not a group of militiamen bent on overthrowing the U.S. government by armed force. No one was dressed in camouflage. No one carried a weapon that I could see. They had come from surrounding ranches in remote rural northeastern California to hear what Nevada's latest Sagebrush Rebellion—also known as the states' rights or county supremacy movement—was doing to fight federal environmental regulations.

I had come from Carson City, two hundred miles to the south, to report on this grassroots revolt spreading across the western United States and to see how close the movement's fiery rhetoric was to real violence. The rally was in January 1995, three months before the bombing of the Federal Building in Oklahoma City. It was two months before a pipe bomb exploded at a Forest Service office in Carson City, and six months before dynamite blew up a forest ranger's van in the driveway of his home there. But it had been over a year since a satchel of explosives ripped through the ceiling of the Bureau of Land Management headquarters in Reno. And it was already well into what many have taken to calling "the war for the West."

The war metaphor has laid siege to the Western imagination for at least a century, but it has overrun the West in recent years. It seems hardly possible to talk about Western environmental issues without resorting to words of war these days.

The wise use movement, ranchers, miners, and loggers, accuse the Clinton administration and environmentalists of waging "war on the West." And environmentalists have taken up the battle cry, accusing the wise use movement, industry, and Congress of declaring "war on the environment."

My head spins. There is so much talk of war in the West that many people worry whether real war is breaking out in the region. Does violent talk lead to violence? How can it? How can it not? These are questions bandied about in a national debate that can never be resolved. Violent acts are facts. Violent talk is talk. The two often come together in stories, but, thank goodness, less often in reality.

Like many journalists, I have dreamed of being a war correspondent. But I never would have imagined I might get the opportunity so close to home. And I hope the nightmare never comes true.

I confess. I have used the war metaphor too. I have written about range wars and water wars. The metaphor seems to come with the territory, perhaps because warrior mythology is buried deep, not just in western American history, but in our psyches.

However, the more I have covered environmental issues, the more I have found the war metaphor too easy and too distorting. Talk of war masks many of the most interesting changes taking place behind the rhetorical conflicts. These are not wars that we are seeing in the western United States. There are plenty of real wars that we hear about every day, in Bosnia, Chechnya—you can fill in the current hot spot.

I once resolved to try to abandon the war metaphor and to try to find new metaphors, new ways of telling the stories of change in western communities and the environment. But I quickly discovered that no matter how hard I tried to change my usage, the metaphor is here to stay. And it's not just the fault of the media's lazy use of language. I found that people on both sides help create and perpetuate the rhetoric. They are attached to the word wars. The metaphor validates their struggles as warriors.

When I looked up "war" in the dictionary, I found another reason the metaphor is so widespread and tenacious. The word "war" is rooted in the French Norman word "werre," which meant "confusion." Thus war has come to mean any kind of confusion and strife.

The war metaphor is only the most glaring way that debates over environmental issues are polarized by rhetoric from environmental and wise use camps. There are others, sometimes serious, sometimes simply silly.

At a conference of the Society of Environmental Journalists, I once listened to a panel of environmentalists and wise use and property rights advocates use up an hour and a half debating whether the wise use and property rights movements were a "mom and pop phenomena" or "not a mom and pop phenomena." Unfortunately, the wider debate has rarely gone beyond that level. And it has often sunk even lower.

Borrowing an exclamation point from Earth First!, a group calls itself People for the West! The Sierra Club promptly dubs them People for the Worst. Environmentalists counter calls for "wise use" by saying it's "wide abuse."

The Southern Utah Wilderness Alliance, an environmental group, came out with an "interpreter's guide for members confused by the rhetoric of the wise use movement." When wise use advocates say "local people," the guide explained, "they mean the nearest anti-environmentalist" and "environmentalists" are "rich newcomers who don't have to work for a living." When they say "wise use of our natural resources," the guide said, they mean "any extractive use of natural products especially if that extraction makes lots of noise, uses motors or goes moo."

It is probably no coincidence that around the same time, the Blue Ribbon Coalition, a wise use group, came out with a "Green Dictionary" subtitled "What they say ain't what they mean." An "ecosystem," the dictionary said, is "any land that someone wants to develop or utilize for profit or recreation." "Overgrazing" is "any grazing, according to environmental doctrine." And since "enviroz have a superstitious fear of chemicals," the dictionary explained, "hazardous chemicals" include "sodium chloride (table salt), H_2O (water) and Coors."

These examples barely scratch the surface of the rhetorical strategies, many with much more serious implications, that Jonathan Lange dissects in "The Logic of Competing Information Campaigns" (chapter 10). He gives names to such tactics as mirror and match, parallel vilification, frame and reframe, select high/select low, vilify/ennoble, and simplify/dramatize.

I find this dialectical analysis useful for understanding these word wars. However, even though I can analyze this endless spin cycle, it is still troubling to me as a journalist who is writing about communities and the environment in the West today where I live. The most discouraging experiences for me personally have come when I called friends and acquaintances on both sides of the debate and found them dissembling to me, trying to put such simple spin on complex stories. On the other hand, the most rewarding experiences have come when I have found people who are really interested in talking about what is going on, even if it does not spin their way.

I thought I had found a way out of this spin cycle with a story that I wrote on mining reform. I had seen the rhetoric on mining reform go back and forth. Then I got an opportunity through two acquaintances, a gold miner and an environmentalist in Nevada, who let me into their own quiet ongoing dialogue. They were John Livermore, a geologist who discovered the Carlin Trend gold bonanza in Nevada, and Glenn Miller, who was for a long time the chair of the mining committee of the Sierra Club.

I saw that there was a rich discussion going on outside of the environmental movement's rhetoric complaining about the $2.50-an-acre mining patent giveaway, on the one hand, and on the other, industry rhetoric claiming that environmental regulations are shutting down mining in this country.

Livermore, Miller, and I traveled around northern Nevada together to several mines. We talked about the issues and where there might actually be reasonable accommodation between industry and environmental concerns in the very heart of the greatest gold boom in American history. I wrote a story about our journey entitled "Mining reform searching for common ground." My editors compared it to the Israeli-Palestinian peace accord signed that same fall of 1993.

I was gratified to find this rich story that hadn't been covered elsewhere right in my backyard. But I was also frustrated to see the story published in *High Country News*, and then see the issue seem to disappear quietly. I wanted to bring this dialogue out into the public realm and show people in my own community that a civil debate is possible, even in an atmosphere polluted by the polarization of word wars.

So I invited some other environmentalists and miners to participate in a panel discussion and public forum at the University of Nevada at Reno. I was warned that it would be impossible to pull it off, that people would "get western" in the aisles—a quaint regionalism for getting violent.

That didn't happen. But I was nevertheless chastened by the experience. Although I proved that it was possible to hold a civil debate, I also got a sense from the three hundred people who showed up— both from the mining industry and environmental groups—that they preferred the word wars. The kinds of questions they asked, the statements they made, furthered the emotional rhetoric of diametrically opposed camps rather than the search for common ground. I realized then that the word wars weren't coming from the people who were most centrally involved in the industry or in the environmental movement. They were coming from the audience, the public.

I had thought that the experience might provide an example for the community of peaceful, practical discussion. But my experiment in what is now widely called "civic journalism" or "public journalism" foundered on the public. The word wars continued.

The debate over mining reform in Congress mirrors this spin cycle. When Republicans in Congress introduced a bill that would charge a 3 percent net royalty on minerals taken from federal lands, environmentalists called it a "sham" proposal. "The miners get the gold and we get the shaft," said one. On the other hand, an industry spokesman said the bill would end the flight of mining overseas, which is causing $2 billion "hemorrhaging" in our economy.

Thus are the parameters of the debate on mining limited by word wars. Lost in the rhetoric on high are the facts on the ground. The public understands neither how mines are developed on public land in this country, nor why exploration is moving overseas. The perpetual spin cycle stymies change. And Congress remains gridlocked.

When Secretary of the Interior Bruce Babbitt tried to build a consensus on grazing reform, he ran headlong into a similar wall erected both by ranchers and environmentalists. In the polarized debate over range reform, rhetoric quickly overwhelmed some of the real dialogue and change that is taking place across the West.

While the ranchers and environmentalists that Babbitt pulled together in Colorado seemed to come to a workable consensus, those talks were immediately attacked by both sides, demonstrating how hard it will be to find common ground in much of the West. On the one hand, environmentalists constantly called up the image of welfare ranchers. On the other hand, ranchers resorted to the desperate claim that reform would drive them out of business. Both sides drew lines in the sand and said, as one environmentalist told me, "We cannot work with these people."

I thought that the situation might be different in the West's water wars. It seemed that a more complex understanding of how people, communities, and ecosystems share watersheds was emerging around the region. However, water is still a treasure trove of word wars.

In the West, the old saw goes, "Whiskey is for drinking; water is for fighting." Or as a Nevada rancher recently said, "You can mess with my wife, but don't mess with my water."

I watched an example of this unfold in my own backyard during negotiations over a settlement of a century-old water war on the Truckee and Carson Rivers in northern Nevada. Even behind closed doors, where negotiations have moved because they cannot take place in the poisoned atmosphere of public debate in the media, polarized rhetoric prevents people from having a real dialogue.

Here, negotiations failed because efforts to buy water for wetlands and change the way the rivers are run were still portrayed by farmers as stealing water. And the farmers would rather go down fighting than change to survive.

In part, this is because the warrior myth of the West lives on. Farmers and ranchers and miners—and now environmentalists, too—see themselves as survivors in a hostile environment. Their identity is wrapped up in not giving in to adversity.

They all want to believe their clippings, many of them headlined with words of war. In this story, however, I believe communities risk misunderstanding the changes they are going through. This is not a war that will be won with spin. The best epithet will not win.

Worse, if war is what we want, we may get it. Lately, it has seemed that we are getting awfully close. The history of the West is full of bravado. But cultural studies of the western frontier, such as Richard Slotkin's *Gunfighter Nation*, and crime studies, such as Roger McGrath's *Gunfighters, Highwaymen and Vigilantes*, a history of violence in mining towns, have shown that the stories of violence have almost always been bigger than the real violence. Nevertheless, when violence seems the only way out, bullets will fly.

I now realize that war is such a powerful metaphor, tied to such a powerful mythology, that it would be impossible to exorcise, even if people wanted to, which it seems they do not. I must confess my own resolve to abandon the war metaphor has weakened considerably. My editors have reacted to the idea with a barely contained yawn, as I find many people do.

After all, war sells newspapers. And war may be one of the richest metaphors that we have, even though it often is misleading. I think we need to use the metaphor more accurately—and more sparingly, I hope—because word wars can make real trouble.

I take some consolation in the number of people who seem to be tiring of these word wars. And I have found some hope in conversations I have had with young people.

I talked to a group of eighth graders who had been brought to the

Win Back the West rally in Alturas by their social studies teacher. "What do you think about what you're hearing?" I asked them. "Is this going to come down to war?"

Spencer Smith, a ranching kid from Surprise Valley in far northeastern California on the border with Nevada, said, "I don't think it will go that far. The government doesn't want that."

"And we don't want that," his friend Connor Nolan added. "We need compromise and communication so you can work with them and they can work with you. I don't want to sit back while they annihilate our way of life. But I think if they look at it positively, we can too, and we can come up with a compromise."

Another boy, Tommy Harris, said, "We can live together in peace, but it will take time. We have to give up something."

"We'll all have to give up something in exchange," Connor added.

I was heartened to find that these kids were seeing beyond the rhetorical war that adults in their community, including some of their parents, were promoting. But I also glimpsed how slender their hopes were and how easily they might be dashed in the word wars and real conflicts that they will undoubtedly face in the future.

As a journalist, I know I have to report on the word wars in the West. But I also believe journalists need to get beyond the rhetoric to get the real stories.

I believe we all have a responsibility to tell true stories about how the West is changing. Our job is nothing less than telling our own story. That goes for all of us, Westerners, environmentalists, wise users, and the rest of us caught in the middle in the West.

Out of the changes we're living through, we may find and create new myths and metaphors, new stories to live by. I think if we do not find ways to talk about and understand changes, we could find ourselves at war over the wrong stories.

Part 3

New Directions

12

Wising Up to the Wise Use Movement

Karl Hess, Jr.

Environmentalists have good reason to worry about the rising star of wise use in the American West. As a broad-based movement with growing public support, it threatens to eclipse demoralized green ranks and to render green causes irrelevant in the shadow of a conservative Congress. However, greens show surprisingly little sign of understanding the bottomline to the wise use resurgence in the West. Other than exposing its defects and excesses, environmentalists have failed, *clearly at their own peril*, to grasp the movement's meaning and the root cause of its stellar rise.

In typical western style, where morality is reduced to the good, the bad, and the ugly, environmentalists have labeled wise use undesirable in every aspect and simplemindedly tagged it the reactionary foil to progressive and beneficent government. It must be so; Wallace Stegner told us as much in his tribute to John Wesley Powell, and Charles Wilkinson and Secretary of the Interior Bruce Babbitt have reminded us of no less in public memorials to Stegner.[1] But misconceptions tragically abound in the western mind, and environmentalists are no exception.

Wise use is not what it appears to be on the plain surface; it is more complex than a simple cabal of conservative ideologues and resource exploiters waging war against an unbridled and inflated federal government. Such men and women do exist, of course, and thrive in every western town, forest, and range. But they are the window dressings and the stereotypical villains that fuel rather than explain the wise-use revolt. As counterintuitive as it may seem, and as contrary to green assumptions as it is, the wise use movement is—and has been for over a century—the standard bearer of more, *not less*, government.

Across the West, wise users have been nurtured on a cornucopia of federal subsidies. On the public lands, they are the children and the champions of the gospel of scientific land management and the sentinels of a command/control natural-resource economy. They are the nation's lingering link to socialism, to a system where the means of production—the natural resources—are owned by the state and the privileges to extract them are granted by politicians, not markets. We may chuckle or sneer at the watermelon derisions heaped on greens by wise users, but the fact remains that environmentalists, not ranchers, loggers, or miners, are the ones who have fought—often without reflecting on the implications of what they are fighting—the rule of cowboy, lumberjack, and hard-rock socialism and the flow of federal dollars that tether the West to its federal master.

Greens are also unable—or unwilling—to grasp the wise use movement's more positive and hopeful side—the elements of its thinking and constituency that are land-friendly and that point toward a West of peace rather than war, a West of neighbors and communities instead of users and special interest groups, and a West of sustainable living for creatures human and not. They miss the all-important point that the good of the western wise use movement is colored and entwined with the bad and the ugly, a circumstance not uncommon in an American West of tarnished heroes and redeemable villains. Yet if environmentalists—indeed all Americans—are to avoid the worst of wise use and to embrace the very best of it, our understanding of wise users should and must be clarified and then resolved.

Wise Use: Tap Root into Big Government

Western wise users, if they were to read Ivan Doig's *Dancing at the Rascal Fair*, would likely find solace for their grievances and support for their cause in the book's poignant encounter between a turn-of-the-century northwest Montana ranching family and the first Forest Service ranger to arrive in that part of the state. Angus McCaskill, immigrant, father, and head of a small ranch in Two Medicine country, is caught off guard by the arrival of Stanley Meixwell, employee of the new U.S. Forest Service. Sensing the import of the ranger's arrival, and troubled by what it may mean, he is unsettled by his son's expectations. "From the instant he reached down to shake your hand, you looked at Stanley Meixwell as if the sun rose and set in him. And I was already telling myself that you had better be right about that."

The young boy was certain he was right; he knew a hero when he saw one. But the father was less sure; he knew, as he watched the man Stanley Meixwell ride away, that the ranger's coming signaled an end to a certain past and the beginning of an uncertain future. It meant a new West, one that might not be to his or his neighbors' liking: "I stood staring for a while at the mountains. National Forest. They did not look like a national anything, they still looked just like mountains. A barbed wire fence around them. It did not seem real that a fence could be put around mountains. But I would not bet against this Meixwell when he said he was going to do a thing. A fence around the mountains not to control them but us."[2]

Federal fences around western mountains are the heart of the wise use beef in the West. For over a century, politicians, policy makers, and functionaries have choreographed almost every facet of life on the high plains, desert grasslands, sagebrush basins, and mountain ranges that make up the nation's arid region. They have told westerners how to settle their lands, how to extract their resources, and how to live their lives. Today, federal ownership controls one-half of the West and federal mandates and environmental laws control much of what remains.

Adding immediacy to the wise-use gripe is the fiscal, regulatory, and management abyss in which the 260 million acres of federal grazing lands hang precariously. The grazing budgets alone of the two western land-managing agencies—the U.S. Forest Service and the Bureau of Land Management—are so large that they could buy out every public-land ranch in the West at fair market value over a period of four years.[3] Indeed, for every two dollars earned in profit by public-land ranchers, the government spends three dollars on grazing administration.[4] No less intimidating are the rules that govern public-land ranching. In the past twenty-five years, the pages of laws, regulations, and policies promulgated by Uncle Sam have come to dwarf the *Encyclopaedia Britannica*. Adding insult to wise-use injury, the 28,000 men and women who ranch in the federal West are outnumbered by just the Forest Service and BLM employees who watchdog the people's land.

Wise-use grievances *seem* valid enough in light of the intrusive role that government has repeatedly played in the region's history. Yet appearances are only skin deep, and in the modern-day West of aggrieved politicians, resource extractors, and recreationists, there is a more profound and troubling truth. Cries of federal bullying and victimization belie the uncomfortable fact that many of the federal fences that now ring the mountains and deserts of the West were built by westerners themselves. They, not some cabal of conspiring bureaucrats, are the architects of big government on the western range; they got the dose of federal governance they demanded and, to their chagrin, an extra ounce in the bargain.

This is not surprising. The wise-use West that now chomps at the federal bit is the West that welcomed federal assistance for over a hundred years with nary a discouraging word. Indeed, the region's taste for big government began early in its Anglo history. Western settlers, seeking security for their families and communities, demanded at the onset federal government protection as they took without consent the lands that rightfully belonged to native Americans. It mattered little to them that in doing so they were violating the very Jeffersonian values that stood behind the 1862 Homestead Act—the inviolate right of all people to have and hold property in land. What mattered was that territories once under the control of native Americans were cleansed of danger and safely opened to white settlement. And it certainly didn't hurt that the military forts and soldiers that followed in the wake of victory, and even in some cases the reservations of conquered Indians, provided the nucleus of new markets to sustain marginal homesteads and struggling governments. "In those rough times," writes Patty Limerick, "Washington was in essence subsidizing a government which had few citizens, no income, and a highly questionable future."[5]

Federal aid to the West only accelerated in subsequent years. Cries of foul play from nesters, farmers, and small ranchers brought the full weight of the federal government to bear on the emerging cattle kingdom of giant land barons and gargantuan livestock herds. By a judicious combination of Supreme Court rulings, presidential orders, congressional statutes, and the U.S. Cavalry, public rangelands were kept open to the cattle and sheep of all Americans.[6] To save the West from itself, the federal government effectively turned its physical landscape into sacrificial lands. It ordained, in the name of equity and fairness, overgrazing as the law of the lawless range, enshrining erosion and desolation in public policies that made ideological sense in Congress but nonsense on the parched, wind-blown basins and ranges of the Rocky Mountain West. At the same time, and by an altogether different logic, the government transferred millions of acres of western land to the Union Pacific, Kansas Pacific, Atchison, Topeka, and Santa Fe, Southern Pacific, and Northern Pacific Railroads. The West needed and wanted railroads. It was as simple as that.

Basically, whatever the West needed and wanted it got from big government. Westerners bought off on the federal damming of the region's rivers without flinching a muscle or suffering an ounce of coercion. They were not victimized by the engineers at the Bureau of Reclamation who wanted to rechannel their life blood, by the politicians who wanted to trade their future for votes, or by the private construction firms that made out like bandits. They did it all to themselves. When the Bureau of Reclamation announced its plan to dam Echo Park, who was on the front lines begging for federal votes and federal dollars? It was the proud and independent people of Vernal, Utah. They, like the rest of the West, greeted every dam and hydroelectric project in the region with wild-eyed enthusiasm. They jumped at the chance to have someone else pay for their prosperity, realizing only after it was too late that the cost of that prosperity was the despoiling of their landscape and the ringing of their mountains with fences strung by miles of federal rules and regulations to protect the West from its own people.

But westerners kept building the federal fences. With their homes Indian-proofed and their fields, livestock, and mines watered from federally tamed rivers, they turned to the catastrophic fires that were vital to the ecological heart beat of the West but that threatened their families, communities, and livelihoods. Rather than use prudence in selecting where they lived and how they worked, they threw themselves at the mercy of a youthful Forest Service that was able and more than willing to put out the flames that so terrified them. They garnered the necessary votes in Washington to finance the most expensive firefighting force known to man, and it hardly cost anything except another fence post or two and another stretch of federal barbed wire. It gave them good seasonal jobs. Later, after the role of fire was better understood, it also gave them decadent wildlands and a new reason to chaffe at the bit of federal intrusion.

Old growth forests went the same way of the salmon and the natural wildfire, and for exactly the same reasons. Federal managers, at the behest of the West, changed the name of the tree-harvesting game in the wake of World War II. They opened up western forests by building thousands of miles of heavily subsidized roads and then disposing of vast stands of old growth timber at below-cost timber sales. Large, commercial timber companies were the biggest and most immediate beneficiaries of new Forest Service guidelines. They, not the small mom and pop logging operations that thrived before the war, had the resources and the markets to level entire mountain ranges of mature timber. Yet, who stood behind the idea of creating national forests in the first place? Who lobbied for the federal appropriations to expand forest cuts, who provided the labor and equipment to do the actual work, and whose communities lived off the fat of the federal tree-cutting machine for so many years? The moms and pops and the little guys didn't do so badly while the trees lasted and the federal dollars flowed so freely.

No one in the West did poorly so long as the dollars flowed. In a fraction of the time it took to settle the Massachusetts Bay Colony, big intrusive government brought subsidized crops to lands that were once desert and subsidized cities to places where once only buzzards dared to dwell. By every measure, the American West was built on federal dollars. The interstate highway system that connects one patch of desert to another happened only because federal dollars flowed easily. Employment in the West skyrocketed because waterless ship-yards were built on the arid plains of Colorado, because air force bases, scientific labs, and federal centers mushroomed overnight, because a slew of federal bureaus provided enough jobs to keep rural outposts from becoming ghost towns, because ten times as many defense dollars were spent in the West as in the rest of the nation, and because ten western states representing less than 10 percent of the nation's population controlled a fifth of the votes in the U.S. Senate.

Today, western wise users are enraged at being victims of federal meddling. Even governors and state legislators are chiming in on the rising chorus of dissatisfaction. Forget the fact that federal jobs help keep western treasuries afloat, such as in New Mexico where Sandia Labs, Los Alamos, NASA, White Sands Missile Range, three air force bases (Cannon, Holloman, and Kirtland), and regional headquarters for the Forest Service, the Bureau of Land Management, the Fish and Wildlife Service, and the Park Service fatten that state's economy. So what if hundreds of rural communities across the West would be nothing but ghost towns today were it not for the free flow of government dollars from the Forest Service, the BLM, the Post Office, and dozens of federally run or financed welfare programs. These are just details. Wise users have their reasons to chew on the bit.

They are fed up with being told what to do, with having every inch of their West pampered and regulated as though they were spoiled children incapable of self-control. They rebel at federal conditions that constrain their sovereignty, and they are maddened by the arrogant displays of power exercised by federal employees. They complain about roads, Medicare, unfunded mandates, and the burdens of the Clean Air and Water Act; and they bristle at the public-land reform proposals of Washington bureaucrats. They just can't take it anymore. They call for states' rights, and they raise the symbolic banner of the victim-ized rancher whose land and livelihood are threatened by a crazy-quilt pattern of undeserved yet oppressive environmental laws and regulations. They're certainly right about oppressive, but they're dead wrong about undeserved.

Ranchers, and most especially the sagebrush rebels who occupy the wise use front, have worked diligently like the rest of the West to erect federal fences around the lands they call home and workplace. History speaks for itself. During the Hoover administration, the western states were offered the possibility of title to the public lands.[7] Public-land ranchers balked at the idea, opting instead for low grazing fees, the Taylor Grazing Act, and continued federal oversight. At the end of World War II, congressional moves to privatize public grazing lands went nowhere as western ranchers went bananas over a cornucopia of federal dollars for range reclamation.[8] Thirty years later, after supporting the 1976 Federal Land Management and Policy Act, which declared public lands forever federal, stockmen traded off private property principles for the promised largesse of Interior Secretary James Watt's "good neighbor" policy. With his blessing, Nevada ranchers joined hands with the Nevada chapter of the Sierra Club to kill President Reagan's modest attempt at privatization, the asset-management program.[9]

Today, sagebrush rebels—many of whom are leaders in the western wise use and private property rights movement—march to the beat of the same drummer. Privatization is too risky. At worst, nonranchers—God forbid, environmentalists—might end up with *their* land. At worst, *they* might have to pay their own way. It's much easier to demand, as have a handful of rural western counties, that Washington turn over authority and public dollars to local jurisdictions—or, for that matter, hand over federal lands to state administration.[10] Either way, public lands stay public and public-land ranchers stay in the saddle.

Western, wise-use stockmen have ringed their mountains and prairies in federal barbed wire by other, more disingenuous means. Staunchly opposed to federal welfarism, they have serendipitously partaken of its benefits. Big government is there when grasshoppers invade their rangelands and when coyotes go after their calves and sheep. All told, taxpayers pay $30 to $40 million a year to protect western stockmen from creatures large and small.[11] Big government is also there with an emergency livestock feed program whenever drought strikes—a natural calamity that now happens with unnatural regularity in a West addicted to federal handouts. Nevada ranchers, the angriest of the sagebrush rebels, now rake in over $18,000 a year for each emergency feed claim.[12]

Federal fences, though, have been built largely to protect ranchers from themselves. In Vale, Oregon, the government spent over $300,000 (1992 dollars) per public-land rancher to stop overgrazing. That didn't work. By 1994, it shelled out another $30,000 to $50,000 apiece on the same stockmen to keep their starving cattle alive on overgrazed ranges. Elsewhere, the story is the same.[13] Taxpayers will spend almost $200 million in 1995 to keep federal ranchers afloat, to kill the brush that comes with overgrazing, to genetically alter livestock so they can graze the poisonous plants that thrive on overstocked ranges, and to pay for the water holes and fences needed to do private business on arid, public lands. In return, public-land ranchers will pay about $22 million in grazing fees in 1995, 50 percent of which will be handed back to them in the form of federally financed range improvements.[14]

Stockmen of all stripes, on private and public lands alike, belie their wise-use cause even further by making mockery of deeply held principles. They speak glowingly of free markets and free enterprise, but when push comes to shove they opt for protectionism and less-than-free enterprise. Western ranchers voted as a block to authorize the USDA to collect *mandatory* per head livestock charges to finance the beef industry's "Real Food for Real People" campaign. And today, most public-land ranchers oppose making federal grazing permits marketable to nonranchers. In a populist twist on real threats to real people, the free market—not a bloated, overregulating government—is what ranchers see as the gravest threat to their tenure on the federal domain. Government fences may be bad in principle, but in practice they sustain the monopoly hold that ranchers have on public rangelands.

Inconsistencies bedevil wise-use rebels on other fronts. They argue for local control and county government as instruments of grassroots democracy. Yet in many locales, their agenda is anything but participatory and democratic. In Bonner County, Idaho, rebels ran roughshod over local citizens and railroaded county government into a land-use plan favorable to their cause. Idaho courts wasted no time killing the plan. In Catron County, New Mexico, the native soil of the Sagebrush Rebellion, county commissioners are intent on grassroots tyranny—on registering environmentalists as dangerous weapons and foiling landowners who might wish to raise wildlife in lieu of livestock. Government pure and simple, even at the local level, is the wise-use tool of practice for a wise-use agenda ostensibly opposed to government in principle.

Sagebrush Rebels and wise users have done their jobs well. Thanks to the big government they built, and its fountain of subsidies, western ranges now hold a third more cattle than the land can sustain.[15] Overgrazing persists, ranges and streams degrade, and deficit ranching thrives at taxpayer expense. Is it any wonder that environmentalists want regulatory fences raised to hem in the public West and to keep out public-land ranchers? They are, after all, the ones who bear the damages with the greatest anguish and pay the bills with most bitterness. At the same time, they lack the most basic privileges afforded to ranchers by government—such as the right to acquire a grazing permit and then to use it for conservation rather than livestock purposes. The wonder is that Sagebrush Rebels and wise users have never caught on, that they have simply ringed their lands with federal fences strung with miles of self-caused rules and regulations.

Environmentalism: Falling for the Wise-Use Line

Environmentalists are adept at seeing the natural-resource damage caused by a century of wise-use traditions in the American West. They are the ones—not the BLM, the Forest Service, the Bureau of Reclamation, or the western land-grant schools—who brought to the public eye the millions of acres of overgrazed federal rangelands, the tens of thousands of miles of eroding, subsidized logging roads, the thousands of miles of degraded streams, the countless mountain ranges scarred by clearcuts and below-cost timber sales and pockmarked by federal mineral giveaways, and the death of the great salmon rivers of the West. They saw through the boosterism that blinded generations of Westerners and they witnessed what ranchers, loggers, miners, and dam builders either missed or did not want to see: the decline and loss of the natural heritage that had made the West such a special home and had set it apart from the rest of the nation.

But environmentalists have their blind spots, too. They see the legacy of wise use with uncanny clarity, yet when it comes to understanding what it is and why it happened, their vision fogs. They swallow the wise-use line, hook and sinker, and they sing the wise-use chorus of victimization wholeheartedly. Like the ranchers, miners, and loggers they berate, they see themselves and the West they love as unwitting victims of other people and outside forces. They embrace, although they would never acknowledge it, the populist reasoning that compels many Sagebrush Rebels and wise use ranchers to lay the blame for "the plunder of the western range [on] eastern capitalists and investment cliques."[16] Private greed and exploitation is the

downfall of the West. Bernard De Voto was right: "The Cattle Kingdom overgrazed the range so drastically that the processes of nature
were disrupted. Since those high and far-off days the [public] range
has never been capable of supporting anything like the number of cattle
it could have supported if the cattle barons had not maimed it."[17]
Edward Abbey was also right: the ruin of the West is the product of
greed and environmental ignorance of cowboys and ranchers. Their
ethic, or more likely their lack of one, reduced the western range to a
"cow-burnt wasteland." "The whole American West," Abbey declares,
"stinks of cattle." They are the pest and plague polluting streams and
infesting "our canyons, valleys, meadows, and forests."[18]

Given such assumptions, is it any wonder that environmentalists
have sought stronger and higher federal fences to ring and protect
western mountains and ranges from the depredations of ranchers and
their wise-use ilk—or that they have sought, like their wise-use foes,
the help of the federal government to quell a complex of threats far
greater than native Americans, drought, fires, and rampaging grasshoppers and coyotes? Certainly their motives differ from those of
ranchers, loggers, and miners, but their support for big, intrusive government is still the same in principle as well as in degree of enthusiasm. Bigger and better government can work for the West so long as
the right people hold the reins of federal power and the purse strings
of congressional largesse. That's been the lesson of 130 years of federal engineering in the arid region. Ranchers proved it true for their
vision of a ranching West with James Watt in 1981, and environmentalists are now working to make it true for their vision of an environmental West under Bruce Babbitt.

Of course, bigger and better government is also a gamble; it entails both winners *and losers.* A victory for wise use—and there have
been many—is invariably a setback for greens. Still, faith in government runs deep among western environmentalists. Its wellspring, in
part, is the kinder and gentler West proffered by Wallace Stegner in
Beyond the Hundredth Meridian. There, Stegner offers an enticing
vision for the region's future, one that comes in the human yet heroic
form of John Wesley Powell, Civil War veteran, western explorer, first
navigator of the waters of the Grand Canyon, and architect of the
National Geographical Survey.

In contrast to his contemporaries, Powell was a man ahead of his
times. He alone understood the enormity of the West, the uniqueness
of its aridity, and the essential need for a benign and enlightened
government to guide it in the direction of cooperation and planning.
Had he lived to this day, Stegner writes, he would have known when

dams were too numerous, clearcuts too large, and forest harvests too extreme. He would have sided with the Sierra Club in fighting the damming of Echo Park. He would have fought to rationally manage the federal lands "according to the principles of wise use for the benefit of the whole nation"; he would have celebrated the reservation of more than a hundred million acres of forest land; he would have basked in the human and environmental triumph and legacy of the Taylor Grazing Act of 1934; and he would have spoken out with Civil War righteousness to defeat "the private interests that he feared might monopolize land [and] water in the West."[19]

Stegner's Powell was and remains the perfect hero for a West torn and preyed upon by the callous and shortsighted forces of wise use. "I fought for the conservation of the public domain under Federal leadership," Stegner quotes Powell, "because the citizens were unable to cope with the situation under existing trends and circumstances."

> The job was too big and interwoven for even the states to handle with satisfactory co-ordination. On the western slope of Colorado and in nearby states I saw waste, competition, overuse, and abuse of valuable range lands and watersheds eating into the very heart of western economy. Farms and ranches everywhere in the range country were suffering. The basic economy of entire communities was threatened. There was terrific strife and bloodshed between the cattle and sheep men over the use of the range. Valuable irrigation projects stood in danger of ultimate deterioration. Erosion, yes even human erosion, had taken root.[20]

Powell *knew* what the West needed. He *knew*, as Stegner recounts in glowing admiration, that no one could guarantee the future of the West "except the American government." He *knew* that even if "government contained quarreling and jealous bureaus, that was too bad."

> If it sheltered grafters as it did so spectacularly during the time of Grant, too bad. If it was too far from the resources in question to make every decision right, too bad. Too bad. But the alternative was worse. The alternative was creeping deserts, flooded river valleys, dusty miles of unused and unusable land, feeble or partial or monopolistic utilization of the available land and water. The alternative was great power and great wealth to a few and for a brief time rather than competence and independence for the communities of small freeholders on which [Powell's] political economy unchangeably rested.[21]

Powell was a white-hatted hero to match the scenery of the western landscape. Sadly, he died before his time. He died too soon to see the glory of the Newman Act and the promise of its offspring, the Bureau of Reclamation. He was denied the sweet victory of watching concrete and steel monuments that glorified federal supremacy over nature span and tame the wild Missouri, Columbia, and Colorado. And even if, as Stegner claims, he would have battled the damming of Echo Park, he certainly would have welcomed the flooding of Glen Canyon. He would have been proud, as was Stegner, of such heroic federal achievements as the Central Valley Project of California; and he would have embraced as a vision come true the Central Arizona project and the production of cheap hydroelectric power in the Pacific Northwest.[22]

Reclamation was, after all, the path to western prosperity and the key to turning western deserts into gardens that would "blossom like the rose." Powell knew this when he addressed Montana's 1889 constitutional convention and predicted that one-third of the state could be irrigated. He spoke of a dammed Montana that exceeded by leaps of imagination the fondest dreams of proponents of reclamation: "It means that no drop of water falling within the area of the state shall flow beyond the boundaries of the state. It means that all the waters falling within the state will be utilized upon its lands for agriculture."[23] Salinized soils, exiled wolves, struggling salmon, and dead and dying rivers aside, Powell had a persuasive and powerful vision for the West. He would have celebrated the heroic making of Marc Reisner's *Cadillac Desert*, a cornucopia of federally subsidized water and energy projects that magically transformed seemingly useless desert into productive croplands and homelands.

None of this should be surprising. After all, as Stegner reminds us, Powell "was always one to take the long view . . . a bureaucrat before the name got either familiar or unpopular." His farsighted vision simply prophesied what the West was fated to become. He had just the right mixture of bureaucrat and idealist to see beyond the hubris and self-deception of the West:

> Both the bureaucrat and the idealist knew that private interests, whether they dealt in cattle or sheep, oil, minerals, coal, timber, water, or land itself, could not be trusted or expected to take care of the land or conserve its resources for the use of future generations. They could be trusted or expected to protect neither the monetary nor the nonmonetary values of the land: even in his day Americans had the passenger pigeon and the buffalo, the plowed and eroded plains, the cutover forests of Michigan, to tell them where "nature and the common incidents of life" would lead us. Later years have added the Dust Bowl and the eroded watersheds to the evidence.[24]

Powell was indeed a visionary man. Stegner, in one of the few understatements of his biography, notes that "Major Powell was never primarily interested in the forests . . . [b]ut he would approve the reservations [of forests] that by the middle of the twentieth century totaled 139,000,000 acres, plus another 21,000,000 in Alaska."[25] Stegner is too modest. Powell was very interested in western forests; so interested that he recommended to Secretary of the Interior John Noble that "the best thing to do for the Rocky Mountain forests was to burn them down." He was dead serious, something he made crystal clear when he proceeded to brag to the secretary "with gusto how he himself had started a fire that swept over a thousand square miles."[26] In fact, he was so interested in western forests that he even promoted overgrazing by sheep in the Sierra Nevada Mountains as "a useful way to keep forest growth down."[27] As one of his associates at the Geological Survey later confided, "it is advisable to cut away as rapidly as possible all the forests [of the West], especially upon the mountains, where most of the rain falls, in order that as much of the precipitation as possible may be collected in the streams. . . . [and] It may be added that the forests in the arid region are thus disappearing with commendable rapidity."[28] Powell cared deeply for the forests, at least in the context that they were depriving the West of sorely needed irrigation water.

Wallace Stegner is silent on these all too human foibles. What he offers in prose is John Wesley Powell, the man of legend and myth today. He is the reconstructed Civil War hero who inspired Interior Secretary Stewart Udall in 1961 to enlist Stegner in the knighthood of John Kennedy's brief but meteoric Camelot and to later name him to the National Parks Advisory Board. He is the patron saint of avant-garde western thinking who helped launch Stegner on a course of environmental fame and a three-year stint as member of the Sierra Club's Board of Directors. He is the inspirational creation that moved a youthful Bruce Babbitt to a born-again experience, to a religious like conversion from being the son of a ranching dynasty to becoming the son of an environmentally progressive West. Powell is the bigger-than-life figure who energized now Interior Secretary Babbitt to push for a National Biological Survey modeled along the lines of the National Geological Survey. He is the quintessential western visionary who excited writer Charles Wilkinson to celebrate Babbitt's ascension to interior secretary as the dawning of a *new West* and to subsequently declare *Beyond the Hundredth Meridian* "the greatest book of the West."[29]

Stegner's version of Powell and the American West is flawed and dishonest. The West he evokes is the West he desperately wanted to believe in. He wanted a hero who could match the grandeur of the western landscape; for that belief he created John Wesley Powell. He wanted to redeem the West from the sins of overgrazing, overlogging, and destructive mining; for those ill-deeds he focused on the private sector, its stockmen, timber cutters, and hard-rock miners. He wanted to affirm and sanctify the positive role of bureaucracy and centralized authority in a postdepression, postwar world; to make that case he envisioned a benevolent government for the West. But none of it was ever true.

Powell was never the social democrat and environmental visionary imagined by Stegner; he was the spirit that dammed the West's great rivers, clearcut its primeval forests, turned its rangelands into permanent fodder for cattle, and parlayed its heritage of Jeffersonian, hands-on democracy into a nightmare of bureaucratic red tape and mounting regulation. He is the soul of wise use—the spirit of progressive and benign government that presumed men and women dedicated to public service and trained in natural resource management could objectively and efficiently discern, pursue, and implement the resource needs of the land and its people.

Simply put, Powell laid the moral and intellectual groundwork for the rise of scientific land management and its institutional embodiments, the Bureau of Reclamation, the Bureau of Land Management, the Army Corps of Engineers, and the U.S. Forest Service. He set the precedent for Gifford Pinchot, the Forest Service's first chief, to declare scientific land management "the one great antidote for the ills of the nation [that would create] the Kingdom of God on earth"—that would ensure "where conflicting interests must be reconciled, the question will always be decided from the standpoint of the greatest good for the greatest number." Above all, he stood for progressive conservation—for what Pinchot would later define as "the *wise use* of the earth and its resources for the lasting good of men [italics added]."[30]

Missing the Forest for the Trees

Wise use is ubiquitous. It has never been the monopoly of ranchers, loggers, and miners—or, for that matter, the private sector in general. It's ingrained in the ethos of government, special interest politics, and the presumptions of federal stewardship of the West. It's not about good or bad uses of the land, although it has a distinct and deserved reputation for the latter. Rather, it's about how land-use decisions are made, whether by well-intentioned or less than scrupulous people. It's the gamble by resource extractors and preservers alike that politics is the cheapest and easiest way to get the resource uses and conservation outcomes they most desire. It's the legacy of the American West, the social and environmental story of ranchers and loggers, hunters and hikers, environmentalists and preservationists, and reborn Wallace Stegners and John Wesley Powells using government to shape and mold the West into a scenery befitting their personal visions.

But if brute facts account for anything, and in the West of personal visions they frequently don't, wise use has been a dismal economic and ecologic failure. The evidence is crystal clear; from the high plains to the Rocky Mountains, and from the intermountain basins and ranges to the Sierra-Nevada and Cascade crests, it simply hasn't worked. And what is just as clear is that federal fences have made little difference. With or without them, the fortunes of ranchers and environmentalists have risen and fallen with the vagaries of politics and the power plays of special interest groups. All that has remained constant is the plight of the Western landscape—the chronic overgrazing of its vast expanses, the trampling of its streams, the mismanagement of its forests, and the continuing struggle of its salmon to overcome man-made barriers in search of steadily diminishing spawning grounds.

Bruce Babbitt, secretary of the interior in the Clinton administration, is a prime example of the wise-use dead end. Cut from the same cloth as John Wesley Powell, his fate was to be the last, great environmental hope in the dying tradition of wise use. He created the National Biological Survey to match the Geological Survey engineered by Powell. He fashioned his own Camelot, bringing together a generation of westerners weaned on the prose of Wallace Stegner and the myth of John Wesley Powell. He promised a kinder and gentler West, one where environmental values—endangered species, biological diversity, and aesthetics—would assume equal standing with the traditional uses of public lands for wood, forage, and minerals. He gave a valiant effort, but in the end his wise-use roots frustrated his vision of a new West. His National Biological Survey died under the 1995 appropriations' axe. And his two years preaching and pushing rangeland reform amounted to little more than a recycled wise-use effort to ratchet up by one more notch the role of government.

In the spirit of progressive conservation, Babbitt proposed standards and guidelines for ecosystem management on public rangelands. New, ecologically sound land-use regulations, he argued, would help heal

degraded grasslands and improve a lackluster tradition of federal grazing management. The idea had merit in principle, but in practice it
never stood a chance. Ecosystem management on a politicized
western range is no ecosystem management at all—and most certainly not on a pampered landscape where subsidies and poorly conceived
public-land policies encourage and reward overgrazing. Babbitt should
have known this, just as environmentalists should have known that wise
use, even when practiced by the environmentally most caring and the
ecologically wisest, is still wise use.

Federal payments to ranchers to reclaim overgrazed grasslands, to
remove brush from poorly managed ranges, and to feed starving cattle on prematurely barren pastures undermine the integrity and good
intentions of ecosystem management. They bail out the worst of stockmen and they keep the most marginal—and commonly the most environmentally destructive—of ranches in operation, frustrating the efforts
of the best and most dedicated federal-land managers. Likewise, the
disincentives of the grazing permit system make mockery of whatever
other advantages ecosystem management might have to offer federally
subsidized, overgrazed ranges. For one, the system fosters overstock-
ing by encouraging ranchers to steward and conserve not the land that
sustains their livestock but the numbers of cattle attached to their
grazing permits. It's a matter of self interest; they can't buy or sell
the public lands they graze, but they can buy and sell the permits
that authorize them to put a fixed number of livestock on the lands
they lease.

Making matters worse, grazing permits limit what stockmen can
do on federal ranges. They can use the grass they lease to grow cattle
and the streams that flow across their federal allotments to water livestock, but they can't use—and profit from—grass to grow wildlife for
fee-hunting or riparian areas for fee-fishing and paid bird watching.
They must put their public grazing lands to uses that are deemed beneficial by public law, even if it means sacrificing wildlife habitat and
polluting mountain streams. Of course, no federal law or federal manager mandates such wise use, but the effect of public-land law is as
good as a wise-use mandate. It pins the fate of grasslands and riparian waterways on the gambit of politics; it makes them at best temporary prizes of conquest for ranchers on one day and environmentalists
on another and, at worst, hostages of a political process predicated on
compromise. It's called multiple use in the context of federal law,
though in the context of western history it's known as the governing
law of beneficial use.

In retrospect, Babbitt's rangeland reforms hardly differed from the counterproposals later offered by Senator Pete Domenici in the 1995 session of the 104th Congress. His Livestock Grazing Act, later renamed for publicity purposes the Public Rangelands Protection Act, suffered none of the environmental subtleties of Babbitt's reforms— such as ecosystem management—and made no pretense of changing how environmental resources are stewarded—such as greater attention to matters of biological diversity and habitat protection for all species. Despite its ecological blinders, though, Domenici's act lay well within the wise-use tradition of Babbitt's more progressive agenda. Both sets of rangeland reform upheld the dominance of livestock grazing on public lands, the primacy of politics in resource allocation, and the crucial role of subsidies in sustaining an ailing system of public-land grazing. Both were wise use to the hilt, empowered and committed to preserving a status quo half as old as the nation.

Living with Wise Users, Not Wise Use

Environmentalists need to wise up to both wise use and wise users. They need to see that the first—wise use—is the legacy of failed politics, the shipwrecked aspirations of well-intended public servants determined to engineer western resources for the sake of the land and the benefit of its people. They need to grasp the elemental truth of Bruce Babbitt's observation that federal-land reform "is the art of the possible," and that in a wise-use West what is possible is hardly nothing at all.[31] And they need to ask, in the context of wise use, what divides ranchers from environmentalists—what pits the values of the stockmen against the values of the urban green? The answer is apparent: it's the dogged reliance on wise use to solve problems that are value laden and deeply personal.

Nowhere is this more evident than in the century-long epic of the wolf in the American West. At first, ranchers were the ones to rely on government to do their bidding, to gun down the symbols of their primal fear, and, as necessary, to pay others to do the killing too. Federal trappers and private bounty hunters were busy in those days, and they did their jobs well. In a few short decades, they erased *Canus lupus* from the western scene.

Today, it's the turn of environmentalists. In fair political turnabout, they are relying on government to do their bidding, to protect and breed wolves, and to release them back into the western wilds. It's the kind of wise use that is politically correct in these verdant times. Still, one wonders what might have happened if federal trappers and private bounty hunters had not extirpated the wolf from the West. What would environmentalists and ranchers be doing today? Would they be such competitors for political power and such irascible foes? And, more important, where would the wolf be in a world without wise use?

Wise users, in contrast, are distinct from wise use. They are not bad people; they are mostly decent men and women operating under bad laws, bad policies, and very bad incentives. Their stellar rise to power in recent years is not part of some Machiavellian plot. Rather, it's just the natural change of the wise-use guard with the inevitable shift in the prevailing political winds. Ranchers, after all, didn't set out to overgraze the West. What happened is much more innocent and yet far more onerous. Public policy failed them, and it failed the land they use. It gave them few, if any, options to destructive grazing in what were then the halcyon days of the federally enforced, open range. And for the western stockmen who overgraze today, public policy marches on mindlessly to the same beat, failing once again the land and its users. Its many-faceted bundle of inappropriate laws, convoluted incentives, and lucrative subsidies are simply too much, too many, and too compelling for men and women of all-too-human flesh.

Those who abuse western grazing lands—or, for that matter, the forests, soils, streams, and wildlife of the West—are responsible for their choices and they should and must be held accountable for what they have done. Yet, it would be a tragic and a costly error to lay at their feet the full blame for what a century of wise use has brought to the prairies, basins, and ranges of the West. Stripped of their wise use powers, wise users are powerless to do many of the things that so anger environmentalists. Conversely, when stripped of their wise-use shield, greens are not the environmental bogeymen of a wise user's nightmare. At worst, wise users and greens can work around each other and, at best, they can be good neighbors in cohesive, working communities. And, in the best of worlds, they can build communities healthy and tolerant enough for even the likes of wolves.

There are, of course, good reasons why western environmentalists and traditional wise users can and should be peaceful neighbors rather than warring foes. Greens, for example, are really part of, not apart from, the property rights movement in the West. For the past quarter century they have been shoulder to shoulder with ranchers and miners in staking their claims to the vast, unowned resources of the arid region. And, like their wise-use counterparts, they have turned to government to sign, seal, and sanctify those claims in an array of federal legislation. They understand the lesson of Garrett Hardin's *Tragedy of the Commons*, the rational mind-set that drives unrestrained resource users to consume and exhaust common resources. They know the ecological costs of the open range of a past century of unbridled use and they accept with a sigh of inevitability the two solutions offered by Garrett Hardin: private ownership, which is as onerous to them as it is to ranchers, and meticulous regulation by government, which is tolerable by default. In the end, they opt for more and higher federal fences, just as wise users have strung miles of federal barbed wire in their struggle against privatization on the western range.

Like their mentor Garrett Hardin, neither greens nor wise users have any sense of a third option for the federal domain—the historical precedent of common resources being managed by small, self-governing communities. Yet such a solution is not far-fetched in a public-land West where meticulous regulations have failed to tame the worst excesses of the tragedy of the commons and where issues of place, identity, equity, and fairness make privatization an undesirable and unlikely social outcome. Little commons scattered among the plains, deserts, and mountains of the West and made up of wise users and environmentalists shorn of their wise-use advantages might well bring closure to the property rights movement in the West—and do so to the mutual benefit of one and all. It might even create space—voluntary space mutually agreed upon by western families, neighbors, and communities—for the triumphant return of the exiled wolf.

This might well happen if Congress allowed a series of experimental, self-governing public-land projects to blossom on the war-riddled, wolf-fearing landscape of the federal West. Carved from local grazing districts or watersheds, the projects would be run by locally elected councils. Voting and membership in the councils would be based on residence within the project area and use of project lands—such as the holding of a "grazing" permit, if such a permit were no longer limited to ranching and raising livestock, or the purchase of an annual access permit, irrespective of residence. Funding and control over management—including the responsibility to find a more peaceful and lasting home on the range for the wolf—would revert to the local level. In turn, keys to success might be how well project lands weaned themselves from federal funding, how well they stewarded their public trusts, how well they functioned as land communities for both humans and wildlife, and how well they served the public's demand for wildland recreation. Federal agencies would steer clear of the projects, only monitoring how well they worked and then reporting to Congress.

Self-governing communities in the public-land West are not as far-fetched as they might seem to greens, wise users, and an American public numbed to the mischiefs of wise use. Local self-governance is a tradition deeply ingrained in the American experience and character. Alexis de Tocqueville wrote in *Democracy in America* that local associations and small communities were the workhorses of American democracy. They, not central government, were the social glue that held the nation intact and the social channels through which the matters of everyday life flowed. Wise users and environmentalists, despite whatever other differences they may have, are uniquely at home beneath the Tocquevillian umbrella of grassroots democracy.

Western stockmen in rebellion against Washington's authority, for example, now embrace place and community as the proper surrogates for a century of federal rule. They argue fervently for government that is closer to home and more responsive to the people who are most affected by its decisions. And although their practice of grassroots democracy is strained by wise-use subsidies and a national wise-use political agenda, their sentiment for hands-on governance is heartfelt and rooted in a long attachment to land and neighbors. In fact, their personal histories on the western range are entwined by a common, communal thread—the neighborly ethic of "barn raising" celebrated by Daniel Kemmis as the common ground of place and community.[32]

Western environmentalists also share an affinity to place and community, though it is an attachment born less from a history of shared experience and more from an ethics of choice and commitment. They seek roots in an all-inclusive community of place. It is, in essence, the span of social and ecological felicities, the self-governed living and working spaces sought by wise users but expanded in citizenship and time to embrace all of nature's parts and all of nature's evolving processes. It is what Aldo Leopold called "the land community"—the immediate and physical locale of place where the boundaries of community are enlarged "to include soils, waters, plants, and animals, or collectively: the land." It is where "the role of *Homo sapiens* [changes] from conqueror of the land-community to plain member and citizen of it."[33]

Almost all of the ingredients needed to build a land community and to nurture good neighbors and lasting peace are there on the western range. Environmentalists and wise users alike are weary from a century of conflict and contention. They long for some kind of final resolution—for some order and meaning out of the chaos of conflicting claims and unclaimed rights that clutter the landscapes of the federal West and that threaten a never-ending tragedy of the western commons. They know, or at least they should know, that the status quo is no longer sustainable, desirable, or debatable. Whether they acknowledge it or not, each one of them has a vested interest in staking out clear, lasting, and secure claims to the West of their various visions.

More to the point, environmentalists and wise users share a deep and abiding affection for community and the land. They may define what they mean by community differently and they may favor uses of the land that are dissimilar, but in practical terms their common anchorage in place is all that really matters. Ideology aside, what counts is where their fealty lies; it lies, as it always has in principle, in the basins and ranges of the Rocky Mountain, Sierra Nevada, and Cascade West. Only in practice, and only by virtue of wise use, have their loyalties waned from time to time.

One ingredient alone is missing in the recipe for strong land communities and small-scale cooperation on the western range. It is the critical awareness of what wise use has wrought and what is now needed to translate loyalty to place into tolerance for diversity on the western range. No matter what others may say, environmentalists and wise users are no more fated to be natural foes than wolves are destined to be the symbolic enemy of people and domestic beast. That they are, even if only in perception, is testimony to the power and persuasion of the wise use message. Yet if environmentalists and wise users would only listen and take heed, they could hear a more compelling and persuasive truth. They would come to understand that what divides them is not the difference in the values they hold, but rather the similarity in the tools they have used to reach those values. They would see the futility of wise-use solutions that leave room at the top for only one set of values, and where the rule of those values is no more fixed than a president's four-year term. They would see the wise-use West for what it truly is: a place where winners are never winners for long and where losers are the rule of the range. And they might just see that their advantage lies in the common ground of community and place. There, decisions that touch the land and its life would be safe from the vacillating machinations of national politicians and the well-meaning flow of federal dollars.

With wisdom and insight of what wise use has done to the West, environmentalists and wise users could begin dismantling the miles of federal barbed wire that have fenced them out of the land communities they envision as home. They could, if they wished, forge an ecumenical West where mutual aid supplants political fiat, where voluntarism and association eclipse reams of regulations, and where the intimate interests of the land community take precedence over the distant interests and passing fads of the national community. Western-ers of all ilks would then be ready for a kinder and gentler sagebrush rebellion—a peaceful revolt that would, in Kemmis's judgment, give "an unusual opportunity for the West to gain some control over its own territory and resources."[34]

Should this happen, the independence that wiser users seek and the expanded community that environmentalists long for might just coa-lesce as one from the building blocks of sand and sagebrush. On such a western range, people would find space for their dreams and elbow room for their ambitions. They would be able to stake secure and last-ing claims to their corner of the West and shed at long last the fear and insecurity that attends the claims of others. Freed from the fences that come with forced integration, westerners of all stripes might also be more receptive to the natural return of the wolf. They might wel-come with tolerant hearts the fateful homecoming of a citizen too-long exiled in the name of wise use. Then, the West will be truly ready for good neighbors and lasting peace.

Notes

1. Wallace Stegner, *Beyond the Hundredth Meridian: John Wesley Powell and the Second Opening of the West* (New York: Penguin Books, 1992), 32.

2. Ivan Doig, *Dancing at the Rascal Fair* (New York: Harper & Row, 1987), 232–33.

3. Karl Hess, Jr., "The West at War with Itself," *Reason* 27, no. 2 (June 1995): 20.

4. Karl Hess, Jr., "Babbitt Inherited a Mess: His Plan Will Make It Worse," *High Country News* 25, no. 20 (1 November 1993): 16.

5. Patricia Nelson Limerick, *The Legacy of Conquest: The Unbroken Past of the American West* (New York: W. W. Norton & Co., 1987), 83.

6. Examples include *Buford v. Houtz*, 133 U.S. 618, the Unlawful Enclosures Act of 1885, Grover Cleveland's 1885 Presidential Executive Order implement-ing the act, and the assigment of army troops to enforce both the act and the order.

7. William D. Rowley, *U.S. Forest Service Grazing and Rangelands* (College Station: Texas A & M Press, 1985), 148.

8. Karl Hess, Jr., *Visions Upon the Land: Man and Nature on the Western Range* (Covelo, Calif.: Island Press, 1992), 111.

9. R. McGreggor Cawley, *Federal Land, Western Anger* (Lawrence: Univer-sity Press of Kansas, 1993), 118.

10. Karl Hess, Jr., "Homage to Catron County," *Northern Lights* 9, no. 4 (Winter 1994): 18–22.

11. Karl Hess, Jr., *Reason* 27, no. 2 (June 1995): 22.

12. Jerry Holecheck and Karl Hess, Jr., "Government Policies and Range Management: The Emergency Feed Program," *Rangelands* 17, no. 4 (August 1995): 133–36.

13. Karl Hess, Jr., and Jerry L. Holecheck, "Subsidized Drought," *New York Times*, 12 December 1994, A15; and Jerry L. Holecheck and Karl Hess, Jr., "Free Market Policy for Public Land Grazing," *Rangelands* 16, no. 2 (April 1994): 64–65.

14. Karl Hess, Jr., and Jerry L. Holecheck, *Policy Analysis* (Washington, D.C.: The Cato Institute, June 1995).

15. Lisa Jones, "An In-Your-Face Range Scientist," *High Country News* 27, no. 8 (1 May 1995): 19.

16. Wayne Hage, *Storm Over Rangelands* (Bellevue Wash.: Free Enterprise Press, 1989), 62.

17. Bernard De Voto, "The West against Itself," *Harper's Magazine* 194, no. 1160 (January 1947): 3.

18. Edward Abbey, "Even the Bad Guys Wear White Hats," *Harper's Magazine* 272, no. 51–55 (January 1986): 53–54.

19. Stegner, 352–62.

20. Ibid., 355–56.

21. Ibid., 362.

22. Ibid., 358.

23. Michael P. Malone and Richard B. Roeder, *Montana: A History of Two Centuries* (Seattle: University of Washington Press, 1976), 180.

24. Stegner, *Beyond the Hundredth Meridian*, 361–62.

25. Ibid., 354.

26. Donald J. Pisani, "Forests and Reclamation, 1891–1911," *Forest & Conservation History* 37 (April 1993): 70.

27. Ibid., 69.

28. Ibid., 70.

29. Charles F. Wilkinson, "A Tribute to the Man Who Imagined the West We Now Seek to Build," *High Country News* (3 May 1993): 16.

30. Gifford Pinchot, *The Fight for Conservation* (New York: Harcourt, Brace and Co., 1947), 95–96; see also Gifford Pinchot, quoted in William Voight, Jr., *Public Grazing Lands* (New Brunswick, NJ: Rutgers University Press, 1976), 45; and see *Breaking New Ground* (New York: Harcourt Brace and Co., 1947), 505.

31. Bruce Babbitt, quoted in Tom Kenworthy, "Babbitt Drops Increase in Western Grazing Fees," *Washington Post*, 22 December 1994, A7.

32. Daniel Kemmis, *Community and the Politics of Place* (Norman: University of Oklahoma Press, 1990), 75.

33. Aldo Leopold, "The Land Ethic," in *A Sand County Almanac* (New York: Oxford University Press, 1949), 204.

34. Kemmis, *Community and the Politics of Place*, 127.

13

The Economic Role of Environmental Quality in Western Public Lands

Ray Rasker and Jon Roush

Assyrian iron, Arabic numerals, Greek philosophy, the Roman phalanx, the British steam engine, American electronics and information technology . . . a nation's wealth is created by intellectual innovation, not mere exploitation of resources.

— Montana Science and Technology Advisory Council

Public Lands and Community Stability

According to a Wall Street cliché, two emotions drive the stock market: fear and greed. Recent history suggests these emotions are at home on the range as well. Western landowners have expressed a litany of fears—some reasonable and some paranoid. The most common denominator is that the government, in league with environmentalists, will take some arbitrary action in alleged defense of a species or a wetland or a wilderness area. The result, these people fear, will be lost jobs, lost profits, economic decline, and whole communities posting "Going Out of Business" signs. To support those fears, people offer endless examples, ranging from anecdotes of beleaguered landowners to scholarly analyses of regulatory cause and economic effect. A domi-

A longer version of this chapter previously appeared as "A New Look at Old Vistas: The Economic Role of Environmental Quality in Western Public Lands," by Raymond Rasker in *University of Colorado Law Review* 65 (1994): 369–99. Reprinted, as abridged and updated, by permission of author and publisher.

nant concept underlies all these examples. It is the concept that has controlled land and water policy in the U.S. West. According to the dominant concept, the appropriation and use of natural resources for private gain is the primary engine of economic growth. Any interference with that engine is presumed to carry inevitable costs for the entire community. With so much at stake, sorting out fact from fiction in the dominant concept is essential. In this chapter, we have attempted that sorting.

We feel compelled to add at the outset that no discussion of land use and economics is value free. We have undertaken this work partly because of deeply held values. We love western landscapes. We believe the United States and the world need sustainable local and regional economies. The diverse cultures of America's West have enriched our lives. Above all, we believe future generations should have a chance to experience this land and way of life, and do so in a flourishing economy.

We explain our values because they are the same values often espoused by defenders of the dominant concept. The West's wise use movement explicitly champions those values. That should simplify the task. When people agree about ends, they should be able to engage a discussion of means. Yet one other difference in values remains. It is a difference in the perceived relationship between the individual person and the community. Most blatantly, the dominant concept opens the door for that other Wall Street emotion: greed. Some people have exploited westerners' fears for their own economic or political benefit. Those people have a stake in maintaining polarization by fanning fear, regardless of the facts. No matter how they rationalize it, those people knowingly sacrifice the common good for their own profit.

Less obvious but no less insidious is a related problem. Our conventional economic theories describe, measure, and value private goods more than common goods. It may be unfair to ascribe this bias to greed, but it undeniably has produced flawed economic analysis. The results are evident in current public policies throughout the United States. For example, consider the policies of the U.S. Forest Service. Even though the Forest Service has, as a manager of public lands, no specific statutory obligation to maintain community stability in resource-dependent communities, the Multiple-Use-Sustained Yield Act requires that multiple uses of the forests be balanced on a sustained yield basis.[1] Through this act, the Forest Service has the authority to consider "community stability," as long as it remains consistent with sustained yield.[2] Because of the emphasis on sustained yield, the term "community stability" is generally meant to apply to timber-dependent communities, or to protect "permanent communities of forest workers who would not have to move on when the local timber supply gave out."[3]

The idea of sustained-yield management was initially to help prevent the boom-and-bust cycles of natural-resource development in the West, Appalachia, and the Lake States by securing a steady supply of timber.[4] According to Schallau and Alston, "the supply role of the Forest Service is associated with long-run stability to the extent that stable and continuous supplies of timber allow firms and communities to undertake substantial investment projects without fear of loss of a source of raw material."[5]

The management philosophy of community stability has therefore been based on the implicit assumption that by altering the supply of raw materials made available from public lands, agencies can somehow fine-tune the direction and stability of nearby communities. As a result, agencies use community economic stability to justify subsidies to extractive industries, such as below-cost timber sales, and the heavy emphasis on commodity extraction are often justified by agencies that cite community economic stability as the rationale.[6]

Even though the origins of the community stability policy are based in timber, concerns over the impact of recreation, water resources, minerals, energy, and grazing also run throughout today's forest plans and environmental impact statements. According to Schallau and Alston, "the forest planning process mandated by the National Forest Management Act brings clear focus and urgency to the community-stability issue by producing comprehensive and long-range management plans for individual forests."[7]

The fallacy of the community stability policy can be exposed at two levels. First, as learned from lessons of the former Soviet Union, centrally planned economies do not work. Even if it were possible to manipulate natural ecosystems—of which we know very little—to produce a steady and predictable flow of grazing, mineral, energy, and timber resources, it is unlikely that the economy of nearby communities would remain stable. Factors such as price, the application of labor-saving technologies, international competition, the availability of capital, and the changing preferences of consumers all play as much a role in determining the health of local resource-dependent industries as does the supply of raw materials from public lands.[8] Second, the premise that public resources such as forage, timber, minerals, and energy can stimulate local economic stability presumes that the local economy is indeed dependent on federally owned resources. All too often the role public-land managers play in community development is based on an antiquated, often mythical view of the economy.[9]

New Economic Realities

The Changed Nature of
Goods Production

Three forces are at work in shaping the world economy. First, the industrial economy is becoming uncoupled from the primary products economy (i.e., raw materials). Many of the most valuable "products" in today's economy, like computer software and medical technology, require very little input of raw materials. Second, in the industrial economy itself, employment has become uncoupled from production. Manufacturing efficiency has decreased the demand for physical labor. Instead, human resources are increasingly applied in terms of research, design, engineering, finance, marketing, and other knowledge-based or value-added applications. Third, capital has become "foot-loose"—money follows good ideas, no matter where they occur on the globe.[10]

As a result of these forces, trade—not just of raw materials, but also human resources and financial capital—has become increasingly international. In the past, a country's comparative advantage was largely a function of its natural-resource endowments and the availability of labor and capital. In today's economy, these factors of production are less important than brainpower.[11] Some of the wealthiest countries in the world, such as Japan and The Netherlands, have achieved high living standards despite the fact that they own few natural resources. Japan, in particular, has excelled in international competition by skill-fully using the full potential of its human resources, relying on the expertise of financial experts, researchers, designers, product design engineers, advertisement specialists, and a whole array of knowledge-based or service professions. Indeed, services have become the fastest growing part of the economy of rich countries, where today over half of the workers are employed in the production, storage, retrieval, or distribution of knowledge.[12] Furthermore, components of manufacturing, such as research, design, testing, and marketing are often "outsourced" or subcontracted to firms, sometimes at opposite ends of the world. Today, where the final product rolls off the assembly line is less important than who adds the most value to production. And, if most of a finished product's value lies in the amount of human ingenuity and modern technology that is applied, then those countries with the best trained and educated workforce will command the largest piece of the economic pie.

Lester Thurow points out that the seven key industries of the next few decades are all "brainpower" industries—microelectronics, biotechnology, the new materials industries, civilian aviation, telecommunications, robots and machine tools, and computers and software. An important aspect of these industries is that they are footloose—they can locate anywhere in the world. According to Thurow: "Where they will locate depends upon who can organize the brainpower to capture them. In the century ahead the comparative advantage will be manmade."[13]

The Role of "Services"

In the jargon of government statistics, the knowledge-based professions are invariably lumped together as "services." However, in today's rapidly changing economy it is difficult to define precisely what a service is, and a lack of understanding has led to some confusion. A common misconception is that the service sectors are composed of people making hamburgers and shining shoes, while in reality, services are a significant force in today's economy. Worldwide, services account for 60 percent of the gross domestic product of rich countries. In the United States, services account for 72 percent of GDP and 76 percent of employment (manufacturing, in contrast, accounts for only 23 percent of America's GDP and 18 percent of all jobs). Since 1982, services accounted for 91 percent of new jobs.[14]

The service sectors are made up of complex, powerful, and often technically sophisticated businesses. They are represented, in part, by those in the knowledge-based professions—the doctors, lawyers, engineers, management consultants, software designers, and data processing and telecommunications specialists. This category also includes the low-paying, cyclical jobs, such as retail sales clerks and hotel maids. Unfortunately, many knowledge-based professions are labeled by government statisticians as services, but these should clearly be separated from the services provided by chambermaids and bartenders. As a recent article in the *Economist* magazine put it: "Policemen and prostitutes, bankers and butchers are all lumped together in the service sector."[15]

An outdated but, unfortunately, all too prevalent way of thinking alleges that service industries do not produce exports and that they are, in fact, "parasitic to goods production."[16] In other words, service industries serve as support functions to manufacturing, and by themselves do not generate new wealth into the local economy. This misconception stems, in part, from the fact that service products are often intangible in nature, making it difficult to see how they might serve as exports. The production of computer software, the invention of an improved chemical formula for a new pharmaceutical product, or advice given over the phone by a broker are all products of the service sector. Rather than being exported via truck or train, like timber or minerals, the service export often travels via mail, telephone, fax, or computer modem.[17]

The distinction between manufacturing and services is becoming increasingly useless. Services, such as design, sales, and engineering, are an integral and necessary part of the manufacturing process, even though they are counted differently in government statistics. Growth in services is more likely an indication of the increased application of knowledge to the manufacturing process; they are part of the assembly line that produces a manufactured product. To accurately account for the different forms of labor on a finished product, it is, therefore, in most instances, no longer relevant to differentiate between manufacturing and services. Manufacturing depends on the application of human ingenuity and management skills (services), and many services (e.g., engineering, biotechnology) exist only because they are applied to manufacturing. Yet other forms of services, such as entertainment, health and education, can exist without the manufacture of a physical product, but nonetheless create viable "exports." According to one recent estimate, about one-sixth of export-related economic activity in rural economies nationwide is associated with producer services, and "these businesses are strongly attracted to rural America due to quality of life considerations."[18]

Overall, services seem to be one area where the U.S. economy is doing well. While the United States trade deficit, in total, has topped $100 billion in seven of the past nine years, American companies that export services have amassed a $59 billion trade surplus. Even against Japan, the United States last year ran a $14 billion trade surplus in services.[19] This is a clear indication that one of the strengths of the economy is the ability to compete in the service or "knowledge" industries.

Economic Changes in the Rural West

The economic history of the rural West is one of a dependence on natural resources; on soils and water for crop and livestock production, on minerals, coal, oil, and gas, and on forested lands for timber. Of course, some gateway communities to national parks, like West Yellowstone, Montana, Jackson, Wyoming, and Estes Park, Colorado, have been able to carve a niche for themselves in the tourism industry. But, for the most part the West is still largely assumed to be dependent on agriculture and the extractive industries.[20] In an article for the *Denver Post,* James McMahon of the Independence Institute wrote, "I ask you to consider for a moment what drives the economy of the West. Look past the major cities into the mountains and plains of rural America. Is it not these very industries—ranching, farming, mining and logging—that provide all of the employment in many of our communities?" In the article McMahon asserted that "western businesses are girding for the battle of their lives as the new administration plans to hike grazing fees, end farm subsidies, impose royalties on mining, and halt below-cost timber sales."[21]

The "goods producing" industries—the extractive sectors and agriculture—are often assumed to be the only "basic" or export-producing industries. This is exactly how the Wyoming Heritage Foundation illustrated its view of reality on the brochure for its 1992 annual meeting: "The Engines That Power Wyoming's Economy." On the cover was a drawing of a locomotive, charging full-steam ahead. On the engine, under the heading of "Wyoming's Economy" appeared "Coal, Trona, Gas, Oil, Agriculture and Tourism."[22] On the cowcatcher were the other industries: "finance, retail, utilities, transportation, construction, services and health." The implication is clear: the "other" industries are of secondary importance; the real economy is driven by resource extraction, primarily, and tourism.

A closer view of economic trends reveals a flaw in this depiction of the Wyoming economy. In 1969, mining (including oil and gas) and agriculture represented 17.6 percent of all employment and 17 percent of personal income in the state. By 1991, the contribution of these industries declined to 12.4 percent of total employment and less than 10 percent of personal income. Even though there has been a decline relative to the rest of the economy, it can be argued that these industries continue to be of importance, particularly for some resource-dependent communities. The trends indicate, however, that mining and agriculture—long the pillars of Wyoming's economy—are not the sources of most new jobs. From 1969 to 1991 over 91 percent of all new jobs have come from industries other than mining, oil and gas, or agriculture. During that time the farming and ranching sectors lost over two thousand jobs. The mining sector added a little over seven thousand new jobs in the last two decades, but today employs less than half of the number of people it did in the oil and gas boom of the early 1980s.[23] The majority of economic growth in Wyoming (76 percent in the last two decades) has been in the "service" industries: retail sales, finance, insurance and real estate, consumer, personal, health, legal and business services, and state and local government. The remainder of the new growth was in construction, transportation, public utilities, and manufacturing.[24] In terms of wages, the new jobs created represent a mix of low-paying jobs and high-wage professions. For example, the average annual wage in the oil and gas industry, the highest paid industry in the state, is $28,000 per annum. Service-related industries that pay similar wages are engineering, architecture, communication-related businesses, and finance. Nor are all extractive related industries high paying. Earnings in the lumber and wood products sector in Wyoming, for example, average $16,000 per annum.[25]

Wyoming's economy has diversified beyond its former reliance on natural resources as the only engine that pulls the economy. The "knowledge" economy described earlier has arrived in Wyoming. For example, Safecard Services, a company that conducts credit checks for financial institutions, recently moved its headquarters to Cheyenne. Using modern telecommunications facilities, the three hundred employees of this $150 million dollar per year firm conduct business by tapping into computer records across the country and communicating with clients via fax and computer. This company does not rely on Wyoming's natural resources for business. Instead, it requires an educated and reliable workforce, and a pleasant social and natural environment. For companies like these, Wyoming's assets lie in its towns and people, and in its amenities. Throughout the West similar trends can be seen. The Rocky Mountain West, for example, has added over two million new jobs from 1969 to 1991, most of them in service-related occupations. Of the new jobs, 38 percent were in personal, consumer, legal, health, and business services, 19 percent were in retail trade, 12 percent were in government, and 9 percent in finance, insurance, and real estate. In 1969, over 11 percent of all direct employment and 9.6 percent of personal income in the region were in the natural resource industries—in either mining, farming, ranching, or in the lumber and wood products industries. By 1991, these industries combined represented less than 6 percent of all employment and less than 5 percent of all personal income. In contrast, in 1991, the service-related sectors represented over 81 percent of employment and 68 percent of labor income. The four largest service employers are also in relative high-wage occupations: health, engineering and management consulting, business, and legal services, respectively.[26]

Throughout the West, the economy has adapted to changing conditions. Despite this, the common mythology is still anchored in the belief that the extraction and export of raw materials are what matters. A commonly heard phrase is "true wealth comes from the ground." Over the last two decades, however, it has become increasingly obvious that wealth also lies in resources that are not based on agriculture or the extractive industries. Although these traditional industries will—and should—remain as integral components of a diverse economy, it is clear that a "rear-view mirror" approach to economic development will not suffice.[27] Communities in the West need to shift their focus from what worked in the past, and ask instead what will work in the future. Economic wealth consists of much more than raw materials. There is also wealth in the quality of the environment for nonconsumptive uses, in the small-town friendliness of western communities, and in the skills and desires of the region's people.

Economic Role of Environmental Quality

Recent economic trends in the West portray a mixed picture. The region has grown, but not in the accustomed ways. Most of the growth has been in service-related industries, while the declines have been primarily in agriculture and resource-extractive sectors. Nor has the growth or decline been evenly distributed. While some areas grew, others declined. Those who lost population generally saw a loss in economic vitality, an increase in unemployment, a relative decline in income, and a high level of out-migration.[28]

The biggest obstacles for rural areas have traditionally been the distance to markets, and increasing competition from abroad in agriculture and manufacturing. Although international competition remains intense, the remote nature of rural communities can, in some instances, be counted on as an economic benefit.

Significant to rural communities is the fact that many of the individuals involved in the "service" or "knowledge-based" forms of production have become footloose. These people are called "lone eagles" by some, a growing group of freelance professionals who are abandoning life in the cities for the good life in the country. This phenomenon is also referred to as "green-fielding," which refers to the migration of entire firms, which move out of cities to escape the expense and hassles of urban life.[29]

With the advent of the fax machine and computer modem, and with access to efficient delivery services like United Parcel Service and Federal Express, many of those who choose to live in rural communities with high amenities can now do so, while at the same time maintaining their jobs. In a recent study on the subject, the Office of Technology Assessment estimates that perhaps the most promising way to make rural communities competitive in a global service-based economy is to improve the communications and information-delivery infrastructure.[30] In some instances, this view has reached the political leadership. For example, Montana senator Conrad Burns speaks passionately of Montanans "telecommuting to work" during the emerging "information age" on "information highways" using sophisticated fiber optic networks, interactive video computers, and other high-tech equipment like phone service, faxes, and modems.[31]

For many rural communities, the economic benefits of living adjacent to public lands has historically been in terms of access to vast repositories of raw material. Because of this economic history, there has been a tremendous bias on the part of public agencies to equate quantitative expansion in commercial activities with social and economic well-being. Lacking is a perspective on economic development that measures the role of quality of life as provided to community residents living next to public lands: the mountains, scenery, wildlife, clean water, wilderness, and other noncommercial amenities.

An independent assessment of the economy of Montana, entitled "The Governor's Council on Montana's Future," showed the economic importance of environmental quality to the future of Montana's economy. At town meetings held throughout the state, citizens were asked to rank the relative importance of different goals and visions. Maintaining a "clean environment" was the highest priority, followed by a "quality education." As strengths and opportunities, the "natural resources" and "quality of life" ranked first and second, respectively. In terms of the biggest weakness, "poor tax structure" was mentioned first, followed by "polarization/partisanship." The report concluded that "Montana's quality natural environment and its strong citizen support for maintaining a sustainable environment and excellent quality of life provide the underlying foundation for the Department [of Commerce] to focus business efforts upon environmental protection."[32]

Like the rest of the region, Montana needs to be viewed as more than a repository of raw material for production. Since 1970, over 150,000 new jobs have been added to the state's economy, not one of them in mining, logging, ranching, or farming.[33] Throughout the West the situation is the same; the key assets are not only the natural capital of the land, but also the intellectual capital of its residents and the friendly, small-town atmosphere—the quality of life. These amenities are economic assets in very much the same way timber and minerals resources are. They serve an important function: to retain existing people and business, and to attract potential entrepreneurs. The implications for public land management are obvious. If public lands play a role in maintaining the quality of life, then land managers can assist rural communities by protecting those qualities.

The Greater Yellowstone Ecosystem

The eighteen-million-acre Greater Yellowstone ecosystem includes at its core two national parks—Yellowstone and Grand Teton—which are surrounded by seven National Forests, land administered by the Bureau of Land Management, state and private lands, and the Wind River Indian Reservation. It is an area that is internationally renowned as one of the most intact temperate zone ecosystems on the planet, as a place where most wildlife species inhabiting the region before the arrival of Europeans still survive, and as a place where large-scale ecological functions, such as wildfires and ungulate migrations still occur with minimal human intervention.[34]

The economic history of the Greater Yellowstone area is similar to much of the West: resource extraction, ranching, farming, and tourism, particularly for gateway communities to the parks, like Jackson and Cody, Wyoming, and West Yellowstone, Montana. Like the new West, the Greater Yellowstone has also undergone a significant change in its economy. From 1969 to 1991, the region added over 74,000 new jobs, the majority (over 80 percent) in retail trade, finance, insurance, real estate, business, education, engineering, legal, and other services, or in state and local government. Over 98 percent of all new jobs in the region and 91 percent of labor income during that time has occurred in industries other than mining, oil and gas, farming and ranching, or manufacturing, which includes the lumber and wood products sector.[35] In addition, nonlabor income, primarily retirement income and money earned from past investments, constitutes 35 percent of the personal income in the region, which is more than two and a half times the income derived from mining, logging, and agriculture, combined.[36]

A frequently heard lament on the transition from timber, mining and ranching to a service-based economy is that high-wage jobs are being lost. Yet, in the Greater Yellowstone region, the largest components of services are in relatively high-wage industries. Twenty-nine percent of services is made up of engineering and management services ($39,376 per annum); another 22 percent is in health services (over $20,000 per annum). Of course, the service sector also includes relatively low-paying industries, such as hotel and lodging (a little over $10,770 per annum). On average, however, the salaries in the service industries are 20 percent higher than the average wages for all other industries.[37]

In spite of these changes, the management priority of the national forests of the region reflects a bias toward commodity extraction and toward a view of "community stability" based on an outdated view of the local economy. Throughout the 1980s and early 1990s, two out of every three Forest Service dollars went toward the production of commodities—timber, oil and gas, minerals, and range for livestock grazing. For some forests, the emphasis on commodity extraction has been even higher. For example, in 1989 the Targhee and Shoshone forests spent 72 and 70 percent of their budgets, respectively, on commodity-oriented expenditures.[38] Yet, less than 5 percent of the workforce in the region is dependent, directly or indirectly (through a multiplier effect) on logging, mining, energy development, and grazing on the national forests. If recreation is included, only 9 percent of the 156,000 jobs in 1989 were dependent in any way on activities that take place in the national forests of Greater Yellowstone.[39]

From the perspective of public-land management, the trends in Greater Yellowstone beg the question: If the region is little dependent on commodities from the national forests, then what is the role of public-lands management in promoting community stability? A clue can be found in research conducted by Montana State University, where researchers surveyed business owners in the Montana portion of the ecosystem. The purpose of the survey was to discover the relative importance of quantitative reasons (e.g., profits, costs of production, taxes) versus qualitative reasons (e.g., scenery, climate, crime rate) in people's decisions to either move to or retain a business in the region.

The study revealed that traditional reasons for locating a business, such as availability of raw materials, the local tax structure, and availability of labor and capital, all ranked comparatively low in people's decisions to move to or stay in the area. In fact, 66 percent felt they "would be more profitable in an urban setting," but when asked "all things considered, would you choose to locate a business here again," 86 percent said yes. The most important reasons cited were, in order, "quality environment," "a good place to raise a family," and "scenic beauty." When the responses of old-timers were compared to newcomers, it was revealed that existing business owners felt even stronger about the importance of quality of life variables than recent newcomers. The implication is that the social, cultural, and environmental amenities of a community are even more important to business retention than they are for attracting new businesses. The study concluded that an important role for public policy is to understand the role amenities have on business owners, and if amenities are a significant determinant of people's decisions to stay in the community, then the role of government should be to protect, and even enhance, the attributes that the community finds attractive.[40]

In the Greater Yellowstone region, the primary stimulus for the economy is the scenery, wildlife, and wild features of the ecosystem, and the unique social and cultural characteristics of the community. Yet, the Forest Service has managed the land with a priority that suggests that the national forests of the ecosystem are the engine that drives the local economy.[41] An alternative strategy for the agency— one that would be more productive economically—is to protect and enhance the elements of the natural landscape that serve to attract and retain people and business.

"Wilderness—Land of No Use"

Perhaps no other issue tests the common knowledge of the western economy than that represented by the bumper sticker that says "Wilderness—Land of No Use." It is emblematic of the utilitarian view many in the West hold, that in order for a resource to have economic value, it must be used. If it is not used, it is assumed to be of no good to society. Minerals can be dug up to produce copper wire or jewelry, rangelands can be grazed to produce beef, timber can be cut to build homes, even elk can be measured in "use values" in terms of expenditures by hunters. But what is the economic value of something that is not used? What is a grizzly bear worth? More difficult yet, what is the value of wilderness, of the habitat of the grizzly bear?

A study by Rudzitis and Johanson illustrates how not using resources can play a considerable economic role. They found that during the 1960s, counties containing federally designated wilderness areas had population increases three times greater than other nonmetropolitan counties. In the 1970s, they grew at a rate twice that of nonmetropolitan areas, and in the 1980s, their population increased 24 percent—six times more than the national average of 4 percent for non-metropolitan areas and almost twice as much as counties in the rural West.[42] In order to test the importance of amenities in people's decision to migrate to areas with high environmental quality, Rudzitis and Johansen conducted a random survey of over eleven thousand migrants and residents in fifteen wilderness counties in the West. They found that economic considerations were important location variables for only 23 percent of the migrants. In contrast, the most important reasons for locating in a wilderness county were the environmental and physical amenities, the scenery, outdoor recreation, and the pace of life. When asked their attitudes toward development, 90 percent of recent migrants and 85 percent of established residents felt that it was important to "keep the environment in its natural state." The authors concluded that "amenities and quality-of-life factors are increasingly important to people's decisions about moving" and that "newcomers appear to want more access for recreational use of wilderness, preservation of established wilderness, and designation of additional wilderness in the same area." Almost 75 percent of the migrants surveyed felt that life was less stressful since they had moved; 91 percent found it more enjoyable; and 89 percent felt happier and healthier since their move.[43]

New Options for Public-land Management Agencies

As the role of public-lands agencies shifts away from facilitating commodity production, an all too immediate tendency is then to assume that the next thing to do is to expand the recreation and tourism roles of public lands.[44] Environmentalists are as guilty of this form of oversimplification as anyone, yet such a strategy may lead to significant environmental costs. An example of the fact that tourism is not an environmental panacea can be found in the plight of the grizzly bear in the Greater Yellowstone ecosystem. Between 1975 and 1987, approximately 127 bears were killed in the ecosystem; 80 percent of the deaths were attributed to interactions with humans.[45]

While there is little room in this paper to extrapolate on the ecological, social, and cultural pressures that tourism growth brings to
rural communities, it is sufficient to say that a complete transition
from resource extraction to tourism misses the point. Community stability can best be ensured by economic diversity. For this reason, the
wisest approach is if there is tourism potential, develop it, but not to
the point where it significantly alters the character of the town. Then,
combine tourism with a small-scale, value-added and sustainable wood
products industry, open a small-business incubator, and build an assis-
ted-living center for elderly residents. In other words, make tourism
one of many different strategies.[46]

The cornerstone to an economic diversity strategy is to create a
favorable business climate and to protect the cultural, social, and environmental qualities that make a community a pleasant place to live
and do business. An investment in infrastructure, such as education
and telecommunications facilities, will also facilitate entrepreneurial
activity. In many instances, the most economically productive role of
public lands is not in resource extraction or tourism, but in protecting
the landscape, the wildlife, the rivers and streams, and the scenery—
all those things that collectively enhance the quality of life for local
residents.

New Challenges for the Environmental
Movement

In the 1800s the challenge for the West was to promote growth—to
make the most use of the natural-resource endowments of the region.
In the 1990s, the challenge is more difficult. The West is not a
single, homogeneous place. It is a mosaic of landscapes, resources,
communities, economies, and cultures—a mosaic of confounding complexity. No one person, agency, or interest can have enough information or wisdom to manage any significant part of the region without
involving others. As in many other environmental issues, we must
master the most difficult of challenges: making decisions about highly
complex systems with low levels of certainty and high stakes.

However we make these decisions, the goal must be to pass our
natural endowment undiminished to future generations. That can happen only if we treat natural systems and economic systems as parts of
a single whole. Sustainable economies require sustainable landscapes,
and vice versa. We must balance private needs and public values. Since

public values include the unpredictable needs of future generations, decision processes must be dynamic and open ended. They must preserve options, and that means we cannot afford decisions that deplete renewable resources. Fortunately, all these principles make good sense economically as well as ecologically.

The challenge is to use our natural endowment intelligently, without despoiling the quality of life for the region's residents, and without foreclosing opportunities for economic diversification. If scenery is part of what attracts and retains modern business activity beyond tourism, then an unsightly clearcut will have more than ecological costs; it will be bad for the economy.

Public lands in the West still contain a healthy "multiple-use" endowment of minerals, timber, oil, gas, and cattle forage. Can the resources be extracted in a way that does not damage the scenery, wildlife habitat, soils, and streams—and in a way that is financially equitable, without the crutch of taxpayer-supported subsidies? In some instances this may be the case. But in the economy of the new West, the concept of multiple use may have begun to lose relevance. Increasingly, the best management option may be "no use." As is the case with wilderness, sometimes the most productive economic role of public lands agencies is to protect the ecological integrity of the land.

A paradigm shift toward a better understanding of the economic role of public lands is necessary and long overdue. There are two reasons supporting this shift. First, past policies simply have not worked. Central planning and the heavy emphasis on a scientific management model have not succeeded in establishing community stability, nor have they led to management practices that protect and nurture the ecological productivity of the land. There are simply too many economic and ecological forces at work to accurately plan and predict for the long-term stability of a community. Furthermore, many times, as in the Greater Yellowstone ecosystem, a community stability strategy that emphasizes commodity extraction has been shown to be counterproductive, particularly when those activities threaten the amenity-based foundation of the new economy.

The new high-tech, knowledge-based, amenity-based economy of the West brings with it a whole new set of problems. As new residents flock to the Rocky Mountain states they also bring with them the danger of loving the place to death. In the Greater Yellowstone ecosystem, for example, the biggest challenge is not job growth but growth management. The influx of recent migrants has resulted in subdivision of agricultural land, and the loss of open space and wildlife habitat. Over a million acres, or more than a third of the region's private lands, have already been subdivided into plots of two hundred acres or less. In places like Jackson, Wyoming, Driggs, Idaho, and Livingston, Montana, a feeding-frenzy mentality has ensued on the real estate market, driving up the cost of living and forcing the local population to commute in from distant bedroom communities. The same story repeats itself in Telluride and Boulder, Colorado, Santa Fe, New Mexico, and other "islands of the lycra archipelago." Pickup trucks are replaced with BMWs, rodeos disappear, and boutiques and espresso shops open up. In short, the Old West is supplanted by a New West, and in the process old and familiar cultures are being replaced by new ones. The resulting social stress this causes is significant and generally poorly handled.

The financial and human capital that is currently being spent on promoting extractive uses of public lands could be redirected toward helping communities deal with these new challenges. For example, savings to the Treasury from phasing out below-cost timber sales, instituting a market price for grazing fees, instituting recreation user fees, and reform of the Mining Law of 1872 could all be applied to helping communities develop the infrastructure and leadership capacity to deal with the challenges of the New West. The expertise of Forest Service and BLM staff can be applied to help communities deal with change in a way that protects the social, cultural, and environmental values of the community. The Forest Service and the BLM can also play a significant role in protecting what little is left undeveloped in the West. As private lands are parceled out for the booming real estate market, public lands will provide the last sanctuary, the last remnants of open space, wildlife habitat, clean water, and solitude. In an article for *Time* magazine, William Kittredge asked, "Is this the old dream—America the beautiful, and I want my share? Yeah, except it may be more accurate to say that this is all that's left of the dream— a hideout in the Rockies, the last safe place. And afterward, in a couple more generations, where will we go then?"[47]

In the early 1980s, the gap between the rich and poor was widening, with its effects being particularly prevalent in rural America, which has a long-standing tradition of being exploited by large outside corporations. As mining companies exploited the land around Anaconda and Butte and as large timber companies created company towns, a culture of dependency was created. Then they left, and on their way out pointed the finger of blame at environmentalists. Working-class people in rural America are being used as pawns in a political game.

A cargo cult economy has been created, and the wise use movement, often funded by large extractive corporations, has tried to perpetuate that way of thinking.

We environmentalists can help the West get out of the box of scapegoating and denial, but only if we also are willing to adapt. New realities in the West have challenged everyone concerned to reexamine assumptions. Economists, landowners, business people, policy makers, regulators, and not least, environmentalists—all must work together to create systems that are sustainable economically and ecologically.

The reexamination already has begun, through a growing number of spontaneous initiatives. For example, for the past several years The Wilderness Society has worked with several rural communities, like Grays Harbor, Washington, and Kremmling, Colorado, to help find ways to diversify resource-dependent economies. A small grants program has been used to help finance innovative solutions to economic and environmental problems, and it has produced a workbook entitled *Measuring Change in Rural Communities*.[48] Working with several small towns, The Wilderness Society conducts workshops on the use of the workbook, which shows residents how to gather and present data on demographic, economic, and fiscal trends. The workshops are conducted in a consensus-based, value-neutral setting. The society is also planning a series of demonstration projects to strengthen the connection between rural economic and ecological health. One project will produce certified (as coming from sustainable, or well-managed forests) paper. The demonstration project will explore the potential market niche for such paper and break the trail for local mills who might survive by occupying that niche. Another pilot program seeks to establish a revolving loan fund to help environmentally responsible small-woodland owners and forest-products manufacturers clear the financial and technical hurdles between them and greater competitiveness in world markets.

None of these initiatives by themselves is the final answer. Nor is The Wilderness Society the only organization trying. Other organizations, like EcoTrust, Sustainable Northwest, the Sonoran Institute, Grand Canyon Trust, the Conservation Fund, and the Corporation for Northern Rockies are engaged in other approaches that complement ours. Environmentalists need to build on such work. The goal should be to help communities that share regional resources work together toward a sustainable future. In such work, environmentalists can be catalysts and sources of expertise, but they will succeed only by sharing power.

The environmental movement faces the challenge of helping to change the dominant economic paradigm without perpetuating polarization. Too often, we environmentalists have ignored our common interest with rural people. We need to join forces with communities that stand to lose from unsustainable levels of resource use. Ultimately that is the only way to defuse the fear and greed that now paralyze the West.

Notes

1. S. Bates, "The Changing Management Philosophies of the Public Lands," *Western Lands Report* 3 (1992), Natural Resources Law Center, University of Colorado School of Law, Boulder.

2. C. H. Schallau and R. M. Alston, "The Commitment to Community Stability: A Policy or Shibboleth?" *Environmental Law* 17 (1987): 429.

3. D. A. Clary, "What Price Sustained Yield? The Forest Service, Community Stability, and Timber Monopoly under the 1944 Sustained-Yield Act," *Journal of Forest History* 31, no. 1 (1987): 4.

4. D. N. Wear, W. F. Hyde, and S. E. Daniels, "Even-Flow Timber Harvests and Community Stability," *Journal of Forestry*, September 1989: 24–28.

5. C. H. Schallau and Alston, "The Commitment to Community Stability," 433.

6. M. Peter Emerson, "An Overview of the Below-Cost Timber Sales Issue," paper presented at a Conference on the Economics of National Forest Timber Sales in Spokane, Washington, 1986; C. H. Schallau, "Evolution of Community Stability as a Forestry Issue: Time for the Dry Dock," in D. C. LeMaster and J. H. Beuter, *Community Stability in Forest-based Economies* (Portland: Timber Press, 1987), 6; R. N. Rasker, N. Tirrell and D. Kloepfer, eds., *The Wealth of Nature: New Economic Realities in the Yellowstone Region* (Washington, D.C.: The Wilderness Society, 1992).

7. Schallau and Alston, "The Commitment to Community Stability," 434.

8. Wear, Hyde, and Daniels, "Even-Flow Timber Harvests and Community Stability," 24–28; S. E. Daniels and B. J. Daniels, "The Impact of Below-cost Timber Sales on Community Stability," *Western Wildlands* 12, no. 1 (1986): 26–30; D. N. Wear, "Structural Change and Factor Demand Analysis in Montana's Solid Wood Products Industries," *Canadian Journal of Forest Research* 19 (1989): 645–50.

9. T. M. Power, "Ecosystem Preservation and the Economy in the Greater Yellowstone Area," *Conservation Biology* 5, no. 3: 395–424 (1991).

10. P. F. Drucker, "The Changed World Economy," *Foreign Affairs* 64, no. 4 (1986): 768–91.

11. L. Thurow, *Head to Head* (New York: Warner Books, 1993).

12. "The Final Frontier" *The Economist*, 20 February, 1993, 64.

13. Thurow, *Head to Head*, 45.

14. "Final Frontier," 63, 64. See also J. B. Quinn and C. E. Gagnon, "Will Services Follow Manufacturing into Decline?" *Harvard Business Review*, November-December 1986, 95–103; and R. B. Reich, "The Real Economy," *Atlantic Monthly* 267, no. 2 (1981): 35–52.

15. "Final Frontier," 63.

16. R. W. Goe and J. L. Shanahan, "A Conceptual Approach for Examining Service Sector Growth in Urban Economies: Issues and Problems in Analyzing the Service Economy," *Economic Development Quarterly* 4, no. 2 (1990): 149.

17. R. Rasker, "Rural Development, Conservation, and Public Policy in the Greater Yellowstone Ecosystem," *Society and Natural Resources* 6 (1993): 177.

18. W. B. Boyers, D. P. Lindahl, and E. Hamill, "Lone Eagles and Other High Fliers in the Rural Producer Services," paper presented at Pacific Northwest Regional Economic Conference, May 1995, Missoula, Montana.

19. R. T. King, "Quiet Boom," *The Wall Street Journal* (western edition), 21 April, 1993, A1.

20. R. Rasker, "Rural Development," 109–26; P. Polzin, "The State and Local Economic Outlook," *Montana Business Quarterly*, spring 1990, 5.

21. J. McMahon, "The Most Pressing Environmental Issue Concerns People," *Denver Post*, 18 April 1993.

22. Trona is a mineral that is used as a source of sodium compounds.

23. U.S. Department of Commerce, "Regional Economic Information System" (REIS CD-ROM computer disk), Bureau of Economic Analysis (Washington, D.C.: 1992).

24. Ibid.

25. U.S. Department of Commerce, "County Business Patterns: Wyoming," Bureau of the Census (Washington D.C.: U.S. Government Printing Office, 1992).

26. U.S. Department of Commerce, Regional Economic Information System.

27. T.M. Power, "Ecosystem Preservation and the Economy in the Greater Yellowstone Area," 396.

28. U.S. Congress, *Rural America at the Crossroads: Networking for the Future.* Office of Technology Assessment, OTA-TCT-471 (Washington, D.C.: U.S. Government Printing Office, 1991).

29. P. Roberts, "Global Villages," *Seattle Weekly* 18, no. 28, (1993): 18–23.

30. U.S. Congress, *Rural America at the Crossroads: Networking for the Future.*

31. U.S. Senate, "Building the roads for the future for Montana," Legislative Alert, U.S. Senator Conrad Burns, 1991.

32. Montana Department of Commerce, *The Montana Future's Project: Report Three*, Governor's Council for Montana's Future, 1992, 3–4.

33. U.S. Department of Commerce, "Regional Economic Information System."

34. D. Glick, M. Carr, and B. Harting, *An Environmental Profile of the Greater Yellowstone Ecosystem.* (Bozeman, Mont.: Greater Yellowstone Coalition, 1991).

35. U.S. Department of Commerce, "Regional Economic Information System"; Power, "Ecosystem Preservation and the Economy in the Greater Yellowstone Area"; Rasker, *The Wealth of Nature*; Rasker, "Rural Development, Conservation, and the Public Policy in the Greater Yellowstone Ecosystem."

36. Rasker, *The Wealth of Nature*, 11.

37. U.S. Department *County Business Patterns*. Bureau of the Census (Washington, D.C.: 1992).

38. R. Rasker, "Rural Development, Conservation, and Public Policy in the Greater Yellowstone Ecosystem," 120–21.

39. Congressional Research Service, *Greater Yellowstone Ecosystem*. The Library of Congress (Washington, D.C. 1987), and Rasker, *The Wealth of Nature*, 16.

40. J. Johnson and R. Rasker, "Local Government: Local Business Climate and Quality of Life," *Montana Policy Review*, fall 1993, 11–19.

41. R. Rasker, "Rural Development, Conservation, and Public Policy in the Greater Yellowstone Ecosystem," 123.

42. G. Rudzitis, "Nonmetropolitan Geography: Migration, Sense of Place, and the American West," *Urban Geography* 14, no. 6 (1993): 574–85.

43. G. Rudzitis and H. E. Johansen, "Migration into Western Wilderness Counties: Causes and Consequences," *Western Wildlands*, spring 1989, 19–23; G. Rudzitis and H. E. Johansen, "Amenities, Migration, and Nonmetropolitan Regional Development," *Report to the National Science Foundation* (Moscow: Department of Geography, University of Idaho, 1989).

44. C. H. Schallau and R. M. Alston, "The Commitment to Community Stability," 8; L. J. McDonnell, "Discussion Paper: The Changing Economics of the Public Lands," *Western Lands Report No. 2*, (Boulder, Colo.: Natural Resources Law Center, University of Colorado School of Law, 1993), 33.

45. D. Amato and D. Whittemore, *Status Report on the Yellowstone Grizzly Bear* (Bozeman, Mont.: Greater Yellowstone Coalition, 1989); Congressional Research Service, *Greater Yellowstone Ecosystem*.

46. For a review of the social and cultural costs of tourism see P. C. Jobes, "The Greater Yellowstone Social System," *Conservation Biology* 5, no. 3 (1991): 387–94; J. D. Johnson, J. D. Snepenger, and S. Akis, "Host Resident Sentiment toward Tourism in a Transitional Rural Economy," *Annals of Tourism Research* (forthcoming); B. S. Martin and M. Uysal, "An Examination of the Relationship between the Carrying Capacity and the Tourism Lifecycle: Management and Policy Implications," *Journal of Environmental Management* 31 (1990): 327-33.

47. W. Kittridge, "The Last Safe Place," *Time*, 6 September 1993, 27.

48. R. Rasker, J. Johnson, and V. York, *Measuring Change in Rural Communities: A Workbook for Determining Demographic, Economic and Fiscal Trends* (Washington, D.C.: The Wilderness Society, 1994).

14

Wise Use Movement and the National Parks

John Freemuth

It may not seem that the national parks would draw much attention from the wise use movement, because the wise use movement tends to concentrate on the use and development of natural resources. Thus much of the wise user's attention is focused on federal bureaus whose policies allow for resource extraction and utilization, notably the U.S. Forest Service and the Bureau of Land Management. National parks are supposed to be areas protected from resource utilization and would seem to lie outside the purview of the wise use movement. Unless, of course, one argues that national parks *should* be opened for resource development, which some in the wise use movement have done. The wise use movement has, however, also had some interesting things to say about the management of national parks under *current* bureau policy. These points raise difficult and provocative questions about the management of these renowned protected areas. In order to understand the movement's arguments, however, some background is helpful.

Statutory Setting

A specific type of use is addressed in the 1916 Organic Act, which created the U.S. National Park Service (NPS) and gave the new bureau its management direction and mission. The relevant section of that act gives the NPS regulatory authority over the parks, to be guided by the act's statement of purpose. That purpose, according to Congress, is to "*conserve* the scenery and the natural and historic objects and the wildlife therein and to provide for the *enjoyment* of the same in such manner and by such means as will leave them *unimpaired* for the *enjoyment* of future generations."[1] I have placed this section's key words in italics: conserve, unimpaired, and enjoyment. These words help create what many have come to call the "use/preservation tension" for park management. Parks, within this tension, are to be used and they are to be preserved. Hence, debate over the amount and type of use of parks relative to park preservation has often occurred, stemming from the language of the 1916 Organic Act.

Later legislation has never made clear which aspect of the NPS mission is to be given priority. Congress and the executive have, on the other hand, muddied up the management waters. Congress has created a large number of unit types for the national park system, units such as national recreation areas, national preserves, and so forth. Thus, of the over 360 units of the national park system, only 54 are national parks. Each unit of the national park system has enabling legislation, which states the "purpose" of the unit created. For example, the enabling legislation for the Glen Canyon National Recreation Area allows, under certain circumstances, for mineral extraction and grazing.[2] Enabling legislation such as this may thus alter the general intent of the 1916 Organic Act by mandating an activity not mentioned in the 1916 statute. In addition, the 1906 Antiquities Act gives the president the authority to create national monuments, which are often, but not always, added to the park system. These monuments have sometimes been authorized with resource extraction permitted.

Use and Preservation

Much of the post-1916 history of NPS has revolved around the bureaus' and others' views on how the parks should be managed. One continuum of the policy discussion concerns whether the "conserve unimpaired" or the "enjoyment" aspects of the Organic Act should be stressed. Environmentalists, some Park Service professionals, and some elected and appointed officials have viewed preservation as the policy "trump." Others such as local communities, park concessionaires, some park professionals, and elected and appointed officials have stressed park enjoyment or visitor use. Thus, it becomes easier to see how the wise use movement might become interested in the national parks.

A second aspect of the policy discussion concerns whether the NPS or others have the most control over park policy. Only the bureau itself consistently supports maximum control over its policies; outside actors support bureau policy-making control to the extent that it reflects their views on such questions as the use and preservation of parklands.[3]

At this point we need to pay attention to the history of park management and the wise use movement's interpretation of that history. The early days of the National Park Service were dominated by the promotion of public use of parks. Scholars have made the point that the parks had to be used in order to develop the constituency necessary to support the new bureau and its activities, and that early and influential NPS directors Stephen Mather and Horace Albright understood this fact.[4]

This pro-use era in park management extended into the 1950s and the Mission 66 program, which was a massive park infrastructure improvement project that took over ten years to develop and implement. Mission 66 also marked a turning point in the relationship between NPS and environmentalists, for two reasons. The first had to do with park use. As Ronald Foresta noted about environmentalist reaction, "Mission 66 was the essence of those things which they detested; it was the sacrifice of preservation to mass use."[5] But the 1960s were also the time of environmental awakening, and parks were being viewed as "important parts of the global ecosystem . . . where nature-altering human activities must not be allowed to take place."[6] It is very possible that ecological concerns were also stalking horses for "mass use" limitation arguments strategically stated in less direct terms.

Preservationist views began to have some effect on the NPS, and how the bureau approached the question of use within the parks. Foresta, in perhaps the most recent definitive look at national park policy, put the new direction in the form of a question: "If the national parks were run with the primary aim of strict ecological preservation, what would distinguish them from mere nature preserves or national wildlife refuges?"[7] The unstated conclusion is that without the co-equal mandate of public "enjoyment," nothing would distinguish the parks from wildlife refuges.

William Brown, a retired Park Service professional, provided one answer to Foresta's question when he posited what he termed an "extreme" consequence of pure ecological preservation: "First, certain parks or segments thereof are designated ecological reserves. Second, scientific study, not enjoyment and use, becomes the controlling purpose in such reserves. Third, traditional park management is relieved in favor of a science management board."[8] Under these scenarios park use is clearly to be subordinated to park preservation, if not prohibited at times.

It is at this point that the concerns of the wise use movement regarding park use and preservation become paramount. In 1989, the movement issued a task force report titled the *Wise Use Agenda*. In that report were several key sections relating to national parks and park management. The report called for a National Parks Reform Act, which would split the current bureau into four distinct bureaus with respective jurisdiction over urban, recreational, historical, and national park units of the park system. This proposal is in sync with other calls to rethink the park system. For example, Robert Nelson recently called for the transfer of recreational and most historic units out of the park system.[9] Thus, the wise use movement appears to part of a larger and growing chorus to restructure and rethink the park system. In fact, there are some professionals within the service who also argue along similar lines, often claiming that urban recreation should not be a part of the NPS mission. This argument, if successful, would lead to the removal of places like Gateway National Recreation Area in New York from the system.

Where the wise use movement is at its most provocative, however, is in its stance regarding park use. First, it calls for a "Mission 2010" program to construct new visitor services in all the national parks, and prioritizes parks in need of this construction. One of the priority units, Canyonlands in Utah, also illustrates a paradox for the wise users. Canyonlands has no overnight services in the park; they are located outside in towns like Moab and Monticello. Presumably, private interests outside the park might become somewhat nervous about new services inside the park, unless they could provide them. Local private sector interests might be at odds with this aspect of the wise use proposal.

More important, however, is the blunt assertion of the wise users that "appropriate overnight visitor facilities should be constructed in all national monuments, national recreation areas, and major historical areas. *Policies that exclude people shall be outlawed . . .* All actions designed to exclude park visitors such as shutting down overnight accommodations and rationing entry should be stopped as inimical to the mandate of Congress for 'public use and enjoyment' in the National Park Act of 1916" (emphasis mine).[10] Here we have it, then. The wise users have made it quite clear that park use is more important than park preservation. In so doing, they have reinvigorated the debate over the purposes of the national parks.

I have chosen to use the term *reinvigorated*, because what the wise users argue for is not an original point of view. Because it is they who have made these arguments, however, the arguments gain much more attention than they would otherwise. Others who have made their own cases for public use of parklands have been ignored by preservation advocates. For example, there was hardly any discussion of Foresta's provocative claim that "first there was the principle of managing a national park, as a park, a place to be used and enjoyed by the citizens of a democracy. Both the idea of the national park as a park, and the idea of a park in a democracy seem to have gotten lost, or at least obscured, in debates about the National Park system in recent years. A park is anthropocentric; its special quality comes from its appeal to humans. It strikes people as grand or sublime, or it just makes people happy to be there, for whatever reason."[11]

Although not as strong a pro-use statement as that made by the wise users, Foresta still makes a vital point. If parks are anthropocentric, then people belong in parks. If parks are biocentric, as others argue they should be, the role of people is more problematic. The wise users are forcing the question in a direct way, challenging environmentalists and NPS to defend any actual or proposed large-scale exclusion of people in the parks in the name of biocentrism or some other "pure" preservation point of view.

There is more to the argument, though. If people do belong in parks, does that mean people in unlimited numbers enjoying a wide range of activities? Would park users become adversely affected by too many park users and thus their park experience would be made to suffer? How about the provision of elaborate and exotic visitor services in national parks? Would this take park use too far? How much and what type of use is "appropriate" in the words of the wise use movement?

Joseph Sax offered one thoughtful answer in his remarkable *Mountains without Handrails*. The book is remarkable for two reasons. One, it is an eloquent argument for a certain type of park experience, and two, it was ignored by the environmental community. Sax reminds us that "most conflict over national park policy does not really turn on whether we ought to have nature reserves, but on the uses that people will make of those places—which is neither a subject of general agreement nor capable of resolution by reference to ecological principles."[12] He goes on to call for what he terms "contemplative recreation" as the guiding principle for the management of park use, where the park visitor sets his or her own agenda relating to experiencing the natural wonders of the park, rather than having the agenda preset by elaborate visitor activities. In addition, he supports developments in the parks as long as they are not "attractions in themselves."[13]

Sax is arguing for a certain type of visitor experience. In some degree then, he might find common ground with the wise use movement in rejecting use limitations on unclear biological principles. But what about the limiting of visitors, in the name of carrying capacity, visitor experience, or some other measure? Here we are on subjective ground. There is, however, some important research being done in a program at Arches National Park. Visitors have been shown photographs of popular park areas, such as Delicate Arch, with various numbers of people superimposed on the landscape. A majority of viewers say that over thirty people in the park area is "too many" for the visitor experience.[14] Such data might lead to more justifiable limitations on unrestricted use of parklands. It is refreshing to learn what park visitors have to say about their experience, rather than having others speak for them.

There are problems here, admittedly. Some environmentalists have found access that allows even thirty people in one place a problem, while the wise users might well feel this to be a limiting of public access. Also, visitors to national parks do not represent a cross section of all Americans. This program also does not speak to the much more thorny problem of closing parts of national parks for reasons other than overcrowding or obvious resource damage, what the wise users might refer to as "policies that exclude people."

Here the wise users' policy recommendations on wilderness are illustrative. They have called for certain areas within wilderness to be "Human Exclosures . . . where people are prohibited altogether, including wildlife scientists who frequently harass to death the very animals they are supposed to protect."[15] On one hand, the wise users are in a bind. Some units of the park system do have congressionally designated wilderness, therefore some parts of some national parks could be closed to visitor use. On the other hand, the wise users are onto something. That "something" might be seen as a demand that NPS policies that exclude people be clearly and directly justifiable. To play a bit with their example of wildlife scientists, it might annoy some people to have an area closed to use in the name of park research, and then to find scientists in the closed area enjoying, hence "using" the resource closed to everyone else.

Use or Preservation?

This discussion has worked itself around a general theme. Are national parks for use, preservation, both simultaneously, or is one more important, but not exclusive, than the other? The importance of the wise use movement's position is that it forces us to rethink and revisit this question. Where sometimes their rhetoric is extreme (I don't think that very many wildlife scientists actually harass animals to death), nonetheless it has taken back some ground seized by the preservation community. Perhaps Wallace Stegner's claim that our parks are "absolutely democratic" can be a focal point for this renewed discussion. Without public use of parks, the parks lose much of their meaning.

Notes

1. 16 *United States Code*, Section 1.

2. 16 *United States Code*, Section 466dd-2, 5.

3. John Freemuth, "The National Parks: Political Versus Professional Determinants of Policy," *Public Administration Review* 3 (May/June, 1989): 278–82.

4. Donald Swain, "The Passage of the National Park Service Act of 1916," *Wisconsin Magazine of History* 50 (October, 1966):4–17

5. Ronald Foresta, *America's National Parks and their Keepers* (Washington, D.C.: Resources for the Future, 1984): 55.

6. Ibid., 97.

7. Ibid., 121.

8. William Brown, "Preamble Grist," *George Wright Forum* 5 (spring, 1987): 8.

9. Robert Nelson, *Public Lands and Private Rights* (Lanham, Md.: Rowman & Littlefield, 195): 324.

10. *The Wise Use Agenda*, ed. Alan Gottlieb and Ron Arnold (Bellevue, Wa.: The Free Enterprise Press, 1989): 10.

11. Foresta, *America's National Parks*, 268.

12. Joseph Sax, *Mountains Without Handrails* (Ann Arbor: University of Michigan Press, 1980), 103.

13. Ibid., 80, 88.

14. Todd Wilkinson, "Crowd Control," *National Parks* 69. no. 7–8, 1995: 39.

15. *The Wise Use Agenda*, 14.

15

End of the Progressive Era: Toward Decentralization of the Federal Lands

Robert H. Nelson

The system of public-land management is grounded in a guiding vision—a basic paradigm—that dates back to the progressive era of the late nineteenth and early twentieth centuries.[1] It is this set of ideas that explains many of the features of the current system: the centralization of land management authority at the federal level; agency ethics of professionalism and expertise; reliance on personnel trained in particular fields of scientific specialization; the view that "politics" is an unworthy influence on agency actions; the emphasis on comprehensive planning as the proper basis for public-land decisions; the specification of agency objectives in physical output (or more recently physical system) terms; the expectation that rational analysis will be able to provide a single definitive answer across the nation to many if not most management and policy questions; and, at the heart of all this, the concept that the management of the public lands is fundamentally a scientific task. Indeed, it was in the Progressive Era that "scientific management" became the official ethos—the core value system of the culture of public-land management.

To be sure, it has been apparent for many years that the progressive vision of scientific management contained at least as much fiction as fact.[2] Politics, for example, has regularly overwhelmed science in the history of public-land management. Part of the reason is that the experts all too frequently have been unable to reach any scientific

This chapter is adapted from "Government as Theater: Toward a New Paradigm for the Public Lands" in *University of Colorado Law Review* 65 (1994): 335, by permission of the author and publisher.

agreement. The progressives, it is now apparent, substantially overestimated the power of the scientific method in studying matters involving human actions and decisions. Yet, no new vision or paradigm has emerged. Although scientific management is still adhered to as a matter of form, it is no longer widely believed.

If a new guiding vision were to arise, it would mean more than a change in agency culture alone. The rise of progressivism at the end of the nineteenth century meant the end of the long standing policy of disposing of public lands to states and the private sector. The emergence of scientific management led to the creation of the Forest Service, Bureau of Reclamation, Bureau of Land Management, and other federal agencies.[3] Today, if the progressive ethos were finally and officially abandoned, the organizational arrangements for the public lands might well change by an equal magnitude (a prospect, it might be noted, that represents one of the main reasons why the federal land agencies are so reluctant to officially abandon progressive ideas).

The likelihood of major institutional change is greater because the current period resembles in a number of ways the late nineteenth century. There was then, as there is now, wide discontent with the workings of the political system. New populist forces have emerged today with particular strength in the South and West, the centers of populist sentiments one hundred years ago as well. The nation is once again experiencing a period of especially rapid economic change, driven this time by forces of international economic competition and the information revolution. Like the end of the nineteenth century, the end of the twentieth century sees the political and economic ideas that have formed the basis for the existing public order under severe challenge. In short, it is not only on the public lands but in many areas of American government that there is a wide public sense of the bankruptcy of an existing system and a resulting crisis of legitimacy.[4]

This chapter reviews briefly the intellectual and political developments that have brought us to these circumstances on the public lands.[5] It then raises some possibilities for a new guiding vision and new set of organizational arrangements for the public lands that could emerge in the next century. To anticipate the conclusions, I am recommending the transfer of most ordinary federal lands managed by the BLM and Forest Service to the states. Each state could then wrestle with its own determination of a proper way of organizing management responsibilities for the lands within the state. The answers might well vary substantially from state to state, a fitting outcome to a new decentralist regime.

Progressive Paradigm

There have been essentially two controlling paradigms over the two-hundred-year history of the public lands.[6] In the nineteenth century, vast acreages of federal land were transferred to private owners under laws such as the Preemption Act of 1841 and the Homestead Act of 1862. Under statehood grants, swampland legislation, and other laws, another huge area, 328 million acres (about 15 percent of the current U.S. land area), was transferred to the ownership of state governments.[7] In the Progressive Era at the turn of the century, however, the federal government gradually began closing off these various disposal vehicles. Except for lands in Alaska, disposal essentially ended with the enactment of the Taylor Grazing Act in 1934.

The federal government was left to manage what is now about 30 percent of the total U.S. land area. In the eleven westernmost lower forty-eight states, federal lands today cover 47 percent of their area. In four states—Alaska, Idaho, Nevada, and Utah—federal lands represent more than 60 percent of the state.[8]

The progressive movement was a driving factor in shaping not only public-land management but also many other elements of American government. The Civil Service Commission, Federal Reserve Board, Federal Trade Commission, Food and Drug Administration, Bureau of the Budget, and other new federal agencies were all created and shaped in significant part according to progressive precepts. Progressivism provided the foundation for the subsequent development in the twentieth century of the American welfare state.[9]

In the Gilded Age following the Civil War, Congress and the executive both were seen as agents of the special interests. The progressives thus were attempting to solve a problem similar to one that exists today: what to do about a failing set of governing arrangements. To simplify matters a bit, their answer was to turn to science. It was an age when science seemed capable of accomplishing anything. Marvelous new inventions were transforming the conditions of daily life; airplanes, moving pictures, electric lighting, and other technological wonders were virtual miracles to many people. New secular faiths increasingly challenged the older institutional religions of America, offering a vision of the attainment of heaven not in the hereafter, but right here on earth.[10] It would be through the systematic application of scientific knowledge—derived from both the physical and the social sciences—to all aspects of American life that this marvelous result would be realized.

Thus, who could question the logic that government should be made scientific as well? If politics was corrupt, the idea would be to re-place politics with science. Experts in economics, forestry, adminis-tration, and other professional fields should replace the political appointees that had traditionally occupied government positions. The university systems and the professions to supply these experts were created in the Progressive Era as part of the grand plan for the scien-tific management of society. The overall result would be an objective and disinterested government, a government that served the overall public interest—rather than the many special interests that up to then had always been clamoring for government favors.

The place of Gifford Pinchot in American history was to adapt these basic progressive themes to the fields of natural resource policy and public-land management. The result was the conservation movement, which argued that the old bromides, the casual rules of thumb, the traditional ways of doing things must be cast aside in the manage-ment of lands and resources. In their place, actions and policies grounded in the technical knowledge of foresters, range-management scientists, wildlife biologists, and other professional experts must be substituted. Among his many efforts in this cause, Pinchot in 1900 became a founder of the American Society of Foresters, whose mis-sion was to spread scientific forestry. In 1905 the Forest Service was created in the Department of Agriculture to serve the progressive vi-sion of the national forests—with Pinchot as the first chief.

To be sure, if the progressive argument were carried to its ulti-mate end, the result might be to banish all politics. Indeed, many socialists in Europe were prepared to reach this conclusion, arguing that all matters in society should be controlled by scientific determi-nations. In America, however, there was a strong tradition that gov-ernment must also mean popular democracy. To combine democratic government with scientific government was sure to be a difficult task. Seeking nevertheless to find a reconciliation, the progressives argued that democracy and science could each have their own separate do-mains in government.

In one domain, democratic politics would set the overall goals and establish the basic values and directions for society. Then, in another distinct part of government, located principally in the executive branch, these values and goals would be implemented.[11] The implementation would be the task of the scientific managers, who would apply tech-nical skills in administrative science and other subjects in which they had been professionally trained. In the scientific parts of government, politics should be strictly excluded. Nothing could be worse than, as the progressives would have put it, to allow "the special interests" into the routine administration of the government.

Rise of Interest-Group Liberalism

A basic challenge to the progressive vision occurred in the years after World War II, as a whole generation of American political scientists made their reputations by describing the continuing large role of interest groups throughout the affairs of government. The progressive design for separate domains for politics and science was simply not holding.

In another especially influential criticism, Yale professor Charles Lindblom described a governing system characterized not by the administrative rationality of the progressive design but by an evolutionary incrementalism that was poorly understood and observed few formal rules. It was a process of "partisan mutual adjustment" far removed from the progressive prescription that well-defined social goals should be set out in advance, and then scientific administrators should devise the most efficient means of achieving them. Instead, the setting of goals, the politics, the administration, and all the many other elements of government were jumbled together. In 1959, Lindblom captured the flavor of this real world of American government in one of the famous articles of post–World War II social science, "The Science of 'Muddling Through.'"[12]

Although most economists limited their study of self-interest to its expression in the context of a market, a few economists also examined the political role played by interest groups in American society. John Kenneth Galbraith captured wide public attention with his "theory of countervailing power."[13] Like many of the political scientists, Galbraith was on the whole optimistic about the results. After all, matters were going well in American life. The economy was growing rapidly, education was improving, people felt optimistic about the future. As a practical matter, interest-group government seemed to work.

By the end of the 1960s, Theodore Lowi was writing about the emergence of a new political philosophy in the United States that he labeled "interest-group liberalism."[14] The old style of liberalism, similar to old-style European socialism, and grounded in the scientific management of society by a technocratic elite, had been abandoned. Instead, at its core the new understanding of liberalism argued that there was no other way in American democracy than to have widespread participation of affected interest groups throughout the decision-making processes of government. Americans had to get over their prudishness about interest groups and learn to let them in and live happily with the results.

Despite the obvious tensions with progressive thinking, these new ideas significantly influenced public-land management as well. Although they were not happy about it, the Forest Service, BLM and other agencies gradually incorporated public-participation requirements of environmental impact statements, land-use planning, and an assortment of other steps that Congress demanded in new laws of the 1970s. In the greatest burst of legislative activity in the history of the public lands, Congress in the space of a few years enacted the Forest and Rangeland Renewable Resources Planning Act of 1974, the National Forest Management Act of 1976, the Federal Land Policy and Management Act of 1976, the Federal Coal Leasing Amendments Act of 1976, the Public Rangeland Improvement Act of 1978, and still other statutes.

These laws provided for greater public inputs into management decisions but at the same time—and confusingly—also sought to revitalize the founding vision of scientific management. The key instrument for this purpose would be comprehensive land-use planning to provide the objective and rational basis for decisions that had been politically driven in the past. Yet, the outcome in the 1980s, and thus far in the 1990s, has been yet another example of the failings of the progressive model. The agencies have stumbled from one unworkable land-use plan to another. At a recent conference, a top official of the BLM reiterated a familiar refrain: "we recognize that our planning systems have been a pretty bad failure."[15]

Land-use planning did, however, have some important practical consequences. It took a great deal of knowledge and skill to master the planning and other new decision-making procedures—to work the new "handles." The practical effects of the new statutory planning requirements of the 1970s were not to achieve professional management; rather, the 1970s laws mainly shifted political power to new groups. The beneficiaries were the individuals and organizations that best knew how to play the game according to the new rules—most often recreational and environmental groups.

The new legislative foundation of the 1970s for the public lands offered, as it appears today, a much compromised and confused version of scientific management. Somehow, and neither the Congress nor the agencies have ever really been able to say for sure, the management of the public lands should be grounded in both science and democracy. The inherent tension between decision making by representatives elected by popular vote, and decision making by a technical elite committed to following rigorous empirical procedures to reveal objective scientific truth, was simply shunted aside once again as irresolvable.

Economists and Environmentalists

Two new sets of players in the 1970s began to have a larger presence in public-land management. One can be called, crudely, "the economists." The second can be called, about equally crudely, "the environmentalists." Although they had many differences, they did share one important conviction. Both were committed to judging the quality of public-land management by substantive standards. It was not enough simply to obtain a satisfactory compromise among the affected interest groups.

For both environmentalists and economists, the basic verdict was negative. Marion Clawson of Resources for the Future (RFF) reached conclusions that were more visible because of his prominent stature in the field of public-land management but were also representative of many other economists. In essence, Clawson found that public-land management was betraying its original mandate that dated back to the Progressive Era. If progressivism was known as the "gospel of efficiency," the public lands were being managed about as inefficiently as they could be. Indeed, Clawson in 1976 described Forest Service management as "disastrous" from an economic standpoint. [16]

The Forest Service made timber investments in forests where returns were very low, ignoring other possible investments with much higher potential returns. In the 1970s, Clawson was one of the early critics of the "below-cost" timber sales of the Forest Service. The Forest Service followed irrational harvesting rules such as the even flow requirement that effectively wasted a large part of the potential economic value of the timber resource. [17] In essence, economic considerations and efficiency played a minimal role in agency decision making.

Economists also identified the problem. It was politics. There was a fundamental conflict between economic decisions and political decisions and, in practice, politics almost always seemed to win out. Clawson's colleague at RFF, John Krutilla, was less pointed but reached essentially similar conclusions. With his RFF colleague Michael Bowes, Krutilla sought to show the Forest Service how to reform its ways. [18] The agency should turn from politics to the systematic implementation of economic analysis as a basis for its decisions through-out its activities.

If they had done so, the public-land agencies might have been better at responding to the major economic changes occurring in the West. Recreational demands rose rapidly in the decades following World War II, as more visitors from all over the United States came to the West. In addition, more retirees, workers for high-tech companies, and other people were coming to live in the West, especially its urban areas. At the same time, the role of traditional public-land uses such as mining and grazing was declining. Yet, even in the 1980s, the budgets and internal workings of the Forest Service and the BLM were not greatly changed.[19]

Part of the problem was that recreation never paid its way. For most recreation there was no fee; and if there was a fee, it was likely to be minimal. So Congress and the public-land agencies had few budgetary incentives to encourage recreational use of public lands. However, there was a more important factor. If public-land manage-ment was driven by politics, not economics, political power in the West was shifting much more slowly than economic power. In a re-gime of politicized public-land management, the agency managers on the ground were simply not free to respond to the changing economic circumstances on the public lands.

To put this another way, how fast would the computer industry have changed over the last several decades if Congress had been required to approve every new computer model proposed? Or, to use another analogy, public-land management suffers from some of the same ad-ministrative rigidities and economic irrationalities—if on a much smaller scale—that afflicted the old planned economies of the former Soviet Union and eastern Europe, where politics also superseded economic considerations.

The Rise of Environmentalism

To be sure, the new pressures on the public land agencies involved more than just shifts in the economics of the West. There were also major changes occurring in basic social values. Much of this was as-sociated with environmentalism.[20]

Like economists, environmentalists were also prepared to judge public-land management by the substantive results—if applying a dif-ferent standard than economic efficiency. Yet, many projects proved just as objectionable to environmentalists as to economists. It was an alliance pioneered in environmentalist and economist attacks on the Bureau of Reclamation whose pork-barrel dam projects environmentalists saw as "raping" and "assaulting" rivers and streams. For many environmentalists, nature unaffected by human impacts assumed virtually a sacred character. In the 1960s, David Brower argued that to build a dam backing water into Grand Canyon National Park would be the moral equivalent of flooding the Sistine Chapel in the Vatican.[21]

The Natural Resources Defense Council (NRDC) in 1974 won a major suit against the BLM over its grazing management. The NRDC argued that cattle were overgrazing and in many cases threatening to damage severely the environment on the public lands. Other groups saw livestock as an unwelcome sign of human presence in areas that should be left wild. Edward Abbey called for the elimination of livestock grazing altogether on public lands. [22]

By the early 1990s, environmental organizations did in fact succeed in closing down timber harvesting over large areas of federal forests in the Pacific Northwest—taking advantage of the presence of the spotted owl and the unusually strong teeth provided by the Endangered Species Act. It was a virtual revolution in public-land policy. Unlike the Rocky Mountains, the federal forests in the Pacific Northwest are some of the prime timber-growing lands in the world.[23] The long-run net value of forgone timber sales by the federal government probably exceeds $20 billion in order to protect the spotted owl (and the ecologies in which it lives, although that is not the official justification).

In the Progressive Era the scientific management goals of conservationists such as Pinchot had mostly won out over the aims of preservationist advocates such as John Muir, the founder of the Sierra Club in 1892. Today, events are moving in the opposite direction. In an epic battle, Pinchot defeated Muir to win approval in 1913 for the construction of Hetch Hetchy dam in Yosemite National Park. It is inconceivable that such a dam could be built in any national park today. In 1903, speaking to the American Society of Foresters, Pinchot could still say without arousing much controversy that "the object of our forest policy is not to preserve the forests because they are beautiful . . . or because they are refuges for the wild creatures of the wilderness . . . but . . . the making of prosperous homes. . . . Every other consideration becomes secondary."[24]

In the current period we are seeing the very concept of "progress" come to be widely questioned. At heart, this development is perhaps best understood as a fundamental change of a religious character in

American life. Since the Enlightenment, belief in reason and progress have been the civic religion of the American people. In a nation that is very diverse in traditional religious terms, this common secular faith has provided a bond to hold together the American national community. Today, this bond is fraying.[25]

Progressive Gospel

In the Progressive Era, by contrast, few people had any doubts about progress. For the progressives, the rapid pace of economic advance would soon transform the human condition; for many true believers, it would mean nothing less than the salvation of mankind here on earth. A leading progressive, the economist Richard Ely, argued that "God has given to his people this world for salvation" and that what we "learn about heaven" in the Bible is in fact meant to apply "for this world."[26] For Ely, who was a founder of the American Economic Association in 1885, the purpose of the social sciences was to assist in this task. In practice, it meant alleviating poverty, improving housing, obtaining better conditions for labor, conserving natural resources, comprehensive land-use planning, and other parts of the reform agenda of the progressive movement. Social scientists were necessary to salvation in this world because they possessed the requisite technical knowledge to achieve such tasks.

There was theology at the heart of the progressive gospel.[27] The progressive faithful believed that it was the existence in the past of dire poverty and material deprivation that explained why so many people throughout history had killed, stolen, cheated, and otherwise behaved so badly. In progressive theology, this was the true source of "original sin," moved from an event in the Garden of Eden to the harsh economic circumstances of history. For this reason, as Ely and many others preached, it would now be possible to attain salvation— the abolition of sin—right here on earth. Modern science and economic efficiency were generating unprecedented material progress. The end of scarcity soon to come would eliminate the cause of past misbehavior in the world, thus bringing on a whole new era of happiness and harmony for all people.

The gospel of efficiency was also the religion of public-land management. A former chief of the Forest Service said that the agency was "born in controversy and baptized with the holy water of reform." Ashley Schiff observed that Pinchot was the leader of a "conservation crusade" the early Forest Service was characterized by an "administrative evangelism" that reflected its "quasi-religious approach." The employees of the Forest Service exhibited a "moral righteousness" that yielded great personal dedication to the mission of scientific forestry.[28] The Forest Service developed an agency culture grounded in a religious commitment to progress. Ironically, this commitment came about even while the progressives were asserting the necessity of a strict separation of scientific administration from social values, religious or otherwise. Indeed, along with the continuing involvement of interest groups throughout land management, the existence of a land-management culture fundamentally grounded in secular religious values has represented a second great contradiction contained within progressivism.

The powers of science that so enthralled the progressives did enormously expand the physical capacity of people to transform the world. Yet, the vast growth of economic capacity in the twentieth century did not produce corresponding gains in moral and political dimensions, making the new scientific powers seem all the more dangerous to many people. As such concerns spread worldwide, other national religions grounded in a belief in the redemptive power of economic progress— most notably communism and socialism—were also losing their hold.

On the Cutting Edge: Deep Ecology and Libertarian Thought

In the United States, the fiercest critics of the progressive gospel are found among two groups not normally considered to have much in common. Both the "deep ecology" camp of environmentalism and the contemporary libertarian movement draw much of their strength from a shared antipathy to the concept that society is a grand scientific system to be designed and managed by experts. Leading thinkers in both groups see scientific management not only as technically infeasible, but as ethically objectionable. Individual actions become no more morally significant than the actions of atoms or molecules obeying a scientific formula. The crucial element of individual freedom of choice—of "free will" in the more traditional theological formulation of the problem—is thereby lost.

In their book *Deep Ecology*, Bill Devall and George Sessions explain that "deep ecology goes beyond the so-called factual scientific level to the level of self and Earth wisdom." They quote approvingly the observation of biologist Neal Everndon that "ecology undermines not only the growth addict and the chronic developer but science itself."[29] The progressive vision of the scientific management of society must be rejected:

> Technological society not only alienates humans from the rest of Nature but also alienates humans from themselves and from each other. It necessarily promotes destructive values and goals which often destroy the basis for stable viable human communities interacting with the natural world. The technological world view has as its ultimate vision the total conquest and domination of nature and spontaneous natural processes. . . . The ultimate value judgment upon which technological society rests—progress conceived as the further development and expansion of the artificial environment necessarily at the expense of the natural world—must be looked upon from the ecological perspective as unequivocal regress.[30]

Similar views can be found among some of the leading spokesmen for contemporary libertarian thought. An antipathy to scientific management is prominent in the thinking of James Buchanan, also a founder of the "public choice" school of economics and the winner of the 1986 Nobel prize in economics. As Buchanan sees matters, the American welfare state originates in the teachings of American progressivism. Buchanan finds that these doctrines have imbued the welfare state with a pervasive "social engineering" mentality. In pursuing a vision of the scientific management of society, government and other welfare state institutions come to play the role of a "potentially benevolent despot."[31]

Speaking with the voice of authority for the national community, the scientific professions are the deliverers of ultimate truths. The commands of the state (speaking for science) must in the end be obeyed, as in older religions the commands of the church (speaking for God) had to be obeyed. In the tradition of Luther, Calvin, and the Protestant Reformation of old, Buchanan sees his mission today to make a modern protest against a new oppressive collectivism. People must shift their fundamental allegiances "from the organizational entity as the unit to the individual-in-the-organization." It is imperative that "man must cling to that uniquely important discovery . . . the discovery of man, the individual human being."[32]

Deep ecology and libertarian thinkers such as Buchanan also agree to a surprising degree on a desirable future direction for society. When perhaps the two leading sources of criticism of the progressive message find themselves in substantial agreement, it may indicate something important about the future—including the future of the public lands. Both are seeking a sharp decentralization of governing responsibilities in the United States.

Buchanan takes his preference for decentralization to the point even of being willing to explore the idea of "secession" of some sections of the United States. He asks, "who will join me in offering to make a small contribution to the Texas National Party? Or to the Nantucket Separatists?" National authority is justified in terms "of such things as 'national goals,' [and] 'national priorities,'" but in fact they are "absurd." The accumulation of power at the center in Washington leads merely to its cynical manipulation by those who are skilled in its methods. It might be added that such an outcome becomes still more likely when the moral force of the progressive gospel—the inspiration for many people in the past to use the instruments of the federal power to do good in the world—is losing its influence in American life.[33]

Not only on the public lands but also in many other areas, a strong new strain of localism and regionalism has emerged in recent years. From Bureau of Reclamation dams to timber harvests to power plants to waste disposal sites to virtually any type of visible project, strong local resistance has often blocked both market forces and central government plans. Local groups are no longer persuaded by the claims of progress, by the argument that they must make sacrifices in the service of a larger and more important cause—the achievement of national economic growth on the path to heaven on earth.

Like Buchanan, some venturesome environmentalists have taken decentralist themes to the point of praising secessionist outcomes. In the popular novel *Ecotopia*, an environmentalist visionary portrays a utopian existence consisting of a pastoral life in the Pacific Northwest. Much of the attraction results from the fact that this region has seceded from the rest of the United States—and from its false value system grounded in the "underlying national philosophy of America: ever-continuing progress, the fruits of industrialization for all, a rising Gross National Product."[34]

Toward Decentralization of the Federal Lands

Much closer to the mainstream, a number of students of the public lands have proposed a sharp decentralization of their management.[35] In making the closing summary at a 1992 public-lands conference organized by the Congressional Research Service, Frank Gregg, the former director of the BLM in the Carter administration, observed that:

We tend to favor decentralization. We see some disjuncture between the levels at which the effects of decisions are felt and the levels at which decisions are made. We are trying to find coordinated ways to focus all the authorities and actions that affect resources and uses at the problemshed level. We grope for ways to apply integrating concepts at the problemshed level which may reflect interactions in natural processes, uses and impacts involving federal, state, local, private ownerships and aspirations.[36]

Decentralization of public-land management would follow in the path of a trend already well advanced in the business world. Many large corporations have cut headquarters staffs and layers of middle management, transferring decision making to local units. All around the world, nations grounded in national creeds of economic progress—communism, socialism, the economic faith of the welfare state—are confronting the erosion of their authority. In the former communist world especially, this erosion has led to a dramatic shift of power away from the center to the regions and localities, in the extreme leading to the breakup of the former Soviet Union.

Decentralization—on the public lands or elsewhere—offers an answer to the fundamental problem of how society can resolve social issues that inextricably mix matters of scientific expertise with matters of basic social values. If the two cannot be separated into distinct domains, contrary to the assumption of the progressives, then decision makers may on the one hand have to be theologians and on the other scientists as well. But where will such people be found? In a society with a pluralism of values, whose values should the national government apply? Must the particular values of one or another politically powerful group be imposed—in the end this means the use of the coercive powers of the federal government—on other groups?

The case for decentralization is that it should in most cases be the values of the people most directly affected that are controlling—and that the only way for these people to ensure that their values prevail is for them to possess the decision-making authority themselves. Scientific knowledge will still be important but an appeal to science will no longer be the basic source of social legitimacy. Local people will not want to look to any experts, even experts that they may hire, to make their value decisions for them. The qualifications for management decision making are not unique to any expert group or technical specialization, partly because expert matters cannot in most cases be separated from religious and other aspects of decision making. To say that local people in the end must make the decisions is also as a practical matter to say that they must rely on their available mechanisms for collective decision making—in other words, on local politics.

The specific mechanisms for achieving such a decentralization can be debated. There are many options as to how far decentralization of authority will proceed—to the state level, to the county, to the local municipality, perhaps to the private individual. However, in the United States, the federal government and the states are the only governments with sovereign status in the Constitution. Local governments are the creation of state governments, and exist under the terms and conditions set by states. It is difficult to imagine a new decentralist political foundation for the public lands that is not reached with the approval and the active participation of the states. While holding a few lands of special national concern in federal hands, I would therefore transfer most of the existing ordinary federal lands—those managed by the Forest Service and the BLM—to the states. The state political process would then be responsible for working out new governing arrangements for these lands.

To be sure, as long as there is a national community and government, decentralization cannot be absolute. Regional and local governance must function within the context of some broad rules. The constitutional protections provided by the Bill of Rights will continue to apply across the United States. Yet, maintaining these and other limited national rules would still leave ample room to increase greatly the autonomy of localities—especially as compared with the existing strongly centralist regimes that have been built on progressive foundations.

A New Paradigm

Many people today seem to have conflicts in their thinking. They cling to Progressive Era rhetoric of the scientific management of society in the public interest even while they feel deep unease about this philosophy. In concrete instances, even self-professed believers in scientific management often strongly oppose those actions that would make this aim a reality. It is an old story in the history of ideas; old orthodoxies often survive for a long time despite growing tension with new ways of thinking. At some point, however, a new paradigm emerges from all the intellectual and social ferment.

As I suggested earlier, public-land management is today ripe for a new paradigm. As a broad concept, such a paradigm might offer a vision of decentralization to meet the demands of a world of growing value pluralism. This pluralism partly reflects the decline of the diverse faiths of economic progress (socialism, communism, the welfare state, etc.) that in many nations once provided the glue of a common culture. The true meaning of "postmodern" may be that we have moved past the age of economic worship—dating back to the eighteenth century and the Enlightenment—and are now entering into a new period of religious experimentation and diversity. The dominance of the secular scientific culture of the twentieth century may be a thing of the past.

Questions as broad as the future of religion obviously transcend the public lands. Yet, it is just these types of questions that may well prove to be the key in assessing the future of these lands. A new decentralist vision for the public lands would not seek any one answer to the question of proper values in the management of the land. Instead, it would rely on experimentation by local communities to build living environments responsive to local values. This concept would meet the needs of a world in which social decision making inextricably mixes considerations of ethics and science.

It would also represent the end of the progressive era of public-land management. It was in the Progressive Era that the federal government ceased transferring lands to states and private owners. Today, as recognition of the practical and moral failure of progressive ideas in the twentieth century reaches the general public, it is time to look once again to states and private owners for a greater role in the new land management system that can be expected in the next century.

Notes

1. Samuel P. Hays, *Conservation and the Gospel of Efficiency: The Progressive Conservation Movement, 1890-1920* (Cambridge, Mass.: Harvard University Press, 1959).

2. See Karl Hess, Jr., *Visions Upon the Land: Man and Nature on the Western Range* (Washington, D.C.: Island Press, 1993).

3. Samuel Trask Dana and Sally K. Fairfax, *Forest and Range Policy: Its Development in the United States* (New York: McGraw-Hill, 1980).

4. Robert H. Wiebe, *Self-Rule: A Cultural History of American Democracy* (Chicago: University of Chicago Press, 1995).

5. See also Robert H. Nelson, *Public Lands and Private Rights: The Failure of Scientific Management* (Lanham, Md.: Rowman & Littlefield, 1995).

6. Paul W. Gates, *History of Public Land Law Development* (Washington, D.C.: Government Printing Office, 1968).

7. Bureau of Land Management, U.S. Department of the Interior, *Public Land Statistics, 1991* (Washington, D.C.: BLM, September 1992), 4.

8. Ibid., 5.

9. See Dwight Waldo, *The Administrative State: A Study of the Political Theory of American Public Administration* (New York: Holmes and Meier, 1984), 19. See also Stephen Skowronek, *Building a New American State: The Expansion of National Administrative Capabilities, 1877-1920* (New York: Cambridge University Press, 1982), 10.

10. See Robert H. Nelson, *Reaching for Heaven on Earth: The Theological Meaning of Economics* (Lanham, Md.: Rowman & Littlefield, 1991), chapter 5.

11. Frank J. Goodnow, *Politics and Administration: A Study of Government* (New York: Russell and Russell, 1967), 83–86.

12. Charles E. Lindblom, *The Intelligence of Democracy: Decision Making through Mutual Adjustment* (New York: Free Press, 1965); see also Charles E. Lindblom, "The Science of 'Muddling Through,'" *Public Administration Review*, spring 1959, 79–88.

13. John Kenneth Galbraith, *American Capitalism: The Concept of Countervailing Power* (Boston: Houghton Mifflin, 1952), 108.

14. Theodore J. Lowi, *The End of Liberalism: Ideology, Policy, and the Crisis of Public Authority* (New York: Norton, 1969).

15. Remarks of Mike Penfold at the Second Annual Western Public Lands Conference, "Who Governs the Public Lands: Washington? The West? The Community?" School of Law, University of Colorado, Boulder, 28 September 1994.

16. See, for example, economists William F. Hyde, "Timber Economics in the Rockies: Efficiency and Management Options," *Land Economics* (November 1981); and Thomas Lenard, "Wasting our National Forests," *Regulation* (July/August 1981); see also Marion Clawson, *The Economics of National Forest Management* (Washington, D.C.: Resources for the Future, 1976); and Marion Clawson, "The National Forests," *Science*, 20 February 1976, 766.

17. Robert H. Nelson and Lucian Pugliaresi, "Timber Harvest Policy Issues on the O & C Lands," in *Forestlands: Public and Private*, edited by Robert T. Deacon and Bruce M. Johnson (San Francisco: Pacific Institute for Public Policy Research, 1985).

18. Michael D. Bowes and John V. Krutilla, *Multiple-Use Management: The Economics of Public Forestlands* (Washington, D.C.: Resources for the Future, 1989).

19. Randal O'Toole, *Reforming the Forest Service* (Washington, D.C.: Island Press, 1988).

20. See Roderick Frazier Nash, *The Rights of Nature: A History of Environmental Ethics* (Madison: University of Wisconsin Press, 1989); also Robert H. Nelson, "Environmental Calvinism: The Judeo-Christian Roots of Environmental Theology," in *Taking the Environment Seriously*, edited by Roger Meiners and Bruce Yandle (Lanham, Md.: Rowman & Littlefield, 1993), 233–55.

21. See John McPhee, *Encounters with the Archdruid: Narratives about a Conservationist and Three of His Natural Enemies* (New York: Farrar, Straus, and Giroux, 1971); and see David Brower, *For Earth's Sake: The Life and Times of David Brower* (Salt Lake City: Peregrine Smith Books, 1990), 368.

22. See Robert H. Nelson, "NRDC v. Morton: The Role of Judicial Policy Making in Public Rangeland Management," *Policy Studies Journal*, December 1985; Edward Abbey, "Even the Bad Guys Wear White Hats," *Harper's Magazine*, January 1986, 53–54.

23. See Elmo Richardson, *BLM's Billion Dollar Checkerboard: Managing the O & C Lands* (Santa Cruz, Calif.: Forest History Society, 1980).

24. Quoted in Orris C. Herfindal, "What is Conservation," in *Politics, Policy and Natural Resources*, edited by Dennis Thompson (New York: The Free Press, 1971), 174.

25. Robert Nisbet, *History of the Idea of Progress* (New York: Basic Books, 1980), chapter 9, questions the idea of progress. See Carl L. Becker, *The Heavenly City of the Eighteenth-Century Philosophers* (New Haven: Yale University Press, 1932) regarding the American people's belief in reason and progress.

26. Richart T. Ely, *Social Aspects of Christianity and other Essays* (New York: Thomas Y. Crowell, 1889), 56–72.

27. See Nelson, *Reaching for Heaven on Earth*, especially 190–95.

28. Quoted in Ashley L. Schiff, *Fire and Water: Scientific Heresy in the Forest Service* (Cambridge, Mass.: Harvard University Press, 1962), 2, 5, 166–67.

29. Bill Devall and George Sessions, *Deep Ecology* (Salt Lake City: Peregrine Smith Books, 1985), 65; Neil Everndon, "Beyond Ecology," quoted *in Deep Ecology*, 48.

30. Devall and Sessions, *Deep Ecology*, 48.

31. James M. Buchanan, *What Should Economists Do?* (Indianapolis: Liberty Press, 1979), 24, 148.

32. Ibid., 157, 173.

33. Ibid., 110–11, 228–29. On the moral force of progressivism, see Robert H. Nelson, "The Theological Meaning of Economics," *The Christian Century*, 11–18 August 1993.

34. Ernest Callenbach, *Ecotopia* (New York: Bantam Books, 1977), 5.

35. See Hess, *Visions Upon the Land*; also O'Toole, *Reforming the Forest Service*.

36. Frank Gregg, "Summary," in *Multiple Use and Sustained Yield: Changing Philosophies for Federal Land Management*, Committee Print No. 11 of the Committee of Interior and Insular Affairs, U.S. House of Representatives (1992), 311–12.

Part 4

Coming Back into the Country

16

Community and the Politics of Place

Daniel Kemmis

Place is a subject much talked about, especially in the inland of the West, a place that is undergoing another population boom from the far western communities of Seattle, Portland, Sacramento, and Los Angeles. Old-timers—who are now becoming a rare breed—talk about how the hills where they once hunted elk are now being overtaken by subdivisions, one ironically called Elk Hills. They lament the recent time they bushwhacked to their secret trout-fishing hole only to find three other anglers there, casting in the same hole. A hunting season on mountain lions has been proposed in areas on the very outskirts of Missoula, because sightings of the cats have increased near the city's boundaries, as those boundaries have pushed themselves into prime lion habitat.

A loss of place doesn't necessarily mean just a loss of physical habitat, physical land, physical space. Loss of place also connotes a loss of the *sense* of place, a loss of feeling a connection with the land around you, what it means to you, brings to you, gives to you. This sense of place is being eroded all across the country as we, as a culture, orient instead to the local mall, the McDonald's, and television advertising that tells us what we're missing by not buying the latest VCR.

There is an underlying current of connection to place that is waiting to be reexposed and reclaimed. In the preamble to Montana's Constitution, the writers ordain the government of the state to achieve

This chapter was condensed from *Community and the Politics of Place* by Daniel Kemmis, © University of Oklahoma Press, 1990 by permission of the author and the publisher. Adapted from the original by Tommy Youngblood-Petersen.

certain specific ends, as most constitutions do. However, the preamble goes on to say, "We the people of Montana, *grateful to God for the quiet beauty of our state, the grandeur of its mountains, the vastness of its rolling plains,* and desiring to secure to ourselves and our posterity the blessings of liberty for this and future generations do ordain and establish this constitution" (emphasis added). Public life, this preamble implies, can be reclaimed only by understanding, and then practicing, its connection to real, identifiable places.

Concomitant with the loss of sense of place is the loss of a sense for public life and public interaction. Government of any size—local, state, national—is viewed skeptically these days, and participation in the labyrinth of political bureaucracies is waning at best. Political apathy, not involvement, covers the general population in a thick passionless malaise. Incumbent bashing is a growing phenomenon in political elections.

The "public" in the republican government that Thomas Jefferson and others worked so hard to help define in our Constitution is disappearing. This loss began with Jefferson's losing of the philosophical battle to Madison and his Federalist cohorts. Our contemporary concept of the public life, of public politics—and the resulting sense of disconnectedness from such—was subtly shaped by these early, and very fundamentally different, philosophies that helped established the political framework of forming colonies into united states.

The Jefferson/Madison Battle

The basic question that Jefferson and Madison attempted to answer through the creation of the United States Constitution was this: Should the burden of solving public problems rest most directly on citizenship or on government? The two arrive at radically different answers.

Jefferson, writing a steady stream of letters from his ambassador's post in Versailles, France, was adamant that the people, the citizenry, had not only the duty but the right to be involved in solving their own problems. To Jefferson, this approach was truly republican. Taking on none of the contemporary political party connotation, the "republican" tradition rested squarely upon a face-to-face, hands-on approach to problem solving, with an implicit belief that people could rise above their particular interests to pursue a common good.

This republican approach to public policy required a high level of interaction among citizens. In particular, it assumed that citizens were presented with many opportunities and much encouragement to rise above a narrow self-centeredness. John Winthrop, the first colonial governor of Massachusetts, called this approach to government "making other's conditions our own." It was a politics of engagement in which people were *engaged* with one another on an emotional level. They worked out solutions for the common good, putting aside their individual needs for the needs of the whole.

How does this more selfless attitude develop? To Jefferson and the civic republicans, as they came to be known, agriculture was the key. Jefferson thought that the way people made their living had much to do with the development of a sense of responsibility, and that farming developed it most consistently. What bothered Jefferson about the nonfarming activities of commerce and manufacturing was the disconnectedness and the anonymity that seemed necessarily to accompany them. Jefferson saw clearly that those who made their living through these activities were wholly dependent upon the choices of utter strangers, known only as "consumers." Jefferson was appalled by the thought of large numbers of people making their living by depending solely upon the choices of other people with whom they had no social or moral ties of any kind.

Farming, on the other hand, by the mere essence of the work itself, developed "civic virtues": plain honesty, industry, and perseverance. Jefferson saw that the new Constitution, as presented by Madison and others, placed little value upon such civic virtues. This was a retreat from republican principles for which, Jefferson believed, the war with England had been fought.

The thread that Jefferson and the civic republicans hung on to was a phrase in the Constitution, kept there by Madison and others most likely to appease these civic republican desires. Guaranteed to all states in the Constitution was a "republican form of government." Jefferson could foresee that the vast, open lands of the frontier would be at once a source of new states, that those states would be republican in the most fundamental sense because open lands would draw people into agriculture, at least as fast as they were drawn into cities and factories. Republican principles would thrive "as long as agriculture is our principal object, which will be the case, while there remains vacant lands in any part of America."[1]

The obvious question is: What happens to Jefferson's ideals when all of the vacant land is gone, an inevitable process that surely even Jefferson was aware of? We will deal with that question in a minute.

For there was another view of how these United States were to be governed, of how the Constitution would be written and interpreted. James Madison and Alexander Hamilton were the leaders of the Federalists, a group that was skeptical at best about the ability of individuals to come to a common decision. They believed that the *causes* of conflict could not be removed, that conflict is simply a part of human nature, and believed only in controlling its *effects*. They were fearful that a majority, having come to a decision in a "republican" way (engaged with each other, working out a solution for the common good) would evolve into a tyrannous insurrection. As a result, the Federalists devised political systems whereby citizens would be kept apart—large-scale decision-making bodies instead of small-scale, face-to-face bodies in the republican style—where there was little room for common goals, the common good, and, therefore, the dreaded tyranny of the majority.

It was at this point that Madison shrewdly turned the republican ideal of open land for the creation of republican states to his advantage. He argued precisely the same point that Jefferson had urged—that the frontier lands of this country were necessary for the healthy expansion of the country—but for a different end. For Madison and the Federalists, an extensive territory was an excellent hedge against tyranny, especially against the tyranny of the majority. "Extend the sphere, and you take in a greater variety of parties and interests; you make it less probable that a majority of the whole will have a common motive to invade the rights of other citizens; or if such a common motive exists, it will be more difficult for all who feel it to discover their own strengths and to act in unison with each other."[2]

Where those advocating a republican form of government stressed the term "public" as meaning that everything appears in public and can be seen and heard by everyone, Madison abandoned the idea of citizens beholding, let alone acting upon, the public interest. It was their private interests that he wanted them to behold, to understand, and to pursue. To this end, the Federalists advocated a series of checks and balances within government, where government was structured to balance private pursuits of individuals so cleverly that the highest good would emerge without any one individual having willed its existence.

Let us return now to Jefferson and his adamant feeling toward open lands. Remember that the western territories, which at that time meant all lands west of the eastern seaboard colonies, seemed almost limitless. To Jefferson these lands were necessary for the establishment of a strong agrarian population, a series of farming communities that would evolve naturally by virtue of their civic values into states with republican forms of government, as guaranteed by the Constitution.

Yet Jefferson must have realized that even the vast lands of the western territories had, eventually, to be filled up. In fact, just a century after Jefferson penned his letters to Madison, the most remote region of the Louisiana Purchase had been admitted to the Union. The admission of these states marked the closing of the old American frontier.

Meanwhile from across the ocean had come a response that, point for point, was exactly the opposite of Jefferson's. Georg Wilhelm Friedrich Hegel argued that a real republic would become possible in America "only after the immeasurable space which that country presents to its inhabitants shall have been occupied, and the members of the political body shall have begun to be pressed back on each other." Hegel even contradicted Jefferson's fundamental argument that civic virtues are more effectively transmitted in rural than in urban settings: "Only when, as in Europe, the direct increase of agriculturists is checked, will the inhabitants, instead of pressing outwards to occupy the fields, press inwards upon each other—pursuing town occupations, and trading with their fellow citizens; and so form a compact system of civil society, and require an organized state."[3]

With the closing of the old frontier, the issue between these two views of civil society would seem to have been firmly joined. If Hegel was right, a civil society could now at last emerge. But if Jefferson was closer to the mark, things would now be likely to become less civil. Let us follow a bit more of our political history to see more clearly where we are in these terms, and who we have become.

Populist Campaign

All was not lost for Jefferson's civil republican ideals as the frontier lands diminished. Almost ironically, with the "closing" of the frontier in the 1890s—with Montana and the Dakotas (1889), and Wyoming and Idaho (1890) being populated enough to be admitted to the Union—came a strong, land-based political movement that came close to establishing itself as the civic republican philosophy that Jefferson envisioned for the country. But the populists, as they came to be known, suffered a defeat from which they, and with them Jefferson's agrarian ideals, never recovered.

The presidential election of 1896, like any political election, can be analyzed in a variety of ways. For our purposes, it represents a turning point in political history, a classic battle between the Jeffersonian ideals of agrarian, engagement-oriented politics, represented by

William Jennings Bryan, and the growing political philosophy of commercial and industrial interests that shapes our contemporary political scene, represented in 1896 by William McKinley.

It might be stretching it to say the election of Bryan could have changed history, but the course of American politics certainly would have shifted, at least temporarily. It is probable that the momentum of capitalist politics would have caught up to the civic republicans. But this is all conjecture. The relevant point that relates to our look at contemporary political thought is that the defeat of Bryan was a decisive setback for the principles of self-government, according to Lawrence Goodwyn in *The Populist Movement*. McKinley and his party ran the first mass advertising campaign that set the course of modern political spending. Big money and big commerce were the winners in this race. What was lost? The fundamental faith of ordinary people in their ability to govern themselves.

Coupled with the growth of U.S. imperialism, which enabled the United States to look outward, again, to a new "frontier," came a significant increase in regulatory bureaucracy that heightened the mechanistic and diminished the face-to-face dimensions of public life. So at the beginning of the twentieth century, citizens were once again "kept apart" by the government's political framework.

Now, at the end of the twentieth century, some citizens are calling for a renewed commitment to small-scale, personal-engagement politics based on a sense of *habitation*, a sense of where one is based, a sense of place. In the end, of course, the point is not what Jefferson or Madison thought, but what we can, should, and will do with the part of the world we call home.

A New Sense of "Being Public"

Our democratic faith has been weakened by a political system (a system that operates with increased regulatory bureaucracy and large-scale government) that frustrates public involvement in the processes of change. The more frustration, the fewer people become involved. For example, Montana has attempted for ten years to pass a wilderness bill for the state, only to be gridlocked time and time again. Public interaction—our way of being public at hearings, public testimony, and public meetings—is unsatisfactory. What do we do?

What "we" do depends upon who "we" are, or who we think we are. It depends, in other words, upon how we choose to relate to each other, to the place we inhabit, and to the issues that inhabiting raise for us.

To Montanans and others in this dry, windy, cold, hot, and remote western region, the place is still largely unpopulated, precisely because of the harsh physical conditions. Even with the increase in "immigrants" to the inland West, studies are showing that a high percentage leave after two or three years due, in part, to unrealistic expectations of climate and more romantic notions of the West not being fulfilled. It seems to come naturally, then, that people tend to define themselves in terms of the land that surrounds them. This is a step in the direction of defining who "we" are.

Wallace Stegner says: "Angry as one may be at what heedless men have done and still do to a noble habitat, one cannot be pessimistic about the West. This is the native home of hope. When it fully learns that cooperation, not rugged individualism, is the quality that most characterizes and preserves it, then it will have achieved itself and outlived its origins. Then it has a chance to create a society to match its scenery."[4] "Cooperation, not rugged individualism" and "a chance to create a society to match its scenery." Powerful words. But what is missing in our society's ability to change?

In an attempt to understand how to cooperate, how to operate as a republic, let's look at the word itself. The Latin phrase for "republic" was *res publica*, the "public thing," a fairly meaningless phrase at first glance. Hannah Arendt says this about the relationship of the public and *res publica*:

> To live together in the world means essentially that a world of things is between those who have it in common, as a table is located between those who sit around it; the world, like every in-between, relates and separates men at the same time.
>
> The public realm, as the common world, gathers us together and yet prevents our falling over each other, so to speak. What makes mass society so difficult to bear is not the number of people involved, or at least not primarily, but the fact that the world between them has lost its power to gather them together, to relate and to separate them. The weirdness of this situation resembles a spiritualistic seance where a number of people gathered around a table might suddenly, through some magic trick, see the table vanish from their midst, so that two persons sitting opposite each other were no longer separated but also would be entirely unrelated by anything tangible.[5]

This vanishing table is the "thing" that would make a "public" possible. It is just this that is suggested by the Montana preamble, where the eminently tangible mountains and plains of the state play precisely the role of gathering people together by simultaneously relating and separating them. Arendt herself does not use the natural world, but rather the human world to define what gathers us together.

The U.S. preamble (and indeed most of what we now call "public" life) attempts to dispense altogether with that gathering and separating "thing." We have severed the public from its republican context. In the process, we have made any real public life all but impossible.

Our question, then, is what happened to the public thing: How did the table vanish? Part of the answer lies in what happened to our understanding of public life at certain key periods in our political history, described in the previous sections. But the demise of public life has to be understood in terms of space (or place) as well as time. Putting it more positively, public life can be reclaimed only by understanding, and then practicing, its connection to real, identifiable places. This is not a particularly easy way for most of us to think about public issues. Thinking of politics in historical terms is second nature, but we tend to be more dubious about the propositions that political culture may be shaped by its place, as well as by its time.

So we have two parties at the table, the rugged individualist and those who endorse the regulatory bureaucratic approach. What is particularly ironic in the West is that a substantial amount of land has been set aside as federal (public) land; that the land became public precisely for the public good, to protect against the negative impacts of individuals who wanted to do their own thing, be it overharvesting of timber, mining next to pristine rivers, or drilling in the midst of sensitive wildlife habitat. But the two parties at the table have lost the table itself. They have lost the process of how to gather around it, and both feel incredibly frustrated: the individualists feel stymied by what they perceive as overly bureaucratic control, and those inclined to the regulatory approach see their dreams stymied by the process of modern politics, which allows initiatives to be blocked, but doesn't seem to allow genuine progress to be made.

The democratic process, the table, does indeed seem to be missing. As it stands now, the parties have the power to veto each other's initiatives, but none has the ability to create successful initiatives. In 1994, the Wilderness Bill was again introduced to Congress and it was again blocked by both sides. As initiatives are blocked, the willingness to try anything new is diminished.

How our society makes decisions is key. "Public" hearings, which are good in the democratic sense of involving the public, have become simply the place where initiatives are blocked. In fact, any genuine "hearing" is absent, partly because the system of hearings, which rightly fulfills two important components of our due process of law of giving "notice" on decisions and providing "the opportunity to be heard," transfers over the responsibility of *hearing* to the decision maker, a third party, *and the public is therefore not required to hear.* The result? What George Will calls the Cuisinart theory of justice: "A good society is a lumpy stew of individuals and groups, each with its own inherent 'principle of motion.' This stew stirs itself, and in the fullness of time, out comes a creamy puree called the 'public interest.' The endless maelstrom of individuals pursuing private goods produces, magically, the public good."[6]

Will deplores the fact that, in this model, none of the individual participants has responsibility for "willing the social good." They are not expected to do any public willing, and by the same token, they are not expected to do any public hearing. So it is that "public hearings" are curiously devoid of that very quality that their name might seem to imply.

This lack of hearing shouldn't be surprising. It is the result of the Madisonian approach that elevates individual rights over communal, group, or societal rights. This "framework of rights" is the framework of individual rights, and the role of public institutions, then, is to provide this "framework of rights," not to choose or impose the common good, but to uphold individual rights (like the right to privacy, the right to property) against infringement by other individuals, or by the government itself. So this is not a substantive choosing of a common good, but a process of weighing, balancing, and upholding rights. This process, this "due process" (giving notice and giving the opportunity to be heard) replaces direct dealings between parties in conflict. The parties don't have to come to agreement or even to hear each other. They have given this responsibility over to "the process," which prevents face to face problem solving resulting in the diminished collective ability to get anything done.

An important question here is, Are values purely private? They don't seem to be, for if values are entirely private, then there is no objective way of choosing among them. But herein lies a tension: public decisions are often based on values (and emotions) even though the decisions have to appear to be based on objective facts (rationality). This tension produces all too familiar public scenes—shrillness and indignation of protest or of "public" decision making and the blocking of initiatives, for protesters realize that they can never win an argument, nor can they lose. This shrillness and lack of forward motion leads to the withdrawal of people from public involvement.

If the privatization of values is at or near the root of this problem, then some conception of shared or communal values must be part of the solution. We must move from "territoriality" (individualism) to "common ground" both literally and metaphorically. Fortunately, there are many ways we can move to common ground, but often we don't realize their existence or realize their potential. Examples abound: 4-H clubs, rural fire departments, and neighborhood watch programs. No one can engage in these social goods in this "practiced way" while maintaining a purely subjective approach to values. Even the homeliest practices instill a sense of the whole, of true "civic virtues" like justice, courage, and honesty.

In the public realm, however, all of these virtues are overshadowed. Robert Bellah and his coauthors in *Habits of the Heart* say that in such instances our language changes from our "second language" of family and tradition to our "first language" of self-reliance. They describe these languages in this way: "if the language of the self-reliant individual is the first language of American moral life, the languages of tradition and commitment in communities of memory are 'second languages' that most Americans know as well, and which they use when the language of the radically separate self does not seem adequate."[7]

Public discourse is couched in the framework of a dichotomy— regulated versus unregulated individuality—and so it is no wonder that people speak publicly in the "first language of individualism." The language of justice and community is pushed to the rear and forced to the forefront is the language of individual survival. The next obvious question then is, What can be done to establish practices that would teach people to act and speak in a truly public way in public?

There are no easy answers, but one aspect is the importance of the specific, the concrete, the tangible, which allows values to become objective and, therefore, public. Lawrence Haworth has perhaps best understood the essential connection between the concepts of community and objectivity: "In any genuine community there are shared values: the members are united through the fact that they fix on some object as preeminently valuable. And there is a joint effort, involving all members of the community, by which they give overt expression to their mutual regard for that object."[8]

Common values, which form the basis for a truly common life, arise out of a context that is concrete in two ways: the actual event or thing that the cooperation produces, such as a 4-H club or a rural fire department, and the actual *places* in which the cooperative efforts took place. To in*habit* a place is to dwell there in a practiced way, in a way that relies upon certain regular, trusted habits of behavior.

Our prevailing, individualistic frame of mind has led us to forget this root sense of the concept of "inhabitation." We take it for granted that the way we live in a place is a matter of individual choice (more or less constrained by bureaucratic regulations). We have largely lost the sense that our capacity to live well in a place might depend upon our ability to relate to neighbors (especially neighbors with a different lifestyle) on the basis of shared habits of behavior. Our loss of this sense of inhabitation is exactly parallel to our loss of the "republican" sense of what it is to be public.

In fact, no real public life is possible except among people who are engaged in the project of inhabiting a place. If there are not habituated patterns of work, play, grieving, and celebration designed to enable people to live well in a place, then those people will have at best a limited capacity for being public with one another. Conversely, where such inhabitory practices are being nurtured, the foundation for public life is also being created or maintained. Wendell Berry's teachings say this about practiced ways of living in places:

> The concept of country, homeland, dwelling place becomes simplified as "the environment"—that is, what surrounds us. Once we see our place, our part of the world, as *surrounding* us, we have already made a profound division between it and ourselves. We have given up the understanding—dropped it out of our language and so out of our thought— that we and our country create one another, depend on one another, are literally part of one another; that our land passes in and out of our bodies just as our bodies pass in and out of our land; that as we and our land are part of one another, so all who are living as neighbors here, human and plant and animal, are part of one another, and so cannot possibly flourish alone; that, therefore, our culture must be our response to our place, our culture and our place are images of each other and inseparable from each other, and so neither can be better than the other.[9]

So we become aware of how places, by developing practices, create culture. The civic republicans, in a sense, take up where this concept leaves off. That is, they recognize the crucial role of practices, not only in the development of culture, but also in the revitalization of public life. Here is how Robert Bellah speaks of what he calls "practices of commitment":

People growing up in communities of memory not only hear the stories that tell how the community came to be, what its hopes and fears are, and how its ideals are exemplified in outstanding men and women; they also participate in the practices—ritual, aesthetic, ethical—that define the community as a way of life. We call these "practices of commitment" for they define the patterns of loyalty and obligation that keep the community alive.[10]

A New Sense of Place and the Politics of Possibility

What holds people together long enough to discover their power as citizens is their common inhabiting of a single place. In Missoula, part of that place is the basin valley in which the small city lies, and because it is surrounded on all sides by mountains, the area of the valley is finite, limited, and therefore fragile. (The sole-source drinking water aquifer lies a mere thirty feet below the surface.) No matter how diverse and complex the patterns of livelihood that arise within that valley may be, no matter how many the perspectives from which people view the valley, no matter how diversely the people value it, there is, finally, one and the same value for everyone. There are not many valleys, one for each of us, but only one valley, and if we all want to stay here, in some kind of relation to the valley, then we have to learn, somehow, to live together.

Before they become citizens, then, people become neighbors, and not just as next door acquaintances. The word *neighbor*, in its Old English rendition, meant something like "near dweller." Neighbors are essentially people who find themselves attached to the same (or nearly adjoining) places. Because each of them is attached to the place, they are brought into relationship with each other. Now some people may actually prefer that they had different neighbors, but because neither of them is about to leave and because their dwelling in this place makes them interdependent, they develop patterns for dwelling near each other, for living with each other.

This concept of "living with" is deeply rooted in various inhabitory practices, one of which is the process of consensus building, which has by now developed some fairly standard operating procedures. One of the guidelines often invoked in consensus decision making is that participants should be looking for solutions that they can all live with. Such an approach can be viewed simply as a matter of compromise and accommodation, and certainly it contains such elements. But the actual practice of finding solutions that people can live with usually reaches beyond compromise to something more like neighborliness—to finding within shared space the possibilities for a shared inhabitation. Such neighborliness is inconceivable without the building of trust, of some sense of justice, reliability, or honesty. This practice of being neighbors draws together, therefore, the concepts of place, of inhabitation, and of the kinds of practices from which civic virtues evolve.

Most people, most of the time, do not think about these features of the art of being neighbors. What they do know is that neighborliness is a highly prized quality of life. Where it is present, it is always near the top of people's lists of why they like a place, and where it is absent, it is deeply lamented. This deep-seated attachment to the virtue of neighborliness is an important but largely ignored civic asset. It is in being good neighbors that people very often are engaged in those simple, homely practices that are the last, best hope for a revival of genuine public life. In valuing neighborliness, people value that upon which citizenship most essentially depends. It is our good fortune that this value persists.

So it is that places may play a role in the revival of citizenship. Places have a way of claiming people. When they claim very diverse kinds of people, those people must eventually learn to live with each other. That is to say, they must learn to inhabit their place together, which they can only do through the development of certain practices of inhabitation. The practices rely upon and nurture the old-fashioned civic virtues of trust, honesty, justice, toleration, cooperation, hope, and remembrance. It is through the nurturing of such virtues (and in no other way) that we might begin to reclaim that competency upon which democratic citizenship depends.

In Missoula, writers and musicians collaborate at the base of Mount Jumbo to tell stories of their place of habitation. It is altogether appropriate in the context of our discussion here that this gathering of people to help spread the art of place is happening at the *public* radio station. The storytelling project is for the citizens of Missoula, the neighbors of Missoula. It is for the people that inhabit this region called the Northern Rockies: the public of this place.

Another Missoula citizen, writing to help save the fragile ecosystem of Mount Jumbo offers this: "Only a five-minute drive from downtown Missoula and a half-dozen steps past the trailhead, and I already feel the change. Cobalt lupines quietly brush my calves and mind, the streetnoise of just moments ago already fading from memory; the pungent scent of yarrow filters out the diesel fuel and rubber; and my eyes are filled with the smooth, open space of the summer-browned grasses of Mount Jumbo."[11]

Notes

1. Thomas Jefferson, *Notes on the State of Virginia* (New York: Harper and Row, 1964), 157.

2. James Madison, "Federalist Paper No. 10," *Notes of Debates in the Federal Convention of 1787* (Athens: Ohio University Press, 1966), 83.

3. Georg Wilhelm Friedrich Hegel, *The Philosophy of History*, trans. J. Sibree (New York: Wiley Cook Co., 1944), 84–85.

4. Wallace Stegner, *The Sound of Mountain Water* (New York: Doubleday, 1969), 37–38.

5. Hannah Arendt, *The Human Condition* (Chicago: University of Chicago Press, 1958), 52–53.

6. George F. Will, *Statecraft as Soulcraft* (New York: Simon & Schuster, 1983), 35.

7. Robert N. Bellah et al., *Habits of the Heart* (Berkeley: University of California Press, 1984), 20–21.

8. Lawrence Haworth, *The Good City* (Bloomington: Indiana University Press, 1963), 86.

9. Wendell Berry, *The Unsettling of America* (New York: Avon Books, 1967), 22.

10. Bellah et al., *Habits of the Heart*, 154.

11. Tommy Youngbood-Petersen, *Mount Jumblo: A Preservation Manifesto*, (unpublished manuscript): 1.

17

Settling America: The Concept of Place in Environmental Politics

Mark Sagoff

Before the American Revolution, Hector St. Jean de Crevecoeur asked "What then is the American, this new man?" and gave an answer we might give today.[1] We are Americans, he suggests, insofar as we take our customs and culture from this new land or, as Robert Frost said at the inauguration of President Kennedy, we are Americans insofar as we belong to—we are possessed by—the land we possess.[2] Our community is bounded not by race, ancestry, or religion but by the history, natural and cultural, of the land we inhabit. We become Americans by becoming native to this place.

Much of what we deplore about the human subversion of nature—and fear about the destruction of the environment—has to do with the loss of places we keep in shared memory and cherish with instinctive and collective loyalty. It has to do with a loss of diversity and an attendant loss of security—the security one has when one relies upon the characteristic aspects of places and communities one knows well. What may worry us most is the prospect of becoming strangers in our own land, of never quite settling into it, of being no more at home here than anywhere. The prospect that a person of European, African, or Asian descent, no matter for how many generations in this country, can never be native to it—never become a "native American"—must be an unsettling one. It commits us forever to the vagrancy of the frontier, to a footloose and pioneering spirit that strikes a claim and then moves on.

This chapter is adapted from an article previously appearing in *Journal of Energy, Natural Resources, and Environmental Law* 12, no. 2 (1992): 349–416.

What Gertrude Stein is reputed to have said about her birthplace, Oakland—"There's no there there"—she later applied to America as a whole: "Conceive of a space that is filled with moving."[3] Our politicians promise to "get America moving again," but Americans are always on the move. "We are in urgent need of understanding places before we lose them, of learning how to see them and to take possession of them."[4] We take possession of places by possessing a history and not simply by making it, as Americans are wont to do, and thus by bringing time into sync with change. Our environment erodes because we do not set roots in it. Wallace Stegner concludes: "American individualism, much celebrated and cherished, has developed without essential corrective, which is belonging. Freedom, when found, can turn out to be airless and unsustaining. Especially in the West, what we have instead of place is space. Place is more than half memory, shared memory." Rarely do Westerners stay long enough to share much of anything.[5]

This chapter will explore and elaborate a concept that mediates between the ideas of nature and of the environment and captures what may be most important in each. This is the concept of place. Commentators tell us that we Americans lack a sense of or affection for places: we do not settle anywhere, but move on, always going to somewhere or something new. The historian Frederick Jackson Turner predicated the development of the American national character on the existence of the frontier—"an area of free land, its continuous recession, and the advance of American settlement westward." The mobile home, the chain store, the fast-food stand, and the commercial strip turn placelessness into a way of life. "In this country, at this moment," writes artist Alan Gussow, "we are very conscious of man as a violator of his environment, a destroyer of the earth's lovely places."[6]

Placelessness and transience triumph in uniformity—the replication everywhere of the standardized surroundings from which one has just fled. This is not just America's problem: it is worldwide. Global unity, we are told, presages global uniformity. Local cultures cannot stand up to forces unleashed by the global economy: "forces that demand integration and uniformity and that mesmerize the world with fast music, fast computers, and fast food—with MTV, Macintosh, and McDonald's, pressing nations into one commercially homogeneous global network: one McWorld tied together by technology, ecology, communications, and commerce."[7]

The expression "McWorld" is novel, but the thought is an old one. Consider this statement: Variety is disappearing from the human race;

the same ways of acting, thinking, and feeling are to be met with all over the world. This is not only because nations work more upon each other and copy each other more faithfully, but as the men of each country relinquish more and more the peculiar opinions and feelings of a caste, profession, or a family, they . . . become more alike, even without having imitated each other.[8]

In this way, Alexis de Tocqueville described in 1830 the effect of democracy on diversity. He thus anticipated the analytic argument Karl Polanyi offered in *The Great Transformation* a little more than a century later. Polanyi understood production as an interaction between people and nature; he conceived economic liberalism in terms of a self-regulating system of barter and exchange. For Polanyi, this system of global markets dissolves the connection between productivity and place, that is, between the economy and the characteristics of local communities. Once humanity in the form of labor and nature in the form of land became subject to price, for example, wages and rents, they had to conform themselves to markets rather than markets to them. The forces of production and consumption wear down the particularities of places and the differences among communities; they relate supply and demand in one abstract universal system of exchange.

The story Polanyi told in his famous book is now a familiar one. Once labor and land were separated from ways of life and subjected to the laws of supply and demand, the atomistic or granular competition of individuals supplanted organic relations between human communities and their natural surroundings.[9] Polanyi continues:

Such a scheme of destruction was best served by the application of the principle of freedom of contract. In practice this meant that the noncontractual organizations of kinship, neighborhood, profession, and creed were to be liquidated since they claimed the allegiance of the individual and thus restrained his freedom. To represent this principle as one of non-interference, as economic liberals are wont to do, was merely the expression of an ingrained prejudice in favor of a definite kind of interference, namely, such as would destroy non-contractual relations between individuals and prevent their spontaneous re-formation.[10]

What is remarkable about this passage is Polanyi's ability to identify the root philosophical contradiction—one that arises within liberal political theory—that makes us at once pursue and yet deplore the destruction of the organic connection between productivity and place. Liberals seek to maintain that connection in the name of protecting diversity, that is, by supporting the ability of many different religious and ethnic communities to maintain themselves by linking people to particular places and ways of life. Yet liberals, by emphasizing the freedom of individuals to make their own bargains in markets that are open on the same terms to all, also embrace an ideal of "arms length" autonomy that conflicts with traditional social relationships essential to cultural diversity.[11] The ideals of freedom and autonomy conflict with those of commitment and belonging—and in America they underlie our St. Vitus's dance. Thus, the conflict obvious in education, family, and health policy between the autonomy of the individuals and the sustainability of diverse communities affects environmental policy as well.[12]

Nature Is Not a Place

The concept of place is distinct from that of nature, because places are cultural artifacts and nature exists apart from culture and in distinction to it. The Romantic imagination, which interpreted nature as a book of divinely authored moral messages and symbols, never counted the ways nature is useful to people. It never took nature so neat or at so short a range. Thus, Ralph Waldo Emerson looked to nature for nothing so ordinary as a living. The Transcendentalist, he wrote, "does not deny the sensuous fact . . . but he will not see that alone." Instead, he looks to "the other end of phenomena," to the universal spiritual lessons they teach. Emerson seems oblivious to the particular in his quest for the universal, as when he writes: "Standing on the bare ground,—my head bathed by the blithe air, and uplifted into infinite space,—all mean egotism vanishes. I become a transparent eyeball. I am nothing. I see all. The currents of Universal Being circulate through me; I am part or particle of God."[13]

One way to illustrate the difference between nature in this Romantic sense and place would be to contrast the currents of Universal Being, which Emerson describes, with those of the Mississippi River. The latter can be much more problematical, especially if you are hauling a load of pig iron. The useful knowledge the river pilot acquires does not come by way of moral transcendence or, for that matter, by way of scientific inference. It comes from practice—from achieving a practical harmony between one's purposes and those of the river.

In Mark Twain's *Life on the Mississippi*, Horace Bixby, a steamer pilot, tells his trainee: "There's only one way to be a pilot, and that is to get this entire river by heart. You have to know it just like A B C." Bixby adds that piloting is not an empirical science: it contains nothing that can be inferred from instruments or written up in formulas. As a collection of empirical phenomena, the river has no shape; it is utterly Heraclitean. When the trainee complains that there are too many facts to learn about piloting, Bixby replies: "No! you only learn the shape of the river; and you learn it with such absolute certainty that you can always steer by the shape that's in your head, and never mind the one that's before your eyes."[14]

The engineer and the hydrologist study the river scientifically, but this would not make them good pilots. On the contrary, their studies usually feed efforts to straighten out the river or to control water flows, thereby making good piloting less important. The painter and poet also describe the river, but the spectacle they see is lost on the pilot. In his attention to minute particulars, the pilot nearly ignores the magnificence of the landscape.

Mark Twain illustrates two approaches to nature—one as spectacle, the other as place—by contrasting the ways the pilot and the passengers experience the river. When the trainee finally learns to be a pilot, he exchanges one aesthetic for the other. Though he admits he made a "valuable acquisition" in learning how to read the water, he adds: "I had lost something, too . . . all the grace, the beauty, and the poetry had gone out of the majestic river." The sense of place, wedding the pilot through practical harmonies to Heraclitean particulars, supplants the spectacle of nature, apparent to the steamboat passengers. The pilot trainee goes further: "All the value any feature of it had for me now was the amount of usefulness it could furnish toward compassing the safe piloting of a steamboat."[15]

A natural landscape becomes a place—"a shape that's in your head"—when it is cultivated, when it constrains human activity and is constrained by it, when it functions as a center of felt value because human needs, cultural and social as well as biological, are satisfied in it. The hunter, trapper, angler, or farmer who comes to terms with nature in particular places in pursuit of specific purposes may get to know its local conditions so intuitively that they get built into his reflexes. This contrasts entirely with the attitude of the outsiders, for example, the tourist who comes to see a spectacle and for whom "nothing has a drift or a relation; nothing has a history or a promise. Everything stands by itself, and comes and goes in its turn, like the shifting scenes of a show, which leaves the spectator where he was."[16]

The Environment Is Not a Place

The concepts of environment and place are far from interchangeable, and the differences in their meanings are profound. Consider, for example, the planetary support systems we threaten by putting too much of certain chemicals into the air. We sometimes speak as if the planet itself had a respiratory system, as if its biospheric organs were continuous with our own lungs, kidneys, or livers. We may view the environment in this way as if it were plumbing; we bother ourselves about it as we do our own health, when we think it needs repair. The environment in this sense is not a place or even a collection of places; rather it constitutes a sort of global infrastructure. Alan Gussow points out, "there is a great deal of talk these days about saving the environment. We must, for the environment sustains our bodies. But as humans we also require support for our spirits, and this is what certain kinds of places provide. The catalyst that converts any physical location . . . into a place, is the process of experiencing deeply. A place is a piece of the whole environment that has been claimed by feelings."[17]

If we turn from the planetary to the local environment, then we think more in terms of natural resources than of biospheric systems. In the past, nearby natural resources had a great deal to do with defining places, and to some extent this continues today. Consider, for example, fishing and watermen communities. The whaling villages of New Bedford and Nantucket, as Melville describes them in *Moby Dick*, once created a powerful sense of community and of place, even though those who frequented them were voyagers. Plainly, the nature of these places had everything to do with a particular natural resource, namely, whales, and therefore with the relationship between these communities and the natural environment.

The demise of the whaling industry illustrates the problem communities face in preserving the ways of life that depend on their proximity to natural resources. Communities of this kind rarely disband because resources run out; rather, the problem is that advancing technologies either glut or otherwise transform markets. The market for whale oil, for example, is not what it was. This is not because of a shortage of whales—the failure to manage the stock on a sustainable basis—but because of the availability of cheaper forms of energy.

The fishing industry of New England—like the whaling industry before it—may be displaced by technological inventions elsewhere, whether by fish factories like those that now fabricate chickens or by the direct culture of fish tissue in vitro. This industry will then go the way of every other in the New England states, a victim not of the poor management of resources but of technological change. The rivers that once powered the mighty textile industry in Lowell, Fall River, and Pawtucket have not dried up, though the industry has; in search of cheap labor it went to the South and then abroad. The southern New England farms that once fed Boston and Providence have reverted to woods or been planted in split levels and condominiums. This has not caused food shortages. Vegetables of all kinds come in year round from California, Florida, Ecuador, and Chile. Clothing piles up from Taiwan. Fish farms in Louisiana and Idaho run in catfish and trout. How, then, have the people and communities of New England maintained themselves? Why do families still live in them?

They have survived because their cultural and social institutions proved sustaining and sustainable—churches, schools and universities, town meetings, libraries, governments, families, and all kinds of associations. While these have kept up with the times, the basic structures and philosophies underlying them may not have changed very much in two hundred years. If you want to understand what makes the economic use of environmental resources sustainable—if you want to know how places survive the vagaries of markets—then look to the relationships, cultural and political, of the people in them. Look for affection not for efficiency as the trait with which people treat their surroundings. Where family and community ties are strong, where shared memories and commitments root people to a place, they can adapt to changing conditions, and they will do so in ways that respect nature and conserve the environment.

The Commons As a Cultural Construct

Aristotle, in describing what we call today "coordination" problems, wrote, "that which is common to the greatest number has the least care bestowed upon it." While the theory of the degradation of common property resources through competitive overuse may have held interest in Aristotle's time, to discuss the "tragedy of the commons" and associated notions of externalities, competitive equilibria, and prisoner's dilemma games today is to connive at criminal boredom.[18] The interesting question is no longer why we waste resources when no rules exist for controlling exploitation. Rather, the question to answer is how communities have historically succeeded in conserving and preserving assets that their members own in common.

As a general rule, societies do not treat common property as everybody's property. Individuals who share fisheries, pasture lands, and forests may have equal rights, but this does not give them open access to the commons without restrictions. Anthropologists point out, on the contrary, that communities sharing resources typically control access to them.[19] Indeed, by forbidding some uses and by permitting others, communities define what the resource is.

Anthropologists urge us to recognize that the ways a commons is used depend on the cultural meanings and not just the economic values that attach to it. As one anthropologist notes: "The definitions of rights, of relative claims, of appropriate uses and users are not only imbedded in specific historical sets of political and economic structures but also in cultural systems of meanings, symbols, and values."[20]

If groups typically find cultural means to regulate common resources, this does not argue for the polemical opposite of "tragedy of the commons" analysis, that is, "romanticized notions of a precommercial, precapitalist past when communal rights preserved the land and permitted all to use it on an equal footing."[21] The success of many communities in regulating without dividing the commons, however, should lead us to ask why we tend today to think of the commons as normally an unregulated or open-access resource rather than as one maintained by cultural practices and societal decisions.

Anthropologists criticize the "individualistic bias of most commons models" because it "underestimates . . . the ability of people to cooperate in commons situations and contributes to the tendency to avoid social, historical, and institutional analysis." The "individualistic bias" leads some analysts to conclude that the commons should be privatized if it is not to be wasted—that individuals should have property rights to portions of it. This suggests that property rights essentially constitute relations between individuals and things—a view many commentators hold.[22]

The alternative is to understand systems of property rights as relating individuals to each other, in other words, as constituting social expectations and practices that make individuals into a community. On this approach, "property rights do not refer to relations between men and things, but, rather, to the sanctioned behavioral relations among men that arise from the existence of things and pertain to their use."[23] If this is true, then the uses of the commons are not simply "given" *ab initio* by the hand of nature and by the needs of human beings. Rather, the "things" individuals share—the character, utility, and extent of the commons—are determined in large part by social perceptions—by a consensus concerning what of value is and is not "there." The value of a commons depends as much on what the community as a whole believes is important as on what individuals wish to consume and use.

Place As *Res Publica*

Hannah Arendt observes that public places bring together people who possess them in common; like a table located between people, it both relates them and separates them. Arendt continues:

> The public realm, as the common world, gathers us together and yet prevents our falling over each other, so to speak. What makes mass society too difficult to bear is not the number of people involved, or at least not primarily, but the fact that the world between them has lost its power to gather them together, to relate and to separate them. The weirdness of this situation resembles a spiritualistic seance where a number of people gathered around a table might suddenly . . . see the table vanish from their midst, so that two persons sitting opposite each other were no longer separated but also would be entirely unrelated by anything tangible.[24]

What Arendt says about a table may also be said about local environments. When we regard these as resources, then we set up all the competitive dilemmas associated with the use of what many people own in common. If we constitute these environs as places, then instead of economic opportunities, what we have are moral and cultural obligations. For individuals to own up to these collective obligations is for them to become a community; it is in itself to substitute an ethic of responsible care for that of regulated competition.

While other species rely on instinct to develop nature into their habitat, human beings have to depend on culture. The traditional work of culture, indeed, has been to make nature into our habitat or home. The word "culture" derives from *colere*—to cultivate, to dwell, to care for, and to preserve—and relates primarily, as Hannah Arendt notes: "to the intercourse of man with nature in the sense of cultivating and tending nature until it becomes fit for habitation. As such, it indicates an attitude of loving care and stands in sharp contrast to all efforts to subject nature to the domination of man."[25]

The appropriate cultivation of nature as habitat—which is neither to preserve nature for its own sake or to industrialize it for the sake of maximizing wealth—may be America's next great moral achievement. The attitude of loving care, far more than that of efficient exploitation, expresses and preserves American culture and, therefore, our character and identity as a nation. This attitude, as Robert Frost wrote in the poem with which this chapter began, has as much to do with giving as with getting and spending. The land was not given to us, Frost wrote, but we to the land:

> Such as we were, we gave ourselves outright
> (The deed of gift was many deeds of war)
> To the land vaguely realizing westward,
> But still unstoried, artless, unenhanced,
> Such as she was, such as she would become.[26]

Notes

1. "He is an American who, leaving behind him all his ancient prejudices and manners, received new ones from the new mode of life he has embraced," J. Hector St. Jean de Crevecoeur, *Letters from An American Farmer* (New York: Penguin, 1981).

2. Robert Frost, "The Gift Outright," in *Complete Poems of Robert Frost* (New York: Henry Holt and Co., 1949).

3. W. Stegner, *Where the Bluebird Sings to the Lemonade Springs* (New York: Penguin Books, 1992), 72.

4. C. W. Moore et al., "Towards Making Places," *Landscape*, autumn 1962, quoted in A. Briggs, "The Sense of Place," *Smithsonian Annual II: The Fitness of Man's Environment* 85 (1968).

5. Stegner, *Where the Bluebird Sings*, 72.

6. F. Turner, *The Frontier in American History* (Tucson: University of Arizona Press, 1896); A. Gussow, *A Sense of Place: The Artist and the American Land* (San Francisco: Friends of the Earth, 1972), 27.

7. James Barber, "Jihad vs. McWorld," *Atlantic Monthly*, March, 1992, 53.

8. Alexis de Tocqueville, *Democracy in America* (New York: Oxford University Press, 1946), 240.

9. For case studies of the organic aspect of the relation of communities to nature, see Robert Coles, *Migrants, Sharecropers, Mountaineers* (Boston: Little, Brown, 1971). Coles quotes one farmer in the deep South: "To me the land I have is always there, waiting for me, and it's part of me, way inside me, it's as much me as my own arms and legs" (Ibid., 411).

10. K. Polanyi, *The Great Transformation* (New York: Farrar & Rinehart, 1944).

11. For a brilliant discussion of this conflict in the history of the American West, see Stegner, *Where the Bluebird Sings to the Lemonade Springs*, chapter 5. Stegner notes that being footloose has always fascinated Americans; it is "associated in our minds with escape from history and oppression and law and irksome obligations" and with absolute freedom (72). Stegner continues:

But the rootlessness that expresses energy and a thirst for the new and an aspiration toward freedom and personal fulfillment has just as often been a curse. Migrants deprive themselves of the physical and spiritual bonds that develop within a place and a society. Our migratoriness has hindered us from becoming a people of communities and traditions, especially in the West. It has robbed us of the gods who make places holy. It has cut off individuals and families and communities from memory and the continuum of time (71–72).

12. The conflict between space and place presents the geographical analogue to the conflict between autonomy and diversity. For an excellent discusison of this see Yi Fu Tuan, *Space and Place: The Perspective of Experience* (Minneapolis: University of Minnesota Press, 1977), chapter 5. Tuan notes: "Freedom implies space; it means having the power and enough room in which to act" (Ibid., 52). He adds: "Space is a common symbol of freedom in the Western world. Space lies open; it suggests the future and invites action" (Ibid., 54). Place, in contrast, concerns commitment and responsibility, actuality rather than potentiality. It is not the realm of conquest but the sphere of concern. Place involves what Tuan calls "an ordered world of meaning . . . and beyond it is . . . space" (Ibid., 56).

13. Ralph Waldo Emerson, *Selected Writings of Emerson*, edited by Brooks Atkinson (New York: Modern Library, 1992).

14. Mark Twain, *Life on the Mississippi* (New York: Harper, 1911), 59, 72.

15. Ibid., 83, 85; see also L. Marx, *The Pilot and the Passenger: Essays on Literature, Technology, and Culture in the United States* (New York: Oxford University Press, 1988); Twain, *Life on the Mississippi*, 85.

16. See R. Hoggart, *The Uses of Literacy* (London: Penguin, 1957); E. Relph, *Place and Placelessness* (London: Pion, 1976), 87.

17. Gussow, *A Sense of Place*, 27.

18. For Aristotle, see Cass & Edney, "The Commons Dilemma: A Simulation Testing the Effects of Resource Visibility and Territorial Division," *Human Ecology* 6 (1978); 372; see also G. Hardin, "The Tragedy of the Commons," *Science* 162 (1968), 1243; for externalities, see, for example, Cheung, "The Structure of a Contract and the Theory of a Non-exclusive Resource," *Journal of Law & Economics* 13 (1970): 45; for competitive equilibria, see Ciriacy, Wantrup, and Bishop, "Common Property and a Concept in Natural Resources Policy," *Natural Resources Journal* 15 (1975); 713; for prisoner's dilemma games, see M. Olson, *The Logic of Collective Action* (Cambridge: Harvard University Press, 1965).

19. See Ciriacy-Wantrup and Bishop, "Common Property," 713–27; Godwin and Shepard, "Forcing Squares, Triangles and Ellipses into a Circular Paradigm: The Use of the Commons Dilemma in Examining the Allocation of Common Resources," *Western Political Quarterly* 35, 265.

20. P. Peters, "Embedded Systems and Rooted Models: The Grazing Lands of Botswana and the Commons Debate," in *The Question of the Commons*, edited by B. McCay and J. Acheson (Tucson: University of Arizona Press, 1977), 177.

21. Ibid., 178.

22. B. McCay and J. Acheson, "Human Ecology of the Commons," in *The Question of the Commons* (Tucson: University of Arizona Press, 1977), 7; see

also, for example, Demsetz, "Toward a Theory of Property Rights," *American Economic Review* 62 (1967): 347.

23.   Furubotn and Pejovich, "Property Rights and Economics Theory: A Survey of the Recent Literature," *Journal of Economic Literature* 10 (1972): 1139.

24.   H. Arendt, *The Human Condition* (Chicago: University of Chicago Press, 1958), 52–53. Daniel Kemmis places Arendt's discussion of *res publica* in the context of Wendell Berry's *The Unsettling of America*:

> We have given up the understanding—dropped it out of our language and so out of our thought—that we and our country create one another, are literally part of one another; that our land passes in and out of our bodies just as our bodies pass in and out of our land; that we and our land are part of one another, and so cannot possibly flourish alone; that, therefore, our culture must be our response to our place, our culture and our place are images of each other and inseparable from each other, and so neither can be better than the other.

See D. Kemmis, *Community and the Politics of Place* (Norman: University of Oklahoma Press, 1990), 7.

25.   H. Arendt, *Between Past and Future: Eight Exercises in Political Thought* (New York: Viking, 1968), 311–12.

26.   Robert Frost, "The Gift Outright," in *Complete Poems of Robert Frost* (New York: Henry Holt and Company, 1949), 467.

18

Peril on Common Ground:
The Applegate Experiment

Brett KenCairn

For much of its recent history, the Pacific Northwest has served as a resource-extraction colony in service of the burgeoning urban areas to the east and south. Like most colonies, the emphasis has been on short-term profit, often at the expense of both the local landscape and the local people.

The early strategies of environmental protectionists attempting to combat these excesses were primarily legal. Environmental groups fought to protect specific forests, streams, and grasslands through passage of laws to set land aside or regulate its use. Initially small and choosing only winnable high profile areas, the environmental movement grew rapidly and began challenging the extractive industries over all resource use on public lands.

As the two sides dug in, the contrasting worldviews became strikingly evident. For the extractionists, the earth and all its "resources" are the exclusive domain of the human species. For the preservationists, "nature" is the preeminent value. Humans are often considered disruptive forces to be minimized if possible.

Between these two extremes, and largely forgotten, is the traditional conservationist approach of Gifford Pinchot and Aldo Leopold. For conservationists, reciprocity, a relationship with the land that involves both taking and giving back, is the goal of good environmental stewardship. The Applegate Partnership was formed in this tradition.

As in other timber-dominated areas of the Northwest, the public lands in the Applegate Valley had been placed off limits to logging due to the listing of the northern spotted owl as an endangered species. While the federal land-management agencies spent months trying to formulate a management plan that would ensure the survival of the owl, timber and environmental interests waged an all-out war to win public sympathy for their opposing causes. Activists, loggers, state and federal agencies, and the timber industry had arrived at a bitter and hostile impasse.

Seeking a way to end the stalemate, Jack Shipley, a local environmentalist, circulated a proposal for a new watershed management plan that would be based on conceptual agreement between environmentalists, industry, and agencies. What follows is the story of the Applegate Partnership—its struggles and successes, its growth and notoriety, its internal tensions and shifting allegiances. In this story there are important lessons: what is possible when people with disparate interests take the risk to sit down together to work through their differences; what it takes to stay together; and the perils and obstacles that are probably inevitable in any effort that seeks to find common ground in natural-resource policy debates.

Applegate Valley and the Antecedents of Change

The Applegate Partnership emerged amid a unique set of circumstances:

Geography

The Applegate River watershed encompasses approximately 496,500 acres in southern Oregon. This diverse landscape is situated in the world renowned "Klamath Knot," a meeting of several mountain ranges forming a unique east-west/north-south confluence of botanical and climatic influences. Throughout geologic history, this area has served as a refuge for plant species during alternating cycles of glaciation and inland flooding which covered most of the lower lands surrounding this confluence of mountains. As a result, the Applegate watershed is the biological repository that provided genetic material for repopulating much of the Pacific Northwest. Relatives of Siskiyou gene stocks have been found from Alaska to Idaho. The area is recognized as one of the critical biological reserves on the planet.

Social History

Prior to Euroamerican arrival to the area, the watershed was inhabited by two distinct groups of Native Americans, the Takilma and the Dagilma. The Takilma were primarily located on major tributaries, while the Dagilma frequented the many highlands. These people were known as fierce and enterprising. Oral history indicates they frequently traded with the Yakima for weapons up north. The frequent currency was slaves they had captured among the Modoc to the east. Around 1850, gold was discovered in the Jacksonville area just to the south of the Applegate watershed. Soon thousands of miners were marauding about the hills digging and burning their way into modest deposits of a number of precious metals. Placer mining was common, as was floating dredge. Enormous ecological damage took place during this period to both hydrological and forest systems. Today, most forests in the Applegate contain trees approximately 120 years old, corresponding to this period. Later, big ranching and sheep operations ran tens of thousands of livestock in the fragile high-mountain meadows of the area, again seriously disrupting many riparian and native grassland communities. Around 1900, this intense phase of extraction subsided, leaving primarily small subsistence agricultural and timbering operations. Many small saw mills operated up the various drainages, and small to medium farm/ranch operations worked the narrow valley bottoms.

In the late 1950s and early 1960s, many of these smaller operations began to close up shop, unable to remain profitable in commodity markets. Land began changing hands and a new population of urban "back-to-the-landers" began inhabiting the marginal lands. This new social group brought many new perspectives and experiences to the area. Yet despite many cultural differences, the old-timers and the newcomers quickly integrated around essential community services like volunteer fire departments, and both groups frequently joined together in community benefits.

The contrast of values emerged strongly, however, when federal land-management agencies adopted industrial forestry as a dominant management approach. Before the 1960s, timber management of federal forest lands, approximately 70 percent of the watershed, was relatively low impact and low intensity. With the growing pressure of many high-capacity mills in the Medford area, however, federal land managers began using clearcutting and burning strategies refined in the lush forests of coastal Oregon and Washington.

Accompanying this monoculture strategy was the need for ways to impede the natural proliferation of broadleaf trees rather than conifers following a clearcut. Aerial spraying was introduced to kill this "competing vegetation," igniting a firestorm of protest among the "back-to-the-land" community. Soon large-scale protests were taking place at agency offices, and activists were learning how to successfully challenge agency actions in court. Moreover, neighbors began forming alliances to coordinate actions across the watershed. Soon these challenges broadened to include specific timber sales being planned in each watershed. By the early 1980s, groups such as Headwaters and the Applegate Watershed Conservancy were becoming a formidable force. Toward the close of the 1980s, these groups began joining with state and regional organizations such as the Oregon Natural Resources Defense Council and the Sierra Club Legal Defense Fund in linking campaigns and spreading organizing skills.

Politics of Polarization and an Opening for Action

By 1992, the practice of forestry on public lands in the Pacific Northwest had taken a sudden and dramatic reversal. Throughout the 1980s, the public lands of the Pacific Northwest produced over five billion board feet of softwood annually. With the listing of the northern spotted owl and the subsequent federal court injunctions on logging activity that could endanger the owl, logging came to an abrupt halt on most federal lands. As restrictions on logging increased, timber industry interests mounted a loud and well-organized resistance. In many forest-dependent areas, local politicians, community leaders, and even labor-union representatives joined to renounce the listing as well as issue warnings of the impending layoffs and economic disruption these actions would cause. The simplistic struggle between "jobs and owls" had begun.

Jackson and Josephine Counties of southern Oregon were not exceptions to the rancorous conflict that characterized this time. As powerful and growing environmental organizations successfully challenged many timber sales, tensions with the timber industry increased dramatically.

Yet during the spring and summer of 1992, a local environmentalist, Jack Shipley, began circulating a proposal calling for the development of a watershed-management plan for the entire 500,000-acre Applegate watershed, one of seven watersheds in the larger Rogue River basin. This proposal outlined broad concepts of sustainable management, carefully avoiding discussion of specific management techniques. Shipley's goal was to seek conceptual agreement between environmentalists, industry, and the agencies on the goals of management.

Initial responses to the draft were cautious but encouraging from all sides. The draft went through several iterations and eventually inspired Shipley to call a potluck meeting at his home in the Applegate in October of that year. Attending the potluck were people from most of the major interests represented in the watershed and the valley: agencies, environmentalists, industry, farmers and ranchers, and a variety of local residents. Again Shipley structured the gathering to focus on broader values and issues facing the watershed. As people introduced themselves, they were asked to not disclose which interest they represented or organization they worked for, but to simply say what was important to them about the watershed. In this context loggers spoke of taking their grandchildren hunting and fishing in the watershed, environmentalists described their concern over the loss of jobs and economic opportunities for local residents, agency people related their sadness over the ways the land had suffered under human management, and everyone described their concern over the many growing threats to the larger health and resilience of the watershed. Most participants left the meeting with a renewed hope that common ground was achievable.

At the end of the meeting, a group of eighteen people volunteered to go forward with refining the manifesto of sustainable management that Shipley had been circulating. This group in turn selected a group of nine with nine alternates who would become the guiding board for what was then named the "Applegate Partnership."

The board-selection process is one of the important characteristics of the partnership's legacy. From its inception, the partnership was catalyzed by an individual who offered a vision that drew in other participants. This core group then considered who the essential stakeholders were and collectively identified the particular individuals within those groups who were most respected and most likely to be capable of working with those sharing different views or values. There were no elections. People were asked to come to the table as individuals first and as representatives of their interests or organizations second. This fluid dynamic between individual and interest has proven to be one of the most interesting and challenging aspects of the partnership's history, as we will see in a moment.

The Partnership's "Crusade"

For almost three months the partnership avoided publicity. During this time, the various constituencies drafted and finalized a common vision statement and organizational objectives. Over a process of weekly meetings and more frequent committee work, a consensus for proceeding emerged. One of the delightful events that took place during this period underscores the political ambiguity that initially provided a niche for partnership initiatives. In December of 1992, the partnership hosted regional forester John Lowe of the Forest Service, and BLM state director Dean Bibles on a tour of the Applegate. After flying them over the watershed in timber industry helicopters, they were deposited in the backyard of a local resident. In his small front room, more than twenty partnership participants shared beans and cornbread with the two agency heads and described their plan for formulating a watershed management approach.

At the end of the presentation, the partnership invited the officials to ask questions and describe their impressions of the effort. After a long silence, the Forest Service official looked around the room and asked "Who gave you the authority to do this?" During the ensuing silence partnership members looked at one another until someone replied, "I guess we did!"

The symbolic power of this gathering of previous adversaries was not lost on these agency officials. Still immobilized by legal and political gridlock institutionalized by timber and environmental interests, these officials sensed a potential opening for resolving the timber dispute. They pledged their support and endorsement of local agency participation in further development of these ideas.

Not long after this event, President Clinton announced his intention to convene a forestry conference in Portland, Oregon, to initiate efforts to resolve the forest crisis. In preparation, he sent his cabinet secretaries to the region to identify issues and opportunities. Bruce Babbitt was invited to visit with the partnership. In an event similar to the previous meeting with agency heads, Babbitt helicoptered in for a brief living room meeting where he heard about the "partnership alternative."

Babbitt left the meeting noticeably impressed with the apparent effectiveness of the partnership's collaboration between agency, industry, and environmental interests. Soon the partnership appeared in both administration and agency briefing papers. With this notoriety came a seemingly unending stream of requests for appearances at events ranging from conferences of professional mediators and facilitators, to the Society of American Foresters national convention, and a meeting with the vice president's environmental advisor. Ever-increasing amounts of partnership volunteer time and resources were consumed by these requests.

The release of the president's forest plan sealed the partnership's fate as a "poster child" for collaboration. In the hastily appended "Option 9," the scientific team proposed the creation of ten "Adaptive Management Areas" (AMAs). These were to be areas in which greater flexibility would be allowed for experimentation with new techniques and approaches to forest management, including greater participation by local groups. The Applegate was named as one of the ten AMAs and profiled as a model for this concept.

However, this effort to institutionalize the partnership model was to have serious negative consequences for both the partnership's own initiatives and the larger movement toward community participation in forest management in the Northwest.

Dissension at Home, Disenchantment Abroad

The partnership identified four major goals in its work to formulate a watershed-based approach to management of the Applegate. These goals were to:

1. conduct a comprehensive ecological assessment of the entire watershed identifying the critical concerns, priority areas for restoration action, and key opportunities for sustainable use;
2. develop a comprehensive community assessment evaluating the major social and economic issues facing the more than ten thousand residents of the watershed and mechanisms for addressing these issues in the context of watershed management;
3. initiate efforts leading to near-term forest products projects capable of generating economically viable resources compatible with an overall forest-health emphasis;
4. create a research and monitoring strategy capable of evaluating and improving the activities taken in the watershed including the creation of a comprehensive Geographic Information System database compiling all available data on the watershed.

Without resources of its own, the partnership relied on participating organizations to bring the necessary resources to the table to accomplish these tasks. A local nonprofit represented on the board, the Rogue Institute for Ecology and Economy, took the lead in the community assessment and community outreach efforts. Environmental and industry representatives also began working with the agencies to formulate a strategy for an ecological assessment. Local and regional educational institutions, as well as the Forest Service's research branch, were courted in an effort to secure research and monitoring funding. With such far reaching ambitions, the partnership was ever aware that proof of its viability meant getting some sort of sustainable forest products project to happen. The first attempts at generating activity involved reviewing revised agency timber sales, which were adapted to meet a list of criteria (biodiversity, community benefit, protection of old growth, etc.) developed by the partnership. This approach quickly produced dissent from agency planners and managers who resented an outside board attempting to direct their management activities. Many of these sales were under injunction and would only have been possible with some form of injunctive relief. Consequently, this emphasis on defining viable forest products opportunities also created powerful resistance from within the environmental community, who did not support many of these sales despite their modification.

After stepping back to evaluate this experience, partnership representatives, led by environmentalists on the board, proposed an entirely new project that would attempt to demonstrate the types of forest health-based prescriptions being discussed within the group. The Forest Service eventually endorsed the idea and named the new project "Partnership One."

Planning for Partnership One was a remarkable experiment in participation. Numerous field trips with partnership representatives and others generated many different ideas about prescriptions and strategies. Several field days even included test paint markings in which environmentalists and industry people were given paint guns and asked to show how they would mark the stands for retention and harvest. Unfortunately, these experiments were poorly documented and when the initial draft Environmental Assessment was released, many discrepancies and misunderstandings began to surface. In one incident, an argument surfaced over whether there would be a maximum allowed harvest diameter of large trees. Although the dispute was eventually settled in favor of the environmental interests who had raised it, it created substantial friction within the partnership and fueled suspicion in the environmental community.

The Tyranny of Process

At the same time, a growing chorus of prominent regional environmentalists were beginning to openly attack the partnership. With the selection of Option 9 as the preferred alternative, the partnership was visibly linked to the Adaptive Management Areas, which many environmentalists viewed as a ruse to create areas with fewer logging restrictions. Internal conflicts within local environmental groups over the strategies of the partnership intensified. One of these groups demanded more and more stringent guidelines for all communication and outreach regarding the partnership. All outgoing communications, including a video produced on the philosophy of the partnership, were subjected to intense scrutiny and calls for modification. The formerly informal partnership meeting process was repeatedly challenged by those who felt their views were not given equal consideration. More and more partnership time was consumed negotiating the process by which anything was to be done.

The Tyranny of Personality

At the same time, key individuals in the partnership balked at the types of changes being proposed. In certain cases, long-held patterns of gruff talk and angry outburst were called into question. In other instances, the loose and sometimes unaccountable promotion of partnership views by some partnership participants were scrutinized. As the group settled into patterns over time, many of these idiosyncrasies were simply tolerated. Problems were overlooked in large part because the only thing holding most participants at the table was their own personal will and inclination. At various times in this period, a number of key participants would issue subtle or overt messages that they might abandon the effort.

Throughout this time, participants struggled to address these problems. Two professional facilitators alternated attendance at the weekly meetings to provide some degree of guidance and, when necessary, mediation. A number of members consistently acted as ambassadors between feuding participants and their groups.

Headwaters Withdraws

Eventually the stress created by participation in the partnership became too great for the key environmental group represented on the partnership, Headwaters, to sustain. Conflict over strategy had already led to the request for a partnership advocate's resignation from Headwater's board. A deepening conflict between Headwaters' staff and board over strategy loomed. The organization was also under intense pressure from some of its allied organizations who had taken openly hostile positions against the partnership. Finally, Headwaters announced in the spring of 1994 that it was resigning from the partnership.

Paradoxically, the Headwaters representative, a cofounder of Headwaters and a long-term resident in the Applegate, elected to stay on the partnership board and simply switched his official affiliation to the local watershed group he chaired. However, the well-publicized move by the Headwaters organization was quickly picked up by local newspapers and used to cast doubts on the integrity of the partnership. In an editorial based on no follow-up investigation, the *Medford Mail Tribune* raised suspicions that the partnership was compromising its environmental values. Rumors began to spread widely in both agency and environmental circles that the partnership was dead. Many of those spreading these rumors, both agency and other, spoke with noticeable satisfaction.

The FACA Debacle

Despite the Headwaters withdrawal, partnership participants all agreed that they were committed to going on. Work continued on the various projects including supporting the Forest Service in final preparations of the Partnership One forest-products sale. Then, just months later, the agencies announced that they were being ordered by the Clinton administration to formally withdraw from the partnership.

As part of its strategy to challenge the Clinton administration's Northwest Forest Plan, the timber industry had discovered an obscure and little-used law passed in the early 1970s to limit the influence of special interest groups on federal decision-making processes. This law, the Federal Advisory Committee Act (FACA), stipulated that agencies were not allowed to meet regularly with nonagency groups in any context that could be construed as giving consensual advice or recommendations about agency actions. In a lawsuit filed in U.S. District Court, the timber industry won its case. Although the judge ruled that noncompliance with the law had not significantly altered the outcome of the process and allowed the forest plan to stand, he issued a stern warning to the administration that any further knowing violations of the law could jeopardize the forest plan. The administration ordered the agencies to stop attending partnership activities.

The effect on everyone was dramatic. Agency participants struggled valiantly to persuade their superiors to find ways to continue participation. Administration officials met repeatedly with the partnership and other community-based collaborations to try to formulate mechanisms for continued involvement. In the end, however, in order to protect the political capital already invested in the forest plan, the Clinton administration directed the agencies to publicly withdraw from regular and active participation in the highest profile partnership groups. Number one on the list for withdrawal was the Applegate Partnership.

Guidelines were eventually released that enabled agency participation at a reduced and carefully prescribed level. Key agency personnel continued to participate throughout this period due entirely to their own personal commitment to the partnership process. With the eventual approval of the forest plan, this distancing of agency personnel has diminished. Unfortunately, months of potential action and substantial stocks of trust and goodwill were also squandered in the process.

Quiet Steps toward Renewal

For many who watched the partnership, the measure of its success or failure was whether or not it could facilitate any sort of forest products outputs. This yardstick was constantly in the background of industry statements about the partnership, and it was frequently the most persistent question from agency representatives. As the months passed, the partnership was clearly failing to improve the gridlock in forest-product activities.

Measurable Successes in Restoration

At the same time, a stalwart core of partnership participants was steadily making progress in formulating a comprehensive watershed restoration strategy through support made available by two state programs, Oregon's Watershed Health Program and the Governor's Watershed Enhancement Board. As a result of the Watershed Health Program, the Applegate Partnership was designated a Watershed Council and given over $400,000 to implement watershed health projects. These included assisting farmers to improve irrigation-water utilization, anadromous fisheries improvements, riparian-habitat restoration, and tree planting. Despite the continued preoccupation with creating forest-products projects, these efforts began to create visible successes in the watershed and dramatically increased the exposure and support of the partnership among area residents. As part of this restoration program's outreach efforts, the partnership secured funding for a watershedwide newspaper featuring articles written by both resource specialists and local residents on issues related to forestry, farming, ranching, economics, and local culture and history.

As the notoriety of the partnership waned in the larger political arena, its popularity waxed in the local watershed. Gradually the partnership's principal participants have become involved in a much broader circle of land-management issues in the watershed, including innovative strategies for grazing management, new approaches to water management for anadromous fisheries restoration, and alternatives to suburbanization and loss of farmlands.

Another Bold Proposal

Despite these successes in restoration and community outreach, a central mission of the partnership continues to be the demonstration that sustainable forest management is possible. Out of the frustration engendered by the FACA mess, several partnership members began working with the Aerial Forest Management Foundation to formulate an independent plan for watershed management. The plan proposed congressional funding for a partnership-directed environmental impact statement and subsequent implementation plan covering activities on over twenty thousand acres a year over the next ten to fifteen years. The plan was quickly in circulation among key congressional and administration staff. Suddenly both the agencies and Headwaters were attending partnership meetings and attempting to influence development of the proposal.

Today, after long negotiations and restructuring, the process is going forward as a comprehensive watershedwide fire-management program. Four partnership members are participating in the "coordinating" group (though FACA requires that they simply represent themselves and are not consulted as a group for advice). The program will likely result in a fascinating planning process in which industry, environmental groups, agencies, and educational institutions will all have the opportunity to assist in formulating strategies that address both fire and forest health concerns. The partnership anticipates that this project will make substantial contributions toward an integrated watershed-scale landscape-management strategy.

Reflections on the Partnership Experience

As I look back over the almost three years of effort, which has given life and richness to the Applegate "experiment," I am aware of a number of powerful themes that have shaped the outcomes of our work.

The Importance of Precipitating Events

It is conventional wisdom among community organizers and others working to facilitate change that the most effective moments for encouraging such shifts come during times of crisis or conflict. This was clearly true in the Applegate case. The powerful incentive that brought the timber industry to the table was the near-total stoppage of all logging in public forests. Industry representatives on the partnership board were explicit from the beginning that they hoped that the partnership's efforts could lead to some form of injunctive relief or greater flexibility to allow some form of forest-products sales to go forward.

The environmental community's goals were more complex. Many of the long-time activists were also community residents and had seen how the politics of conflict had turned neighbors against each other and created a climate of anger and suspicion within the community. Many also recognized the real economic hardships that forest-dependent families were experiencing. For the agencies, the partnership was clearly a way of attempting to rebuild lost credibility as institutions able to mediate balanced use of the public lands. Finally, for the community, it was a way to try to take back a sense of control over its own destiny. Many, if not most, local residents had come to feel that all major decisions affecting the land and lifestyles they cherished were being made by people living far outside the valley.

Many of these circumstances have now changed dramatically with the lifting of the injunction and the new Republican agenda in Congress. But for the partnership to continue to be an appealing venue for any of these major interests, it will be necessary for each major interest to recognize continuing value in collaboration rather than returning to the "timber war" postures.

Communities of Interest and Communities of Place

From the beginning, the partnership has attempted to play two concurrent but perhaps fundamentally incongruent roles. In the larger public view, the partnership was initially a place where three major interests—industry, environmental, and agencies—were apparently working through their differences and formulating mutually agreed-upon solutions. At the more local level, the partnership represented a particular community's attempt to regain real influence over the forces that were affecting its destiny. So at one time, the partnership was attempting to be a high-profile forum for major communities of interest to work through their problems (which would theoretically provide models relevant to the larger sphere of conflicts between these forces) *and* a very local attempt to demonstrate effective community participation in developing sustainable forestry alternatives.

Although some may disagree, I argue that one of the reasons the partnership began to run into so much opposition was because it in fact began to succeed in creating a space at the table of decision making and power for local people. This fundamentally disrupted and challenged the preexisting distribution of power. Sworn enemies, including both the timber industry and the environmental community (both regional and national), not to mention the regional and national levels of the land-management agencies, were all accustomed to existing rules of the game. These rules dictated that decisions were going to be made at higher levels in a struggle of lawyers and lobbyists. When suddenly an upstart local group began to pull many of these decision-making processes out of Washington back to the local level, vested stakeholders in all three of these major "communities of interest" were threatened. So we see the terrific paradox in which both the timber industry and environmental groups at regional and national levels began using the Federal Advisory Committee Act to try to stop planning activities that gave more power to locally based decision making. This struggle over power is far from over.

Partnerships As Catalysts Versus Representative Democracies

To juxtapose anything "versus" a phrase including "democracy" would seem like a losing battle from the beginning. Yet I would like to suggest an enormous challenge facing "partnerships" is the propensity for being pushed into the role of a body attempting to "represent" the interests of many major interests in a struggle. The work of many sociologists, anthropologists, and social workers clearly demonstrates that informal organizations are crucial to the care of people and resources because they are neither hierarchical nor do they rely on systematic and regular selection processes to establish leadership and coordinate action. Instead, they utilize more horizontal systems of association, relation, and friendship to organize and mobilize community resources.

One of the fatal flaws in groups who have attempted to assert leadership during times of crisis is their attempt to superimpose a representative democratic process on essentially informal community problem-solving processes. The Applegate Partnership struggled frequently with this ambiguity. From the outset, outside forces—be they agency officials, politicians, or media—have encouraged or portrayed the partnership board as "representing" the major interests involved or the community as a whole. This is clearly not the case. No one organized elections in any of the major interest-group constituencies or the community to select the board members. Instead they were identified and approached largely on the basis of their reputations as people capable of working with others of different views or backgrounds. Therefore, I would argue that the most valuable role of partnership is as a catalyst that can identify viable responses to vexing situations by knowing and thinking through the integration of the various interests, needs, and capabilities of the key stakeholder groups. This is a far less glamorous role than that of representative. It means participants are less the highly visible spokesperson, and more the inconspicuous facilitator within their respective constituencies. It is my belief that this is a role we are poorly prepared for in our political system because of our increasing reliance on formal representative processes.

The Essential Role of Individuals As Catalysts

Moving beyond the status quo requires someone who has the energy, ideas, and resources to make a system shift. The Applegate Partnership has not only met weekly for almost three years, it has had countless thousands of additional volunteer hours contributed by a number of key individuals in essential networking, evaluation of options, planning, fundraising, and so on. In the case of the Applegate, much of this volunteer labor was possible because several key partnership members were not compelled to be a part of the daily wage-labor workforce, whether because they were financially independent or had a working spouse. In addition to these volunteer hours, several participating organizations lent their support staff to partnership activities. If we are to evaluate the essential ingredients necessary to create a major effort to effect change, we should not underestimate the importance of these volunteer and in-kind resources. This compels us to consider how costly the shift toward two-income households has truly been to the social capital of our communities.

Redefining the Role of Communities in Ecosystem Management

One of the pivotal challenges facing the Applegate Partnership and all resource-based rural communities is in defining their roles in the larger social struggle to create more sustainable patterns of land management. To do so, rural communities must redefine the themes of the discussion currently used in evaluating how or whether to try to provide support for rural areas.

Currently, most discussion about rural assistance seems cast in terms of conducting damage control or triage with suffering communities. In practice, pioneering work in rural-community assistance is demonstrating how rural communities are in fact the essential foundation of any effective ecosystem-management effort. Diverse, resilient, and adaptive rural communities containing well-trained, technologically sophisticated and adequately capitalized workers and enterprises must exist if we want sustainable forests, farms, rangelands, and waterways.

Incongruent "Rates of Return"

Several years ago a local environmental group involved in formulating sustainable management guidelines for their particular mountain area invited the chief forester from a major timber company to speak at one of their events. In the discussion that followed, this industry forester very openly acknowledged that one of the dilemmas he faced was trying to make forest systems with an intrinsic rate of return of around 6 percent compatible with financial systems that expected a minimum of 10 to 12 percent return. Clearly, he was pointing out that he had no choice but to overharvest the forests he was responsible for in order to meet the financial goals of the organization that controlled both him and the land he managed. There is a comparable dilemma facing community-based organizations and partnerships as they attempt to facilitate fundamental changes in the role of communities in resource management and the ways the community attempts to solve problems. Real change takes time, generally far more time than the rates of "return" that political institutions, interest organizations, or funding sources demand. Not all interests in the partnership are willing or can afford to wait.

Conversely, the partnership's acceptance and support among the local community seems to be continuing to build as people have gradually come to recognize that the partnership was willing to endure hardships and show long-term commitments. If we want to support and empower more problem solving and innovation at the local level, we must be willing to put in place mechanisms of support that recognize longer time horizons.

Building Federations of Rural Communities

Finally, it is clear that no single rural community, partnership, or bioregional group is going to be capable of mustering the necessary political force necessary to change some of the basic impediments to sustainability. Tax and environmental policies that favor short-term profiteering, market supports that encourage raw-resource extraction, labor policies that fail to build high skills, investment policies that lead to capital flight, power and water policies that fail to adequately reinvest in the source watersheds—all of these must be reconsidered and in many ways restructured.

To make their voices heard in the political debate, rural communities will have to find ways to join together. A variety of institutions already exist to exert such an influence. Unfortunately, these institutions are often narrowly representative. Frequently they are directed by a small leadership elite that has had long-standing control of the political context of a particular rural region. In other cases, these institutions are controlled by large corporate interests with little long-term stake in the well-being of either rural landscapes or rural people.

For those of us who are continuing to work together in the Applegate Partnership, these issues are just one part of the messy but never dull struggle to keep hope alive. Perhaps more than anything else, it was hope that founded the Applegate Partnership and a stubborn hold on this hope has sustained it. For most of us it is the hope that we can still overcome our differences and work together to solve some of our problems before it is too late. Otherwise there seems little else to place our hope in. Certainly there is peril in partnership. Yet how much greater will be our peril without.

19

Tough Towns: The Challenge of Community-Based Conservation

Graham Chisholm

Beginning in the late 1980s, the national environmental organizations faced a strong challenge not just from a growing wise-use and property rights movement, but from an increasing number of locally based environmental initiatives critical of the national groups for engaging in "politics as usual."[1] Despite the tremendous differences between the wise use movement and local environmental activists on these issues, they both were arguing that the national environmental groups were run by bureaucrats too focused on "Beltway" politics and hopelessly isolated from the everyday realities in local communities. There is a strong current driving politics back to the local level.

The wise use movement has moved quickly to take advantage of the 1994 elections to move legislation that would undermine gains achieved by the environmental movement, in part, by turning over significant authority to local and state entities. The national environmental organizations are fiercely opposing this "rollback" due to suspicions about the uneven fate of environmental oversight at the state and local level. Despite this concern within the environmental movement about turning over decision making and oversight to local and state entities, there are many flourishing local environmental initiatives, including partnerships and consensus groups, seeking to resolve conflicts at the local level or on the ground.

This renewed focus on working at the local level and engaging communities is an important direction in the environmental movement. It is an important counterbalance to a tendency to downplay local communities and their economies in significant pieces of environmental legislation. At the same time, it is important to avoid romanticizing communities. Communities have their own histories, factions, and

279

conflicts that often make resolution of conflicts difficult. In addition, conflicts are not necessarily more legitimately resolved at the local level as often there are broader regional or national interests involved.

This chapter focuses on The Nature Conservancy's efforts to restore the Lahontan Valley wetlands and achieve a complex, multiparty settlement of issues related to water use on the Truckee and Carson Rivers (see Figure. 19.1) in order to explore the challenges of community-based conservation. It makes the case that a successful and sustainable settlement of conflicts, particularly on public-resource issues, requires that environmentalists, particularly those associated with large organizations, get back into communities. Until environmentalists recognize the value of community-based conservation, and better understand communities and take their needs seriously, we will not succeed in developing a sustainable conservation strategy in rural America and will create fertile ground for its opponents. Environmentalists should have no illusions about the real challenges of working with communities and strategies are needed to match the landscape.

Restoring the Lahontan Valley Wetlands

Beginning in 1989, The Nature Conservancy (TNC), in conjunction with the U.S. Fish and Wildlife Service, the State of Nevada, and the Nevada Waterfowl Association, entered the water-rights market in Fallon, Nevada, to purchase water rights to benefit the Lahontan Valley wetlands.[2] Historically, the Carson River terminated in the Lahontan Valley creating an expansive mosaic of wetlands critical to hundreds of thousands of nesting and migratory shorebird and waterfowl species on the eastern edge of the Pacific Flyway. Development of the Newlands Project, the oldest federal reclamation project, beginning in 1903, directly affected these wetlands, which have shrunk from a preproject total average of 150,000 acres to fewer than 10,000 acres today.

The fledgling water-rights purchase program was assisted in 1990 by the passage of federal legislation, the Fallon Paiute-Shoshone and the Truckee-Carson-Pyramid Lake Water Rights Settlement Act of 1990 ("Settlement Act"), which seeks, among other things, to redress the adverse environmental impacts of the Newlands Project on the adjacent Lahontan Valley wetlands.[3] The Settlement Act recognizes that the wetlands require an increased and reliable supply of good quality water if they are to be sustained. It directs the secretary of the interior to acquire, from willing sellers, sufficient water and water rights to sustain, on a long-term average, approximately 25,000 acres of primary wetlands.[4] Although the Settlement Act was hailed as a landmark settlement of a ninety-year conflict over water resources and a remarkable effort to integrate competing water needs, not all issues were settled and not all parties were satisfied by the legislation.[5] The majority of irrigators based in the communities of Fallon and Fernley

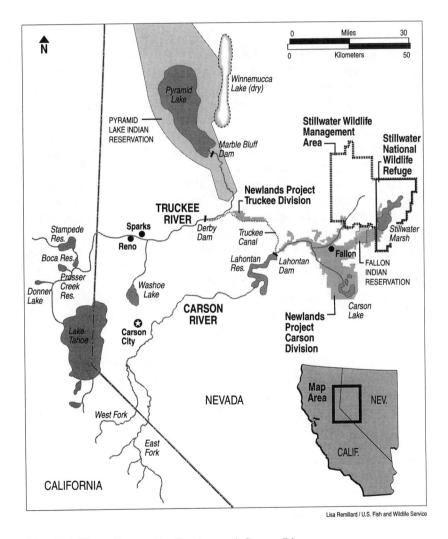

Fig. 19.1 Water Use on the Truckee and Carson Rivers.
Source: Lisa Remillard/U.S. Fish and Wildlife Service

resent and continue to oppose, not only the overall Settlement act, but a large-scale water-rights acquisition program in particular. In order to purchase water rights, it has generally been necessary to purchase both land and water. Although the purchases to date have focused primarily on marginal agricultural parcels, there is a strong concern within the community that any reduction of the irrigated agricultural land base will undermine the entire farm economy.

How, in light of the public resentment toward the Settlement Act within the Newlands Project, can the ambitious wetlands-restoration program move forward? After some initial purchases, TNC and its partner the Environmental Defense Fund (EDF) believed that the restoration program needed to make every effort to address local concerns about the purchase of water rights.[6] Further, it was assumed that the best hopes for restoration would be through reaching a comprehensive "second generation" agreement on issues not settled or anticipated by the Settlement Act. TNC and EDF maintained that the wetlands' restoration could only be successful if the local community embraced wetlands restoration as an important community goal.

The wetlands have long been part of the Lahontan Valley's way of life going back to the "Cattail-Eater" people who resided in the valley for thousands of years before European settlers arrived in the 1850s. Today it is rare to find long-time local residents who do not have memories of hunting, fishing, or visiting the wetlands. Further, the Truckee-Carson Irrigation District (TCID) was instrumental in setting aside both the Stillwater Wildlife Management Area (1948) and the Carson Lake and Pasture (1928) as important sites for wildlife, grazing, and hunting purposes. For most of this century, support for the wetlands was easier to the extent that the wetlands could be sustained through the diversion of large amounts of Truckee River water. In fact, the Newlands Project's impact on the Lahontan Valley wetlands was somewhat masked by the project's ability to divert an average of 50 percent of the Truckee River's flow over into the Carson River basin. The trouble was that this benefit was adverse to Pyramid Lake, the natural terminus of the Truckee River. As the federal government and the Pyramid Lake Paiute Tribe were successful in legal and administrative efforts to reduce diversions out of the Truckee River in order to benefit Pyramid Lake and the endangered cui-ui fish by tightening project conveyance efficiency, the wetland's dependence on the project's excess drainwater became apparent. With this supply in jeopardy, it became even more imperative to secure a manageable and dependable source of water for the wetlands primarily through water-rights acquisition.

The initial local reaction to the start of the wetlands water-rights acquisition program in 1989 was guardedly supportive. The TCID passed a resolution supporting the acquisition of up to twenty thousand acre-feet of water rights.[7] Ted DeBraga, TCID's chairman and board member for twenty years, was the first to sell water rights to benefit Stillwater Marsh.

However, there are limits to the local support for the purchasing of water rights. The bitterness over the Settlement Act and the increased scope of the restoration program led to growing unease about the buying of water rights within the Newlands Project. Although the wetlands acquisition program has raised opposition, local support for the wetlands, particularly when the question of how to sustain them is not addressed, remains relatively strong.[8]

Local concerns about the wetlands acquisition program center around the overall scope of the acquisition program and its impact on the agricultural sector, local drinking water supplies, and Fallon's quality of life.

Working with the Community

Although the TNC-EDF team realized that successful restoration would require, among other things, an effort to integrate the needs and concerns of the Fallon community, it was not until October 1992 that the necessary funds were raised to hire me as the regionally based project director to work on Truckee-Carson water issues. My primary focuses were to work closely with the Lahontan Valley community, seek to develop consensus proposals to restore the wetlands, and work to initiate a "second generation" negotiation with a neutral facilitator.

The initial task was geared toward "mapping the community" by attending community meetings and visiting with a broad cross section of the community. Although initial meetings were with the more obvious political and business leaders, it was also important to seek out individuals from different circles in the community who, over time, served as important bellwethers for testing ideas and gauging reactions. It was also important to look for the emerging leaders who are likely to assume leadership within the community in the next decade.[9] This "mapping" helps to better understand the various factions and interests within the community, and ultimately assists in evaluating what makes the community tick and how it is changing. The strength of this analysis ultimately helps in developing solutions that not only work for your objectives, but also that genuinely address the concerns and needs of the community.

A drive into Fallon these days quickly dispels the notion that this is just an agricultural community. In fact, the agricultural sector continues to shrink as other sectors boom. The Fallon Naval Air Station, home of the "Top Gun" flight training school, provides more than one quarter of the local jobs. The area's 30 percent population growth in the last decade is linked not just to growth in Fallon, but also to its proximity to Reno, Sparks, and the Carson Valley. Not surprisingly, albeit more slowly, this change is transforming the community's political leadership. The old leadership based in the water-user community and TCID are no longer the only players. The new leadership is still more fluid and emerging, but seems to mingle a younger generation who left the farm (and Fallon), but return to Fallon largely for lifestyle reasons with newcomers to the community.

The economic and demographic changes in Fallon have generated concerns, shared by many communities throughout the West, about the loss of quality of life, loss of agricultural lands, and how to manage growth and the issues related to growth. These were issues that were accentuated by the water-rights acquisition program, but were problems confronting the community nonetheless. The acquisition program raised additional issues about the impact on the agricultural land base, loss of economic activity, concern about checkerboarding the irrigation project, and making it hard for those remaining in agriculture to keep on farming. A number of early water purchases also raised issues related to whether the program would encourage subdivisions once water was removed from farms.

Recognizing that if the acquisition program was to be successful, it needed to incorporate local preferences where possible and be part of a broader communitywide discussion about the program and more generally about growth, TNC and EDF explored a number of proposals, including: (1) the use of a locally developed land rating system to evaluate potential purchases for the acquisition program; (2) reducing the proposed level of fee acquisitions by mixing it with water leasing; (3) supporting the development of a locally based restoration trust to oversee the leasing program and land conservation needs; (4) facilitating land exchanges to promote growth in areas of the community considered appropriate for growth by local government; and (5) developing a land bank to keep highly productive agricultural land in production.

These ideas, particularly the development of a land-rating system to direct the acquisition program toward agricultural lands considered less valuable from a community and agricultural perspective and the land-exchange mechanism, were explored through a number of groups over several years. The groups sought to hammer out proposals to address these community concerns, while also allowing the acquisition program to move forward. The hope was to receive community endorsement for the proposals and incorporate them into the acquisition program through a comprehensive "second generation" settlement agreement.[10]

The investment made by TNC to become an active part of the community and move beyond its narrow acquisition role paid off. Regardless of what members of the community thought of the organization as a whole or about the acquisition program, there was a recognition that an investment was being made to listen to the community and try to develop solutions that worked. There were also important limits to becoming a part of the community, because given the intertwined nature of the Truckee and Carson Rivers through the Newlands Project, it was important for TNC to avoid becoming too closely associated with just the Lahontan Valley and Fallon as that would make it difficult to work with the Pyramid Lake Paiute Tribe and upstream interests.

In addition, there is some question as to what is a legitimate role for TNC within the community: should we merely be bystanders watching change occur? Should we encourage change by siding with new groups? Or would siding with a new group delegitimize the group among certain segments of the community? It is apparent that given our role in the community, it is difficult to merely be a bystander. Yet, the dangers associated with taking sides within the community are many.

The Community Creates a New Voice

While willing to work with all parties, the development of a broad-based community entity called the Lahontan Valley Environmental Alliance (LVEA) opened an important opportunity. TNC decided not to join LVEA, but expressed a willingness to work with LVEA, as it had done with Lahontan 2000, an educational forum for the community on water issues and a catalyst in LVEA's formation. The reason for not joining was an unwillingness to be too closely associated with local solutions that work for Fallon but are adverse to Pyramid Lake and other interests within the Truckee-Carson system. In fact, this case illustrates one of the potential pitfalls of trying to solve problems at a community level when the definition of community is too narrow.

The LVEA does, however, provide a forum to bring the various disparate local governing entities together, as well as a forum to bring new community members into the discussion about the community's future, particularly in regard to water issues. It was apparent that until the community was a community and had a vehicle to discuss the choices it should consider making about its future, it would be very difficult to reach a comprehensive settlement. The LVEA certainly holds the promise of forming a broad-based community position in negotiations with the Pyramid Lake Tribe, the federal government, and upstream and environmental interests, and proved important in the "second generation" negotiations that started in September 1994.

Rolling the Dice: Going to the Table

One of TNC's chief objectives was to help initiate facilitated negotiations among all the major parties in the Truckee-Carson watersheds in order to resolve issues not anticipated or resolved by Congress in 1990. These negotiations could also reduce the uncertainties associated with the water-rights acquisition program making a long-term restoration strategy more likely, while simultaneously addressing community concerns about the acquisitions. The opening for negotiations came following a U.S. Senate Water and Power Subcommittee field hearing chaired by Senator Bill Bradley in December 1993. It was billed as an oversight hearing that would lead to additional federal legislation addressing the Newlands Project.

During an informal meeting with TNC in June 1993, a number of community leaders had already indicated their willingness to participate in mediated negotiations at the regional level. With the knowledge that the valley, particularly the agricultural community, was open to negotiations under certain circumstances, TNC approached Senators Reid and Bradley about convening negotiations and providing stakeholders, including the federal government, an opportunity to reach a mediated settlement. In addition, this approach was discussed with all major parties in an effort to build support for comprehensive negotiation. The effort TNC had invested in working with the Lahontan Valley community made it easier to discuss this proposal and build confidence in the proposed negotiations.

Following an April 1994 hearing on the Newlands Project in Washington D.C., both senators' offices expressed a willingness to ask a mediator, Gail Bingham of RESOLVE, to undertake a preliminary assessment of the opportunities for successful negotiations. Based on Bingham's initial findings and her ability to gain the confidence of all parties, particularly the agricultural community, Senator Reid convened negotiations in September 1994. As the negotiations opened, all parties noted that, unlike past negotiations, the Lahontan Valley was seemingly fully represented with a large delegation supporting three representatives at the table.[11] The three included a member each from the Newlands Water Protective Association (NWPA), a water-rights advocacy organization, LVEA, as well as Mike Clinton, a consultant to LVEA from Bookman-Edmonston, who had extensive experience in settlement negotiations. It was hoped that he could help hold the diverse valley delegation together.

The composition of LVEA's delegation, and the developments leading up to the negotiations, pointed to an important shift in the valley. There was a growing sense within the community that the broader interests of the community would be better represented by an entity like LVEA. The mood favored moderate members of the community who were open to negotiations and willing to work with Senator Reid, the author of the 1990 Settlement Act. The NWPA's more militant rhetoric was viewed by some within the community as an embarrassment. In addition, the old fight strategy advocated by some water-rights holders simply had exhausted itself for many in the valley.

The subtle shift in the valley's balance of power, and its tenuous nature, is significant because shortly after the start of the negotiations the 1994 congressional elections changed the political landscape. Although the negotiations continued for five months, it became clear that the change in Washington, D.C. provided an opening to revive the exhausted story that now was not the time to settle because a new congress (or the courts) would deliver a better deal. This renewed, and ironic, hope that Washington, D.C., would reverse past decisions also was able to rally some of the undecideds to the old battlelines using the rhetoric of the "war on the West." The negotiations came to a close without a comprehensive settlement.

What Happened? Some Important Lessons

Tracing the causes for a failure to reach a settlement initially leads one back to the November 1994 election. The broad political environment and the uncertainties associated with the new Congress simply precluded a settlement at this time. This points to a real challenge of efforts to resolve conflicts at the local level: it simply is not realistic to assume that you can operate at the local level and ignore broader policy debates. In fact, the notion of "local" is quickly losing any meaning. Rural communities increasingly look alike and are more likely to be integrated into the mainstream economy and political scene. Westerners also have a particular problem as we like to think we can ignore the federal government, while we remain entirely intertwined with it. The simple lesson is that the broader political environment matters.

In addition, there is an important issue related to the pace and timing of the negotiations. Perhaps the negotiations simply came too quickly for the valley. It is easy to assume an actual community exists when in fact rural communities have managed to successfully find accommodations among factions and interests that reliably work only when that community is asked what it opposes. The cohesiveness may fall apart as soon as it is asked to define what it wants for its future. It certainly takes time to nurture. In other words, was the community ready to make the type of tough decisions it needed to make in order to reach a broad settlement? The LVEA was simply too new an organization to be expected to hold such a diverse community of interests together and make the type of decisions required to sign a settlement.

Further, one needs to consider how a community's mythology about its past, in this case about the pioneer myth of persevering against the desert, affects the views of its leaders about its future. In the case of Fallon, this is an important component. Any settlement proposal that stands half a chance of succeeding needs to overcome the power of the past. Communities that are strongly rooted in their vision of their own past—whether accurate or not—are often only able to compare the future against the past, and not against some alternative future. This makes it difficult to settle. In these cases, a strong leadership backed by a broad consensus can help a community consider its future alternatives and create an atmosphere that makes settlement possible. In this case, the new leadership may have needed more time to expand its base and frame new visions of the future so that it could answer challenges by others holding up the promise of a better deal outside of the negotiations.

Where to from Here?

The challenge is to keep faith in a community-based strategy once a negotiation of this magnitude fails. It also means committing scarce

financial resources to pursuing a less-certain goal—somewhat less attractive to project funders. However, for the work to continue it requires choosing the right strategy, particularly as a number of the major
parties return to litigation.

In an increasingly polarized setting, the wetlands need strong advocates and this will require a remobilization of the Lahontan Wetlands Coalition as the wetlands' strongest defenders. The coalition is
a diverse group representing environmentalists, waterfowl hunters, and
others who came together originally to represent the wetland's interests during the 1990 settlement negotiations. Although less active since
the 1990 Settlement Act passed, the group has the ability to
build a broad coalition in support of the wetlands. It will also mean
that the water-rights acquisition program should continue moving forward.

However, TNC also remains committed to deepening its involvement with the community. This new role will focus less on trying, in
a polarized setting, to cobble together new settlement proposals, but
more on establishing the first wetlands visitor and educational center.
It means working with community members who see the wetlands as
a part of the community and extending a hand to local efforts to put
forward constructive proposals. It is TNC's assessment that now would
be the wrong time to simply step back from our cooperative work with
the community, despite the substantial investment of resources required
to keep a community presence. TNC's relationship with the community
is built on developing a cooperative relationship and exploring ways
to narrow our differences. As with any community there is an element of trust that goes both ways, and the valley will be interested to
see if TNC is willing to remain engaged over the long term.

Keys to Success

The environmental movement's ultimate success in developing a sustainable strategy to protect our natural heritage and environmental
health will require that it take seriously the internal and external criticism of the movement as out of touch with the realities at the local
level, particularly in rural communities. It will mean articulating an
economic vision that speaks to communities long ignored by the movement. For a movement whose rapid success since the 1970s focused
its largest organizations on "Beltway" politics, the current backlash
and attempt to devolve decision making to the states and local communities is an important reminder that it has neglected to develop a

strong community-based strategy. Without working cooperatively with communities, the environmental movement may become less relevant and increasingly open to challenge as the losers band together in a politics of resentment.

At the same time, it is important not to get carried away with the current enthusiasm about "community." Working in and with communities is challenging and potentially unsatisfying. The term "community" is often too rigid and leads one to conceive of communities as unified entities capable of action when in reality we are often confronted by fractious entities that are bundles of, often diverging, interests. Working in and with communities is challenging and will require a long-term commitment.

The environmental movement should avoid slipping into the tendency to view community as a more appropriate realm for resolving conflicts by being granted a higher moral standing as the political arena closest to the citizen. In a period of great frustration where communities are facing economic and political changes that are changing their traditional positions, there is a tendency to want to turn inward and merely solve the problem at the local level. This turning inward into the community runs the risk of ignoring that there are many conflicts that can no longer legitimately be resolved within the community, but must be resolved through solutions that bring in neighboring communities and far away cities. The current political swing, despite some of the overreaching, particularly in regard to rolling back decades of strong bipartisan agreement on environmental reforms, should be read as an important signal to the environmental movement that it needs to reflect on its strengths and weaknesses. Once the rhetoric dies down, the movement will face the task of articulating an economic and political vision that demonstrates it recognizes the economic plight of dislocated communities. It will need to bring in constituencies that have not traditionally considered themselves environmentalists.

Working in and with communities will help build these bridges, but the environmental movement needs to be realistic about the challenge. Engaging communities requires a willingness to take the time to learn the community from top to bottom and appreciate that communities have their own goals. It also means becoming a part of the community with a recognition that you need to choose, and stick to, an appropriate role. From that point on, you need to be flexible, adaptive, and patient both in tactics and strategy. Above all, the best laid plans may not succeed due to factors far beyond your control.

Notes

1. The groups have been critical of the established group's orientation toward regulation of dangers to health and the environment and giving up a strong no-compromise stance against polluters. These groups have also challenged the established group's general neglect of minority communities.

2. In order to benefit the wetlands, an application to change the place and manner of use must be submitted to the Nevada State Engineer. Once approved, the wetland management agencies effectively hold a right to call for water, similar to any other irrigator with the Newlands Project.

3. Public Law 101-618, 104, STAT.3289.

4. The U.S. Fish and Wildlife Service's draft Environmental Impact Statement released in July 1995 maintains that somewhere between 75,000 and 133,000 acre-feet of water rights will need to be purchased from within the Newlands Project to maintain an average of twenty-five thousand acres of wetlands.

5. The Settlement Act did incorporate an agreement between the States of California and Nevada on the allocation of waters on the Truckee and Carson Rivers, incorporated claims settlements against the federal government by the Fallon Paiute-Shoshone Tribes and the Pyramid Lake Paiute Tribe. In addition, the act provided an innovative water-banking scheme to provide drought-storage protection for Reno and Sparks in exchange for better flow management for the endangered cui-ui fish.

6. The EDF has been involved in the Truckee-Carson watersheds since 1986 and actively sought to involve TNC in a water-marketing program. The EDF and TNC formed a joint venture partnership for this project in 1989. The partnership emphasized developing the necessary technical and analytic tools and skills to undertake a broad program to advance creative solutions integrating competing water needs in the Truckee-Carson system.

7. Policy position adopted 7 October 1988 and revised on 7 December 1988.

8. Many residents of the Lahontan Valley express strong support for the wetlands, but maintain the view that wetlands have suffered as a result of federal actions taken to benefit Pyramid Lake at the terminal end of the Truckee River. These actions included an end to Truckee River diversions simply to generate hydropower at Lahontan Reservoir on the Carson River and increased efficiency levels for the Newlands Project. The wetlands benefited from the large amounts of drainwater from the relatively inefficient irrigation project. The difficulty with this explanation is that it directly pits the wetlands against Pyramid Lake. Therefore, so long as the wetland's water source is met through increased Truckee River diversions, adverse to Pyramid Lake, local support for the wetlands is high. The difficulty comes when agriculture and the wetlands are competing for a diminishing supply of water.

9. In fact, I use the term "community" with some caution because it has become clear that the community is divided and evolving.

10. TNC and EDF had been slowly developing a "second generation" settlement concept paper based, in part, on my discussions with stakeholders, including parties in Fallon. The concept paper served as the basis for our position in the

negotiations convened in September 1994 and was an effort to carefully address all legitimate interests within a realistic water budget for the Truckee-Carson system.

11. During the 1989–90 negotiations, the valley had been generally represented by TCID and local government. The TCID was viewed as the dominant player in the valley.

20

The Wilderness Killers

Tom Wolf

Man has won. The wilderness killers have lost. They have written their own death warrants in killing, torture, blood lust, almost fiendish cruelty.

—Arthur Carhart and Stanley Young,
The Last Stand of the Pack

It may be possible for some Coloradans to reconsider coexistence with the wolf. This opportunity arises at a time when elsewhere in Colorado the habitats of predators are rapidly disappearing. The remote, obscure Sangre de Cristo Mountains present us with the chance to reinvent our relationship with wolves—our fellow predators—the chance for mutual respect.

Private individuals, working on private land, have already begun the miracle of raising the Sangres' wolves from the dead. Hope lurks at the private, nonprofit *Mission: Wolf* compound on the Sangres' eastern edge. *Mission: Wolf* began as a refuge for abandoned wolf hybrids. Then it grew into an effort to educate Coloradans about the wolf through "ambassador wolves," who visit school children. Today, some thirty wolves and wolf hybrids pace their chainlink compound, living on roadkill from the Sangres' burgeoning elk and deer herds. Local ranchers kick in cattle carcasses. At night, howls echo over the nearby one hundred thousand acres of the Wolf Springs Ranch.

This chapter previously appeared in *Colorado's Sangre de Cristo Mountains* by Thomas J. Wolf. Copyright 1995 University of Colorado Press. Reprinted by permission of the author and publisher.

This area is the real-life scene of many of the bloody, steel-jawed, poison-laced stories from *The Last Stand of the Pack.* Consider "The Greenhorn Wolf." In 1923 she was the "last native renegade gray wolf in Colorado." A professional wolfer named Big Bill Caywood terminated her with strychnine.[1]

Local ranchers had offered bounties for wolves up to the turn of the century, but business was slow. With fewer and fewer wolves, private individuals found each additional kill more difficult and expensive. Cost-efficiency flew out the window when the federal government started wolfing seriously in the Sangres. Big Bill's employer was the Bureau of Biological Services, an agency of the federal government—and bureaucratic ancestor of today's U.S. Fish and Wildlife Service (FWS). In 1914, Congress started the eightball rolling toward the wolf in Colorado with its first appropriation for exterminating wolves: $125,000. No numbers exist on the cost-efficiency of Big Bill's efforts.

The people in the communities around the Sangres still live close to animals—close enough to travel the conceptual distance needed to work together with wolves. Now, my neighbors around the Sangres have the chance to heft the burden of our responsibility toward our fellow predators. Animal trainers know the perils and rewards of this responsibility. They learn the all-important lesson of humility. They know that training means mutual mastery of a common language, a code by which an animal can tell you more than you may want to know about what it perceives when perceiving you. Remember Aldo Leopold's famous passage from "Thinking Like a Mountain"?[2] Now, rethink the "green fire" that died in that old wolf's eyes. Do wolves and official wilderness really belong together? Not in today's Sangres. Not yet, anyway.

❈   ❈   ❈   ❈   ❈

Conservation pioneers like Arthur Carhart and Aldo Leopold left us the concept of wilderness without major predators—wilderness without biodiversity—which is like religion without God, or Self without Other. They baked us quite a cake with their zoolike wilderness; and then frosted their creation with impoverished concepts of wilderness carrying capacity. In Carhart's case, that carrying capacity tended to be cultural, aesthetic. His colleagues called him "the beauty Doctor." In Leopold's case, wilderness carrying capacity leaned toward the biological. Typical for its time, Leopold's ecology offers productivity and efficiency at the price of disorder and diversity. Together, these two giants impart to us the newly (1993) ordained Sangre de Cristo Wilderness as cathedral. We have little idea what role wolves might play in such an ecosystem. We know only this: when important pieces are missing in the predator category, the whole threatens to unravel.

If only we knew where halfway was, we might meet the wolf there—in that landscape in the Sangres—and in that landscape of the mind where we both fear and respect each other. It's not like there was any shortage of prey for any kind of predator. Thanks to the Colorado Division of Wildlife's all-too-successful game-management programs, today's Sangres overflow with elk and deer in such numbers that human hunters cannot keep pace with the increase.

If they were alive today, what would Leopold and Carhart say? What advice would they have for the predators of the Sangres as we enter wilderness status? What would these Olympian figures make of the stark contrasts in ecological health between the worthless Sangres and the place that ecologists love to compare with the Sangres: Rocky Mountain National Park?[3]

Can there—should there—be a balance between predators and prey in the Sangres? During much of the year, the feeding habits of elk and cattle are indistinguishable—especially when neither is subject to wolf predation. When we see cattle beating out riparian zones on nearby Forest Service land, we beat our breasts and call it overgrazing. When we see the same phenomenon involving elk or deer, we call it "natural" management—an excuse for doing nothing.

Elk were rare in the Sangres by 1878 and extinct before 1900. The current population started from Wyoming stock railroaded into the Sangres in 1922. That population expanded again until World War II, when poachers shot out what did not starve in competition with vastly increased cattle herds. In 1947, there were no elk in the Sangres.[4]

Now no sheep, only a few horses, and only a couple hundred cattle graze public lands in the Sangres. Now nonmigratory elk and seasonally migratory recreationists number in the tens of thousands, nicely demonstrating that managers can meet cultural and biological carrying capacities while ignoring biological diversity. Some of these elk so closely resemble cattle in their behavior that they spend all their lives on subdivisions, former grazing allotments, and private ranchlands.

Is this a success? Will the population collapse when range quality finally declines? Is this "success" also due to the rarity of predators?

That's what Aldo Leopold's orderly ecology determined. Yet even Leopold's famous Kaibab Plateau deer case study now seems deeply flawed. The traditional explanations for the population eruption were predator control and protection of does from hunting, while the decline was thought to have resulted from loss of food supply and habitat caused by overpopulation. But a closer, more recent look at the Kaibab demonstrates that such vagaries as prior grazing by domestic livestock, fire control, and drought were much more important than Leopold's culprits.[5]

Ungulate populations are not self-regulating in chaotic disturbance ecosystems like the Sangres (or like the Kaibab). The Sangres owe their current "success" in red-meat production to a long series of easy winters, to nearly fifty years of relative freedom from domestic livestock grazing, and to aggressive fire-control policies made possible by large expenditures of federal funds that have no financial relationship to the market value of the resources "protected."

This success is also due, in part, to the cooperation of private landowners, who can qualify for wildlife-damage payments if their haystacks and alfalfa fields suffer. Since everyone benefits from such programs, including thriving populations of bears and lions, it is hard to see why such programs should not include the wolf.

※   ※   ※   ※   ※

Maybe a quarter century ago, it was rare to encounter bears or lions in the Sangres. Now I often pause and reflect at the smell of acorn-heavy bear scat. Or I startle at the sight of lion tracks daintily set on top of mine when the next day finds me retracing a ski track. Does this mean that the Sangres will soon be unsafe for humans? Hardly, for unlike ungulates, the populations of big, fierce animals can be self-regulating. They don't necessarily need our help. They have their own ways of making themselves scarce.[6]

Only the zeal and the limitless funds of the federal government would push predator "control" to extinction. Only the bear and the lion could escape the fate of the wolf, and then only because the heavily glaciated Sangres present such rough, broken country to hounds and horses.

Such insights about different species' abilities to regulate their populations were not obvious to observers like Carhart and his colleague, Stanley Young, principal biologist of the U.S. Biological Survey, and source for the parables of butchery that adorn their book.

Carhart dedicates *The Last Stand of the Pack* to Young and the predatory animal hunters of the biological survey: "They are the friends of all animals; the compassionate, regretful executioners of animal renegades when such outlaws must die that other wildlings may live."[7]

When it was almost too late, biologists learned that big predators are extinction-prone. Reasons include a dispersed food supply, high metabolic demand, low metabolic rates, and the limitless subsidies even today driving such federal programs as wilderness recreation, public-lands grazing, and predator control. Yet it is becoming increasingly clear that without big predators, ecosystems like the Sangres simply unravel in ways that make restoration unthinkable. Further, without their adjacent big private ranches, the long, skinny Sangres make no ecological sense. At three hundred fifty thousand acres, they barely nudge the island biogeographers' minimum of five hundred square miles. Such biologists have calculated habitat needs for the wolf in southern Colorado. Each wolf would require about ninety square miles of habitat.[8]

Plans to maintain biodiversity in the Sangres also become nonsense without including both large, private lands, as well as the Great Sand Dunes National Monument and its backcountry, the Medano Creek watershed. Traffic on the Medano Pass road must travel east through Wolf Springs Ranch, probably the best potential wolf habitat in the Sangres. No one has explained to the owner of this ranch how and why he should put up with this traffic's impacts on his experimental "Ranching for Wildlife" operation. Colorado's "Ranching for Wildlife" program represents our belated and grudging admission that private individuals and government agencies must team up to manage land in ways that might keep whole ecosystems intact. This program is the key to restoring the wonder that once was Medano Pass, for out to the west lies the 80,000 acre Rocky Mountain Bison Ranch, while out to the east lies Wolf Springs Ranch—and *Mission: Wolf*.

In 1984, the Park Service and the Forest Service joined local citizens in renaming the peak to the north of Medano Pass Mount Herard. This act monumentalizes the obvious: Medano is the center of the Sangres—and an extraordinarily fertile place, especially for predators. The story of Ulus Herard shows this. His father had first seen Medano Canyon in 1849 on his way to the California gold fields. He later returned with his family to the Sangres, where he positioned himself on Medano Creek.

When Ulus was a young man, in 1878, a mule kicked him in the head, leaving him stone deaf for life. Ulus's disposition (and his attitude toward the government) did not improve when his wife ran off with a forest ranger. Local legends abound detailing Ulus's revenge. Ulus ran anywhere between fifteen hundred to six thousand cattle on a huge realm of around 125,000 acres that stretched east from today's Great Sand Dunes, over Medano Pass, and down to Redwing and Gardner. He also is said to have run a thousand horses.[9]

Forest Service files overflow with reports about the adverse consequences for rangelands and watersheds. Predators of all kinds attempted to reap this whirlwind, as evidenced by the many stories of Ulus's prowess in slaughtering his competitors. He claimed a hundred lion kills, as many black bears, and even a few grizzlies and wolves. Anyone who considers the Sangres a poor candidate for predator propagation and reintroduction should study Herard's story—not to cluck disapproval, but to see what potential lurks there for the future. A Mount Herard overlooking a healthy wolf population would be well named indeed!

While the Denver-based Carhart was drawing up his vast recreational plans for the Sangres, Herard's tale exemplifies what was really going on in the Sangres. How did this split between recreation and biodiversity develop? How did Beauty lose contact with Beast?

❅   ❅   ❅   ❅   ❅

"The Sangre de Cristo is a range that is wonderful in the massing and march of peaks, cliffs, lakes, forests and streams," said Arthur Carhart in 1920.[10] Carhart's career shows how the Forest Service got started pursuing cultural (and budgetary) goals at the expense of biodiversity. As the Forest Service's premier "Recreation Engineer" (his actual title), he had to move quickly to make his mark when he was hired in 1919—at a time when the Park Service was threatening to elbow the Forest Service aside in the competition for congressional favor. In the entire twenty-year history of the young Forest Service, Congress had never made an appropriation for recreation, and recreation was what the Sangres seemed to offer, as the Sangres' depleted ranges yielded dwindling grazing revenues.

Sensing an opening, the resourceful Carhart immediately descended upon the otherwise worthless San Isabel National Forest with the kind of staff officer bravado that makes common line people cringe, grimace, and roll their eyes. In the Forest Service's quasi-military line of authority, Carhart would ordinarily have made himself as welcome as wasps. But the San Isabel had been blessed with an extraordinary forest supervisor, Al Hamel, who discerned unsung values in the Sangres.

In the spring of 1919, the two men toured the San Isabel by automobile—an important breakthrough. They knew that the automobile would make national forest recreation accessible to even more people than those who presently traveled by train to the national parks. In contrast to the perceived elitism of the Park Service's offerings, Carhart and Hamel viewed the national forests as levelers, as democratizers, as extensions of the Jeffersonian concept that every American should "own" workable land, whether the crops be potatoes or patriotism.

Taking his cue from Gifford Pinchot, Carhart bitterly attacked those who would reserve parts of the forests for private use or special interests. He did not oppose private interests as such. In fact, he organized and encouraged them. He opposed private greed at public expense. Unfortunately, Carhart did not see that predator extermination programs benefited only special interests in the livestock, hunting, and recreation industries.

Carhart presented his plans to Carl Stahl, then regional forester. Ever alert to land-grabbing, budget-busting threats from the nascent National Park Service, Stahl had to endure the presence of Rocky Mountain National Park in the midst of national forests under his administration. Trail Ridge, the alpine highway bisecting the park, must have seemed a brilliant and threatening move in that high-stakes game. The Park Service had already cut its deals with the railroads, who were only too glad to run lines to major terminals at the showier parks. How could Colorado's dispersed and difficult-to-access national forests ever compete? Which agency would control the future of automobile-powered mass recreation?

Stahl wisely sent Carhart south to New Mexico to meet with Aldo Leopold, then the assistant district forester in Albuquerque. They met on 6 December 1919, at a time when Leopold's energies were hellbent on the eradication of predators, not the edification of tourists. Leopold saw sportsmen as the political allies of the Forest Service's future. Carhart presented his older colleague with a bold new bridge between their obsessions. The two men agreed that wolves and other major predators had to go, but they also agreed that some Forest Service lands should be maintained in what they saw as a "natural" state. Somehow, the flash of friendship between these freethinkers begot wilderness.

In 1922, Carhart the utopian dreamer submitted a plan to the sober Stahl. He proposed expansion of the Forest Service's recreation budget to $56,000, together with hiring five fellow landscape architects. Instantly, alarms blared. Opposition to his plans came not only from grazing, mining, and timber interests, but from the Park Service's bulldog of a Director, Steven Mather. In a memo to Carhart, Mather said that only the parks were set aside for recreation. According to Mather, the lines had been drawn. National forest lands were to be used strictly for watershed protection and commodity production. Fearing both bark and bite, Stahl was not the first forester to backpedal at the snap of Mather's jaws.

After this interagency mauling, Carhart then had to deal with a congressional whipping—a stingy recreation appropriation of $900, compared to the $125,000 appropriation for exterminating wolves. Disgusted with lack of congressional support and Forest Service political compromises, Carhart quit in 1922. Yet Carhart never lost the clarity of his dedication to beauty—or the confusion of his feelings about beasts.[11] He simply learned his lesson about changing bureaucracies from the inside.

He also took his love for mountain glory into private practice. His career highs include the Denver Mountain Parks system, the Denver Capitol Complex, the campus of Denver University, and Colorado Springs's sprawling Myron Stratton home. Far from losing his interest in Forest Service, he continued to lobby Congress to force the Forest Service to develop the kinds of regional recreational plans he had first conceived for the Sangre de Cristo Mountains.

In an avalanche totaling five thousand publications, he hammered away at a theme he established in his "San Isabel National Forest Recreation Plan." Therein he forecasts

> a time when in all of the Forests of the Nation a really comprehensive plan for regional development will be in force and, by a correlation of the recreational use with other activities and a full utilization of that use consistent with the best use of the Forest, will give to the people of the Nation the fullest return possible from their Forests. The San Isabel Plan is a pioneer plan of the type, but it is so well founded on common sense need and rational utilization of possibilities that it will probably stand for a long time as the model of big recreational planning in our Forests. This plan is truly an answer to a recognized need and a step towards full Forest utilization.[12]

Ever upbeat, Carhart labeled the forest "the San Isabel Playground." He had big plans for developing the former tollroads over Hayden and Mosca Passes, connecting the latter with Medano Pass and with Pass Creek Pass—all to be year-round roads. A believer in the teeming masses-moving power of railroads, Carhart, like so many Americans of his time, also saw the potential for the automobile, which would pioneer beyond the rail terminals to access a "system of uniformly built, uniformly managed hotels, working together." In blazing whirls of energy, he organized tours in terms of aesthetic climaxes, where he generously, guilessly sited hotels, auto camps, tent camps, picnic camps, lookout points, trails, and support industries.

For Coloradans, Carhart's brief career with the Forest Service was at least as influential as Leopold's long one. Far from a failure, he showed how later generations might push the Forest Service into big, bold recreational planning of a sort that now comes back to haunt the Sangres as they enter their designated Wilderness era. Yet Carhart's legacy also includes other ironies and ambiguities. Today's Forest Service still strives to keep the Sangres safe from predators. By filling the Sangres to the brim of their cultural and biological carrying capacity, Carhart's and Leopold's heirs jeopardize the Sangres' biodiversity.

We err if we snicker at Carhart's idealism. We follow the straight and narrow path if we compare his zeal with our latter-day zeal for admitting—or readmitting—wolves into the realms of considerability, whether those realms be morality or markets. Or better, both.

Notes

1. Arthur Carhart and Stanley Young, *The Last Stand of the Pack* (New York: J. H. Sears, 1919), 267. Some say that the last Colorado wolf died in the San Juan mountains in 1945. See "Colorado Wolf Tracks," *Sinapu* 2, no. 2 (Summer 1992). "Sinapu" is the Ute world for "wolf." Sinapu is also an organization dedicated to the return of the wolf to Colorado. Contact Sinapu, Box 3243, Boulder, Colorado 80307.

2. "We reached the old wolf in time to watch a fierce green fire dying in her eyes" (Aldo Leopold, *A Sand County Almanac* [New York: Sierra Club/Ballantine Books, Inc., 1974], 138).

3. Karl Hess, *Rocky Times in Rocky Mountain National Park* (Boulder: University Press of Colorado, 1993).

4. Anonymous, "History of the San Isabel National Forest," on file at the San Carlos Ranger District, Canon City, Colorado.

5. For a history of Leopold's thought on this subject, see Aldo Leopold, *Game Management* (New York: Scribners, 1933); Aldo Leopold, "Deer Irruptions," *Wisconsin Conservation Bulletin*, August 1933; and John Mitchell and Duane Freeman, *Wildlife-Livestock-Fire Interactions on the North Kaibab: A Historical Review* (Fort Collins, Colo.: Rocky Mountain Forest Range Experiment Station, USDA Forest Service, 1993).

6. John Terborg, "The Big Things That Run the World—A Sequel of E. O. Wilson," *Conservation Biology* (1989).

7. Carhart and Young, *Last Stand*, 270.

8. Tony Povilitis, "Applying the Biosphere Reserve Concept to a Greater Ecosystem" *Natural Areas Journal* 12, no. 1 (1993).

9. Jack Williams, "A Biography of Ulysses V. Herard," manuscript in the Great Sand Dunes National Monument library, no date. See also Steven Trimble, *Great Sand Dunes: The Shape of the Wind* (Southwest Parks & Monuments Association, 1978); and Walter E. Perkins, "Historical Sketch, San Isabel Forest Preserve," manuscript on file at San Carlos district, San Isabel National Forest (1922).

10. Arthur Carhart, Recreation Engineer, San Isabel Forest Recreation Plan, 1920. Document on file at San Isabel Headquarters, Pueblo, Colo. The issue of Carhart's versus Leopold's wilderness paternity has sparked a good deal of sterile debate. My point is that they were both wrong if you look at what actually happened to biodiversity on the lands they wanted protected. See Donald Baldwin. The Quiet Revolution: *The Grass Roots of Today's Wilderness Preservation Movement* (Boulder, Colo.: Pruett Press, 1972).

11. Robert Cermak, "Plans Must Be Big and Broad: The Beginning of Recreation Planning on the National Forests," undated document (probably 1970), San Isabel National Forest. See also Arthur Carhart, "Passes over the Blood of Christ," *Westerner's Denver Posse Brand Book* (Denver, 1946), 183–200; Arthur Carhart, *Colorado* (New York: Coward-McCann, 1932). For further background on the wolf, see L. David Mech, *The Wolf* (New York: Garden City Press, 1970); David Brown, ed., *The Wolf in the Southwest* (Tucson: University of Arizona Press, 1983); Stanley P. Young and E. A. Godman, the *The Wolves of North America* (Washington, D.C., 1944); and, Jenks Cameron, *The Bureau of the Biological Survey* (Washington, D.C., 1944); and *The Papers of Stanley Young*, Denver Public Library, Western History collection. These contain his correspondence with Carhart.

12. Carhart, San Isabel Recreation Plan.

Epilogue

Taming the Wolf

Philip D. Brick and R. McGreggor Cawley

In *Of Wolves and Men*, Barry Lopez struggles to understand the hatred that ranchers and bounty hunters have for wolves: "It was as though these men had broken down at some point in their lives and begun to fill with bile, and that bile had become an unreasoned hatred of many things. Of laws. Of governments. Of wolves. They hated wolves . . . because they seemed to be better off than they were."[1] As if confirming Lopez's assessment, one disgruntled logger and wise use advocate from Montana complains that environmentalists and federal land managers "turn our homes into their playgrounds, destroy the economy of our communities, wipe out our families . . . because, in their eyes, what we do and how we live has no value. But we're not disposable. We're not some inconvenience society brushes aside like a piece of lint simply because of where we live or what we do for a living." While perhaps an overstatement, the intensity of the remark obviously goes beyond a simple disagreement about the appropriate management regime for the federal estate. It is a statement of fundamental alienation from someone who sees government not as merely a nuisance but as a threat to their way of life.

In most wise use stories, environmentalists are invariably characterized as uncaring "elitists" and "outsiders." At one level, this is merely a rhetorical ploy—an attempt to "demonize" environmentalists. Yet, amid changing social and economic conditions in the West, the environmental movement has often appeared insensitive to the plight of those who live near the areas it hopes to save. In some cases this insensitivity may emerge from a combination of deeply held environmental convictions and a belief that western commodity interests lack an appreciation of the special character of the places in which they live and work. But the causes of conflict run much deeper, and cannot be addressed with greater sensitivity alone.

303

Traditionally, the environmental movement has walked a narrow path between two competing but not necessarily exclusive traditions. The first tradition expressed a faith in technocratic and scientific control as the means to carry out the progressive management of natural resources. Progressive management, in turn, was defined in terms of improving the material conditions of human communities. Thus, scientific management was thoroughly anthropocentric. The second tradition celebrated all that is wild, and relied on what Stephen Fox has called "amateur politics" to ensure that wild areas were "saved" from the self-indulgent appetites of industrial society.[2] In many important respects, this tradition was the precursor of the contemporary biocentrism. By paying close attention to these traditions, and the tensions between them, we might be able to better understand the nature of contemporary federal land arguments.

For instance, John Muir, who is widely recognized as one of the patriarchs of the second tradition, frequently phrased his positions in overtly misanthropic ways. "I have precious little sympathy for the selfish propriety of civilized man," Muir once opined, "and if a war of races should occur between wild beasts and Lord Man, I should be tempted to sympathize with the bears."[3] This statement, as Muir himself, can easily be relegated to the archives of history. Yet, the sentiment is still very much alive. Consider Dave Foreman's view of humanity: "In our decimation of biological diversity, in our productions of toxins, in our attacks on the basic life-support system of Earth, in our explosive population growth, we humans have become a disease—the Humanpox."[4] Foreman, in turn, is one of the founders of Earth First!, which was a self-conscious attempt to revitalize the spirit of environmentalism.

To be sure, this sentiment is not shared by all in the environmental community. Alluding to characterizations like Foreman's, Al Gore argues: "The obvious problem with this metaphor is that it defines human beings as inherently and contiguously destructive . . . the internal logic of the metaphor points toward only one possible cure: eliminate people from the face of the earth. . . . Another problem with this metaphor is its inability to explain—in a way that is either accurate or believable—who we are and how we can create solutions for the crisis it describes."[5]

On the one hand, arguments within the environmental community tend to undermine the unified front that helped the movement sustain momentum during the 1970s. On the other hand, these arguments provide useful ammunition for opponents of environmentalism. For instance, Ron Arnold's assertion that environmentalism contains a "dark strain of anti-humanity that despises everything human," is not so easily dismissed when viewed against the backdrop of comments like those of Muir and Foreman.[6] These arguments also have a direct bearing on public interpretations (and reception) of policy initiatives.

As noted in our preface, land managers have embarked on "ecosystem management" as a way to resolve the acrimony in the policy arena. Viewed in one way, ecosystem management can be understood as a revitalized version of the older scientific management tradition. It is an attempt to harness the tenets of ecology as the scientific foundation for land management. Yet, biocentrists have phrased their attacks against the anthropocentric posture in terms of ecology. Thus, neither ecology nor ecosystem management can be viewed as simply "science," a point amply demonstrated by the reintroduction of wolves to Yellowstone.

For land-rights activists, the Yellowstone wolf introduction offered a classic example of environmentalists creating a threat in their garden with apparently little concern for the people who live and work there. For environmentalists, it was an important symbolic statement that affirmed that ecosystem (and biocentric) values must supersede anthropocentric desires. And when Interior Secretary Babbitt characterized wolf reintroduction as making the Yellowstone ecosystem complete, it seemed, at least to land-rights advocates, that a biocentric posture had been adopted by powerful players in the national policy process. It is not surprising, therefore, that land-rights advocates would direct their animosity at both environmentalists and land managers. Biocentrism may be an appropriate vanguard concept for a movement out to remake modern society, but environmentalists (and land managers) often forget how commanding (and callous) they may appear to others.

To this mix can be added the curious play of bureaucratic solutions and the illusion of control. Despite their other differences, both environmental traditions have understood their efforts in terms of invoking government intervention. Though perhaps less pronounced, there is nevertheless a relatively clear strain in the land rights movement that also seeks to influence the character of government intervention. It might be, however, that too much faith has been placed in the bureaucratic tradition at the expense of exploring creative alternatives emerging from individual actions.

This is not to suggest that a focus on the machinery of laws and regulations is not necessary and important work. But the disconnect between support for environmentalism in the polls and the current structure of natural resource debates should tell us something. Emphasis on influencing the machinery of government does more to create passive audiences than active publics, and does little to truly engage a vast constituency of citizens concerned about the environment. The individual is always one step removed from any real connection to the land. It is precisely here that the weakness of "checkbook" activism can be identified. Urban environmentalists, regardless of how much money they can contribute to environmental causes, or how many letters they write to Congress, have difficulty participating in natural-resource policy debates without the assistance of bureaucratic procedures.

A conversation between a central Oregon public-land rancher and an environmentalist from Portland is indicative of the problem. The rancher, Doc Hatfield, suggested that "you environmental folks are as phony as a three dollar bill. All you do is moan and complain and file lawsuits. Show me one place where you've ever improved one acre of ground!" The environmentalist, a member of the Isaak Walton League, replied, "I thought you understood we don't have any land to improve or manage. The federal agents and the ranchers do that. The only way we can make change is by working with the laws that govern the land."[7] To restore a place for individual initiative, it must be possible to make the "visible hand" of individual commitment supplement the "invisible hand" of impersonal bureaucratic procedure.

Perhaps the alienation we feel toward government and toward each other is not unrelated to a sense that we lack frameworks that can channel and celebrate individual initiative and caring for our common environment. This is not a new problem. Writing in the final years of the Great Depression, Aldo Leopold describes the predicament of the conservation-minded farmer:

> Doesn't conservation imply a certain interspersion of land-uses, a certain pepper-and-salt pattern in the warp and woof of the land-use fabric? If so, can government alone do the weaving? I think not. It is the individual farmer who must weave the greater part of the rug on which America stands. . . . This raises the question: is the individual farmer capable of dedicating private land to uses which profit the community, even though they may not so clearly profit him? We may be over-hasty in assuming that he is not.[8]

Coming from someone who is widely recognized as an early advocate of biocentrism, this is truly a remarkable statement. Could it be that the actual distance between land-rights activists and environmentalists is not as wide as it sometimes seems?

Think back over the collection of essays in this volume. To be sure, there are many points of disagreement. Yet, there are also underlying themes that unite them. Most prominent among these themes are a commonly shared sense of place and a belief that old approaches simply don't work. Perhaps these themes point to what a revitalized environmental movement might look like. Rather than loud national debates about an abstract entity called the "federal lands," carried out by abstract players called "environmentalists," "land-rights activists," and "bureaucrats," future discussions would focus on specific places where real people live, work, and play. In suggesting this possible future, we have no illusions. The essays in this collection clearly demonstrate that a "sense of place" does not mean a shared vision about the character of specific places. Moreover, the essays also demonstrate that discussions about place will not go smoothly, nor be settled quickly.

Notes

1. Barry Lopez, *Of Wolves and Men* (New York: Scribner, 1978), 138.

2. Stephen Fox, *The American Conservation Movement: John Muir and His Legacy* (Madison: The University of Wisconsin Press, 1981).

3. Cited in Bob Pepperman Taylor, *Our Limits Transgressed: Environmental Political Thought in America* (Lawrence: University of Kansas Press, 1992), 86–87.

4. Dave Foreman, *Confessions of an Eco-Warrior* (New York: Harmony Books, 1991), 57.

5. Al Gore, *Earth in the Balance: Ecology and the Human Spirit* (New York: The Penguin Group, 1992), 217.

6. Ron Arnold, *Ecology Wars: Environmentalism As If People Mattered* (Bellevue, Wash.: The Free Enterprise Press, 1987), 35.

7. Discussions with Doc and Connie Hatfield, April 1994. A similar account appears in Sharman Apt Russell, *Kill the Cowboy* (Reading, Mass.: Addison-Wesley, 1993).

8. Aldo Leopold, "The Farmer and the Conservationist," in *The River of the Mother of God and Other Essays by Aldo Leopold*, edited by Susan L. Flader and J. Baird Callicott (Madison: University of Wisconsin Press, 1991), 260.

Index

Abbey, Edward, 170, 222
Acid rain, 31
Aerial Forest Management Foundation, 272
Alliance for America, 51; credo, 123
American Forest Council, 146
American Forest Resource Alliance, 141–42
American Land Rights Alliance (National Inholder's Association), 41, 133n21
American Legislative Exchange Council, 116, 130
American Society of Foresters, 223
Americans With Disabilities Act, 64; and Nuisance Law, 65
Ancient Forest Campaign, 18
Andrus, Cecil 39, 52
Animal rights movement, 5
Anthropocentrism, 25, 304
Antiquities Act of 1906, 208
Applegate Partnership, 261–74
Arches National Park, 212
Arendt, Hannah, 241, 257
Army Corps of Engineers, U.S., 50, 69, 123
Arnold, Ron, 15, 116, 304–5
Articles of Confederation, 90–93
Assets Management Program, 28
Atlas Shrugged (Rand), 55
Audubon Society, 9, 17

Babbitt, Bruce, 1, 52; and Applegate Partnership, 266; and environmentalists, 170; and grazing reform, 155; and John Wesley Powell, 173; and Wallace Stegner, 161; and western land reform, 177; and "wise–use dead–end," 175; and wolves, 305
Babbitt v. Sweet Home, 48, 124
Baca, Jim, 52
Bellah, Robert (*Habits of the Heart*), 244, 245–46
Berry, Wendell, 245
Beyond the Hundredth Meridian (Stegner), 173
Billy the Kid, 90
Biocentrism, 25, 304–5
Biodiversity, 5, 9, 112–14, 121, 298
Bizzarro, 27, 28
Blue Ribbon coalition, 31
Bonner County, Idaho, 168
Brennan, William, 46
Brower, David, 222
Bureau of Land Management (BLM), 39, 40; bombed headquarters in Reno, Nevada, 151–52; and Catron County, New Mexico, 88; Coordination of Planning Efforts, 78, 82; and forestry practices, 137; grazing budgets, 163; Frank Gregg on decentralization, 227–28; imper-

viousness to reform, 109; and local economies, 76; local governments and land–use policies, 78; and neopopulist anger, 123
Bureau of Reclamation, 165, 172, 222
Burford, Bob, 46, 49
Burke, Bill, 41
Bush, George, 49, 66–67, 116, 141

Cadillac Desert (Reisner), 172
California Coastal Commission, 47; *California Coastal Commission v. Granite Rock Co.*, 97–98
Callahan, Debra, 20
Callenbach, Ernest (*Ectopia*), 227
Campbell, Benjamin Nighthorse, 52
Canyonlands, Utah, 210
Capitalism, 17
Carhart, Arthur, 294, 298, 299
Carrying capacity, 16, 17, 211, 294, 295
Carter, Jimmy, 39; and War on the West, 87
Cascade Holistic Economic Consultants (Randall O'Toole), 112–13
Catron County, New Mexico, 88, 95, 99, 110, 168. *See also* County Movement; Bureau of Land Management
Catron County, New Mexico, Interim Land Use Policy Plan, 89, 94, 100; constitutionality, 97; custom and culture, 89; and Native Americans, 90; and nullification of federal laws, 95, 97; preamble, 94; and state land use planning, 98
Center for the Defense of Free Enterprise, 41
Chafee, Senator John, 53
Cherokee County, Georgia, 44
Civil Rights Act, 64; and Nuisance Law, 65
Civil War, 94
Class, 8, 9

Clawson, Marion, 221
Clean Air Act, 42, 97; and custom and culture, 99
Clean Water Act, 43, 49, 53, 55, 69, 99
Clearinghouse on Environmental Advocacy and Research (CLEAR), 22
Clinton, Bill, 46, 53, 63, 87, 108, 266, 270
Coase, Ronald, 125
Cockburn, Alexander, 22
Commons, 55, 114n1; conservation of, 255; tragedy of, 56, 178, 255; western, 181. *See also* Taylor Grazing Act
Community, 180, 286, 288; and BLM, 78; building through compromise, 178; common values, 244, 257; communities of memory, 246, 255; and deep ecology in technological society, 226; as direct democracy, 274; economy vs. local community characteristics, 251; and environmental policy, 151; and environmental strategies, 109, 111, 275; and extractive industry subsidies, 187; Fallon, Nevada, demographics, 284; and federal land managers, 73–74; and Forest Service, 75, 186; and gateway communities, 191; individuals and interests, 265; land communities vs. national community, 182, 229, 274, 288; and livelihood, 37; local, 73, 82, 142, 229–30; and local natural resources, 254; loss of tax base, 73; neighbors, 181, 246–47; "outdated views" of local economy, 196; and pilot programs, 202; politics of conflict, 273; quality of life, 197; relationship between individual and community, 186, 226, 243–44, 305; and Republican versus

Democratic biases, 114; romanticizing of communities, 280, 290; self–governing experimental communities, 179–80; and sense of place, 181, 236; stability, 74, 199; stabilization plans, 79. *See also* Applegate Partnership; Community–based conservation; Local government; Local environmental movements

Congress: 104th, 6, 48, 53, 113, 130, 177; "burst of legislative activity," 220; Continental, 94; land-use policies, 164; mining reforms, 155; and power over public lands, 96; Provincial, 94

Congressional Research Service, 66, 227

Conservationists, 261

Constitution 42, 49; and Anti-Federalists, 93; civic virtues, 237; Constitutional Convention, 92; and "credible interpretation," 127; and decentralization, 229, 236 (*see* Jefferson, Thomas); Just Compensation Clause, 121; Petition for Redress of Grievances (First Amendment), 83; Property Clause, 96, 125; and Shay's Rebellion, 89; Supremacy Clause, 96–98; and takings, 56, 60, 68

Contract with America, 53

Council on Property Rights, 51

County: and Articles of Confederation, 90; Boundary County, Idaho, 93, 168; county ordinance movement, 124; Crooked Lake County, 125; government, 83; mythmaking, 90; rights, 7; supremacy, 11, 87. *See also* Catron County, New Mexico

Cushman, Chuck, 116

Custom and culture: and concept of place, 249; and cultural diversity, 251–52; culture and place, care vs. domination, 257; and management of commons, 255–56; nature vs. place, 252; taking possession of place vs. placelessness, 250; productivity and place, 251; residents vs. tourists, 253. *See also* County; Place

Dams, 111, 164–65, 223, 255

Dancing at the Rascal Fair (Doig), 162

Deep ecology, 18, 25, 225–27

Defenders of Property Rights 52, 115–16, 117

Defenders of Wildlife, 112, 113

Delene, Richard, 45

Democracy in America (Tocqueville), 180

Department of the Interior, 28, 39, 40, 52, 141; and forest management, 74; and M & J Coal, 64; and origins of Sagebrush Rebellion, 116; and nullifying the Surface Mining and Control Act, 66

De Voto, Bernard, 170

Doig, Ivan (*Dancing at the Rascal Fair*), 162

Dolan, Florence, 51

Dolan v. City of Tigard 47, 122

Dole, Bob, 54, 60, 63

Domenici, Pete, 177

Donald, Judy 21

Dubos, Rene, 2

Ducks Unlimited, 114

Dudley, Barbara, 21

Dust Bowl, 59, 172

Dylan, Bob, 8

Earth Day, 42

Earth First!, 18, 37, 107, 142, 153, 304

Echeverria, John, 54

Echo Park dam, 165, 171, 172

Eco-bunnies, 30

Eco-feminism, 5

Eco-fetishism, 20

Eco-ideology, 16–24

Economic Impact Statements, 31

Economy and land use, 186; James Buchanan, 226; central planning, 200, 222, 226; decline in faiths of economic progress, 230; economic diversity, 199; economy of wilderness, 198; Richard Ely, 224; environmental quality, 193–95; global economy, 188, 250–51; Greater Yellowstone economy, 195–97; *Measuring Change in Rural Communities*, 202; multiple use vs. no use, 200; private vs. public goods, 186; public-land management myths, 188; quality of life, 197, 199; resource-based "primary engine" of economic growth, 186, 191; "services," 189–90, 196; tele-commuters, 194; "theory of countervailing power," 219; Wyoming's economy, 191–93

Eco-socialism, 17, 25

Ecosystem (definition), 3

Ecosystem management, 5

Eco-terrorists, 142

Ecotopia (Callenbach), 227

Edwards Aquifer, 44

Ehrlich, Paul, 110

Ellen, Bill, 50

Emerson, Ralph Waldo, 252

Eminent domain, 56, 121. *See also* Constitution, Takings

Empson, William, 19

Endangered Species Act (ESA), 28, 36, 43, 48, 141; and lawsuits, 146; and 1988 local government amendments, 81; local government participation, 79; and market strategies, 110; as perverse incentive to defy stewardship, 124; and private property takings, 69; and Progressive Era, 223; and Property Rights Protection Act of 1995, 53; purposes and requirements defined, 80, 137; and snail darter, 107; weaknesses and hybrid strategies, 112

Endangered species protection, 44, 53, 112, 133n26, 223, 261, 264, 282. *See also* Spotted owl

Environment and Public Works Committee, 53

Environmental backlash, 55, 118

Environmental Conservation Organization (ECO), 51

Environmental Defense Fund (EDF). *See* Lahontan Valley Wetlands

"Environmental ethic," 54, 55

Environmental Grantmaker's Association, 18, 22

Environmental Impact Statements, 31, 42, 48, 77; state and federal vs. local plans, 79

Environmentalism/environmentalists, 10, 17, 19, 169, 177, 222

"Environmentalism's Articles of Faith," 16

Environmental Law Institute, 118

Environmental laws, 6

Environmental movement, 5, 107, 304

Environmental policy strategies, 108, 109, 110

Environmental Protection Agency (EPA), 42, 46, 49, 50, 97, 123

Environmental quality, 193

Environmental regulation, 41, 98

Epstein, Richard A., 63, 66, 116, 125

Establishment interventionists, 17, 24

Executive Order 12630, 48, 66, 116

Fairness to Landowners (Peggy Reigle), 121

Federal Advisory Committee Act, 270, 274

Federal Bureau of Investigation (FBI), 50

Federalists, 66, 237–38, 234

Federal Land Management and Policy Act of 1976, 167
Fifth Amendment, 47, 48, 49, 60, 66
First Amendment, 47, 83
First English Evangelical Church v. County of Los Angeles, 46
Flicker, John, 9
Floodplains, 69
Florida Rock v. U.S., 47
"Fly-In for Freedom," 51
Foreman, Dave, 107, 304
Forests: "doing their part in the economy," 74; and federal management, 165; fires, 165; forestry practices, 136–37; as local concern, 75; old growth, 137; and John Wesley Powell, 173; and public debate, 136; and rhetorical strategies, 140, 142
Foundation for Research on Economics and the Environment (John Baden and Tim O'Brien), 112–13
Fourth Amendment, 47
Fried, Charles, 66
Frost, Robert, 249, 258

Galbraith, John Kenneth, 219
Garden scenario, 2, 224
Gateway communities, 191
Gateway National Recreation Area, 210
Glen Canyon Dam, 172; National Recreation Area, 208
Global warming, 31
Gore, Al, 304
Gorsuch, Ann, 46
Gorton, Slade, 48
Gramm, Phil, 53
Grazing permits, 176, 222
Green Lantern, 27
Greenpeace, 17
Greens, 5, 8, 161, 178
Greenwire press service, 53
Grizzly bear, 198

Habitat, 48, 80
Hardin, Garrett, 178–79
"Harm," 48
Hatch, Orrin G., 63
Hazardous waste, 43
Helvarg, David, 22
Herard, Ulus, 297–98
High Country News, 154
Hodel v. Indiana, 64
Hodel v. Irving, 46
Holmes, Oliver Wendell, 42, 46, 56
Homestead Act, 164, 217
Hoover, Herbert, 167
Huffman, James, 34
Hutchison, Kay Bailey, 53

Indian tribes. *See* Native Americans
Industry, 8, 9
Inholders, 123
Interior. *See* Department of the Interior
International House of Pancakes (IHOP), 64
"Inverse condemnation," 48

Jefferson, Thomas, 236–39. *See also* Federalists
John Birch Society, 21
Jones, Paul Tudor II, 50
Just Compensation Clause, 121

Kittredge, William, 201
Kleppe v. New Mexico, 96
Kosinski, Alex, 47
Kreiger, Martin, 2

Lahontan Valley wetlands, 282–87, 289. *See also* Wetlands
Lamb, Henry, 51
Land management/land planning, 73, 76–78, 82, 98, 188, 200. *See also* Economy and land use; Sandra Day O'Connor
Land-rights movement, 5–10; national networks, 119, 123; origins, 115; and public delibera-

tion, 128; as rooted in rival cultures, 118; and wolves in Yellowstone, 305

Land-rights movement rationales: Equity, 120–22; Libertarianism, 127; New populism, 122; Privatization, 124

Land use. *See* Economy and land use; Public land management

LaRouche, Lyndon, 21

Last Stand of the Pack, The (Arthur Carhart), 297

League of Conservative Voters, 52

League of Women Voters, 63

Leopold, Aldo, 180, 261, 294, 296, 306

Liability planning, 68

Libertarian movement, 225

Life on the Mississippi (Twain), 252

List, Robert, 40

Little Red Riding Hood, 1, 2, 7

Livelihood, 37

Livestock Grazing Act, 177

Lobbies, 146

Local environmental movements: 279, 280, 290. *See also* Applegate Partnership

Local government: difficulty of local control, 274; and ESA, 81; and general public, 77; participating in federal land-management decisions, 76, 78, 82; protecting local economies, 81; protecting tax base and private property rights, 73. *See also* Bureau of Land Management; Community; U.S. Forest Service

Love Canal, 59

Lovejoy, Arthur O., 15

Loveladies Harbor v. U.S., 47

Lucas, David, 47, 51

Lucas v. South Carolina Coastal Council, 47, 51, 69, 121, 126

Machine in the Garden, The (Leo Marx), 15

Madison, James. *See* Federalists

Manifest Destiny, 28

Marx, Leo, 15

Marzulla, Nancie and Roger, 68. *See also* Defenders of Property Rights

Mazurek, Joseph P., 98

Meese, Edwin, 66

Metaphor, 2, 16, 152, 156, 304

Michigan Department of Natural Resources, 45

Militia, 7, 8, 21

Mills, Ocie and Carey, 50

Mining, 64–65, 263

Mining Law of 1872, 28, 33, 201

Moby Dick (Melville), 254

Motorized-recreation-vehicle clubs, 18

Mountain States Legal Foundation, 125

Muir, John, 42, 223, 304

Multiple Use: "Multiple Use Strategy Conference," 29; Multiple-Use-Sustained Yield Act, 186; "prizes of conquest," 176; of public lands, 88–89, 137, 200

Myths, 35, 156, 288

Nash, Roderick, 2

National Biological Survey, 173, 175

National Environmental Journal, 16

National Environmental Policy Act (NEPA) 42, 48, 99, 104n46, 147

National Federal Lands Conference, 7, 90, 99

National Forest Management Act, 28, 36, 137, 147, 187

National forests, 196, 299, 300

National Inholder's Association, 41

National parks, 2, 191, 207, 210, 211, 212

National Resources Defense Council, 222

National Wild and Scenic River System, 39

National Wildlife Federation, 17, 60
National Wildlife Refuge System,
39
Native Americans, 77–79, 90, 164,
262–63, 282, 286
Native Forest Council, 17
Native Forest Network, 18
Natural resource industries, 4, 268,
271
Natural resource policy debates, 262
Nature Conservancy, 17, 114, 280–
90
New Deal, 63, 107
New Ecological Paradigm, 118
New populists, 122–23, 128
NIMBY, 126
Nims, Fred, 51
*Nollan v. California Coastal Coun-
cil*, 46, 122
Northern Lights, 37
Nozick, Robert, 127
Nuisance law, 65

O'Connor, Sandra Day, 46, 97–98
Office of Management and Budget
(OMB), 62
Of Wolves and Men (Lopez), 303
Oklahoma City Federal Building,
151
Old growth forests. *See* Forests
Old West vs. New West, 201
Oregonians in Action, 51
Organic Administration Act of
1897, 2, 74, 207
Organic gardening, 4
Ortega y Gasset, José, 15
Overgrazing, 168, 295
Ozone depletion, 31

Pacific Legal Foundation (PLF), 51,
118
Pastoral ideal, 15, 19
People For The West! 8, 31, 37, 41,
153
Perot, Ross, 133n26
Pilon, Roger, 63

Pinchot, Gifford, 33, 42, 124, 174,
218, 223, 261
Place: 10, 244–46, 250, 251, 253,
254; connection to place, 235–
36, 307; loyalty to place, 181;
personal-engagement politics,
240. *See also* Custom and culture
Plager, Jay, 47
Polanyi, Karl (*The Great Transfor-
mation*), 251
Political Economy Research Center
(PERC), 124
Political lands, 34
Political Research Associates, 41
Political vision, 10
Populism, 239–40
Powell, John Wesley, 161, 170–74;
myth of, 175
Preemption Act, 217
Progress, 25, 223–26, 230
Prometheus Unbound (Shelly), 23
Property rights: and Catron County,
94; as civil rights issue, 54, 64,
127; and community stability,
81; Defenders of, 68; and environmental ethics, 54; and failures
of referenda, 62; grassroots 51,
52; and models of commons, 256
(*see* Community); movement, 39;
as only effective form of environmental protection, 55; private–property rights, 11; property
value, 129; protection of by
environmental laws, 60; revolt,
50; "unfounded" basis of, 59
Property Rights Impact Statements,
31
Property Rights Protection Act of
1995, 53
Prosser, Dean William, 65
Protected species, 44
Public land experimental projects,
179–80, 297
Public land management: and commons, 255; controlling paradigms, 217, 230; decentraliza-

tion, 225–27; and democratic process, 242; economists and environmentalists, 221–29; failings of progressive model, 220, 230; gospels, 224–25; historic basis, 215; and interest groups, 219–220; localism and regionalism, 227; Gifford Pinchot and scientific forestry, 218; Progressive era, 217; science and social values, 228; scientific management, 216; and spotted owl, 223; transfer of control to the states, 216, 229

Public life, 243, 244, 245

Public Rangelands Protection Act, 177

"Ranching for Wildlife," 297

Rand, Ayn (*Atlas Shrugged*), 55

Reagan, Ronald, 28, 45, 49, 66, 167

Reardon, Harry, 49

Reclamation, 172

Recreation, 196, 198, 211, 222, 297, 299

Reed, Ed, 40

Rehnquist, William, 46, 47, 133–34n33

Reisner, Marc (*Cadillac Desert*), 172

Resource conflict, 135, 257

Resource Conservation and Recovery Act (RCRA), 43

Resources for the Future, 221

Revolt of the Masses, The (Ortega y Gasset), 15

Rhetorical strategies, 139–48, 152, 153, 155

Ripeness, 47

Rogue Institute for Ecology and Economy, 267

Romantics, 252–53

Roosevelt, Franklin, 33

Roosevelt, Theodore, 42

Roush, John, 9

Sagebrush Rebellion, 5, 28, 29, 40, 45, 49, 50, 54; and big government, 168–69; and Catron County Ordinances, 96; and county supremacy movement, 87; and Department of the Interior, 116; "kinder, gentler" rebellion, 182; and privatization, 167; Win Back the West rally, 151

Salmon, 165, 169, 271

Sax, Joseph, 54, 211

Scalia, Antonin, 46, 98, 121, 126

Scheffer, Victor B., 16

Schmidt, John R., 61

Sea Shepherd Conservation Society, 18

Secretary of the interior, 3, 98

Shipley, Jack, 262, 264

"Shoot, shovel, and shut up," 112, 133n26

Sierra Club, 22, 111, 114, 171

Simon, Julian, 110

Smith, Loren, 47

Snider, MacWilliams Cosgrove, 20

Society of Environmental Journalists, 153

Some Versions of the Pastoral (Empson), 19

Southern Utah Wilderness Alliance, 153

Spotted owl, 7, 113, 136, 138, 140, 144, 223, 261, 264

State Environmental Policy Act (SEPA), 44

State Implementation Plan (SIP), 42–43

State regulatory schemes, 44

States' rights movement, 94, 122

Stegner, Wallace, 161, 170, 173, 174, 213, 241, 250

Stein, Edith, 16

Stone, Judge Harland, 127

Sunstein, Cass (*After the Rights Revolution*), 128

Superfund, 43, 55

Superman, 27

Supreme Court, 51; consistent takings rule, 67; *Keystone* decision (coal mining), 64; and Property Clause, 96–98; and Surface Mining Control and Reclamation Act, 64; and takings, 60, 61–62, 66; takings rulings, 116

Surface Mining Control and Reclamation Act, 59, 64, 66

Sustained-yield management, 186–87

Sutherland, Rick, 111

Swainston, Harry, 40

Swamp pink, 44

Symms, Steve, 67

Takings, 42; and 1993 Concrete Pipe decision, 60; balancing values, 121; and civil rights, 64; conservatism of recent rulings, 116; costs of, 62; to counter government regulation, 66; "disastrous consequences of," 62; Richard Epstein, 63, 66; erroneous beliefs about, 59; and ESA, 43; Executive Order 12630, 66, 67; and Fifth Amendment, 41, 46, 47, 54, 66; as "flawed caricatures of constitutional rules," 61, 68; "flaw in takings bills," 67; government agency's responses to, 62–63; and Oliver Wendell Holmes, 46, 64; and H.R. 925, S. 605, 60, 63; and "impact analysis," 48, 53, 67; "impossible premise," 67; and *Lucas* case, 126; mandated compensation for, 53; and M & J Coal, 65; market transaction rationale, 125–26; and mitigation, 54, 65; and nuisance laws, 65; opponents of, 63; payoffs, 62; perverse disincentives of, 56; Roger Pilon and Cato Institute, 63; and property value, 129; and protections from mining activities, 64; as

"radical premise" (Associate Attorney General John R. Schmidt) 61; and Reagan administration, 66; "real purpose," 68; Referendum 48, State of Washington, 62; Supreme Court decisions, 60, 68; as threat to environmental safeguards, 60, 65, 68; and voter responses, 62

Taylor Grazing Act, 76, 167, 171, 217

Thoreau, Henry David, 45

Tidwell, Moody, 47

Timber industry, 140, 262, 264, 270, 276

Tocqueville, Alexis de, 180, 251

Tourism, 198–99, 253

Tragedy of the Commons (Hardin), 178–79

Trout Unlimited, 114

Truckee-Carson Irrigation District (TCID), 283. *See also* Lahontan Valley wetlands

Truman, David, 130

Truman, Harry S, 94

Turner, Frederick Jackson, 250

Twain, Mark, 252–53

Twenty-Five Percent Fund Act, 75

Udall, Stewart, 173

Unification Church, 21

United States v. Carolene Products, 127

University of Washington Institute for Public Policy Management, 62

U.S. Fish and Wildlife Service (FWS), 44, 48, 79, 113, 123, 138, 144

U.S. Forest Service, 74; budget allocations, 196; and Catron County, 88; and Crooked Lake, Michigan, 125; as "disastrous" from economic standpoint, 221; and economic stability of local communities, 75, 76, 82, 186;

and environmental regulations, 98; forest fires, 165; and forestry practices, 137; grazing budgets, 163; imperviousness to reform, 109; "New environmental agenda," 141; pipe bomb in Carson City, 151; planning regulations, 77, 78; and recreational fees, 113–14; religious commitment to progress, 225

Van Leuzen, Marinus, 50
Vinson, Roger (Judge), 50
Voluntarism, 182, 275

W. Alton Jones Foundation, 20, 22; Environmental Grass Roots Program, 21
War Against the Greens, The (Helvarg), 22
War on the environment, 152
War On the West, 87, 152, 157, 287
Washington Contract Loggers Association, 145
Watershed management, 262, 265, 271, 283
Watt, James, 5, 28, 46, 167, 170
Webster, Noah, 54
Western Ancient Forest Campaign, 146
Western States Land Coalition, 31
Wetlands 43, 49, 121; and community, 289; denial of permits, 69; and federal regulation, 50; Lahontan Valley, 280–85; myths, 69; and Property Rights Protection Act of 1995, 53; redefinition, 126; and Settlement Act, 280–81
Wild and Scenic Rivers, 88, 95
Wilderness, 2; and Catron County Interim Land Use Policy Plan, 88, 96; "land of no use," 197–98, 200; Leopold and Carhart, 299; and market strategies, 110; Sangre de Cristo, 295; Wilderness Bill of 1994, 242
Wilderness Act of 1964, 15, 36
Wilderness Society, 9, 20, 22, 141–42, 202
Wild horses, 96
Wildlife preserves, 17, 209
Wilkinson, Charles, 161, 173
Will, George, 243
Win Back the West, 151
Wise use "ideas," 31
Wise use movement, 7, 11, 18, 28; and big government, 168–69; and "cargo cult mentality," 201–2; its failure, 175; and federal agencies, 166; and federal subsidies, 162–64; and ideological blinders, 114; as "legacy of failed politics," 177; lobby, 146; "Mission 2010," 210; and National Parks, 207 (*see* National parks); as pacifists in the War on the West, 162; potential for compromise, 181; as response to national environmental strategies, 109, 279; rationale, 124; as rising star, 161; "strategies," 29; ubiquity, 174; "values," 186; *Wise Use Agenda*, 209; "wise-users," 178
Wolves, 177–79, 182, 293, 294–95, 297, 299, 301, 303
Worldviews, 2, 18
Wyoming Heritage Foundation, 191

Yandle, Bruce, 126
Yeats, W.B., 151
Yellowstone, 2, 9, 29, 194–97, 198–99, 200, 305

Zoning, 82, 126, 128, 129
Zumbrum, Ron, 51

About the Contributors

Ron Arnold is executive vice president of the Center for the Defense of Free Enterprise in Bellevue, Washington. He has written widely on the environmental movement.

Philip Brick is associate professor of politics at Whitman College in Walla Walla, Washington, where he teaches international and environmental politics. He received his B.A. in government from Lawrence University of Wisconsin and his Ph.D. in political science from the University of California at Berkeley.

Karen Budd-Falen is an attorney and with her husband, Frank Falen, is the owner of Budd-Falen Law Offices in Cheyenne, Wyoming. She has worked as an attorney at Mountain States Legal Foundation, and is author of *Ecosystem Management: Will National Forests be "Managed" into National Parks?"* (Yale University Press, 1991).

R. McGreggor Cawley is associate professor of political science at the University of Wyoming, and author of *Federal Land, Western Anger: The Sagebrush Rebellion and Environmental Politics* (University Press of Kansas, 1993). He holds M.A. and Ph.D. degrees in political science from Colorado State University.

Graham Chisholm lives in Reno, Nevada, where he works for The Nature Conservancy as the Nevada Special Projects Director. He previously worked as Senator Bob Kerrey's aide on natural resource issues in Washington, D.C. He received his B.A. in political science from Creighton University, and his Ph.D. in political science from the University of California at Berkeley.

John Christensen is a free-lance writer in Carson City, Nevada. He recently completed a special three-year project as Great Basin regional editor for *High Country News*. He also writes about people and the environment for Pacific News Service, a San Francisco-based wire service.

Gus diZerega is research associate at the Institute for Governmental Studies at the University of California at Berkeley. diZerega received his B.A. in political science and history at the University of Kansas, and his Ph.D. in political science at the University of California at Berkeley. He has published extensively on environmental topics in both the academic and popular press.

Kirk Emerson is completing her Ph.D. in public policy and political science at the School of Public and Environmental Affairs and the Department of Political Science, Indiana University at Bloomington. She received her B.S. from Princeton University and her masters in city planning from Massachusetts Institute of Technology. A professional planner for eight years, she specialized in natural-resource planning, wetlands regulation, and affordable-housing policy.

John Freemuth is associate professor of public administration and political science at Boise State University, where he specializes in public land policy and administration. He is the author of numerous publications, including *Islands Under Siege: National Parks and the Politics of External Threats* (University of Kansas Press, 1991).

Karl Hess Jr. is a senior fellow in environmental studies at the Cato Institute in Washington, D.C. He holds a B.A. in economics from the University of Virginia, M.A. in history from the University of Virginia, and Ph.D. in ecology from Colorado State University. He has written extensively on western issues. His books include *Visions Upon the Land: Man and Nature on the Western Range* (Island Press, 1992) and *Rocky Times in Rocky Mountain National Park: An Unnatural History* (University Press of Colorado, 1993).

Daniel Kemmis is mayor of Missoula, Montana, and author of *Community and the Politics of Place* (University of Oklahoma Press, 1990) and most recently, *The Good City and the Good Life* (Houghton Mifflin, 1995).

Brett KenCairn is the executive director and cofounder of the Rogue Institute for Ecology and Economy in Ashland, Oregon. He is also a board member of the Applegate Partnership in southwestern Oregon. He has worked for the last 12 years in a range of nonprofit organizations involved in community organizing, sustainable agriculture, and ecological restoration. He received his B.A. in cultural anthropology from Princeton University and his master's in Community and Regional Planning from the University of Oregon.

Jonathan I. Lange is professor of communication and director of training and organizational development at Southern Oregon State College in Ashland, Oregon, where he teaches organizational communication, communication theory, and negotiation and conflict management. He received his B.A. from Pennsylvania State University, his M.S. from Portland State University, and his Ph.D. from the University of Washington. For two years he was the cofacilitator for the Applegate Partnership.

Nancie G. Marzulla is president and founder of Defenders of Property Rights. She played a key role in several successful state and federal lawsuits and was the first cochair of the U.S. Federal Circuit Court of Appeals Natural Resources Committee. She assisted in drafting property rights legislation for the 104th Congress, and consulted on numerous state bills. She holds a masters degree in public administration and a law degree from the University of Colorado. She was an appointee in the Reagan Justice Department, and was a litigator in private practice prior to founding Defenders of Property Rights in 1991.

Robert H. Nelson is a professor at the School of Public Affairs at the University of Maryland and a senior fellow of the Competitive Enterprise Institute in Washington, D.C., and of the Center for the New West in Denver. From 1975 to 1993, he was a member of the economics staff of the Office of Policy Analysis, the principal policy office serving the secretary of the interior. He is the author of *Zoning and Property Rights* (MIT Press, 1977), *The Making of Federal Coal Policy* (Duke University Press, 1983), *Reaching for Heaven on Earth: The Theological Meaning of Economics* (Rowman & Littlefield, 1991), and *Public Lands and Private Rights* (Rowman & Littlefield, 1995).

Ray Rasker is an economist for The Wilderness Society and lives in Bozeman, Montana. He holds a Ph.D. in economics from Oregon State University, a master of agriculture from Colorado State University, and a B.S. in wildlife biology from the University of Washington. He has authored numerous articles on land management, wildlife economics, and the changing economy of the west.

Scott W. Reed is a member of the Idaho bar and has practiced extensively in natural resources and environmental law. He received his A.B. from Princeton University and his L.L.B. from Stanford Law School. He is currently the attorney for the plaintiffs in *Boundary Backpackers v. Boundary County*, Boundary County No. CV-93-9955.

Jon Roush is president of The Wilderness Society. He received a Ph.D. in English from the University of California at Berkeley. He has taught medieval literature at Reed College, been a foundation officer with the Carnegie Corporation of New York, and served The Nature Conservancy as executive vice president. For ten years he was a full-time rancher in Montana. He has published articles and book chapters in the fields of management, conservation, education, literature, and the arts.

Mark Sagoff is senior research scholar at the Institute for Philosophy and Public Policy in the School of Public Affairs, University of Maryland. He is author of *The Economy of the Earth* (Cambridge University Press, 1988), a Pew Scholar in conservation and the environment, and president of the International Society for Environmental Ethics. Sagoff has an A.B. from Harvard and his Ph.D. (philosophy) from Rochester and has taught at Princeton University, the University of Pennsylvania, the University of Wisconsin (Madison), and Cornell University.

Donald Snow is the founder and associate editor of *Northern Lights Magazine* in Missoula, Montana. His books include *Inside the Environmental Movement,* and *Voices from the Environmental Movement*, both from Island Press. With Deborah Clow, he edited the anthology *Northern Lights: A Selection of New Writing from the American West*, (Vintage, 1994). A native of Hiawatha, Utah, he holds a B.A. in English from Colorado State University and an M.S. in environmental studies from the University of Montana.

Glenn P. Sugameli is counsel, National Office of Conservation Programs, National Wildlife Federation. He received his B.A. from Princeton University and his law degree from the University of Virginia School of Law. His publications include "Takings Issues in Light of *Lucas v. South Carolina Coastal Council*" (1993); and "Species Protection and Fifth Amendment Takings of Private Property" (1995).

Tom Wolf received his Master's in Forestry from Colorado State University and his Ph.D. in English and American Literature from the University of California at Berkeley. He is a freelance writer and adjunct professor of Southwest studies at Colorado College. He is author of *Colorado's Sangre de Christo Mountains* (University Press of Colorado, 1995). He has worked for The Nature Conservancy, is senior fellow at the Gallatin Institute, and is a member of the Society of American Foresters.